D1756844

From Generation to Generation

Shmuel N. Eisenstadt

Third Edition

Transaction Publishers
New Brunswick (U.S.A.) and London (U.K.)

This edition copyright © 2003 by Transaction Publishers, New Brunswick, New Jersey. Originally published in 1956 by The Free Press.

All rights reserved under International and Pan-American Copyright Conventions. No part of this book may be reproduced or transmitted in any form or by any means, electronic or mechanical, including photocopy, recording, or any information storage and retrieval system, without prior permission in writing from the publisher. All inquiries should be addressed to Transaction Publishers, Rutgers—The State University, 35 Berrue Circle, Piscataway, New Jersey 08854-8042.

This book is printed on acid-free paper that meets the American National Standard for Permanence of Paper for Printed Library Materials.

Library of Congress Catalog Number: 2002075478
ISBN: 0-7658-0971-0
Printed in the United States of America

Library of Congress Cataloging-in-Publication Data

Eisenstadt, S.N. (Shmuel Noah), 1923-
    From generation to generation / Shmuel N. Eisenstadt.—3rd ed.
      p.cm.
    Includes bibliographical references and index.
    ISBN 0-7658-0971-0 (paper : alk. paper)
      1. Age groups. 2. Youth. 3. Intergenerational relations. 4. Conflict
of generations. I. Title.

HM721 .E57 2002
305.2—dc21
                                    2002075478

To Shulamit—yet again

Contents

Preface

The republication of *From Generation to Generation*—almost half a century after its first appearance in 1956—constitutes a good occasion for a look at the way in which the problem or problems of youth and generations developed in modern and above all in contemporary societies, the different approaches to the analysis thereof in the social sciences, and the place of the analysis presented in the book in the framework of such analyses and some indications of how to go beyond such analysis.

I have attempted here to address these problems by including in this edition several new chapters dealing with these problems, which were published after the first two editions—1956 and 1968—of the book, as well as by including a new introduction.

The first such chapter is "The Archetypical Patterns of Youth," published in *Daedalus* in 1962. In this I attempted to present a broad critical framework for social analysis of the problems of youth, which went in several ways beyond the arguments presented in the book, by putting a greater emphasis on the cultural dimension in the conceptions of youth. The second chapter, on the student rebellions of the sixties and seventies, "Contemporary Student Rebellions—Intellectual Rebellion and Generational Conflict," published in *Acta Sociologica* in 1971, addresses the problems of youth as manifest in the student rebellions, placing special emphasis on the antinomic elements that were central in the students' movements of that period and which constituted a rather new component in the development of youth activities. In the third additional chapter, "Youth, Generational Consciousness, and Historical Change," published in 1988 in a volume on *Perspectives on Contemporary Youth* by the United Nations University, I have placed a much greater emphasis than before on problems of generational consciousness.

In all these chapters there is a double shift of the analysis presented in *From Generation to Generation*. The first shift is a theoretical one, from the most structural-institutional analysis presented in the original book to a growing emphasis on the importance of the cultural definition of youth and generations in different societies. The second shift is a greater emphasis on the changes in the cultural program of modernity, above all in contemporary "postmodern" societies and their impact on the conception of youth and generational problems they entail.

Using these shifts as a springboard, I present in the introduction to this Transaction edition an overall view of the development of theoretical and historical problems of youth as I see them today.

Introduction to the Transaction Edition

Transformation of the Problem of Youth in Contemporary Societies

I.

The starting point of my analysis is the fact that in the last thirty or forty years, after the great students' revolt of the late sixties, some new tendencies have appeared on the scene with respect to what one could call in old parlance "the youth problems" in modern societies. One very interesting characteristic of this new scene is that people tend now to talk much less about the youth problems. There are different concrete problems of different youth groups or sectors: problems of socialization, of adolescence, of vocational guidance and the like. But somehow the talk about the youth problem, which was quite central for some time in the social sciences and in general public discourse in the interwar period and also after the Second World War, has become much weaker. This is connected with the fact that the dramatic sort of confrontations of generations, which we witnessed often in the nineteenth and twentieth centuries until the students' revolt, have also lately become weakened in many ways. These confrontations may, of course, come back, but, for the time being, they have weakened, and it would be interesting to understand the reasons for this new development.

In order to present some very tentative hypotheses about the reasons for this development, I want to place these phenomena in a somewhat broader framework, namely the framework of different modes of youth formations in modern societies, their relations to the cultural and political programs of modernity and in changes in the programs, and to ask what the social forces are that have continuously influenced the constellations of youth problems in modern societies. I want to analyze what has been changing in the constellations of these forces and how such changes are affecting the contemporary scene.

What then are the major social and cultural forces that have influenced different youth formations—different formations of youth and youth problems have always existed—in modern society or in modern societies? The first and the most obvious of these, in some ways the seemingly simplest to analyze, is the division of labor as it developed in modern societies and its consequences. Among these consequences the most important has been the growing specialization—occupational, economic, educational—of different institutional arenas, the growing specialization of different social roles, the diminishing role of the family in the occupational scene, the growth of education, the growth of formal education, the growth of transitional periods in which young people are neither within the family nor yet fully in society. These processes have been going on continuously, changing, of course, in their concrete constellations as they become more and more complicated and diversified. Such diversification is a crucial aspect of the contemporary scene. The outcomes of these processes have been studied for many years. *From Generation to Generation*[1] emphasized this problem of how as results of this growing complexity of the division of labor, the diminution of the place of the family, and the like, there emerged in modern societies a great variety, a great plethora, of youth cultures or subcultures. Some of these subcultures were organized by youth groups themselves, sometimes by different socializing agencies, some a combination of the two. The multiplicity of youth cultures and subcultures has been a continuous fact in modern societies—and will continue to be so, unless modern or what is now called postmodern society changes so dramatically that the reasons for the emergence of these subcultures, as generated by the social division of labor, disappear, which seems to me to be rather doubtful.

II.

The second social process, which as far as I know has not been emphasized enough in the literature as a force shaping the formation of different types of youth subcultures and youth phenomena in modern societies, is the mode of the contrast, of cultural definition of social roles, of the relations between social roles and different social life spaces as they have developed in modern societies, all rooted in the continual development of the cultural and political program of modernity and in changes thereof.

Among the most important aspects of the cultural program of modernity as it developed until about the last thirty years, has been a strong tendency to construct a very clear demarcation between different social categories, to construct very clear boundaries between them, very clear categorization of different life spaces.

Indeed, one of the basic characteristics of so-called "modern" societies has been a very peculiar combination of, on the one hand, semantic, ideological distinctions between different arenas of life, together with the development of very specific symbolic institutional and organizational linkages between them on the other hand. Among such major semantic distinctions were those between family and occupation, work and culture; between public and private realms; between different age spans; between the sexes; and between different social classes within each of which the former distinctions were elaborated in different constellations. At the same time these different arenas were connected symbolically, organizationally and institutionally in several distinct ways. On the personal level these arenas were connected through a clear structuring of life spans, of patterns of life careers, of different strata of population, and of different sectors within them.

On the macro-societal level these different semantic arenas were closely connected on the one hand by the strong emphasis on economic-industrial development and technological-economic creativity, and, on the other hand, the creation of new types of major sociopolitical centers as major arenas in which the charismatic dimension of the ontological and social visions prevalent in these societies should be implemented.

Needless to say, while this vision of modern and industrial society—as portrayed in both scholarly literature and in more general discourse—was certainly not accepted within all sectors of modern societies, there can be no doubt that it has been, for a very long period of time, the most predominant and hegemonic one. Even those who opposed it—the romanticists, the prophets of Entzauberung like Nietzsche or Max Weber with his image of the iron cage of modernity—opposed *this* specific mode of structurization of modern society and cannot be understood except in terms of their references to it.

The very category "youth" is indeed one central illustration of such a classification. It is the specific category "youth"—not just the acknowledgment that there are young people, not even the acknowledgment of age differences, of age groups, but the development of the very distinct social category "youth," that is important here. Some possible beginnings of such categorization can indeed be identified in ancient Greece and Rome, and there are kernels of this in other civilizations, but such a distinct overarching classification has appeared only in modern societies.[2]

Interestingly enough, this has been also—until some later developments—the only category in modern societies that is based on age differentials. Only lately the same is beginning to be true of old people. "Adult" is not the counterpart of "youth," it is a different dimension or category. No adult movement has ever developed in modern societies. Youth, from some time at the beginning of the nineteenth century, has constituted one of the clearly defined distinct categories in modern societies, a very central social category, and it seems to me that such sharp categorization of youth may be weakening now. But youth was not of course the only such social category. All the major roles—occupational, gender, or political all the major life spaces have been clearly defined with relatively fixed boundaries.

III.

This mode of definition of different roles, life spaces and of interconnections between them, is not necessarily connected with a high level of differentiation, of social division of labor. For instance, if we look at Japanese society, we shall find a society in which a high complexity of social division of labor is not connected with the same mode of characterization of life spaces. Life spaces are organized in different ways, the boundaries are not so clear, and the transitions between boundaries are not as clear as in modern Western societies.[3] In Western societies some of these transitions may have been confrontational ones: others may be non-confrontational, peaceful transitions, but the clear categorization of boundaries denotes also a rather clear mode of transition between such categories.

It was these definitions that shaped many of the patterns of behavior, self-perception and self-definition of large sectors of modern Western societies. Such demarcation became synonymous with what was called somewhat later "bourgeois revolution," but it is not necessarily related to "bourgeois" in the economic class sense, because it affected the lives of other strata; it was forceful also in other sectors of the population such as the working classes. It continued to be even much more forceful in some places, for instance until lately in the Communist regimes of Eastern Europe, and to some degree in the mature phases of the Kibbutz.

A very important aspect of such distinction was, of course, also that distinction between social strata or classes. Each class had its own social space, which was more or less clearly defined and the transition between them was not easy. Even social movements, such as the socialist movements, that aimed to improve the place of a certain social category in overall social life, in the political standing, in economic standing did not necessarily aim to do away with the clear boundary differences between different social categories. Social movements did not necessarily deny the existence of such boundaries.

IV.

The distinct modern category of youth developed within this framework definition of social roles and spaces. One of the most interesting aspects of this process was the fact that youth was seen by itself—i.e., by young people, adolescents and would-be adolescents—but very often to some degree also by other groups, especially in rapid historical situations, as a potential carrier of the charismatic, pure, pristine virtues which became lost through the development of the modern division of labor. This was due to the fact that youth was seemingly the major category that was not *within* the division of labor. Of course it was strongly influenced by the division of labor, but it was presented as if it was, as it were, highly constrained by this division of labor and basically beyond it. And because a large part of the aspirations of modern social movements, ideologies, has been oriented against the alienating aspects of the social division of labor, and aimed to overcome them, youth could easily become also the carrier of those pristine charismatic virtues which one would like to see recrystallized in the rather mechanized world of modern division of labor. Thus, youth has become not only the clear category based on age differentiations but a distinct category imbued with many antinomian, confrontational distinctive potentialities.

V.

The full impact of these potentialities can only be understood in connection with the third major factor which has greatly influenced the formations of youth in modern societies, namely the basic characteristics of the major social movements. The major characteristic of the "classical" modern social movements was the attempt to reconstruct the centers of the society. It was these centers of society, the new national centers, the centers of new nation-states and of class societies that have been the major foci of the classical social movements— national, class movements and the like.

Thus, these movements constituted an inherent part of the cultural and political program of modernity as it was institutionalized in Europe in the nineteenth and twentieth centuries. In the initial stages of the development of modern and industrial societies, most movements of social protest revolved around the revolutionary image or images of the broadening of the scope of participation and channels of access to the centers; of changing or reconstructing their cultural and social contents, solving the problems of unequal participation in them and finding ways to attenuate or overcome, through the policies of the center, the most important problems arising out of industrialization. It was the reconstruction of the centers of societies or of their collective boundaries that constituted the major goals of most social and national movements in the first period of modernity, and these centers and collectivities were perceived as embodying the most important charismatic dimension of the modern sociocultural order. It was the attempt to construct "nation-states" and the ideology of "class struggle" as envisaged by the various nationalistic movements and by most revolutionary and reformist societies that epitomized such characteristics as basic components of the cultural program of modernity.

Among these social movements there arose also different youth movements—some of them revolutionary, confrontational, ideological—which took part, especially in periods of great historical changes in this great effort, or series of efforts, of the charismatic reconstruction of the center. In such situations of intensive change, which abounded in the nineteenth and early twentieth centuries, youth movements have become, at least in some continental European countries, an extremely important component of the numerous social movements that attempted, often in a confrontational way, to present a new charismatic vision of the center.

The dramatic, charismatic confrontational youth movement, with strong components of generational conflict, rooted in a strong generational consciousness, consciousness of distance and difference between generations, a distance expressed in the symbols of youth which constituted a dramatic and powerful image in social reality, has also become a very powerful image in the study of youth. Large parts of the literature on youth movements, and on youth problems, have indeed been greatly influenced by these movements and have assumed, as it were, that these movements constituted the natural manifestations of youth in modern societies.

VI.

Until now, such movement—or movements—of this type have been the student movements of the late sixties. These movements exhibited already rather distinct characteristics. First of all, they were widespread, much more widespread and international, worldwide, than any of the preceding youth movements. Second, they were characterized by a strong combination of intellectual antinomianism and intergenerational confrontation; and their aims were seemingly also oriented to the transformation of the center, the creation of a new center, an entirely new society. But here there emerged a rather complicated and, to some extent, paradoxical picture. One the one hand they obviously failed to change or break down the centers of society. The centers were very resilient. The political regimes did not on the face of it change; they dealt quite efficiently with these movements. There was no breakdown of any political regime because of these movements, although there were wide sectors of the public that saw a strong revolutionary potential in them. Yet, paradoxically, on the other hand, these movements have themselves to some extent at least either indicated or have become closely interwoven with some very far-reaching changes in the structure of their respective societies. They heralded far-reaching changes in the mode of the definition of social roles and of social life spaces in contemporary societies, and also great change in the place of the political center of charismatic vision of society. Indeed all these changes culminated in a radical transformation in the entire cultural and political program of modernity, in what has been called perhaps not very felicitously in the postmodern direction.

First of all, far-reaching changes have taken place in the older semantic, ideological distinctions between different arenas of social life. There have developed strong tendencies to the blurring or recombination of some at least of these arenas and to the crystallization of a multiplicity, plurality of semantic-ideological connections between such arenas as public and private, work and culture, occupation and residence, and to the emergence of the new types of definition of various life styles in terms of such connections.

Second, there developed a strong tendency to the dissociation of most of the major roles, from encompassing, society-wide, symbolic and institutional frameworks. Occupational, family, gender and residential roles have become more and more dissociated from "Stande," class and party-political regional frameworks. Such various roles tended more and more to crystallize into continuously changing clusters, with relatively weak orientations to broad frameworks in general, to the societal centers in particular.

Third, there has taken place a redefinition of many roles and role clusters—especially the occupational and citizenship roles. Thus, for instance, in the occupational sphere, there has developed first, the growing inclusion of community or "service" components into purely professional and occupational activities; second, there tended also to develop a growing dissociation between high occupational strata and "conservative" potential and social attitudes, creating generations of executives and professionals with political and cultural "leftist views" and with orientations to participation in some of these new "permissive enclaves" or subcultures.

In the political sphere there have developed tendencies to the redefinition of boundaries of collectivities; to growing dissociation between political centers and the major social and cultural collectivities;

and to the development of new nuclei of cultural and social identity which transcend the existing political and cultural boundaries and hence also the redefinition of the citizenship role.

Fourth, one of the most important institutional changes connected with those tendencies has been the development of various structural, semi-liminal enclaves within which new cultural orientations, new modes of search for meaning, often couched in transcendental terms, tend to be developed and upheld—partially as counter cultures, partially as components of new culture.

VII.

The combination of these changes in the semantic definition of different arenas of social life and of structural changes gave rise to a growing diversification of the process of strata formation, to the development of a diversified criss-cross of political, sectorial and occupational formations.

Thus, instead of the situation characteristic of the "modern" and "industrial" society, in which different strata had relatively separate cultural traditions with distinct common political symbols, there has continuously developed greater dissociation among the occupational, cultural and political spheres of life. Different strata have no longer separate, totally different "cultures" as before; they tend more and more to participate in common aspects, foci and arenas of culture in general, and mass culture in particular.

These developments have given rise to very complicated differences in styles of life among different status groups; to new status sets, to new patterns of status or class conflict and struggles, new types of "status" or "class" consciousness; to the weakening of any overall, especially "class" or "social" ideological orientations, in the crystallization of such consciousness.

Concomitantly, a new and distinct type of status struggle has developed around the various welfare benefits distributed by the state. The major focus of these struggles has crystallized around the state as a distributive and, to a smaller degree, also regulative agency, as can be seen in the high incidence of strikes and of struggle around social welfare benefits, and to a large degree focused on the attainment of different entitlements in the form of social benefits and the like. By its very nature, this struggle was occupationally dispersed with but little overall ideological political orientation.

While the concrete "economic" foci of such status or "class" struggles have become dispersed between the different types of demands of various occupation groups towards the state, the political and ideological expressions of status consciousness have become less and less focused around such economic problems and much more, even if in a rather vague and unfocused way, around the development of distinct styles and patterns of life.

These changes in the nature of political and class struggles became closely related to a more general tendency toward what may be called the decharismatization of the political centers. Contrary to the earlier modern period when—especially in Europe—as we have seen, the nation-state and "class" center were conceived as the major foci of the charismatic dimension of the social order, as loci of the sacred, and their construction or reconstruction according to some charismatic vision constituted major foci of political struggle, the contemporary political centers, especially in Europe, are not perceived in such a way. The search for the sacred, for some charismatic vision has moved to other social spaces—above all to the various structural enclaves referred to above, to different patterns of quality of life.

This decharismatization of the center was also connected with a great shift in the nature of historical consciousness prevalent in contemporary, as compared with "classical" modern, societies. Great historical changes have, of course, been taking place in Western societies, but these societies become less historically conscious, the tendency of the conception of history as moving to some definitive goal—according to some grand narrative—has become greatly deconstructed. All these developments have indeed entailed far-reaching transformation of what has been envisaged as the epitome of the classical program of modernity—namely the prototype of the classical model of the nation state or revolutionary state—that model of which constituted the focus of the major social movements mentioned above.

VIII.

These two trends—the weakening of the clear boundaries of roles and clusters of roles, the greater diversification of such different clusters, and the development of the tendencies to search for semi-charismatic fulfillment within various different enclaves of quality-of-lifestyles, or in movements which ask for life spaces, but not necessarily for full reconstruction of the center—have become central in contemporary societies and have had, indeed, far-reaching impact on the nature of the orientations of protest that developed from the sixties onward. They became indeed reflected in the development of new types of social movements—starting with the so-called "new" social movements, beginning indeed with the student movements of the late 1960s and early 1970s, such as women's and ecological movements, numerous ethnic and separatist movements, and somewhat later fundamentalist and communal religious movements that emerged within Muslim, Jewish, and Protestant communities.

The common denominator of many of these new movements is that they do not see themselves as bound by the strong homogenizing cultural premises of the classical model of nation-state, especially by the places allotted to them in the public spheres of such states. All these developments precipitated the resurrection, or rather reconstruction, of hitherto "subdued" identities—ethnic, local, regional, and transnational—and their positing into the center of their respective socieites, and often also in the international arena.

It is not that the new social sectors do not want to be "domiciled" in their respective countries. Indeed, part of their struggle is to become so domiciled, but rather on new, as compared to classical models of assimilation, terms. They aim to be recognized in domestic public spheres, in the constitution of civil society in relation to the state as culturally distinct groups, and not to be confined only to the private sphere. They do indeed make claims, as illustrated among others in the recent debate about *laicité* in France, for the reconstruction both of new public spaces as well as the reconstruction of the symbols of collective identity of their respective states.

At the same time, while the identities that are promulgated in these movements and settings are often very local and particularistic, they tend also to be strongly transnational or trans-state, connected with broader civilizational or religious frameworks, often rooted in the great religions: Islam, Buddhism, and different branches of Christianity, but reconstructed in modern ways. In this transnational capacity, the new social movements have also become active in the arena of world politics. Many of the separatist, local, or regional settings, as well as, for instance, the ecological movements, developed direct connections with transnational frameworks and organizations such as the European Union. But it is mainly the various religious, especially fundamentalist movements—Muslim, Protestant, Jewish—that have risen to prominence on the international scene through the utilization of intensive social networks of an intra-religious or inter-religious character.

This new development entails also the transposition of the religious dimension, which was delegated or confined to private or secondary spheres in the classical model of the national-state, into the central political and cultural arenas, and its significance in the constitution of novel collective identities. But the resurgence of religion does not entail a simple return of some traditional forms of religion, but rather a far-reaching reconstitution of this religious component.

X.

All these contemporary movements are indeed modern, comparable in many ways to communist or fascist movements, yet they do evince some very important distinct characteristics which distinguish them from these earlier ones. The crucial difference lies in their perception of the confrontation between the basic premises of the cultural and political program of modernity as it crystallized in the West and in the non-Western civilization, with far-reaching implications for the domestic and international political arenas. These movements, including significantly many of the postmodern ones which emerged in the West, attempt to dissociate completely Westernization from modernity. They deny the monopoly or hegemony of Western modernity and the acceptance of the Western cultural program as the epitome of modernity. This highly confrontational attitude to what is conceived as Western, is closely related to an effort to appropriate modernity and the global system on their own non-Western, often anti-Western, yet modern terms.

XI.

All these processes—the restructuring of boundaries of roles and of life spaces, the decharismatization of the political centers, the weakening of historical consciousness as a basic component of collectivities' self-identity—led to far-reaching changes in the conceptualization of the youth problem in contemporarian societies.

These developments do not, of course, do away with various effects of the growing specialization and differentiation of the division of labor and continue to go on, as does also more and more specialized education, as well as the weakening of the place of the family in the occupational scene. Accordingly different youth groups, youth formations—spontaneous or organized by others—do develop continuously. But these formations become much more diversified than they used to be, because division of labor itself is continuously becoming much more diversified and also because the former sort of sharp divisions between different classes, different occupations, different professions, different stages of education, have, as we have seen, become a bit blurred. Side by side with the growing diversification of youth formations, new modes of the generational confrontation do develop.

But at the same time there has taken place a far-reaching change in the conceptualization of the "youth" problem. Perhaps the most important indication of such changes is that, as indicated at the beginning of our discussion, there is much less talk about *the* youth problem. Youth is not perceived as a homogeneous category, nor is it any longer necessarily the confrontational category it used to be. It is not even necessarily any longer always a focus or carrier of potential charismatic qualities; in other words there has taken place a very interesting, very difficult to grasp, and very important change—mainly decomposition— of the overall category of youth. Again, it does not mean that there will be youth problems, neither does it mean that there will be no family generational confrontations. But with the generational differences and the extent to which they are connected with distinct "youth consciousness societies," they will become much more defined—to no small extent because of the great change in historical consciousness, in the consciousness of historical transition to which I have referred above. Interesting indication of this process can be found in the new fundamentalist and cultural-religion modernities. While many younger people play a very important role in many of these youth formations their goals are usually not defined in terms of "youth" or age but rather in that of their overall collective visions.

The preceding observations are, of course, only preliminary indications and pose important challenges for all those who study youth and the relations between youth generations on the one hand, and modernity on the other. To attempt to analyze it in the contemporary scene is to take into account, to some degree at least, some of the forces I have mentioned above.

NOTES

1. S. N. Eisenstadt (1956 and 1968), *From Generation to Generation,* Glencoe, IL: The Free Press, 1956.

2. See in greater detail, Eisenstadt: *From Generation to Generation,* op.cit., S.N. Eisenstadt, *Japanese Civilization in a Comparative View,* Chicago: University of Chicago Press, 1995.

3. S.N. Eisenstadt, *Japanese Civilization,* op. cit.

INTRODUCTION

Sociological Analysis and Youth Rebellion

Since the publication of this book, interest in intergenerational problems and relations and in youth activities has vastly increased —as has the volume of writing on these subjects. Fifteen years ago, however, this concern was generally confined to the scholarly fields of comparative sociology, anthropology, education, and psychology, and, to a lesser degree, to contemporary history. This interest developed as a result of the emergence of youth rebellions and revolts starting in the late fifties with the appearance of the Teddy Boys and the Halbstarke, carrying over to the Hippies and Beatniks in the beginning sixties, and culminating in the great upsurge of student revolt at the end of the sixties. These movements tended to be regarded as one of the major developments on the contemporary scene. To some they foretold the failure and death of modern civilization. To others they were the forerunners of a new civilization.

The flood of writing that has accompanied these movements —journalistic reporting, polemical debates, and attempts at scholarly analyses—has attained a degree of currency unparalleled since the attempts to analyze the German youth movement.* Until the end of the fifties, the major thrust of scholarly research

---

* See K. Mannheim, "On the Problems of Generations," in *Essays in the Sociology of Knowledge.* London: Rutledge & Kegan Paul, 1948.

involving these problems was directed toward explaining the phenomena of age groups, age-grading "tribal" societies, and examining the varieties of specific sociological settings in more developed and especially industrial societies in which the various types of youth culture or juvenile problems developed. Some researchers also dealt with some of the specific social setting of such groups, such as the school or place of employment. Others tended to emphasize the specific behavioral patterns of different age categories in general and youth in particular in such areas as political behavior or leisure-time activity. Among sociologists and anthropologists, the study of juvenile delinquency constituted a very important, relatively autonomous field of both theoretical and applied research.

Writings by psychologists mainly took two major directions. One was the study of the psychological or socio-psychological aspects of adolescence in various modern social and educational settings, again with special emphasis on problems of juvenile delinquency. The second, and probably theoretically newer and more exciting direction, involved the study of identity-formation among youth in modern societies, with Erik Erikson contributing the most important single line of development. The historical or historical-sociological approach has been concerned with some of the specific historical patterns of childhood or youth formation and with identity formation in contemporary cultures and societies.*

II.

These various lines of research have been set within the framework of the existing disciplines, growing out of their internal development and often closely related to practical problems.

---

* See E. H. Erikson (ed.), *Youth, Change and Challenge*. New York: Basic Books, 1963, published previously as a special issue of *Daedalus* in 1961.

Perhaps one of the best indications of these various developments can be found in many of the anthologies and readers published on this subject. Some of the most representative are: Ludwig V. Friedenburg (ed.), *Jugend in der Modernen Gesellschaft*. Koln, Berlin: Kiepenhauer & Witsch, 1965 or D. Rogers (ed.), *Issues in Adolescent Psychology*. New York: Appleton Century-Crofts, 1969.

Compared with many other fields of social research, these approaches revealed a relatively high degree of continuity.* Moreover, there tended to develop, even if as yet not very advanced, some degree of overlapping and cross communicationg—a mutual opening up among these various fields. Even such fields as delinquency and correction, which seemed mainly self-sustaining, tended to open up a bit—toward, for instance, clinical psychology. Thus, for instance, relatively far-reaching contacts were established between sociologists and historians on the one hand and among psychologists, sociologists and historians on the other. One important meeting point was the study of identity, reflected in the works of Erikson, Lifton, and later on, Kenniston.** Such openings, however, not only were gradual but also, to a large degree, were set by the internal traditions of various disciplines.

One of the most common foci of such initial cross communication was situations of transition, whether from tribal to detribalized communities or new nations or from one type of modern economic or technological or political setting to another. Among such situations of transition, several seem to have attracted special attention. One entailed broadening the base of education, especially in many European and Western societies, through the establishment and spread of general education. Another involved changes in the structure of employment resulting from policies of general employment and the onset of automation. A third had to do with post-revolutionary situations, with the institutionalization of revolutions, first in Russia and later on in the many new states of Asia and Africa. Especially in the new nations the emergence of "new" political generations and the various expres-

---

* One of the best illustrations of such continuity with regard to this field in general can be found in P. Abrams, "Rites de Passage: The Conflict of Generations in Society," Journal of Contemporary History, Vol. 1, Jan. 1970: 175-190.
** E. Erikson, Identity and the Life Cycle. New York: International Universities Press, 1959. See also J. R. Lifton, "Individual Patterns in Historical Change: Imagery of Japanese Youth," Journal of Social Issues, XX (4), 1964: 96-111; and "Japanese Youth. The Search for the New and the Pure," American Scholar, 30(3), Summer, 61:332-334. Also, K. Kenniston, Notes on Committed Youth. New York: Harcourt Brace Jovanovich, 1968.

sions of their generational consciousness in the political life of these countries caught the attention of many scholars.*

III.

By the end of the sixties this relatively "quiet, natural" progress of scholarship dealing with youth had changed markedly. By then all these various trends of research had in one way or another converged in the great upsurge of interest in intergenerational conflict, with the growing alienation of the young, and with student radicalism and rebellion.**

Although much of the writing that was done during this period centered around ideological and political polemics, some of it tended to combine ideological criticism with the analysis of the more theoretical premises of many of the existing scholarly analyses, often linking them directly to more central problems of sociological analysis. These reevaluations have not, in themselves, been very new; most of them already had appeared in scholarly journals. But as youth and intergenerational relations have now become so prominent and have acquired new dimensions, these various criticisms and discussions have become much more relevant. The various sociological analyses were provided, in a sense, with more crucial, semi-experimental instances through which their conceptual tools and concrete analyses could be tested or at least more fully examined.

IV.

What then can be learned from this shift from an academic to a more general approach to the problems of youth and from the attempts made to deal with these problems fifteen years ago in this book? It would be out of place and of little interest to

---

* See, for instance, A. Zolberg, "Youth as a Political Phenomenon in Tropical Africa," *Youth & Society*, I(2), Dec., 1969: 199-219.

** One of the best bibliographies of this kind has been compiled by P. Altbach, *Students, Politics and Higher Education: A Select Bibliography.* Cambridge, Mass.: Harvard University Center for International Affairs, 1967.

discuss some of the *specific* criticisms of various aspects of the analyses presented in this book. To the best of my knowledge none of those scholars, whether reviewers or researchers who referred to the book in their own work, brought out arguments or evidence invalidating the major hypothesis of the book— namely, *that age groups in general and youth groups in particular tend to arise under conditions of non-familial division of labor;* i.e., ". . . in those societies whose main integrative principles are different from the particularistic principles governing family and kinship relations." Nor have the more specific hypotheses concerning how specific types of age or youth groups develop been challenged.

But if the general and specific hypotheses of this work were not invalidated, two more general interconnected criticisms were often raised against what was assumed by several scholars to be the basic approach of the book, an approach often attributed to or connected with some basic theoretical issues in sociological analysis. The first such criticism emphasized that, with its heavy structural-historical emphasis, the book was "ahistorical" or "anti-historical," and, second, that largely because of this characteristic it could neither account for nor predict the development of more specific types of youth activities or orientations that would develop in some historical situations in societies or in specific sectors of societies (the student rebellion for instance).* Although some of those scholars based their criticisms mostly on the presumed fact that a relatively large part of the book was devoted to primitive and historical rather than to contemporary societies, others tended to take exception to its heavy structural-functional bent, which, they felt, made it difficult, if not impossible, to analyze more dynamic, changing historical situations.

The general question that such criticisms raise is whether or not this or any other type of structural analysis can in itself explain or perhaps even predict how specific types of institutional and group patterns in general develop and, in our case here, of

---

* See F. H. Tenbruck, *Jugend und Gesellschaft*, Freiburg, 1962; P. Abrams, *op. cit.*; and Puetro Bellasi, *Rivolta Studentesca e Canpus Universatri*. Milane: Franco Angeli Editore, 1968, p. 24.

how different types of youth and generational activities and symbols take form. Emanating from this general question is the more specific one of whether or not the specific variables which may provide some explanations of a specific case can be derived from general categories (such as employed in the basic hypotheses of the book) or whether general variables are unrelated to those specific attributes of social situations by which more concrete situations can be explained.

The question also exists whether or not there is a contradiction between these general variables and the more specific ones—i.e., whether such general hypotheses are confirmed or disproved by examining concrete situations. This question is, of course, of a different order from the first two, because the very possibility of such a contradiction already assumes the existence of a logical connection between these two levels of explanation.

v.

I myself, since the publication of this book, have taken up some of these questions in my works on sociological theory and on youth problems. Several years ago, for example, I pointed out some of the general theoretical inadequacies in attempting to explain the ways in which certain types of organization based on age tend to crystallize in terms of how universal societal and psychological needs become structured or organized in societies based on a non-familial division of labor.*

". . . These needs have been shown to be, first, the general societal need or structural prerequisite of a society for the socialization of the young and of their development into adults and, second, the need of growing individuals to attain personal identity and social status within their society. It is these general needs which seem to serve as the background for the development of more specific motivations which activate people to undertake membership in different age-groups. Under such conditions there develops, according to this hypothesis, a double tendency or

---

* See S. N. Eisenstadt, *Essays on Comparative Institutions*. New York: John Wiley & Sons, 1965, pp. 11-13.

propensity—the propensity of the adolescent to join youth and age-groups and the propensity of the society to organize such groups.

"These hypotheses and specifications did not, however, deal with several crucial aspects of the problem. They did indicate the nature of the people, that is the adolescents, whose needs for attainment of personal identity and social status were structured under these conditions so as to predispose them to join or become members of age-groups. Here, as in the former case of marriage norms, these people or positions constitute a universal category within the society, and hence the general societal need for socialization is naturally manifest in their own need for attainment of social maturity. But, on the other hand, these hypotheses, and the analyses brought in for their support, did not indicate systematically enough the kind of roles and positions whose occupants are especially sensitive to the needs of the adolescents and the nature of the resources through which the various organizations capable of gratifying such needs could be organized. . . .

". . . Similarly, it was assumed that in most cases (with rare exceptions) there would exist some leader or leaders willing and able to respond to such needs and to organize the youth groups. The possibility that such leaders might not exist was not raised at all. Similarly, the exact ways in which different types of leaders or representatives of the broader institutional structure with different resources at their disposal tended to organize different types of age-groups were not adequately analyzed. The differences in the structure of age-groups were related to broad structural characteristics of the societies, such as the extent of specialization or of achievement orientation that prevailed within them, but the exact mechanisms through which these characteristics facilitated the organization of different types of age-groups by different leaders was not satisfactorily specified. Because of this, the processes of change and possible extinction of any given form of age-groups were also not adequately treated. . . ."

In more general terms the question involves who is especially sensitive to the needs of "the" society in general, and, with respect to the questions considered here, to the need to explain more fully the relations between adolescents and such potentially institutional entrepreneurs, as well as the possibility of incompatibilities, contradictions, and conflicts between the two. Such an explanation could also help analyze in greater detail the variety of ideological youth rebellions.

VI.

Before attempting a fuller explanation of all these problems, however, we must take into account two other closely related aspects of the phenomena of youth.* One is what may be called the cultural-symbolic dimension or image of youth and its relation to the symbolic dimensions of the social and cultural order. Of special importance here is the fact that age and age differences in general often serve as a focus of various basic, charismatic qualities, such as vigor, purity, and sanctity—qualities that also constitute important components of the charismatic elements of the social and cultural order and of symbols of collective identity in most societies.

Second, and especially important in this context, is the dimension of time—the interrelation between personal perception, social and cosmic time, and time sequences. As I have pointed out** ... "The whole problem of age definition and the linkage of personal time and transition with cosmic time become especially accentuated in the age span usually designated as youth. However, great the differences among various societies, there is one focal point within the life span of an individual which in most known societies is to some extent emphasized: the period of youth, of transition from childhood to full adult status or full membership in the society. In this period the individual is no longer a child (especially from the physical and sexual point of view) but is ready to undertake many attributes of an adult and to fulfill adult roles. But he is not yet fully acknowledged as an

---

* See S. N. Eisenstadt, "Archetypal Patterns of Youth," in E. Erikson (ed.), *Youth: Change and Challenge, op. cit.*, pp. 24-43.
One of the few scholars who has emphasized this dimension is B. Bettelheim, especially in his *Symbolic Wounds.* New York: The Free Press, 1964.
** "Archetypal Patterns of Youth," *op. cit.*

adult, a full member of the society. Rather, he is being "prepared" or is preparing himself for such adulthood.

"This image of youth—the cultural definition of youth—contains all the crucial elements of any definition of age in an especially articulated way. This is the stage at which the individual's personality acquires the basic psychological mechanisms of self-regulation and self-control, when self-identity becomes crystallized. It is also the stage at which the young are confronted with some models of the major roles they are supposed to emulate in adult life and with the major symbols and values of their culture and community. Moreover, during this stage the problem of linking the personal temporal transition with cosmic or societal time becomes extremely acute. All cultural definitions of youth describe it as a transitory phase, couched in terms of a transition toward something new, something basically different from the past. Hence the acuteness of the problem of linkage.

"The very emphasis on the transitory nature of youth and of its essentially preparatory character, however, may easily create a somewhat paradoxical situation. It may invoke an image of youth as the purest manifestation and repository of all ultimate cultural and societal values. Such an image is rooted, first, in the fact that to some extent youth is always defined as a period of 'role moratorium'—that is, as a period in which one may assume various roles without definitely choosing any. It does not require the various compromises inherent in daily participation in adult life. At the same time and under certain conditions, however, since it is also the period when maximum identification with the values of the society is stressed, it may be viewed as the repository of all the major basic human virtues and qualities. It may then be regarded as the only age at which full identification with the ultimate values and symbols of the society is attained—an attainment facilitated by the flowering of the cosmos or the society. . . ."

It is the combination of all these components of the cultural definition of youth—its transitory nature, the importance of basic symbols and attributes, and the relation of these symbols to the symbols of individual and collective identity—that also explains why youth may easily become a seed bed of rebellion and antinomian activities and orientations, as well as why many of the most basic themes of antinomianism and rebellion found in human society (the attempts to suspend the time dimension, to negate any institutionalization, to rebel against hierarchy and authority) may easily become focused around the image of youth. Significantly enough, many of these themes can be found—although mostly in a symbolic and transitory way—in many of the formalized ceremonies of *rites de passage* that exist in primitive societies. But in these situations these themes are symbolic and worked out "artificially" in specially transitory situations through which people pass on their way to assuming new roles.

In other societies, in historical situations, and especially in modern societies in general and in the more contemporary scene in particular, the situations in which these themes develop are indeed much more unrestrained and less institutionalized, thus becoming foci of potentially real rebellious or revolutionary orientations.

In order to be able to explain the various ways in which such situations and themes develop in modern societies it is necessary to take into account the general structural conditions specified in this book, as well as the problems of the *process* of institutionalizing various groups in general and youth groups in particular, and the charismatic dimensions of youth.

VII.

It might therefore be worthwhile, first, to see how all these conceptual tools may help us in analyzing and understanding the contemporary youth and intergenerational scene and, second, to re-examine, on the basis of this attempt, some of the broader theoretical implications of such an analysis.

The general causes for the development of modern youth groups and youth problems have been dealt with in greater detail in the book itself and will be only briefly recapitulated here. These causes are related primarily to the development of what has been called the "non-familial" division of labor in society. The process of modernization, of the development of modern industrial societies, is in a way concomitant with the fullest development of this type of social division of labor. Thus, inclusive membership in modern societies is usually based on the universal criterion of citizenship and is not conditioned by membership in any kinship or territorial subgroup. In these societies the family does not constitute a basic unit of the division of labor, especially not in production and distribution, and even in the sphere of consumption its functions are limited. Occupations are not usually inherited. Similarly, the family or kinship group does not constitute a basic unit of political or ritual activities. Moreover, the general scope of the activities of the family has been continuously diminishing as various specialized agencies tend to take over its functions in the field of education and recreation.

The major social developments of the nineteenth century (the establishment of national states, the spread of the industrial revolution, the great waves of intercontinental migrations) have contributed significantly to this diminution. In every new phase of modernization there tends to develop a growing discontinuity between the life of children, whether in the family or in the traditional school, and the "outside" world with its new and enlarged perspectives. To be sure, the extent to which the scope of the family is diminishing in modern societies is often exaggerated. In many social contents (neighborhood, friendship groups, informal associations, some class relations, and community relations), family kinship and status are still very influential. But the scope of these relations is more limited in modern societies than in many others, even if the widespread myth of the disappearance of the family has long since been exploded.

These varied developments were closely related to marked changes in the social functions and organizations of education, which it would be worthwhile to point out here. In pre-modern societies, the process of education was usually divided into several rather compartmentalized aspects. The central educational institutions were oriented mainly toward the education of an elite, and upper strata, and to the maintenance and development of the central cultural tradition in its varied manifestations. The local educational institutions, which were usually only loosely connected with the central ones, were oriented chiefly toward the maintenance of some general, diffuse, and rather passive identification of the various strata with the overall symbols of society. This identification, however, did not permit the local institutions to participate any more closely in the central political and cultural activities of the society nor provide any technical "know-how" which would be appropriate to their position in society. Between the two were several educational institutions which served as either channels of restricted "sponsored" mobility into the central spheres of the society or of some specific vocational preparation.

On the whole, the educational system in these societies was geared to the maintenance and perpetuation of a given, relatively unchanging, cultural tradition and did not serve as a channel either of widespread occupational and social mobility or as a device affording the broader strata overall active participation in the cultural and political order. The type of education given to different classes was largely, although not entirely, determined by their social-economic position. This situation, however, began to change with the onset of modernity, especially after the French Revolution on the one hand and the industrial on the other. Education began to deal with problems of forging new national communities and their common symbols, access to which tended to become more widely spread among different strata. At the same time, it began to serve increasingly as a channel of more general occupational- and allegedly achievement-based selection. Moreover, the system of education tended to become more centralized and unified, thus assuring its permeation into wider strata of the society.

VIII.

All these developments provided the background for the development of the various patterns of youth problems and cultures in modern societies, and they indicate the major types of stress which gave rise to these patterns, as well as the basic directions of reactions to these stresses.

One such focus was closely connected with the changes in family structure and with the growing dissociation between the occupational and cultural worlds of the different generations within the family, and the concomitant weakening of various links among them. A second focus developed around problems of occupational choice, advancement, and selection. A third focus involved the concern with growing demands for participation in the socio-cultural order, and particularly at the centers of these orders.

The attempts of youth in modern societies to react to these stresses manifested themselves (1) in the development of specific types of relatively autonomous youth groups and youth cultures, (2) in a continuously growing gap and discontinuity between the generations, especially during the transition from youth to adulthood, and (3) in the weakening of direct guidance by parents and teachers, and thereby of the relevance, for youth, of adult models.

Although there have been many concrete manifestations of the various youth problems and protests, some have become more prominent than others. One such type, which emerged principally in Central Europe around the middle of the nineteenth century, involved itself in wider social movements or aimed to reform society in terms of distinct, specific youth values.

The second major manifestation of the youth problem concerned "social problems" that grew out of urbanization or early industrialization, and out of migration. The main problems here involved loss of control by the family over its younger members, lack of adequate opportunities and vocational guidance, problems of maleducation, and various types of juvenile delinquency. Of chief importance were the occupational discontinuity and dislocation, and the inadequacy of occupational opportunities and of existing economic and societal frameworks to handle the problem. Between these two types of youth culture or revolt there developed various more informal types of youth groups which permeated all areas of modern society.

IX.

These various types of youth culture that developed during the early stages of modernization tended to exhibit some common characteristics. The close linkage between the growth of personality, psychological maturation, and definite role models derived from the adult world—very strong in primitive and many historical societies—was weakened. Hence, unlike primitive societies, in which these links remained intact, the very coalescence of youth into special groups tended to emphasize their uncertain social and cultural standing. This can most clearly be seen in what has been called the emergence of the problems and stresses of adolescence in modern societies, and the ambivalent attitudes of youth to adult society.

Paradoxically enough, the very process of extending education, of establishing separate, society-wide educational institutions, emphasized the special psychological and social problems of youth and strengthened the ambivalence of youth toward the adult world. This ambivalence was apparent on the one hand in youth's striving to communicate with the adult world and receive its recognition, while on the other hand it appeared in certain dispositions to accentuate the differences between them and the adult, and to oppose the various roles awaiting them in the society and the models presented to them by the adult world. Although their aim was to participate in the adult world, they tended at the same time to reject this world or at least many of its specific roles, models, and assumptions. The ambivalence perhaps could be most clearly seen in the ideologies of modern youth groups. Most of these groups tended to create an ideology that emphasized the discontinuity between youth and adulthood and the uniqueness of youth, but at the same time to indicate that this period, as the purest embodiment of major social cultural values, be recognized and upheld by the adult world.

In many ways youth presented itself, and was to no small degree accepted by the adult world, as the purest embodiment of the central charismatic orientations and symbols of the emerging modern social and cultural order. But this posture also implied, as we have mentioned, that the attitude of most of these youth groups toward adult models was more ambivalent than negative. The type of order that the adults represented was not entirely rejected by the young; rather, they strove either to participate in this order and in the more concrete opportunities available in it (especially economic and occupational) or to re-shape many of its concrete contours and details in order to open it up to wider participation. They did not, however, neces-sarily reject the significance of the type of order that was rep-resented by adult society, or at least what was represented by the aspirations and charismatic orientations of this society.

One important derivative of this fact was that most of the types of youth culture and protest, characteristic of the early stages of modern societies, tended to develop very important—even if often only implicit—assumptions. These assumptions were two. First, there existed some close connection and congruence among the solutions to the problems or stresses arising from all three foci of tensions mentioned above. Second, because of such congruency, the problems of social and cultural identity faced by youth could be solved by participation in these various youth groups within their ambivalent, but not negative, attitude toward social and cultural order.

In terms of the structure of the youth groups, this meant that within most of them there tended to develop some degree of con-gruence in, first, their internal solidarity; second, in the possibil-ities of attaining some adult roles (mostly occupational); and, third, in some participating meaningfully in the broader social and cultural order or even at its centers. Again, the exact ways in which these different elements tended to be combined varied greatly among different types of youth groups—the outright delinquent groups being the only exception. This absence of total rejection of the adult world in most of these youth groups was especially evident in the fact that most of the articulate youth protests were very closely connected with the more general social, national, and political adult protests and that the rebellious youth identity became very closely related to the symbols of collective identity developed more general modern movements of protest. It might, therefore, be worth while here to dwell on some of the major characteristics of movements of protest during the early modern period.

X.

The major thrusts of protest were based on the assumption that most social problems, the problems of meaningful socio-cultural participation and the problems generated by industrialization, could be solved through reformation and reorganization of the political and national centers. These centers were the major focus and framework of charismatic orientations by which the modern social and cultural orders were defined and were the major social and cultural reference points of the individual's identity. They were also regarded as being able, through series of appropriate social policies or through revolutionary changes, to restructure those aspects of modern society which were felt to be most conducive to alienation and anomie.

Thus, during the first stages of the modern period, most movements of social protest evolved from broadening the scope of participation and channels of access to the political and cultural centers, of reforming their cultural and social content, of solving the problems of unequal participation in them, and of finding ways to attenuate, or overcome, through policies of these centers, the most critical problems arising out of industrialization and the development of the capitalist system. It was the solution of these problems that constituted the major goals of most social and national movements during the early modern, and it was these goals which were thought to embody the most important charismatic dimension of the modern socio-cultural order.

From the point of view of our discussion, those initial youth movements which were ideologically oriented were very closely related to such protest movements, and most of them were part of these movements or at least shared many of their assumptions and aims.

XI.

Types of youth problems and forms of youth protest have profoundly influenced the kinds of attitude and social policy that have developed with regard to them. One such attitude was manifest in the interest of all social movements and political parties to absorb the social and political potential of youth groups. Thus, special youth sections were established by most of the political and social organizations that developed in modern societies.

Second, many agencies of "civic education" have developed to direct the potential of youth groups into accepted and "safe" channels and to show how the less developed, more peripheral groups of the society, the majority of the population, could be absorbed peacefully into the central institutions of the society. Specifically, external conditions of life in urban centers were improved and recreational and semi-educational services were provided. In addition, corrective systems, probation officers, juvenile judges, and social workers were added to the scene. Finally, the most encompassing, educational and social policies were adopted which attempted to provide educational facilities for all citizens, and at the same time to respond to problems arising out of the new needs of the economy for different kinds of manpower.

These policies had different starting points. They dealt with different, seemingly even disconnected, aspects of the so-called "youth problem"; they took different approaches; very often they were undertaken by different people and agencies. Yet they shared basic ideological assumptions. Their main aim was to bring youth back into the fold of adult society, and they stressed giving the young a chance to develop social identity. Thus they reinforced the parallel assumptions existing in the major youth groups.

But in fact, especially in education, these policies were based on different orientations and assumptions, sometimes complementary and sometimes contradictory. One approach was to broaden educational opportunities and hence also youth's aspirations. Another was to admit gifted or select groups into the higher echelons of "central" educational and occupational activities. Another was aimed at assuring general participation in the social, political, and cultural orders of society.

Thus, on the one hand, these policies tended to emphasize the general ascriptive right of all citizens to participate, first passively but later actively, in the formation of the cultural and social order. In this way these policies made possible, for the first time since the classical period of the city-states, wide participation in cultural, social, and economic affairs, thus expanding the scope of individual creativity and making an age of plenty an increasingly realizable aspiration.* On the other hand, by emphasizing educational criteria and occupational selection and placement, they restricted participation and called into question its significance, as well as curtailing the vision of plenty.

XII.

But these contradictory implications were not yet fully apparent during the earlier phases of development of modern societies. Later on these problems would develop in almost all major institutional fields.

The most important such developments in the economic field were the bureaucratization of most types of economic markets and the growth of bureaucratization, specialization, and professionalization in the occupational structure, thus increasing the close interrelationship between educational attainment and occupational placement. These developments gave rise to discrepancies and problems in areas such as social mobility, educational selection, and the development of patterns of consumption.

In the field of mobility the most general development was the rise in levels of aspiration among all strata of the population, but without any means to satisfy such hopes. Many elites attempted to develop and maintain types of restricted, "sponsored" mobility, but were unable to confine the aims and goals of the various groups to these limited opportunities. Concurrently, the continuous intensification of "contest" mobility beyond the capacity of many of the existing occupational opportunities and the impact of educational selection continued to make their effects felt.

These problems were closely related to those which arose

---

* See in greater detail Edward Shils, "Dreams of Plenitude, Nightmares of Scarcity," in S. M. Lipset & P. Altbach (eds.), *Students in Revolt*. Boston: Houghton Mifflin Co., 1969, pp. 1-35.

in connection with the various systems of educational selection, systems which, together with universal education, have become fully or partly institutionalized in many modern societies. Perhaps the most extreme examples evolved in England and in Sweden, but they can be found in one way or another in almost all countries. One of the most important developments here was the increase in the number of different types of "drop-outs," extending beyond the older type of professional, "intellectual," or student unemployment to the lower echelons of the secondary and primary schools.

The drop-out problem was seriously complicated by the continuous bureaucratization and centralization of the labor markets, by the increased need for the state and communal agencies to provide both work and educational facilities, and by the fact that in many countries (as today in many new states) the government became one of the most important dispensers of professional prestige occupations. One important result of these developments was the fact that many groups were relegated early in their lifetimes to occupations which restricted the possibility of later mobility; they thus developed feelings of frustration and helplessness within a relatively expanding society and economy. The tendency to early marriage, which among students and lower-class families has become very widespread in many contemporary societies, became closely related to these developments.

Another tendency, in a sense contradictory, tended to develop here among those strata of the population which did go on to college. Here, as Parsons and Platt have very convincingly shown, the college situation and setting has created a new "post-adolescent" stage of transition to more complicated levels of structural differentiation and socialization, with new levels of severe "anxiety." *

Another area which affected youth was the growing emphasis on consumption. The area of choice grew, as did awareness of choice and pressures to exercise it. The result, paradoxically, was the homogenization of patterns of consumption growing

---

* Talcott Parsons and Gerald M. Platt, "Age, Social Structure and Socialization in Higher Education," *Sociology of Education* XLIII(1), Winter, 1970: 1-36.

out of direct access by youth to many amenities of adult society with seemingly little need for direct guidance by adults. But, at the same time, given the realities of income distribution, this very expansion of the scope of consumers' choice tended also to give rise to a growing feeling that real or imagined opportunities were being restricted. It was here that the contradiction between the dream of plenty and the realities of even an expanding economy could become most acutely felt.

XIII.

Parallel developments occurred in the cultural sphere, which added to the difficulties of forging a meaningful relationship in terms of personal identity with the continuous processes of historical change sweeping over the world. Perhaps the most important single, overall development in this field—which in a great variety of ways has been common to many different countries—has been the transfer of emphasis from the creation of and participation in the future-oriented collective value to the growing institutionalization of such values. This development has been closely related to an important shift in the whole pattern of protest in modern societies. Here, as in so many other cases, when many of the initial charismatic orientations and goals have become at least partially institutionalized (through the attainment of political independence, broadening of the scope of political participation, revolutionary changes of regimes or the development of welfare state policies, and the like) they give rise to new processes of change, to new series of problems and tensions, and to new foci of protest. It is important to emphasize that the same is true of youth movements and activities when the goals and values toward whose realization these movements aim become institutionalized by being accepted as part of the structure of their societies. This has indeed happened in most modern societies. Thus, in Russia, youth movements became fully institutionalized through the organization of the Komsomol. In many European countries the institutionalizing of youth groups, agencies, and ideologies came through association with political parties, for through acceptance as part of the educational system. In the United States, many organizations (such as the Boy Scouts) have become an accepted part of community life and, to some extent, a symbol of differential social status. In many Asian and African countries, organized youth movements have become part of the official educational organizations.

These various processes of institutionalization of collective charismatic values shifted the focus of protest in modern societies in general and of youth protest in particular. This new focus of protest and dissatisfaction was of several kinds. After the establishment of modern "social" centers, the most visible and vocal ones, and in a sense also the most continuous ones, were those focused around the claim of groups which still felt themselves to be deprived or underprivileged in their access to the center, or in the relative benefits which they received. Here, special minorities—national and ethnic groups in European societies, Negroes in the U.S., and in general the lower, poorer groups which were ignored by the welfare state—were the most important focus and bearers of protests and dissatisfaction.

This feeling of incomplete institutionalization was also strong in a second type of protest, which tended to develop after the initial insitutionalization of modern centers. This type was oriented chiefly toward the growing feeling of being manipulated by the incumbents of the political and cultural centers, even if formal and symbolic access to them has been attained—or to some degree especially because such access had indeed been attained. This protest was very often related to difficulties in attaining actual access to the centers because of their growing complexity. In more contemporary stages of development of modern societies, there arose many new types of social or cultural protest, borne by relatively non-deprived and relatively non-manipulated groups, although often joining with more deprived groups. The most important element of these new types of protest was strong scepticism toward the new modern centers, a lack of commitment to them, and a tendency to be unresponsive to the institutional and symbolic demands of these centers.

All these changes have also been associated with a marked decline of ideology in the traditional nineteenth-and early twentieth-century sense and a general waning of traditional political-ideological interest. This decline, in turn, has been connected with a growing feeling of spiritual or cultural shallowness in that the new social and economic benefits accruing from the welfare state or from the "consumers society" are spiritually and culturally shallow. This tendency is intensified by the fact that in many countries, be they the new states of Asia and Africa or post-revolutionary Russia or European welfare states, the new generation of youth and students faces not only reactionary parents but also successful revolutionaries who have become part of a new "establishment," creating a new collective reality which youth has to face, a reality that evinces all the characteristics of a bureaucratized establishment but at the same time presents itself as the embodiment of revolutionary collective and spiritual values. The tendency also was reinforced by a weakening in the ideological dimension of the Cold War and by the consequent loss of negative images and symbols.

XIV.

Within this general framework of cultural developments several special developments or processes stand out. One is what may be called the breakdown in continuity of historical consciousness or awareness. The new generation has not experienced a worldwide depression or two world wars, which were crucial in the formation of their parents' attitudes. What is more significant is that the parent generation failed to transmit to the new generation the significance of these historical events, partly because of the institutionalization of their collective goals and their growing affluence.

The very emphasis on the new goals has increased a tendency to stress the novelty of the world created by the parents—a tendency taken up and reinforced by the younger generations.

Another cultural process—closely related to the preceding one and especially prominent in Western European societies and in America in particular—has been the reversal of the hitherto existing relation between the definition of different age-groups and the possibilities of social and cultural creativity. Youth has come to be regarded as a preparatory stage leading to independent and creative participation in social and cultural life, as the very embodiment of permissive, often unstructured creativity. Only later, as adults, would constraints of a relatively highly organized, constrictive, meritocratic, and bureaucratic environment have to be faced. It probably was not these constraints as such (which in themselves probably were not stronger than those in most past societies) but rather the discrepancy between the permissive premises of family and educational life and the realities of adult life which tended to create the feeling of frustration and disappointment among youth.

XV.

Many of the processes of structural and cultural change and contradiction analyzed above tended to impinge most intensively on the social and cultural situation of youth and on the concrete manifestations of youth problems and protest. Several such repercussions can be singled out. The areas of social life that the specific youth and student culture encompasses have tended to expand continuously. First, they have extended over longer periods, reaching, through the impact of the extension of higher education, to what before was regarded as early adulthood.* Second, they tend more and more to include areas of work, of leisure-time activity, and of many interpersonal relations. Third, the potential and actual autonomy of youth and youth groups, and the possibility their members have of direct access to work, to marriage and family life, to political rights, and to consumption has greatly increased, while their dependence on adults has greatly decreased. Paradoxically enough, the growing direct access of young people to various areas of life has given rise to a growing insecurity of status and self-identity and a growing ambiguity in adult roles.

This insecurity and ambiguity tends to be increased, first, by the prolongation of the span between biological and social maturity and by the extension of the number of years spent in basically "preparatory" (educational) institutions. Second, it

---

* See Parsons and Platt, *op. cit.*

is enhanced by the growing dissociation between the values of these institutions and the future occupational and parental roles of those participating in them. Third, it is magnified by the fact that for a long period of time many "young" people may as yet not have made any clear occupational choices or assumed any occupational responsibilities or may be dependent on their parents or on public institutions for their economic needs, while at the same time they constitute an important economic force as consumers and certainly exercise political rights.

In turn, this situation may become intensified or aggravated by the growing demographic preponderance of the "young" in the whole population and by the increasing possibilities of ecological mobility.*

XVI.

Thus there tended to develop in many contemporary societies, particularly in the highly developed and industrialized ones, a whole series of structural and symbolic discontinuities, all related to the development and spread of the institutional and symbolic dimensions of modernization. These discontinuities often may culminate in a crisis or weakening of authority, evident in the lack of development of adequate role-models and in the erosion of many of the bases of legitimacy of existing authority. As a result of all these processes, the possibility of linking personal transition to social groups and to cultural values, so strongly emphasized in youth movements, has been considerably weakened. In general, these developments have soiled the image of the societal and cultural future and have deprived it of its allure. Either the ideological separation between present and future has diminished, or the two have tended to become entirely dissociated. The first of these conditions has led to what Reisman has called "the cult of immediacy"; out of the other has arisen a total negation of the present in the name of an entirely different future. Both are totally unrelated to any consciousness of the historical past.

---

* See A. Sauvy, *La Montee des Jeunes*. Paris: Colman-Levy, 1966.

XVII.

Many of these structural and cultural changes, contradictions, and discontinuities tended to affect most directly the social and cultural situation of youth and the concrete manifestations of youth problems and protest. All these elements have given rise to new types of youth problems and protest. Some of the older types of problems still persist, but the new types of youth culture, protest, and rebellion are more varied and prominent than those that developed earlier in the modern period. They differ from one another in many criteria: internal cohesion, continuity, span of membership, and the nature of the symbols around which their identity develops. They range from relatively mild emphasis on the activities of youth up to openly rebellious attitudes toward adult society. They vary in attitude toward the basic occupational social, communal, and leisure activities; in their aspirations with regard to these activities; and in their self-perception in terms of these values and of the general society, of their own place or places within it and of the possibilities open to them to advance within it. They vary also in their attitudes toward the older generation, both on a personal level as models of their own future roles and powers in society and as channels of transition within it.

And yet, despite these many differences, these new protests tend to evince certain common characteristics. Within most of these new types of youth groups and protest, a growing dissociation tends to develop among the elements which we found coalesced in youth movements and rebellion in the earlier developmental stages of modern societies—i.e., in the internal unity of the youth groups and the expressive interaction of their members, in their orientation to the attainment of occupational and other "adult" roles, and to participation in social and cultural orders and centers. It is this dissociation, along with the feeling of members of these groups that they cannot forge a meaningful identity within the different types of youth culture, which constitute the most important characteristic or syndrome of the new types of youth and student rebellion and protest. Perhaps the most important derivative of this dissociation is the tendency toward a far-reaching, extreme break between the world of the young and of the adult—the feeling of the younger generation that the adult world cannot provide them with any significant models for their own rebellion and for the establishment of their own identity—even negative ones. Hence youth, in its more extreme responses, develops a totally negative attitude toward the basic premises of the modern social and cultural order and denies the significance or legitimacy of the claims that these centers may make on the young.

The foci of protest tend to shift from demands for greater participation in national-political centers or from attempts to influence their socio-economic policies to new directions. The most important of these directions seem to be, first, attempts to "disrobe" these centers of their charismatic legitimacy and perhaps of any legitimacy at all; second, continuous searches for new loci of meaningful participation beyond these existing socio-political centers and the concomitant attempts to create new centers which would be independent of them; third, attempts to couch the patterns of participation in their centers not so much in socio-political or economic terms, but more in symbols of primordial or of direct social participation.

Thus it seems that these developments touch not only on some of the most important structural developments in post-modern societies, but also on the relations of these developments to some of the basic symbolic constituents of these societies—to basic components of the definition of their socio-cultural orders as well as of their cultural, collective, and personal identities.

Significantly enough, many of these new orientations of protest were also directed not only against the bureaucratization and functional rationalization connected with growing technology, but also against the supposed central place of science and scientific investigation as the basis—or even one of the bases—of the socio-cultural order.

These phenomena seem to be rooted not only in the structural derivations that attend the institutionalization of modern charismatic symbols and centers and in attempts to solve modern social, political, and economic problems, but also in what Weber called the "demystification of the world." This demystification focuses on the possibility that participation in the existing social and cultural orders and their centers may indeed be meaningless, that these centers can lose their aura, that the Emperor may indeed be naked. Thus arises a new type of social alienation derived not only from the feeling of being lost in a maze of large-scale, anonymous organizations and frameworks, but also from the meaninglessness of participating in political and national centers.

These centers may be losing their special place as the loci of participation in a meaningful socio-cultural order, and as the major social and cultural referrents of personal identity. There tends to develop as a result a growing feeling of lack of congruence between the quest for participation in the charismatic dimension of human and social existence and these specific types of social and political centers.

XVIII.

Against this background one can understand why youth and student protesters and rebels deny the possibility of developing their identity through some reference to the existing centers. This denial may take a wide variety of forms, from apathy to destruction of property and interpersonal aggressiveness to symbolic confrontation with the central authorities of the society. Its more extreme manifestations usually have assumed, first, a combination of aimlessness, of destructive actions and interpersonal aggressiveness, and/or an emphasis on direct expressive activities and a relative weakness in establishing stable frameworks, groups, and relations. Second, they appear as direct violent confrontations with the representatives of the existing order.

These more extreme manifestations of the new type of youth culture and rebellion often taken on the form of sectarian, totalistic, and self-enclosed groups, seemingly similar to extreme religious revivalist and/or pietist groups. They tend to evolve a great variety of old and new symbols—be they those of saints, martyrs, monks, or heretics—manifesting their heresy in new styles of dress, sexual and communal identities and attitudes, and emphasizing in this way the various basic components of the primordial imagery of youth.

While these attitudes and symbols become most fully articulated in the more extreme, self-enclosed groups—be they hippie colonies or "revolutionary" student groups—in a less extreme form they tend also to pervade wider circles of youth and adult alike.

But these characteristics and orientations have manifested themselves in different ways in various types of new protests and rebellion. Thus, for instance, they revealed themselves in the marked change that developed in the overall trend of juvenile deliquency in many countries: a continuous increase in the more violent types of delinquent activities as against the more traditional petty crimes against property.

Among the Teddy Boys or lower-class Halbstarke, composed largely of drop-outs, this denial could manifest itself in a strong emphasis on the internal solidarity of the peer-group, a purely adaptive relation to the occupational structure, together with apathy toward participating in any broader community, political, or cultural order. Among other lower-class and lower-middle-class drop-outs it manifested itself in a growing general apathy toward the family, with only minimal solidarity even among their peer groups.

Among the Hippies we find a similar denial of the meaningfulness of the existing institutional framework, and especially of its meritocratic, competitive, and achievement-oriented activities and frameworks. The Hippies, however, have attempted to transfer the internal solidarity of the groups into a more general subculture, segregated from the existing order and serving potentially as a starting point for a new social or cultural order.* Among the radical students, especially those from the upper or upper-middle groups, this dissociation and negation manifest themselves in a more general or even total negation of the existing social and political order, and in attempts to overthrow it through series of violent confrontations. Here this negation is oriented against the symbolic and institutional premises of the existing

---

* See on the Hippies Jesse R. Pitts, "The Hippies as Counter-Meritocracy," *Dissent*, July-August 1969: 326-338; and Nathan Adler, "The Antinomian Personality: The Hippie Character Type," *Psychiatry* XXXI, 1968: 325-337.

order. In their extreme manifestations they aim not only to establish a separate subculture but to destroy the existing order in the name of their primitive values and orientations. At the same time, unlike the Hippies, they seem to develop much less cohesive internal social relations.

Of special interest here is the attack on the university. In many cases the student outbursts are, truly enough, sparked by the traditional and authoritarian structure of the university, or by its growing bureaucratization and a consequent widening gap between faculty and students. But paradoxically enough, very often it is the very students who deny the possibility of finding any acceptable models within the adult world who also complain about the lack of such contact.

This paradox does, however, point out some of the basic roots of the attack on the university, some of the reasons why the university is chosen as one of the focal symbols and objects of total attack against the existing order. It is not that the various bureaucratic or meritocratic features are necessarily much more refined or rigid in the university than in other organizations and institutions, but rather that here the contradiction between them and the demand for broader participation in the social and cultural orders tends to become much more salient and articulated. The university is regarded as the logical area for encouraging and permitting such participation, and as the very place in which the quest for such creativity could be institutionalized. In this way the university has tended to become the major focus of legitimation of the modern social order and the attack on it indicates not only dissatisfaction with its own internal arrangements but also with the fact that it serves as one mechanism of occupational and meritocratic selection. The choice of the university as the object of attack emphasizes the denial that the existing order can realize these basic premises of modern life: to establish and maintain an order which could do justice to the claims to creativity and participation in the broader social order and to overcome the various contradictions which have developed within it from the point of view of these claims. It is, of course, very significant that this denial is also often shared and emphasized by many of the faculty itself, which evinces in this regard some of the guilt feelings alluded to above of the parent generation in general and of the intellectuals among them in particular. Within the university basic themes of youth rebellion become firmly connected with those of intellectual antinomianism. It is here that the rebellion against authority, hierarchy, and organizational frameworks, fed by the dreams of plenty and of permissive unstructured creativity, tends to become particularly prominent, especially since the university serves also as the institutional meeting point between the educational and the central cultural spheres of the society.

Perhaps the most significant fact about these movements against the university is that they develop throughout the world in macro-societal situations which are structurally basically different—in the centers of highly developed modern societies as well as in emerging societies, both of which are perceived by those participating in them as symbolically similar. Those participating in them tend to develop rather similar attitudes toward the symbolic aspects, toward the premises and promises of modernism and toward situations of relative deprivation with regard to these premises and promises.

The fact that the bases of such deprivation or discontinuity differ greatly does not necessarily diminish their symbolic affinity, which cuts across different historical and social situations. In the emerging countries the contest is mainly between traditional and modern norms and habits, in communist regimes between an authoritarian regime and those who went to extend liberty, and in the highly industrialized societies mainly between the sons of affluence and the structural-organizational aspects, of their affluent society. In a sense this symbolic affinity is reinforced by just such a broad structural variety, aided by the role the university plays in the spread of modernization. This crucial place of the university and of the rebellion against the university in the whole panorama of the contemporary youth scene also points to one of its major specific characteristics—namely, the combination of generational conflict with intellectual antinomianism. It is this combination that is perhaps one of the great "innovations" of the contemporary scene and it might be worthwhile to expand on it in somewhat greater detail.

XIX.

Intellectual antinomianism is not something new in the history of mankind. It constitutes an extreme manifestation of the tensions and ambivalence between intellectuals and authority which to a large extent are given in all human societies. These tensions and ambivalence are rooted in two distinct, yet strongly interconnected, bases. One is the close relation between the activities and orientations of intellectuals and those of the authorities and holders of power, in the formation and crystallization of the specific cultural and social contours of the charismatic orientations and symbols of any society or civilization and of its tradition and centers. The second is the close relation between some at least of the skills and technical knowledge of some groups of intellectuals and the organizational exigencies of exercise of power and authority in any society. *

This tension is due not only to the antithesis, often stressed in Western thought, between the organization and exercise of power and participation in the maintenance of broad sociocultural order—although this antithesis may indeed constitute an important basis of this tension. Inherent in this tension is also the fact that the charismatic qualities of social order—and the quest to participate in them—are not focused or centered in only one institutional sphere, and that they become dispersed, albeit differentially, in all institutional spheres. This in itself tends to explain to some extent, both the plurality of authorities in any society, the "natural" predilection of the holders of political power to attempt to monopolize and regulate the central institutions of the society and its charismatic orientations and their ultimate impossibility to do so.

The potentially "antinomian" tendencies of intellectuals become especially articulated, insofar as the tensions between them and political authorities tend to converge with some of the

---

* See, for instance, E. Shils, "Intellectuals," *International Encyclopedia of the Social Sciences*. New York: Macmillan and The Free Press, 1968; K. Mannheim, *Ideology and Utopia*, and *Man & Society in an Age of Reconstruction*. London: Oxford University Press, 1933 and 1934; and the selections in G. B. de Huszar (ed.), *The Intellectuals, A Controversial Portrait*, New York: The Free Press, 1960.

major themes of protest, rebellion, and heterodoxy. Such themes have been continuously recurring in the history of human societies and civilizations and have been largely rooted in the tensions inherent in any process of institutionalization of social life, in general, and of authority in particular.

Among these themes is, first, the tension between the very complexity and fragmentation of human relations inherent in any institutional division of labor, as against the possibilities of some total unconditionality of participation in the basic social and cultural order. Parallel to this are the tensions inherent in the temporal dimension of the human and social condition, in the tensions between the deferment of gratification in the present as against the possibility of attainment in the future.

Hence many movements of protest tend to emphasize the suspension or negation of the structural and organizational division of labor in general, and to emphasize the ideal of "communitas" of direct, unmediated participation in the social and cultural orders. They tend also to emphasize, together with such participation, the suspension of the tensions between "productivity" and "distribution" and tend to merge these two together through a basic commitment to the unconditional participation in the community.

Similarly, many such movements display a strong emphasis on the suspension of the differences between various time-dimensions—between past, present and future—and of the relation between such dimensions to patterns of allocation of rewards.

The two institutional-symbolic foci around which the ambivalence to traditions and orders tend to converge are, first, those of authority, especially as vested in the various political and cultural centers, and second, the system of stratification in which the symbolic dimensions of hierarchy are combined with structural aspects of division of labor. It is thus that symbols of authority and of hierarchy constitute the most common objects of ambivalence and foci for demands for change in any society.

These various tendencies to heterodoxy, antinomy, and rebellion are most clearly articulated by intellectuals, but it would be wrong to assume that they are oriented only against the political authority. They may also be oriented against intellectual authority, and it is perhaps in this direction that the antinomian tendencies of intellectuals may tend to become most clearly articulated.

Needless to say, such antinomianism is an extreme phenomenon very often found only within small groups of intellectuals and which tends to develop under very specific conditions. Yet it may also be an important ingredient of the orientations of wider groups of intellectuals, an ingredient which under certain conditions may indeed become more widespread. And indeed the conditions conducive to a more pervasive spread of such antinomian attitudes and dispositions have been most prevalent in modern societies, and in contemporary ones in particular, and they are closely related to the very spread of modernity, if its structural characteristics and of its ideological premises and symbols, which we have analyzed above.

XX.

Thus we come back to the analysis of the specific conditions under which these different types of youth groups and manifestations of youth rebellions tend to develop in modern societies, and to the question of whether such specific conditions can indeed be derived from the general concepts and hypotheses of this book, taking into account the additional analytical concepts and dimensions mentioned in this introduction—the dichotomy between the symbolic, charismatic dimensions of youth and the problems of institutional entrepreneurship. Insofar as any specific data on the distribution of youth cultures exist, they do indicate that the development is closely connected with the different impact of the various new elements in the occupational and cultural spheres which we have pointed out previously. But there are as yet little exact data.

One of the types of youth rebellion on which there tends to exist relatively full data is the radical student. * Here we may

---

* Among the most valuable collections of data and analysis of this problem is the July 1967 issue of the *Journal of Social Issues*, XXIII (3); see also S. M. Lipset (ed.), *Student Politics*. New York: Basic Books, 1967, and S. M. Lipset and P. Altbach (eds.), *Students in Revolt, op. cit.*

quote from Abrams, who both summarized data from Lipset and Altbach and pointed out some additional dimensions of the problem:

". . . This [i.e., Lipset's and Altbach's] research suggests that activists include a tiny proportion of the age span of youth and a small proportion (hardly ever more than 10 percent) of the total body of students. Second, it suggests that activists are disproportionately recruited from privileged social backgrounds; that they come typically from comfortable professional homes and themselves expect to do well in their careers. Again, activists tend to have parents whose own values are liberal and who have been relatively permissive in the way they brought up their children. Fourth, activists seem to have been disproportionately successful at school, to do better academically than non-political students and to be more intellectually disposed. Finally they tend to be concentrated in institutions which even among universities place a particular emphasis on liberal, intellectual and academic values and which, physically, are either very large or very concentrated". *

Beyond these data Abrams also specified some conditions that give rise in modern societies to specific youth consciousness, saying that ". . . Paradoxically, then, age becomes important as a basic for social action in societies where it is ceasing to control access to social status. How far the resulting cultural and political innovation on the part of the young will crop into movements of youth 'for itself,' movements actually articulating the idea of generational conflict, and how far the theme of generational conflict will 'take' in the society at large is, however, a separate matter. It will depend in part on the extent to which particular groupings of young people are objectively victimized by the social system as well as being subjectively perplexed by it—the closing down of educational opportunities in late-nineteenth-century Russia had a lot to do with the recruitment of highly educated young people to the cause of revolution. It will depend in part on the relative unavailability

* See P. Abrams, "Rites de Passage," *op. cit.* p. 186. The research he refers to is S. M. Lipset & P. Altbach, *Students, Politics and Higher Education in the U. S.,* in S. M. Lipset, *Student Politics, op. cit.,* pp. 199-253.

of other symbols of protest and solidarity—the pre-emption of class by compromised organizations such as the CGT and the Labor Party for example. And it will depend finally on the extent to which the society provides settings for interaction among numbers of young people which are at once concentrated geographically and relatively well insulated from the adult world—settings in which there is no one but the young and in which all the young share common predicaments, including exclusive relationships of subordination to adults, universities rather than factories therefore. If the environment is favorable in all three of these respects the young are almost certain to define their experience in terms of a conflict of generations. . . ."

Thus whatever data do exist, both on student radicals and other types of youth organizations and rebellions, point out the importance of the central mechanisms emphasized in this book—the "discontinuity"—especially between family and the broader institutional setting—and the necessity to extend and refine this concept. It was indeed sometimes questioned whether this concept was adequately applied to the more specific type of rebellion by rich youth where seemingly there does exist a high degree of continuity between the permissive and liberal values of the family on the one hand and of the schools or especially universities on the other. *

A closer look at the data does however indicate that such discontinuity does exist in these cases, except that it may tend to become transposed beyond the direct opposition between family on the one hand, and educational and occupational sectors on the other, to the different sectors of the society through which youth passes, and that therefore the foci of such discontinuity tend to become, in modern societies in general and in contemporary societies in particular, much more diversified. They may include discontinuity between the family and the educational and occupational spheres, between the family and educational

---

* See for instance Richard Flasks, "The Liberated Generation: An Exploration of the Roots of Students Protest," *The Journal of Social Issues,* XXIII, 1967: 52-75; and *idem*: "Social and Cultural Meanings of Student Revolt: Some Informal Comparative Observations." Paper prepared for presentation at meetings of American Association for the Advancement of Science, Dallas, Texas, December, 1968.

institutions on the one hand and the occupational sector on the other, between the productive and the consumer roles in the economic sector, between the values and orientations inculcated in the family and the educational institutions and the central collective symbols of the society, between the premises of these symbols and the actual political roles of the parents and young people—thus ultimately cutting across family roles themselves.

XXI.

The available data also bear out that age groups, particularly youth, are especially sensitive to various types of discontinuity and may therefore tend to develop under such conditions a growing predisposition to self-awareness and to the development of new collective symbols. In addition, these data point out that under such conditions youth itself may become a focus of wider rebellion or dissatisfaction for some members of its own age group, as well as for others. But this does not necessarily mean that youth either simply creates new symbols or that it merely accepts whatever new symbols are provided by various institutional entrepreneurs from their own fold or from the society at large.

The process through which the various symbolic dimensions of youth become components in the definition of the cultural and collective identity constitutes, in all such situations, part of a continuous cultural, social, and political struggle involving a search for new bases of authority. This process necessarily varies a great deal according to the type of discontinuity, and since such discontinuities may vary within any single historical society or sector thereof, so also variation develops to a highly differentiated degree even within the same sector or "class."

Similarly, the differences in the extent of self-consciousness, creativity, and historical impact of specific generations—a problem already taken up by Mannheim*—tend to vary greatly in modern, even more than in historical, societies.

All these variations seem to be related to different types of

---

* See K. Mannheim, "On the Problem of Generations," *op. cit.*

discontinuities, and it is still one of the major tasks of social research in this area to analyze more systematically the relations between such different types of discontinuity and different types of youth rebellion. But it should again be stressed that in most modern, and especially contemporary, societies there exists a very large variety of such types of discontinuity and that it is not the more dramatic ones that necessarily are also the more prevalent ones.

XXII.

Thus we come here to the problem of the possible impact of all these developments on the format of modern society. It is, of course, difficult to predict the long-range impact of these new types of protest and rebellion on the structure of modern social, political, and cultural orders. Some may see them as the harbingers of an entirely new civilization, of the same order as the various sects which developed at the end of the Roman Empire and which ushered in the Christian era. But even if one made no such extravagant prediction, there can be no doubt that these developments will have several important repercussions on the structure of modern societies. Perhaps the most important thing is to recognize both the continuous ubiquity as well as the mutability of the conditions that give rise in modern and modernizing societies to continuously changing and new types of youth rebellion, protest, organizations, and activities. Second, especially in industrial societies, youth rebels are a minority in their respective age groups, minorities which tend to crystallize under the rather specific conditions outlined above.

Thus, it seems quite true that, despite the great upsurge of continuous youth rebellions, it is doubtful whether youth in modern industrial societies will develop into a continuous organized political force capable of continuous organized political, activities. Only in very exceptional circumstances—the early solidifying of a new political system and the consequent lack of availability of adequate openings, for example—will the political struggle become couched—as it tends to be in some African states —entirely in terms of "generational groups." But even then, with regard to any specific generation it will be a passing, although continuously recurring, phenomenon.* Moreover, only in relatively few cases may these movements or parts of them become allied with some of the existing leftist parties. I refer here to the rapidly urbanizing and industrializing parts of Latin America or Italy, where conditions may develop not unlike those that prevailed in the early European industrializing societies. In European countries themselves the major shift may be in the direction of a growing "political radicalization" of the younger generation of "bourgeois" families as against a growing conservatism of those of the workers.**

But whatever the direct impact of these movements on the workings of existing political systems, organizations, and groups, some other long-range repercussions of theirs may indeed be discerned, even if tentatively. One impact will be the development of new targets of continuous protest which will add, in both organizational and symbolical terms, to the available reservoir of models and of traditions of protest in modern societies. This indicates a very important shift in the focus of protests in modern societies. As already mentioned, the major shift here is away from greater participation in national political centers or from attempts to influence socio-economic policies in new directions. The most important of these attempts seem to be, first, to strip these centers of their charismatic legitimacy—and perhaps of any legitimacy at all; second, to search continuously for new areas of significant participation beyond these existing centers to create new centers which would be independent of existing ones; and third, to couch the patterns of participation in these centers not so much in socio-political or economic terms, but in symbols of primordial relations or of direct social participation.

In a sense, these new targets of protest go back to anarchist traditions in which protest orientations were not focused around political participation or were at least ambivalent to it. But since these movements of protest arise from the institutionalization of

---

* See A. Zolberg, "Youth as a Political Phenomenon in Tropical Africa," *op. cit.*

** See R. Inglehart, "The Silent Revolution in Europe—Intergnerational Change in Six Countries," unpublished paper, University of Michigan, 1970.

former goals which assumed some congruency between the charismatic social, political, and cultural centers and their economic activities, they may already denote new dimensions of change in modern societies.

It seems that the more extreme of these movements, and especially those of the students, will constitute continuous reservoirs of new types of revolutionary activity, a revolutionary activity which will be fed and reinforced by the continuous spread of modernization throughout the world and by the problems and aspirations it raises. Most of these movements and ideologies will be leftist oriented, thus continuing the predominent leftist bent of most modern student movements; but the degree of their organizational proximity to leftist, socialist parties will vary considerably and on the whole will probably be rather ambivalent than discontinuous.

Given their pronounced predilection against any "establishment" orders and organizations as their basic ideological and antinomian orientations and the transitory nature of their membership, these revolutionary groups and activities will develop into full-fledged, organized, and continuous political organizations or parties only under some of the exceptional conditions specified above. Indeed, they may perhaps be swallowed up by some new movements and thus lose their own distinctiveness. They may be effective, however, by cooperating with various other parties or movements and by shifting the focus of political issues, influencing the selection of candidates, guiding public opinion, and changing the whole climate of political opinion—and as has been indicated above, also changing, to some degree at least, the social and economic bases of political radicalism and conservatism.

XXII.

But the spread of such various types of youth cultures and rebellions probably will not be limited only to spectacular political moves and developments. On a less dramatic and centrally visible plane, but probably more widely pervasive, they may also constitute reservoirs of continuously changing new cultural or ideological movements, fashions, and activities—in dress, artistic styles, or new patterns of leisure-time activity. It may well be that one of the most lasting of their effects will be in the development and extension of new, loosely, yet continuously connected, expressive subcultures, of which that of the Hippies is presently the most prominent but certainly not the only one

The development of such subcultures may provide an indicator or some broad, long-range shifts in the sphere of values and orientations—in general, a shift toward or rebellion against what has been called "humanistic" or "sensate" orientations, a general antidote to the more "this worldly" ascetic values derived from the Protestant Ethic and especially their later organizational and institutional derivatives.*

But it is rather doubtful whether these movements also will be able to destroy the organizational bases of those structures, although in their more destructive manifestations they may indeed seem to be very forceful. Rather, their effect might probably be more in the direction of limited, yet probably quite far-reaching, structural effects. One such effect may be the development within modern societies of areas of permissiveness closely related to some of the new subcultures alluded to above—areas in which some people may participate fully or in a more transitory fashion, areas which will institutionalize the extension of individuality beyond the more bureaucratized, meritocratic occupational and administrative structures.

Within the framework of some of these bureaucratic organizations, there also may develop a marked shift toward greater participation of constituent groups, as well as a broader (community or political) definition of goals, in some cases giving rise to far-reaching restructuring of such goals by the incorporation of new social, community, or "societal" goals and orientations.

It will probably be in the educational sphere (in the structure of universities, in particular) that these developments might indeed create some of the most far-reaching changes. Such changes

---

* See Barbara G. Myerhoff, "New Styles of Humanism; American Youth," *Youth & Society*, I (2), 1969: 151-179.

may occur not only in the internal governing of the university*
but also in dissociating various activities such as research and
undergraduate and graduate teaching and some societal functions
—the general-educational, professional preparation, and occupational selection.

These developments may also give rise to a rather new type
of youth symbolism and to a new definition of youth as a stage
of life.

Several of the characteristics of this stage—the "openness" with
which a direct relationship to the central symbols of the society
is maintained and the high level of concern with them, without
at the same time the necessity of involving a high degree of
commitment to them; the possibility of overcoming all the nega-
tions or contradictions between the dreams of plenty and the
experiences of modern life also tend to become disconnected
from any specific chronological stage or age and they could
become, as Kenneth Kenniston has indicated, a sort of cultural
stage, which in principle people of all ages could participate in
—even if only in a transitory phase.

This tendency may be easily reinforced by the adult's own
ambivalence toward the central symbols of the society and the
contradiction and tensions between these symbols and the realities of modern life.

Another effect of these developments may be a redefinition
of many roles and role clusters, especially occupational and citizenship roles, the beginning of which can already be discerned in
many places. In the occupational area there tends to develop,
first, a growing infusion of "service" components into pure professional and occupational activities.

Second, there also tends to develop, as in Japan and to some
degree in the U.S. and Western Europe, a growing dissociation
between high occupational strata and "conservative" political
and social attitudes, creating generations of high executives with
politically and cultural "leftist views" oriented toward participation in some of these new "permissive enclaves" or subcultures.

These developments may both institutionalize and reinforce

---

* See on this point the Winter 1970 issue of *Daedalus* on "The Embattled
University."

some of the structural and symbolic discontinuities we already have analyzed and weaken the importance of the occupational dimension in the status system of modern societies. In the political sphere, they may give rise to a redefinition of boundaries of collectivities, may lead to growing dissociation between political centers and the social and cultural collectivities and to the development of new nuclei of cultural and social identity which transcend the existing political and cultural boundaries. Many of these tendencies may be contradictory, many mutually reinforcing, and which of them will indeed become predominant depends on the specific constellations of the various conditions specified above.

But whatever the specific constellation of such conditions, given the general trends of development inherent in the spread of modernizations, these movements and their repercussions will be with us for a long time, even if with continuous ups and downs. These ups and downs and diverse activities and influences of these groups will vary considerably according to the types of discontinuity that develop in various sectors of the society and to the extent to which new authority patterns and role models will become successfully accepted and institutionalized.

Thus, we see that not all these changes are directly effected by issues of the relations between systemic, structural, or functional sociological theory and analysis and the explanation of unique historical events. We have seen how the initial analysis presented in this book was based on a somewhat formal structural functional model and had to be "opened up" to account for additional components—the cultural symbolism of youth and its relation to the formation symbols of collective identity; the cultural conception of personal, social, and cosmic time; and the processes by which the various predispositions engendered in given structural, cultural, and organizational settings are taken up and crystallized into specific organizational and symbolic patterns.

The necessity for such explication does not invalidate the legitimacy and fruitfulness of structural analysis and the hypotheses derived from it, nor does it invalidate the systemic nature of social order and the systemic interrelations between its components. Rather, it stresses the importance of not assuming any relations between such basic components as given and fixed, and points out the necessity to supplement and explicate the relation between relatively broad structural categories by specifying the actual mechanisms and processes of institutional interpersonal interaction.

In general theoretical terms, it indicates, first, that although the structural division of labor has to be taken as a given "evolutionary universal" of any human society, this fact does not explain the conditions of development of any specific type of division of labor, of any concrete social institutional type, and, second, that any such concrete type of division of labor develops through such institutional and interpersonal interaction.

Although this approach stresses that any such organization and institution is built up through the varied responses and interactions between different people or groups, it also emphasizes that the individuals or groups who engage in such exchange or interaction are not randomly distributed in any society. Such interaction occurs between people in different cultural, political, family, or economic positions. These positions may result from former processes of institutional exchange. The very aspirations and goals of people are influenced significantly by their placement in the social structure and the power they can exercise thereby. The resources which are at their disposal—manpower, money, political support, or religious identification—are determined by these institutional positions and vary according to the specific characteristics of the different institutional spheres. These resources serve as means for implementing various individual goals, and they may in themselves become goals or objects of individual endeavor. Such resources always evince some tendency to become organized in specific, autonomous ways according to the specific features of their different institutional spheres.

Any given situation of change opens up a variety, although not a limitless one, of possibilities for the development of new types of institutional, organizational, and behavioral patterns. Hence, as has already been pointed out, in the crystallization of institutional frameworks a crucial part is played by those people who evince a special capacity to set up broad orientations to propound new norms and to articulate new goals. The same, of course, applies to the analysis of age groups and youth activities, which we have attempted to present in this book and this introduction.

In these analyses we have attempted, first, to specify the general structural conditions that give rise to age groups and youth movements. Second, we have attempted to derive from these categories and assumptions the condition that could explain a great variety of various specific types of organizations and activities. Last, and especially in this introduction, we also have tried to identify the specific mechanisms that activate the potentialities created by those general and specific conditions and have attempted to show how these may indeed vary and change in different social, historical circumstances. We have seen that the sociological analysis of these specific circumstances has to be attempted in structural terms and be based on general and comparative hypotheses and that it is only through such general analytical and comparative studies that predictions of single situations are possible and can be attempted. But even if all these attempts are successful, they do not obliterate the differences between historical and sociological analysis—although they certainly indicate points of possible convergence.

February, 1971   S. N. Eisenstadt

Foreword

The purpose of this book is to analyze the various social
phenomena known as age groups, youth movements, etc.,
and to ascertain whether it is possible to specify the social
conditions under which they arise or the types of societies in
which they occur. It is the main thesis of this book that the
existence of these groups is not fortuitous or random, and that
they arise and exist only under very specific social conditions.
We have also attempted to show that the analysis of these conditions is not only of purely antiquarian or ethnological interest,
but that it can also shed light on the understanding of the conditions of stability and continuity of social systems.

The problem of age groups has been in the forefront of what
may be called the comparative study of institutions from the
beginning of scientific anthropology. Schürtz's classic essay on
"Altersklassen und Männerbünde" attempted to show the importance of these groups in the general evolutionary development of human society. With the decline of evolutionary schemes
the theme was taken up on a comparative ethnographic basis by
R. Lowie in his various analyses, summed up in *Primitive Society*. Since then interest in the problem has abated somewhat,
although the problem of youth movements, youth cultures, etc.,
has quite often been discussed in sociological literature. It is our
hope that this book may renew this interest to some extent, and
show the importance of the subject for a comparative analysis
of social structures.

The analysis presented in this book is based on a comparative study of various societies—primitive, historical and modern. We have perused most of the known anthropological, ethnological and historical studies which are relevant to our problem and in which the existence of age groups, youth movements, etc., is mentioned. We have also used most of the sociological and socio-psychological researches on adolescence, peer groups and youth movements in various modern societies, as well as various surveys of these problems. We have attempted to analyze the social structure of those societies in which age groups exist, and to compare them with one another and with societies in which age groups do not exist. On the basis of this comparison we could test the hypotheses on which this study is based, validate and elaborate them. The comparative analysis was done in two different, although interconnected, ways. First, we compared total societies. This was done particularly within the scope of primitive and historical societies. Secondly, and mostly within the scope of modern societies, we compared various sectors and segments of total societies, and various special groups. Here the analysis was structural to a lesser degree, and more focused on internal organization of groups, attitudes of their members, etc.

In addition to the numerous source materials, we have also drawn heavily for both types of comparative analysis on the research project on Youth Culture and Youth Movements in Israel, executed under the joint direction of Dr. J. Ben-David and the author, by the Research Seminar in Sociology of the Hebrew University. The results of this research project, in which we have attempted to combine the structural and the psychological approach, will be published separately and will, we hope, provide a further elaboration of the hypotheses presented in this book.

In the various comparative studies we have attempted to utilize only such material as would make the more or less complete analysis of a given society possible. We felt that only in such a way could the hypotheses presented in the first chapter of this book be fully and fairly tested; hence we tried to minimize references to those sources in which only a general indication of the existence of age groups is given, without a full analysis of their social setting. Although these sources were usually mentioned, it was expressly stated to what extent our analysis was based on them.

It would perhaps be worth-while to indicate here the general plan of the book. In the first chapter the general problem of the place of age differences in the social system is discussed, and the basic hypotheses on the conditions under which age groups arise are presented. In the second chapter we present descriptions of some typical age groups, so as to enable the reader to get a direct impression of both the general structure of age groups and their variety. On the basis of these descriptions the most important differences in the structure of different age groups have been indicated, to be investigated later on. Most of the descriptions of age groups given in this chapter are taken directly from the ethnographical or historical sources, with only minimal modifications. In the third chapter the basic hypothesis of the study, namely that age groups exist in universalistic societies (i.e., in societies in which the family or any other particularistic group is not the basic unit of the social division of labor), is tested on the basis of comparative materials. In the fourth chapter we take up the various differences in the structure of the age groups noted at the end of the second chapter, analyze them systematically and relate them to different structural principles of social organization. In the fifth chapter a special type of age group which arises in certain familistic societies is analyzed. In the sixth chapter we attempt to explain the conditions under which age groups and youth movements perform integrative functions in society, or become foci or deviance.

It is, of course, obvious that it was impossible to describe or account for all the great variety of phenomena of age and youth groups. Much has yet to be done in this respect and if the analysis provided in this book will be found to serve as a useful beginning, it will perform its function.

The research work on which this book is based has been carried on for more than four years. During that period I have incurred the debt of many persons who have helped me, either through discussing with me the problems connected with the work, criticizing the various tentative formulations I have made, or aiding me to obtain various materials.

I should like first to thank my friends at the Hebrew University with whom I was able to discuss the problems of this research. Foremost among them is my esteemed teacher, Professor M. Buber, to whom I am indebted for my initiation into sociology in general, and who spared neither time nor attention in discussing these problems. Among my colleagues I should like to extend my thanks to Dr. J. Ben-David, Dr. C. Frankenstein, Dr. Y. Garber-Talmon and Dr. J. Katz for their valuable suggestions and discussion, and to Dr. Ben-David and Dr. Katz also for very careful reading of the manuscript, and Mrs. R. Weinberger for some research assistance. My students who have participated in various discussions and seminars on these problems have also helped a great deal in the clarification of many points. I would like also to thank my friends Dr. A. Fuchs, Dr. Ch. Wirszubski, and Mr. Z. Zucker (Jaawetz), for help in the work relating to Ancient Greece.

I have also had the benefit of the criticism and discussion, both written and oral, of many friends abroad, among whom I should like especially to thank Miss E. Bott, Professor R. Firth, Professor D. Forde, Professor M. Fortes, Mr. M. Freedman, the late Professor Th. Geiger, Professor M. Ginsberg, Professor M. Gluckman (and his seminar in Manchester), Dr. A. Inkeles, Professor C. Levi-Strauss, Professor S. F. Nadel, Dr. J. Peristianyi, Professor I. Schapera, and Dr. D. M. Schneider. Some parts of this book, especially those dealing with the psychological aspects of adolescence, owe much to the work of Prof. E. H. Erikson, to several discussions with him and in the seminar which he conducted in Jerusalem in 1953.

This book has been greatly influenced by the work of Prof. T. Parsons and it is with great pleasure that I record both my general debt to his work, as well as my gratitude for several discussions of the subject of this book with him, and for his careful reading of the typescript and commenting on it.

The greatest debt of all I owe to Prof. E. A. Shils, but for whom this book would never have been written and published in the present form. He has discussed with me in great detail the problems and plan of the book, helped me to grasp the main problems of sociological analysis and to apply them to the problem of age groups, encouraged me to write up this work, has read its various drafts and helped to improve them by very detailed comments. If this book will be found to have any merit most of it will be due to his advice and discussion, although neither he nor any of the other friends mentioned are responsible for its drawbacks.

I should also like to thank Professor J. N. Demareth for lending me a copy of his Ph.D. thesis on "Adolescent Status and Personality," and the staffs of the Jewish National and University Library in Jerusalem, of the British Library of Economics and Political Science, the Royal Anthropological Institute, the International African Institute, the Oxford Institute of Social Anthropology and the Musée de L'Homme for their help in gathering the source material for this work.

I would like also to thank Dr. G. S. Wise, Chairman of the Board of Governors of the Hebrew University, whose grant for sociological research has enabled the execution of the research on Youth Movements in Israel.

Last but not least I would like to thank Mrs. Judith Schorr for her invaluable help in improving the style of this work and in preparing the various drafts of the manuscript, Mrs. Sh. Weintraub for help in improving the English of the book and Miss H. Tenenbaum and her staff for their typing.

Center for Advanced Study
 in the Behavioral Sciences.
August, 1955

CHAPTER I

Age Groups and Social Structure:
The Problem

I   Age and differences of age are among the most basic and crucial aspects of human life and determinants of human destiny. Every human being passes through different ages within his lifetime, and at each age he attains and uses different biological and intellectual capacities. Every stage in this progression constitutes an irreversible step in the unfolding of his life from its beginning to its end. At each stage he performs different tasks and roles in relation to other members of his society: from a child he becomes a father; from a pupil, a teacher; from a vigorous youth, a gradually aging adult.

The gradual progression and unfolding of power and capacities is not merely a universal, biologically conditioned (inescapable) fact. Although the basic biological processes are probably more or less similar in all human societies, their cultural definition varies—in details at least—from society to society, and all of them have to cope with the problems ensuing from this fact of age. Exactly what these problems are we shall try to explain a little later. At this point it is important for us to see that in every human society this biological process of transition through different age stages, the process of growing up and of aging, is subject to cultural definitions. It becomes a basis for defining human beings, for the formation of mutual relationships and activities, and for the differential allocation of social roles. Although the significance of different ages and the extent and boundaries of the years which form relatively unitary age categories or age grades vary from society to society, we know of no society[1] which does not differentiate between various "ages" and does not define them through the norms and values of its cultural tradition. In every society the basic and common biological facts are marked by a set of cultural definitions which ascribe to each age grouping (or, to use the more technical term, age grade[2]) its basic characteristics.

What is the general nature of these characteristics? Despite the great variety of detail, some common features can be discerned. An "age grade" is usually defined in the broad terms of a general "human type," and not of any specific, detailed trait or role. The vigorous young warriors of a primitive tribe, the "wise old men," do not refer to any detailed, specific activities, but to a more general, diffuse pattern of behavior that is proper to a man at a given stage of life. It is true, of course, that sometimes specific activities are thought to be characteristic of a given age, such as excelling in the warlike courage of the young, exhibiting physical prowess, etc. These activities, however, are not the only specific traits which by themselves define the "nature" of a given age; they serve, rather, as symbolic, sometimes even ritual, expressions of a more general pattern of behavior. A cultural definition of an age grade or age span is always a broad definition of human potentialities and obligations at a given stage of life. It is not a prescription or expectation of a detailed role, but of general, basic role dispositions into which more specific roles may be built, and to which they may be ascribed.* At the same time it is not merely a classificatory cate-

---

* In this work some technical sociological terms will be repeatedly used. These terms were mostly coined by T. Parsons and E. Shils. (See T. Parsons and E. Shils, *Towards a General Theory of Action*, Harvard 1951 and T. Parsons, *The Social System*, Glencoe 1951.) As they may be somewhat unfamiliar to the nonsociological reader, we shall explain them briefly here. The most important of these terms are: role, pattern variables of value orientations, and the five pairs of pattern variables: affectivity—affective neutrality, self vs. collectivity orientation, universalism—particularism, achievement—ascription, and diffuseness—specificity.

According to this analysis a society or a group is a system of positions and *roles*, filled out by the different individuals. The *role* is the basic unit of social interaction. It comprises only a segment of an individual's total behavior. Any individual performs many roles in the society—those of son, father, worker, member of associations, etc. The important fact about

gory as it is sometimes used in statistical censuses. However explicit its formulations, it always involves an evaluation of the meaning and importance of the given age for the individual and for society, thus giving it a fully ideological connotation. It contains certain definite expectations of future activities, and of relationships with other people at the same or at different stages of their life career. In terms of these definitions people map out, as it were, the broad contours of human life, of their own expectations and possibilities, and place themselves and their fellow-men in various positions, ascribing to each a given place within these contours.

This brings us to the second basic characteristic of the role expectations of age grades, namely, that no such single expecta-

---

roles is that they organize an individual's behavior towards other individuals in very distinctive patterns.

Every role involves an interaction between at least two individuals. In every such interaction and role there are inherent several possibilities of behavior, several alternatives which are dilemmas between which the individual has to choose; they give rise to the five "pattern variables" or "value orientations" which define these alternatives.

The first alternative is that between pattern variables of affectivity–affective neutrality. There are roles in which the individuals may seek immediate gratification in the actual social action in which he is engaged. Here he chooses affectivity, or direct expressive gratification. On the other hand there are roles in which the individual is carrying out his act in the pursuit of a remoter end. These are the more *instrumental* roles, where affective neutrality is chosen.

The second alternative is that between self or collectivity orientation. There are roles (such as the business man) in which it is permissible to seek one's own ends. On the other hand there are roles (for instance, doctor, priest, etc.) where one should conduct oneself with an orientation to the collectivity and its welfare and ends.

The third alternative is that between universalism and particularism. There are roles, the occupier of which is expected to behave in terms of general *universalistic* categories to which those with whom he interacts, belong. A doctor must treat all his patients alike, and a civil servant all those who come to him on public business. In other roles (such as in relations between relatives), the proper way is to behave in a special way towards other people according to their *particular* relation to the individual.

The fourth alternative is that of achievement vs. ascription. How does one judge the incumbent of a role—by his performance, efficiency, achievement in any field, or by what he *is*, by his qualities—whether aesthetic, or hereditary or his just being a member of a given group or category of of people—in other words, of his *ascriptive* position.

The last alternative is that between diffuseness or specificity. The performance of a given role sometimes demands a diffuse range of duties, as tion stands alone, but always constitutes part of a series. The characteristics of one age grade cannot be fully understood except in their relation to those of other ages. Whether seen as a gradually unfolding continuum or as a series of sharp contrasts and opposed characteristics, they are fully explained and understood only in terms of each other. The boy is seen to bear within himself the seeds of the adult man; or else he must, as an adult, acquire new patterns of behavior sharply and intentionally opposed to those of his boyhood. The adult either develops naturally into an old man or decays into one. (But the one can be understood only in terms of its relation to the other.) Only when taken together do they constitute the entire map of human possibilities, of the potentials of human life; and as every individual usually has to pass through all of them, their complementariness and continuity (even if defined in discontinuous, contrasting terms[3]) become obvious.

The same holds true—although perhaps with a somewhat different meaning—for the age definitions of the two sexes. Each age grade is differently defined for each sex, and these definitions are usually related and complementary, as the "sexual image" and identity always constitute a basic element of man's image in every society.

II   How can we explain the universal fact that in every society age differences and similarities enter into the formation of that society's "human images," into the cultural definition of man's life and destiny? And why are these definitions always diffuse and complementary?

It seems that these facts are rooted in some of the necessities and exigencies of social life. The main preconditions of these universal facts are the following: (a) the plasticity of human nature; (b) the exigencies of socialization and learning; and (c) mortality and population changes within the social system.

One of the main tasks facing every society and social system, is to provide for the perpetuation of its own structure, norms,

---

in mother-child relations, or general in relations between friends; while in other situations one has mainly to provide a single, specialized service—as a clerk in a bank, etc.

values, etc., in spite of the changes continuously wrought in its composition by deaths and births. For this reason the individual's passage through different age stages is not only his private concern, but a matter of crucial importance to the whole social system, emphasizing the potential dangers of discontinuity and disruption, and the necessity of overcoming them. That is why the individual, at every moment of his life, not only performs given roles and interacts with other people, but is also obliged to ensure some degree of continuity of the social system through this performance. In other words, the roles performed by the individual at any given stage of his life span must be defined in such a way as to "sharpen" and emphasize his relations with people on different points of the scale of personal development, i.e., his role as either a transmitter or a recipient of the cultural and social heritage. Thus the individual's place on this continuum becomes of crucial importance for the definition of his own roles and activities and as regards his expectations vis-à-vis other people.

The main ways in which the transmission of the social heritage is effected and the basic preconditions of this transmission tend to emphasize the stress laid on different ages. This transmission is made possible by the plasticity of human nature, i.e., by the fact that the behavior of the human being is not determined by his biological inheritance, but that on the contrary, this inheritance is so shaped that it can become effective only through learning and acquisition of non-inheritable, biologically nontransmissible patterns of behavior.[4] Even the process of maturation of the various inherent biological qualities of an individual is a very slow one, and is dependent to a very large extent on constant interaction with, and learning from, other people. The plasticity of human nature, its inherent capacity for learning and for the acquisition of patterns of behavior, as well as the long period of the child's dependence on adults, are the basis on which social continuity (the transmission of the social heritage) is built. This process of learning is not, however, a mechanical process of a laboratory type, through which the individual acquires various discrete traits. Outside very narrow limits, human learning, and particularly the gradual, continuous learning characteristic of the growing baby and child, can be effected only through socialization, i.e., through communication with and learning from other human beings with whom he gradually enters into some sort of very generalized relationship.[5] Although we have no detailed knowledge about the process of socialization, some facts seem to be beyond dispute: (a) Socialization is effected through the child's attachment to adults (at first to his mother or mother-substitute, to his father, then gradually extended to other people), i.e., it is based on the fact that these adults are desired by the child as objects of his actions; (b) the nature of this attachment is diffuse and generalized, i.e., it is centered on these adults' total personalities, on their general dispositions towards the child (their love of the child), and not, at least at first, on specific actions; (c) the security of such an attachment is a basic precondition of the child's development as a social being, i.e., the development of his capacities for role expectations and role performance; (d) through socialization (effected primarily within the family) the child develops generalized, primary role predispositions; (e) on the basis of these general predispositions more detailed and specific roles are learned in various specific situations.[6] The possibility of interaction with other people, especially with adults, and the securing of a continuous attachment to them constitute perhaps the most basic necessity of the human personality, without which its development and integration cannot be achieved or maintained. The most important mechanisms of learning are rooted in this general necessity—especially the mechanism of identification, i.e., the process through which the desired adult becomes a model for general orientations.[7]

This crucial importance of attachment and identification in the process of learning (i.e., in the process of transmission of the social heritage and maintenance of social continuity) accentuates the difference between various age stages. The child must necessarily learn his behavior from a given adult, older than himself, and in this child-adult relationship age differences are necessarily stressed and emphasized as justification and explanation of the demands made by the adult on the child. These demands are always made in terms of the adult's social experience, knowledge, understanding, etc., i.e., in terms of his position in the life space as related to (or opposed to) that of the child. The process of socialization and learning necessarily involves a normative and evaluative element, and the demands made on the child throughout this process are made legitimate in terms of the differential evaluation of the adults' social experience as compared to that of the child. The adult is described as more experienced, as wiser and better, as a repository of the moral virtues towards which the child has to be educated. It is because of this that he has authority, that he commands respect and has to be obeyed. This emphasis on age is usually accentuated by the fact that, throughout the period of socialization, the child is not the only one in his age span, but one of a group of children whose basic similarity is felt by them and stressed by the adults.

This emphasis on age differences, on the relevance of age as a qualification and obligation for the performance of various roles, is also greatly influenced by the cumulative aspect of different types of knowledge which are necessary for the performance of different roles, and the acquisition of which consumes time and therefore also implies age progression. The same holds true of various physical capacities required for the performance of various roles—capacities which may be related to different stages of biological development.[8]

The two main characteristics of differential age definitions— diffuseness and complementariness—can also be best explained in relation to the exigencies of socialization and of transmission of the social heritage. If the emphasis on age differences stems from the basic characteristic of socialization—the child's attachment to, and identification with, adults and the general contacts of children with each other and with adults—it necessarily bears the imprint of their diffuseness and generality, and its main function is, then to develop the child's various general role dispositions and to enable him to enter into general relations with other people in his society. This is effected mainly through the extension of the adult's relations towards the specific child to include many of both his and the child's contemporaries. One of the most important mechanisms of such extension, with which we shall concern ourselves later on in this book, is kinship-terminology extension.[9]

The complementariness of the diffuse age definitions is also easily understood when we consider their place in the process of socialization. The function of differential age definitions is to enable the individual to learn and acquire new roles, to become an adult, etc., and in this way to maintain social continuity. Emphasis is laid on the difference between child and adult in order to enable the child to become an adult; and his identification with the adult can be maintained only if he sees himself in a meaningful relationship (even if this be opposition) to the adult. But even more important is the fact that ultimately the child has to become an adult. Therefore he must develop some expectations towards his future roles as an adult, to include them in his life-expectation, in his own perception of his future. Such a relationship cannot be maintained if age differences are stressed as completely dichotomous and unrelated. The necessity of maintaining the continuity of the individual's progression through the different age stages calls for some complementariness of the differential age definitions.

III   It becomes understandable from the foregoing that age definitions and differentiation are of great importance both to the social system and to the individual personality. For the social system it serves as a category according to which various roles are allocated to various people; for the individual, the awareness of his own age becomes an important integrative element, through its influence on his self-identification. The categorization of oneself as a member of a given age stage serves as an important basis for one's self-perception and role expectations towards others.

The importance of age grading may be further analyzed if we take up some more specific problems involved in the process of socialization.

The successful development of patterns of behavior which conform to the norms and role expectations of a society involves a high degree of personality integration and concomitant development of special attitudes within the individual's personality. Among these, the individual's attitude towards authority and his co-operation are most crucial for the proper functioning of the personality within the social system. These attitudes may be subdivided into three main categories: the ability to obey persons in whom authority is vested; the ability to co-operate with equals; and the predisposition to accept responsibility and assume authority in relation to other people. In a society almost every individual is called upon to perform roles involving all of these three dispositions, and without them he is probably unable to achieve a full realization of his status in society.[10] These attitudes and general role dispositions are learned in the process of socialization and through the child's interaction with his "socializing agents." Here again the emphasis on age differences—the differential role allocation based on age differences—becomes crucial. The relations between different age grades are necessarily defined in authoritative terms, and the adult socializing agent is the first prototype of authority that the child encounters. Their mutual relationship determines the child's readiness to accept authority, and, later, to undertake responsibility and exert authority through the internalization of the adult's "image." One of the basic components of the complementariness of age grade definitions is their differential authority structure, i.e., the extent to which authority is exercised by one age grade and accepted by the other. Through the acting out of various roles on members of age grades other than his own, the individual develops general predispositions towards acceptance and exercise of authority, and the differential role allocation on the basis of age (and the concomitant differential age definitions) facilitates this development by sharpening and focusing differences of authority on the difference in life span and social experience. Likewise it may be surmised that co-operative patterns of behavior are developed mainly through co-operation with age mates, i.e., those whose position within the life span is not significantly different from one's own, as in relations with them no severely authoritarian element exists in the definition of the situation.[11]

We find thus that relations between different age grades are necessarily asymmetrical from the point of view of authority, respect and initiative. The elder age grades usually exert some authority over the younger ones; they can direct, formally or informally, their activities and command their respect. This basic asymmetry of power and authority is characteristic of the interaction between different age grades and generations as a whole. It may be somewhat informal, as in cases of people with small age differences (e.g., elder boys, etc.); in other cases it may be formalized and officially prescribed. But it constitutes a very important element in the relations between various age grades and emphasizes the complementariness of age images and expectations. The strong emphasis on the respect due to elder people, i.e., to age, is, as we have already seen, a basic prerequisite for the successful maintenance of social continuity.[12]

IV   The crucial importance which age differentation and the interaction of members of different age grades possesses for the continuity of the social system can be most clearly seen in the fact that in most societies the attainment of full membership is defined in terms of transition from one age grade to another. As is well known, the exact age spans, which are defined in a unitary way and differentiated from other age spans, vary from one society to another, both in their age coverage and in the number of age grades between which they differentiate. There is, however, one focal point within the life span of an individual which is to some extent emphasized in most known societies, namely the achievement of full adult status, or full membership in the social system. Within all societies there is some definition—whatever the degree of its formalization—of the "adult man" or full member of the society, and of the point at which the individual may acquire all of the paraphernalia of full status and enter the first stages of the adult age span. This entrance usually—and, it seems, necessarily—coincides with the transition period from the family of orientation to that of procreation, as it is through this transition that the definite change of age roles, from receiver to transmitter of cultural tradition, from child to parent, is effected. One of the main criteria of adulthood is defined as legitimate sexual maturity, i.e., the right to establish a family, and not merely the right to sexual intercourse. This crucial change of the individual's age roles, when the two age definitions still interact within him, is emphasized— more or less strongly—in practically all human societies. At the various ceremonies enacted at this point—*rites de passage* of different kinds[13]—the interaction between the different age grades and generations is intensified in various symbolic or ritual ways. Here also the basic characteristics of the age definition are brought sharply into focus: its relation to the total "human image" in which the individual's appreciation of himself is stressed by the juxtaposition and integration of bodily (sexual) images and of evaluative norms; it is here that the double complementariness of sex-age roles finds its most articulate expression.

The best concrete examples of the ritual dramatization of this period or span of transition are the initiation ceremonies of various primitive tribes (or, with somewhat different emphasis, nuptial ceremonies of peasant folk societies). As anthropological literature abounds in detailed descriptions of these ceremonies, we shall not go into details; we shall merely attempt to analyze their most salient features. These may be summarized as follows:

(a) In these rites the pre-adult adolescents are transformed into full adult members of the tribe, the transformation being effected through

(b) a series of rites in which the adolescents are symbolically divested of the characteristics of youth and invested with those of adulthood from a sexual and social point of view. This symbolic investment, which has deep emotional significance, may have various concrete manifestations: bodily mutilation, circumcision, taking on of a new name, symbolic rebirth,[13a] etc.;

(c) the complete symbolic separation of the adolescents from the world of their youth, and especially from their close status attachments to their mothers; i.e., their complete "male" independence and autonomous male image are articulated (the opposite usually holds true of girls' initiations);

(d) dramatization of the encounter between the different generations, a dramatization which may take the form of a fight, competition, etc., and in which the basic complementariness— whether of a continuous or discontinuous type—is stressed; thus, in all initiation rites the members of different generations must act together, the ones as teachers, the others as "students." The elders sometimes assume frightening forms and stress that without them the adolescents cannot become adults. Quite often the discontinuity between adolescence and adulthood is symbolically expressed in the "rebirth" of the adolescents—in their symbolic death as children and rebirth as adults;

(e) transmission of the tribal lore and generalized patterns of behavior and attitudes, both through formalized teaching and through symbolic ritual activities of different kinds. This transmission of the lore and role dispositions is combined with

(f) relaxation of the concrete control of the adults over the erstwhile adolescents, and its substitution by more generalized, internalized and symbolic controls; and with

(g) investment of the new members of the adult age span with authority-exercising roles; i.e., the substitution of concrete external controls by more internalized ones is clearly connected with the individual's changing position in the authority scheme.[14]

Most of these dramatic elements can also be found, although in a somewhat more diluted form, in various traditional folk festivals of peasant communities, especially those (such as rural carnivals) in which youth and marriage are emphasized.[15]

While this dramatization of the period of transition to adulthood is not found in all human societies (especially not in those of the more "modern" type), wherever it does exist, it brings into very sharp focus all the basic elements and functions of the differential age definitions and their crucial role in social continuity; the same holds true also of the general emphasis on the period or stage of transition to adulthood.

Here, the problem alluded to earlier is further clarified: the expectations which are directed towards individuals with respect to their age constitute one of the strongest, most essential links between the personality system of individuals and the social systems in which they participate.[16] On the one hand, they are among the major criteria by which an individual defines his rights and obligations in relation to others; they also serve to define the types of units within the social system, to which various tasks and roles are allocated. The importance of differential age definitions, both for the individual's self-perception and for the continuity of the social system, can be most clearly seen in negative cases, i.e., when this continuity is broken in one way or another such as in delinquent and revolutionary youth groups of various kinds. Whenever this happens, the difference between various generations and age groups may become accentuated and sharpened to the breaking point, and the younger generation may develop a self-image completely opposed to the complementary image of the adult generation and rebel against it. One of the best examples of this is the German youth movement, or even, in broader terms, the whole modern Romantic movement, in which the extreme opposition between generations was stressed by means of an emphasis on a new type of man.[17] We shall return to this subject in subsequent chapters of this work.

V   Our analysis has shown that the interaction of members of different age grades is essential for the working and continuity of the social system. It is not only that people of different ages act together in the social system, but that their interaction is, to some extent at least, couched and defined in terms of their relative ages. This may take on a variety of forms. First, certain roles may be allocated on the basis of age, e.g., various roles in the family, in the sphere of authority, or in the economic and occupational spheres. The general division of labor in a society is necessarily based to some extent on age differences, and various social units may be regulated according to the criteria of age. Thus the right to take up a given occupation may be conditioned on the attainment of a certain age, and the same may apply in other social spheres and roles.

Moreover, even when age does not serve as an explicit criterion of allocation of roles, it very often influences it to a considerable degree, e.g., in the rules of seniority existing in many formal organizations, in the general assumption that for certain occupations and professions, like medicine, law, etc., experience is of great importance, etc.

In addition, age grading obviously implies that those belonging to a given age grade usually have some similar and common experiences; they may be required to behave in many respects in a similar way and to have similar relations with members of other age grades. They have, on the one hand, many common values, interests and expectations, while on the other hand they have many common points of contact with members of other age grades. Our main purpose here is to understand the ways in which both the common experiences of a given age grade within a society, and their relations with other age grades, are organized. There are here two main and interconnected problems with which we have to deal. The first problem is the extent to which various roles are allocated on the basis of age. Under what social conditions is age a decisive criterion for role allocation and for determining the boundaries of groups? The second problem is: Does the potential community of interest of members of the same age grade lead to any concrete interaction, such as belonging to a similar age group, and if so, to what extent? In other words, to what extent does belonging to a common age grade serve as a basis for allocating membership and defining the boundaries of groups within the society? We shall deal with the second problem first because this will make the analysis of the second easier.

If our previous analysis is correct, we should surmise that age homogeneity as such, i.e., belonging to the same age grade, should not, usually, serve as a criterion. Our analysis has shown that the importance of age grading for social continuity entails the complementary interaction of different age grades. Consequently, while members of a given age grade have many similar characteristics, their interaction (in so far as it is arranged in terms of age) should be mostly with members of other age grades, so as to assure this complementariness and the continuous interacting of the different generations. Although interaction with age mates (equals) is obviously important (especially as concerns the development of spontaneous co-operation and of orientations towards wider universal norms of interaction), the analysis as presented until now suggests that age-heterogeneous groups —in which the complementariness of age grades is constantly articulated and stressed—are of greater importance than age-homogeneous ones, which may have only a transitory or subsidiary character. This is especially so because groups such as the family which are based on age heterogeneity, may also include some subsidiary age-homogeneous relations, while groups various subgroups within these organizaztions. Thus, even from age grades. The same applies to other, more formalized structures —such as churches, armies, etc. There, too, age plays an important part in the allocation of roles; senior positions are, to a large extent although not entirely, given to older, more experienced people. These older people have authority over the younger ones, more recently recruited; and although the criterion of age is not the most important one for the allocation of roles in such organizations (sometimes expert, specialized knowledge is much more important), still, by and large, asymmetrical interaction between different age grades is present in these organizations. On the other hand, members of the same age grade form various subgroups within these organizations. Thus, even from these examples it can be concluded that age-heterogeneous groups are the most common, and perhaps the only ones, that can exist in a society.

And yet this conclusion from our analysis is, to a very large extent, contradicted by facts. Although there exist (as will be shown in detail below) many societies in which this holds true, in others it is not so. In the latter societies there exist many groups of great importance in the social system in which social membership is explicitly allocated to members of the same age grade, and the boundaries of these groups are defined in terms of age homogeneity. Primitive age sets, age groups and age regiments, the youth dormitories of many Indian tribes, modern youth movements, peer groups, juvenile gangs—all these are clear examples. Thus we are faced here with a problem which requires an explanation: It is this problem which constitutes the main theme of this book. How can we account for these facts? Can they be explained in terms of our previous analysis, or do they contradict it entirely? We shall try to prove here that they can be explained in terms of that analysis, through a more rigorous derivation and modification of our basic assumptions. We shall see that these age groups may—and quite often do—perform the same functions that we have postulated for the interaction of age-heterogeneous elements, as agencies of socialization of the individual and as mechanisms of continuity of the social system. Our problem, then, will be to find what conditions of the social system favor or, alternately, prevent the emergence of age groups, what kinds of groups can be age-homogeneous, and what their functions are within the social system. In order to be able to construct a hypothesis which would account for these different conditions, we should first elaborate certain points in our previous analysis.

VI   First we should define more precisely the exact sociological meaning of age-heterogeneous and age-homogeneous relations and groupings. The two types of age relations share some common characteristics which are very important for our subsequent analysis: In so far as actors categorize themselves on the basis of any age distinctions (whether similarities or differences), their mutual orientation is based on ascriptive and not achievement criteria. According to the former analysis, all age criteria are diffuse, and consequently all relations patterned according to these criteria have a diffuse orientation too.

But beyond these similarities there are some important differences in the structure of age-heterogeneous and age-homogeneous groups. In so far as any relationship is defined on the basis of age heterogeneity, it emphasizes differences in age; while age homogeneity implies, within a certain range, similarity in age. In the first type of relationship the mutual orientation of the actors (in so far as it is at all defined in terms of age) is governed by their relative ages and their relative positions in the life cycle. The fullest expression of such a relationship is the principle of (relative) seniority which is fully elaborated in some kinship systems.[18] In the second relationship *relative* age and differences in age become less important, and it is the *common* experience of similar age, the occupying of an absolute position in the scale of age grades, that is important here. In the first, particularistic, hierarchically asymmetrical and usually personal relations prevail. In the second, we find a greater emphasis on common experience and basic equality. Here the age relations are much more inclusive and unitary, and less stress is laid on the relative positions of superiority and inferiority of different age grades. These are expressed, if at all, in intergroup, and not in individual relations. Hence, although the basic criterion of membership is also particularistic, the internal organization of the group is much more open to universalistic arrangements and orientations. Such orientations are usually implicit, to some extent, in most of the informal children's groups, even in particularistic societies. But they may become clearer and much more articulated in the fully age-homogeneous groups.[18a]

On the basis of these distinctions we may now begin to analyze the conditions under which each of these groups exists. The starting point of our discussion should be the fact that in any society whatsoever the first and most basic relationship into which an individual enters is of the first type, i.e., age-heterogeneous, ascriptive, particularistic and diffuse. These criteria characterize the family relationships in all societies, and these groups and relations are the first and most basic socializing agents in any society. Even in those societies in which we do find age-homogeneous groupings and role allocation, such groupings become effective only at some later point of the individual's life span, after a period of life spent within the fold of the family and regulated by kinship relationships.

What is the significance of these features of family life for the individual and society? Their main significance seems to lie in the fact that they indicate the various types of social relations and activities which are combined within the family. It is the combination of these various activities (which will shortly be enumerated) that enables the family to perform its socializing function and to be a mainstay of social solidarity and continuity. Within the family the individual learns both the various types of activities demanded of him as a full member of society, and the various ways of overcoming the tensions and frustrations inherent in orderly social life. It is within the family that the infant learns gradually to postpone the immediate gratification of his needs and to regulate his behavior according to various norms and rules. While during the first stages of life an infant no doubt strives for a maximum of immediate gratification, he gradually learns, through his relations with his mother, father, etc., to regulate the conduct by which he attains these gratifications. All this is bound to cause severe frustrations and tensions in the child.

The tensions are probably most acute because of the stress laid by his parents on the importance of regulated instrumental activities, i.e., activities which are only means to further ends, but do not in themselves give *immediate* satisfaction or gratification. The child learns the various instrumental skills and relations, their regulation and the overcoming of the tensions inherent in them through his constant attachment to adults and identification with them. The assurance of such attachment constitutes, as we have seen, the basic need of the developing personality. This attachment constitutes the basis for the development of identification, which has already been shown to be one of the most important mechanisms of learning and socialization. In the process of socialization within the family, security of attachment and of maintenance of solidary relations with adults is assured only in so far as the individual learns both the various instrumental skills and relations and the rules according to which they are regulated. Thus we find within the family a threefold process of learning: (a) learning of instrumental activities which are (b) regulated according to certain patterns, or values, (c) on the basis of solidarity with adults and other members of the family. In this way the tensions and frustrations arising out of instrumental activities and out of the necessity to postpone gratification and to see others (and to be seen by them) as means to ends, is alleviated here by the achievement of solidarity and expressive gratifications in certain patterns of behavior. Thus the children are assured of the love of their parents if they behave according to the rules set up by the parents, and this assurance of love is one of the most important gratifications that the child receives if he learns to behave in the proper way. Moreover, some of the activities demanded of the children—and of the parents—are pursued in the name of the solidarity of the family, for the sake of the common well-being and goals of the family. The importance of co-operation within the family, for the family, is inculcated in children and is shown also in the behavior of adults. Thus it is understandable that the important feature of family life is that the instrumental activities are regulated according to solidary and expressive criteria and are subordinated to them. This is so during the process of socialization, and it is on this basis that the individual develops a coherent personality and identity. But these relations continue beyond socialization within the family, and also regulate all adult activities in the family. Family life on the adult plane entails many instrumental activities and relations with regard to possessions, property relations, etc., and encompasses a wide circle of persons. All these activities, however, are regulated, as during the earlier period, within the limits of solidary and expressive relations. It may thus be said that the family constitutes a social group or system which maintains a constant balance between these various types of activities, which overcomes in this way the tensions accruing from the necessity of regulating instrumental activities, and which, consequently, maintains the individual's emotional stability and security, as well as social solidarity and continuity.

The family structure also facilitates the development of those integrative mechanisms of the personality which are related to the attitude towards authority. The nuclear family usually consists not only of parents and children, but also of siblings, among whom there usually exist, within the framework of family relationships, a basic age homogeneity and equality.[19] These relations, however, are secondary and subordinated to the more authoritative relations between parents and children. These authoritative relations may be extended also to relations between siblings, if one sibling becomes identified with the parents through his seniority.

This balance between instrumental, solidary and expressive relations is not, however, confined to the nuclear family only. It is extended in all societies to a much wider circle of people, through kinship extension. This term really implies two different, though interconnected, things: extension of kinship terminology and relations to people beyond the membership of the nuclear family; and the extension of familial group solidarity and group identification beyond the nuclear family group.

With regard to the first, this extension is usually effected through the mechanisms of generalization and identification with the general behavior patterns of the primary objects of attachment (parents and siblings) to other persons, who in their turn may have served as such objects for the parents.[20] The child's behavior patterns towards its parents and siblings are extended to other people, who are "equated" with the parents and siblings. The famous principle of "equivalence of siblings" formulated by A. R. Radcliffe-Brown is one of the clearest examples of such kinship extensions.[21] The significance of this extension is far-reaching: Only through such extension may the patterns of behavior and solidarity, learned within the nuclear family, be transferred to a wider cluster of persons who are outside the extended kinship group and whose relations with ego necessarily comprise a wider cluster of instrumental activities (mutual rights, duties, possessions, etc.), and among whom the individual must find his mate for the establishment of his family of procreation.[22]

From the point of view of personality structure, kinship extension enables the young person to maintain his emotional security while more detailed, specific skills and patterns of behavior and need dispositions for the performance of more instrumental roles are being developed. Emotional security is maintained through a transfer of attachment and identification to people less directly related than parents and siblings; in relations with them immediate gratification must continue to be renounced. From the point of view of the social system, the transfer and maintenance of solidarity within a wide nexus of relationships—which may sometimes even comprise the whole collectivity—is effected through kinship extension.

The extension of solidarity is effected not only through the extension of kinship terminology, but also—and perhaps mainly—through the establishment of corporate groups wider than the nuclear family and yet based on common descent, real or imaginary. While kinship terminology regulates the relations between kinsmen, both paternal and maternal, who may live in many different family units, and be widely dispersed within a society, there may also exist many corporate groups based on common descent. The extended family, the lineage, the clan and the moiety are outstanding examples of such groups which may exist in different societies. By the very nature of any kinship terminology, and the regulations of incest exogamy, all those comprised in it cannot form one group. Such groups, e.g., lineages, can be formed only through the exclusion of certain categories of kinsmen and strong emphasis on other categories. These categories become the group's symbols of identification, as for instance the belief in a common ancestor prevalent in various lineages and clans. Identification and collectivity orientation engendered in the fold of the nuclear family are transferred by the individual to these groups. They are not, however, merely groups of people who are emotionally attached to one another. These groups are usually also bearers of corporate rights, and constitute juridic units within the social system. They serve, then, as bases for the allocation of roles and facilities, and as bearers of collective identity within the social system.

VII   Kinship relations and common descent groups form the two main possible types of extension of behavior developed in the family. When both operate in a society, they are usually complementary, the centrifugal tendencies of one being balanced by the centripetal tendencies of the other.[23] In both of them the basic criteria of ascription, diffuseness and particularism, as well as, in different degrees, the collectivity orientation of the family, are operative, and they regulate a much wider sphere of relations, mutual rights and duties. Within the framework of kinship relations and extended family groups, the scope of instrumental relations is already much greater and wider than within the nuclear family. The extent of juridic, semi-contractual relations is greater, and many more types of economic, political and other activities are related to them. Still, the basic framework of these relations is that of solidarity and it is regulated according to the value orientations outlined above. For this reason, both kinship extension and extended family groups are important for the socialization of the child and for the gradual extension of his relations and activities. Already within the nuclear family the child acquires some general dispositions towards his kinfolk, the patterns of his duties and obligations towards them. As he grows up and extends the sphere of his activities, these latent dispositions become more and more important and definite. In this way the continuity between pattern of socialization and later stages of life is maintained.

Kinship relations, like family relations, are organized on age-heterogeneous allocation of roles. Through the various mechanisms of sibling equivalence, the patterns of authority and respect which exist in the nuclear family extend to the relations between different generations of kinsmen. In this way the balance between instrumental and expressive gratification is extended to a wider sphere of activities, and kinship relations and descent groups serve also as extensions of the family in fulfillment of its functions: the integration of the personality and the maintenance of the social system.

Kinship relations and descent groups, however, cannot by themselves maintain the social structure or integrate personality, and in all societies there always exist other spheres and principles of institutional arrangements and roles: economic, political, religious and status relations and the value orientations related to them.

Not all these various institutions are confined to the family and kinship unit; some of them at least are regulated according to value orientations quite different from those of the family. Thus economic relations always have a stronger leaning towards universalism and specificity, while political, religious and other activities may in some societies also be regulated according to more specific and achievement-oriented rules, and the qualities which determine political citizenship may be other than age and blood ties. Every society has, then, some spheres which are regulated according to criteria different from those of the family. Therefore, the particular pattern of balance among instrumental, solidary and expressive relations existing within the family is not automatically maintained in all other spheres. It can be achieved only if the principles which regulate family life—ascription, diffuseness and particularism—are uppermost in the value system of the society, and regulate and limit all the other spheres and values. Such a situation is parallel to that of the family in which instrumental and universalistic relations are not completely nonexistent, but only subordinated to solidary and expressive norms.

In so far as such criteria govern the various institutional spheres of the society, the extension of solidarity and identification, based mainly on age-heterogeneous relations and united in kinship relations, can be relatively smoothly effected. It may also be assumed that in these cases the criteria of age are of relatively great importance in the allocation of roles and tasks within the social system. In so far, however, as these criteria are not the ultimate criteria which regulate the various institutionalized roles and relations and are not uppermost in the value system of the society, there must occur a "breaking point" in the smooth transference of identification and solidarity based on age-hetero-geneous relations. In these cases, and in the exact structural positions of the social system, where roles become institutionalized according to different criteria and values, there arises a tendency towards age-homogeneous relations and groupings directed towards the transference of identification and extension of solidarity from one set of relations to another, different one, structured according to different criteria.

As this constitutes the central theme of this work, we must explore it further. This hypothesis is based on the assumption that in so far as the general system of norms of the social system harmonizes with those of the family (even if the family and kinship unit does not constitute the basic unit of the society), the transfer of identification and extension of solidarity is a relatively smooth process, since the individual is enabled to attain his full membership status within the social system through patterns of behavior acquired within the family unit. When, however, the main integrative principles of the social structure differ from those regulating family and kinship behavior, this smooth growth from familial to civic or other corporate solidarity is impossible, since the individual has to change the patterns of his behavior at a certain point of his life career in order to be able to achieve full status within society (the same holds true, of course, of any subsystem within the social structure); and the solidarity of the social system can be effectively maintained only by patterns of behavior different from those existing within kinship units. In universalistic-achievement societies (like the modern American society) an individual cannot achieve full status if he behaves, in his work, according to the ascriptive, particularistic criteria of family life; such behavior would also prove a strain on the social system.[24] The patterns of orientation characteristic of the family being restricted, there occurs in such cases a defensive reaction in the direction of age-homogeneous relations and groups.

VIII As far as the development of the individual personality is concerned, the belonging to a different age grade (e.g., the adult in his relations to the child) provides a symbolic focus, identification with whom (through the acquisition of broad role dispositions, harmonious or compatible with those of the adult) helps the child to become a mature member of his society. If the patterns of behavior appropriate to a full-fledged member of society in the most important of his statuses differ from those enacted within the child-adult (or kinship in general) relations, identification with the adult will be incomplete; or the identification may be imperfect for other reasons. In such cases there takes place a differentiation between *general* identification with the adult—the taking over of his general dispositions—and the performance of definite, specific roles with him. In order to achieve full social maturity the child must divest himself of at least some patterns of behavior which he has enacted vis-à-vis this particular adult or adults. The child's and adolescent's self-image includes many future expectations which differ from the roles he performs in relation to his parents. The modern father in urban Europe and America does not usually behave similarly at home with his family group and in his place of work. And if his child is to achieve occupational status of some sort he must learn to behave differently than he does with regard to his father within the scope of their family life, although his general orientation to the occupational field is derived from his identification with the father. In such cases the child must, as it were, detach himself to some extent from the adult identification of his childhood days, and his life expectations must go beyond the actual roles and concrete identifications of that period.

This necessity of detachment from the age-heterogeneous element is especially acute in those cases in which the integrative principles of the society are universalistic. The transition from particularistic to universalistic relations is probably most difficult from the point of view of the personality, as it necessitates a rather strong change of emotional attitudes towards objects and of criteria governing the individual's relations with them, and endangers the emotional security of attachment inherent in particularistic relations. Other pattern variables, such as specificity and achievement orientation, may sometimes be compatible with a kinship-regulated division of labor if the kinship groups become the main units of specialization and achievement. This can seldom occur, however, under a universalistic principle of allocation. In these cases, the potential strain on the personality is great, as the particularistic, age-heterogeneous object of attachment is not, in the details of his behavior, a sufficient "guide" to the attainment of social status.

Under these conditions, we assume, the individual develops need dispositions for a new kind of interaction with other individuals which would make the transition easier for him. This transition requires that the individual learn to act according to universalistic criteria, i.e., to choose his objects, behave towards them and expect behavior from them according to generalized, universalistic standards without relation to his particularistic attributes; and the expectation of such relations may endanger the individual's emotional security. Therefore he seeks such objects of action as would, on the one hand, enable him to retain some extent of general emotional security, and, on the other, provide him with relations of a different, wider scope than those of the family and enable him to act according to other criteria and orientations than those which are most prominent in age-heterogeneous relations. The element of emotional security—even within these wider criteria of membership—can be achieved only if he is accepted in his own right (or is sure of being accepted as such) and as a "total" personality; and if the sharing of certain goals and experiences provides him with solidary group relationships. In other words, he seeks relationships which would be ascriptive, and yet based on different qualities than blood ties (e.g., friendship), and to a large extent diffuse, solidary and collectivity-oriented; or he seeks membership within a specific type of *primary* group whose membership and behavior are regulated accordingly. At the same time he expects the content of these relationships to be patterned not on that of the family of orientation, but mainly oriented towards the possibility of entering into relations with any member of his society who would have these qualities.

Of all kinds of relationships, those with age mates, with members of age-homogeneous groups, are probably the only ones fitted for these types of need dispositions. They are, as we have seen, ascriptive while their diffuseness is "guaranteed" by the diffuseness of age definitions. They also have an inherent tendency towards solidarity because of (a) the common definition of life-space and destiny; and (b) the common sharing of emotional strains and experiences during the period of transition and emotional stress. These stresses are various and manifold. The age mates have similar sexual needs, heterosexual strivings and fears, which may be connected with the necessity of going out of the family at the crucial age of sexual maturation. They usually feel the same weaknesses and uncertainties as regards their future roles and a common need for community and participation. They may even, in some cases, have some common spiritual, ideological needs of "finding themselves," of forming their identity. For all these reasons they are naturally drawn together.

Groupings of children or adolescents are common in every society, no matter what its structure. In all societies children are drawn together for various reasons, play together—often at being adults—and thus learn the various types and rules of co-operative behavior and some universalistic norms which are of secondary importance in these societies. But it is only in universalistic societies that these groups become more articulated and develop a strong common identification based on the various needs mentioned above.[25]

These groups develop, in part, as a defense against the expected future roles, an attempt to maintain a pattern of relations differing from that expected in the future. But, on the other hand, orientations—latent or manifest—towards these future roles already exist within these groups, as they exist in most children's play groups in any society. These two attitudes—defense against future roles and orientations towards them—are present in all these age groups and form some of their main components.

IX　　A parallel argument may be traced as regards the continuity and solidarity of the social system. Inasmuch as the main integrative principles of the social system are different from those regulating family and kinship behavior, it is obvious that the solidarity of the latter is not sufficient to ensure the continuity and solidarity of the whole system.[26] Such solidarity depends on some definite integrative mechanisms which define the boundaries of individual and collective goals and values, giving primacy to the latter values. (Even if purely individualistic value patterns predominate, the allocation of roles and values necessitates some extent of collectivity-oriented regulation.) In the case of a universalistic society the collectivity orientation of the kinship system and descent groups cannot, then, be simply extended to that of the whole social structure. The allocation of facilities and rewards within the social system is not based, in this case, solely on kinship criteria, and the rewards inherent in interaction in kinship situations are insufficient to maintain continuity of *motivation* and of solidarity.

The allocation of roles, facilities, etc., on the basis of universalistic (and achievement and specificity) criteria, and through allocative agencies and groups distinct from kin and descent groups, puts a strain on the solidarity and stability of the social system in several ways. First, it upsets, as it were, the balance between expressive, solidary and instrumental orientations inherent in the kinship and descent system. Universalism, achievement and specificity orientations tend to broaden the scope of both purely instrumental relations and individualistic values. Moreover, in universalistic societies there is an inherent tendency for instrumental, solidary and expressive roles to be segregated in different sectors and groups, in each of which one of the value patterns is supreme. Consequently, the regulation of rights, duties and possessions is not fixed by one hierarchy of values, and there is a greater scope for different orientations and principles of allocation.

Secondly—as follows from the above—compatibility between the allocation of roles and of rewards is not as smoothly or almost automatically achieved as is the case in kinship systems. There exists a stronger element of contingency in the regulation of roles and rewards and a larger element of risk in the achievement of rewards and gratifications. This element of contingency can be seen most clearly in the fact that the secure, stable, particularistic boundaries of groups and mutual rights give way to unspecified universalistic relations, in which anyone may claim certain rights. Under these conditions the relations between various age grades, which are so necessary for the continuity of a society, may become strained. Age-heterogeneous relations, manifested in family and kinship relations, also become segregated in special spheres. The attitudes of authority and respect and the solidarity which they engender are not, as it were, automatically transferred to other spheres of the society. There arises then the problem of maintaining an overall solidarity despite the segregation of the various spheres, and of finding ways of transferring the basic solidarity of the family and kinship units, even if in a somewhat different way, and according to some different criteria, to the nonfamilial spheres.

The attainment of such solidarity cannot be assured without linking kinship relations to those of other spheres, and without providing an allocative principle which would maintain the primacy of expressive and solidary orientations and gratifications in a different form. For this reason integrative agencies and groups based solely on instrumental orientations and criteria would also be inadequate. There arises within the social system a functional necessity for an allocative principle which would ensure stable gratification (i.e., would be based on both diffuseness and ascription), without being circumscribed by the narrow boundaries of the membership of kinship and descent groups or any other partial group based on particularistic criteria which impede the attainment of overall solidarity. In other words, this principle should make possible the maintenance of stable, expressive gratification and solidarity through interaction with all members of the society, and at the same time adapt these gratification to collective goals. This principle we assert, must be that of age-homogeneity, because (a) age-heterogeneous principles, which are always rooted in the family situation and related to it, are excluded by definition due to their inherent inadequacy to maintain the solidarity of the society; and (b) other integrative principles which do not stress the age element at all (such as achievement orientation, specificity, etc.) would not ensure the primacy of *expressive* orientation in relation to *all* members of the social system.

The importance of the age criterion in this context is emphasized by the fact that all these problems of extension of solidarity and transfer of identification follow from the individual's transition from one stage of his life space to another, and are always necessarily related to his expectations in relation to various age grades and to his attitudes of respect, of authority, etc., towards these ages. This is clear from the fact that in all such cases the "age grade" most emphasized is that covering the span between the individual's leaving his family of orientation and establishing his family of procreation. We have seen earlier that this span is of greatest importance in the interlocking of different generations and in the mutual interaction of age-heterogeneous persons. Societies in which the overall integrative mechanisms are not harmonious with the patterns regulating age-heterogeneous (kinship) relations utilize this span of life for the establishment of the solidarity of the age-homogeneous groups, and the attainment of full social maturity (status) is effected not only through the interaction of the different generations and age grades in one group, but also, to a very large extent, through emphasis on age group solidarity, and through the corporate interaction of different age grades, each of them organized in an age-homogeneous group.

We see, then, that allocation of roles and constitution of groupings on the basis of homogeneous age is necessary from the point of view of the social system no less than for the personality integration of the individual. There is, then, a basic congruence between the two. This congruence does not, however, involve complete compatibility and harmony. The individual may, under certain conditions, find objects of gratification of his dispositions in age-homogeneous relations which are not institutionalized in the social system. The complete harmony or compatibility of the two occurs only under specific conditions, which will be investigated later in this work. Although we have couched our analysis in explicitly "functional" terms, i.e., in terms of the functions which the age groups perform for the integration of personality and the solidarity and continuity of the social system, we do not assume a complete identity of these two functions, and what may be functional from the point of view of one system may be dysfunctional from the point of view of the other.[27]

The extent of harmony and compatibility in age groups between the objects of the individual's need dispositions and the official roles allocated to him within the social system will be one of the central problems of our analysis. It might be mentioned here, however, that the existence of various juvenile delinquent groups clearly shows that such compatibility is by no means inevitable, and constitutes one of the best validations of our hypothesis.

On the basis of the previous discussion we may now proceed to formulate our hypothesis. In societies which are regulated by universalistic criteria and values which, by their very nature, differ from those of the family and kinship units, the members of the society develop, at the points of transition from kinship to otherwise institutionalized roles, a need to interact and establish social relations which are regulated according to diffuse and ascriptive criteria and qualities other than blood ties which may be common to all members of the society. They develop a need to establish, or join, primary solidary groups which are regulated accordingly and which are partly defense against their future roles and partly oriented towards them. The groups most suited for these purposes are age-homogeneous groups, in which the human image of a given age grade becomes an important symbol of collective identification.[28] Within these societies allocation of roles and definition of groups tends to be made on the basis of age-homogeneous criteria. The scope of these age-homogeneous groups ("age groups") is confined to the "transitory" sphere between kinship relations and those regulated by pattern variables of achievement and specificity. Their function is to extend the solidarity of the kinship system to the whole social system through emphasis on diffuse age group membership.

This hypothesis does not assume that in all "universalistic" societies age groups extend to the whole of the social system;

it is contended that they extend to those spheres of roles which are not institutionalized according to non ascriptive and non diffuse criteria. In other words, institutionalization of roles on the basis of age homogeneity is limited by the extent to which the integration of the social system is based—within the basic universalistic allocation of roles—on specialization and specialized units.

This hypothesis does not, of course, deny the necessity for age-heterogeneous relations within the social system. It only assumes that within special types of societies the interlocking of different age grades does not take place only within age-heterogeneous groups, but also through the corporate inter-action of age-homogeneous groups, which may or may not maintain the general types of mutual attitudes (respect, etc.) between age grades. The extent to which they do, and, in general, the way in which intergeneration relationships are organized in these societies, will be one of the main points of our analysis.

This discussion brings us to another problem with which we are concerned and which was mentioned earlier—namely, under what conditions the criterion of age becomes important for the general allocation of roles in the society. We may suggest here that the importance of this criterion depends on the degree of harmony between the general integrative principles and value system of the society and the main characteristics of "age" as a social category, or, in other words, the importance of age as a criterion for allocation of roles increases in proportion as diffuse, ascriptive and particularistic value patterns predominate in the value system of a society. It is, of course, important what qualities are emphasized, whether those related to some biological facts, blood ties, etc., or others, related mostly to member-ship in various groups not based on hereditary criteria. Obvi-ously, in the first case the importance of the criterion of age would be greater. In universalistic societies the importance of the criterion of age, although smaller than in comparable par-ticularistic societies, will grow in proportion as ascriptive and diffuse orientations prevail.

Our hypothesis has hitherto dealt with relationships be-
X   tween family and kinship groups, on the one hand, and
other institutional spheres of the social structure, on the
other, and we have assumed that age groups arise when the role
dispositions inculcated within the family (and kinship) situation
are incompatible with those of the total structure, and therefore
prevent the individual from achieving a mature status. The
impediments to the achievement of full social status and of the
concomitant change in one's age position are not necessarily
limited, however, to the relations between the family unit and
the total social system. Such impediments may also develop
within the structure of the family and descent group. Here, two
institutions or institutional elements constitute such inherent impediments: (a) the institution of authority; (b) the institutional
element of incest taboo and prohibition of sexual relations within
the family unit. We have seen earlier that relations between
different generations necessitate a strong element of authoritarianism which is, of course, basic to the maintenance of the family's
main socializing functions. This authoritarian element may become so strong as to impede the younger members' attainment
of full social status and assumption of authority-exerting functions. All possibility of access to the different facilities which
constitute necessary conditions for the attainment of full social
status may be blocked. Economic facilities (an independent
household, etc.), ritual and political facilities (the performance
of some ritual and political roles) may here be included, as well
as the facilities necessary for establishing a new family of procreation and attaining legitimate sexual, procreative maturity—
such as the economic facilities necessary for a bride-price, etc.

The incest taboo and prohibition of sexual relations within
the nuclear (usually also the extended) family may become so
severe as to prohibit any manifestations of sexual prowess within
the family unit, and may in this way impede the achievement of
full sexual maturity while the individual is still living within
the family of orientation. Such prohibitions usually take the
form of emphasis on ritual avoidance, especially between in-laws
of different generations.[29]

The two types of impediments—those caused by the blocking of access to facilities and those caused by stretching and sharpening the incest taboo—may, of course, become interconnected in concrete cases (as when, for instance, the elders use superior ritual power based on the incest taboo in order to refrain from providing their sons with bride-price); but they are analytically separate.

In so far as such impediments to the attainment of full social maturity and status exist within the family or kin unit, harmonious interaction between the generations is endangered at the most crucial point, and tensions between them tend to be accentuated. Transfer of identification is here different from that described for universalistic societies. There the object of identification can represent only general dispositions and not concrete roles, but no inherent necessity exists for inadequate identification with these general dispositions and with the object as such. In the families with which we are now dealing, the process of identification used is somewhat inadequate because of the various conditions, analyzed above, which impede the attainment of full status within the family. In these cases solidarity and complementariness of age definitions within the family are weakened and the "inferior" members of the family unit tend to overemphasize their mutual solidarity vis-à-vis the older generations, instead of almost totally subordinating it to the overall solidarity of the total family unit. The age-homogeneous element, which exists, as we have seen, within every family and kinship unit, tends to become accentuated, and age-homogeneous groups arise. As these groups have their origin in the tension between generations, and as their function is to find outlets for these tensions, they may function either as mechanisms of secondary adjustment, or in some cases as starting points for deviant groups.[30] As a result, their structure differs in important points from that of age groups which arise under the conditions stated in the first hypothesis. We shall investigate these differences below.[31]

The distinction between the two types of conditions which give rise to age groups, and between the consequent types of age groups, is mainly an analytical one. In reality the two types of conditions and age groups may often co-exist. In Chapter V we shall analyze these cases in great detail.

XI The broad hypothesis of this work can now be formulated in more precise and formal terms:

A. The criterion of age as a principle of role allocation is most important in those societies in which the basic value orientations are harmonious with those of the human image of age, i.e., particularistic, diffuse and ascriptive. In such societies we usually find that the family and/or kinship unit is a basic unit of the social division of labor. The age-heterogeneous relations of these units are the basic forms of interaction between age grades, while age-homogeneous relations are only of subsidiary importance.

B. Age-homogeneous groups, on the other hand, tend to arise in those societies in which the family or kinship unit cannot ensure, or even impedes, the attainment of full social status by its members. There may be two types of conditions and societies in which this takes place.

1. Those social systems in which the allocation of roles, facilities and rewards is not based on membership in kinship—or otherwise particularistically defined—units and criteria. In these societies the important institutionalized roles of the system are independent of the family and other particularistic units. In such societies, characterized by universalistically determined integrative mechanisms, roles and role dispositions incorporated within the family and enacted within it are not harmonious with the wider social system, and identification with age-heterogeneous members of the family does not ensure the attainment of full social maturity and status and full participation within the social system. In these cases the solidarity of age-heterogeneous relations tends to be broken, and there arises a tendency towards the emergence of age-homogeneous groups. This tendency arises because (a) the individuals develop need dispositions for role performance based on ascriptive, diffuse, universalistic and solidary criteria; and (b) role and reward allocation based on these criteria intensifies the solidarity of these social systems.

These criteria are applicable in terms of group boundaries, to age-homogeneous groups only.

The scope of activities of these age groups is limited to institutionalized roles enacted between the family and kinship unit and other spheres integrated according to criteria of achievement-orientation and specificity; in other words, the scope of age group activities is inversely related to the extent of group specialization within the basic, universalistic framework of the society.

2. When the structure of the family or descent group blocks the younger members' possibility of attaining social maturity within it, because (a) the older members block the younger ones' access to the facilities without which the performance of full adult roles is impossible; and/or (b) the sharpening of incest taboos and restrictions on sexual relations within the family unit postpones the young members' attainment of full sexual maturity.

It should, of course, be clear that these are but very broad, overall hypotheses which will have to be differentiated and more precisely formulated throughout this work. Here we have stated only the most general conditions under which age groups tend to occur, and we have not yet differentiated between various types of age groups and their interrelations with various aspects of the social system. The differentiation and elucidation of the problem and of the hypotheses will be the task of subsequent chapters. But even this analysis has shown that the conditions under which age groups occur are closely related to the basic preconditions of existence and continuity of social systems, and that age groups take part in the performance of some of the basic tasks of a society. The exact nature of these tasks differs, however, between different societies, according to the tasks that other groups perform in these societies.

CHAPTER II

Some Types of Age Groups

In this chapter we shall describe some typical age group systems of various societies. Hitherto we have been discussing age groups in general without calling attention to differences between them. We discussed them also in the abstract, without describing them concretely in any detail. In this chapter we shall give rather detailed descriptions of various types of age groups, using in so far as possible the original descriptive material of ethnographers, historians and modern sociologists, with only slight changes and paraphrasing. We shall not describe and enumerate here all the societies in which age groups are found. We shall rather describe some age group systems which seem to be most representative of a much wider range. In each case we shall also indicate briefly in which societies we find similar organization and characteristics of age groups. All the age groups dealt with here will represent, on the whole, the main types of age groups known to exist in various societies. We shall not give here detailed analysis of the societies in which these age groups are found, but shall dwell only on the internal organization of the age groups.

The age groups presented here—and those discussed in the whole book—belong primarily to three types of societies: a. primitive tribes and societies (e.g., most of the African societies analyzed here, the Plains Indians tribes, etc.), b. historical or semi-historical societies (e.g., the Nupe and Mende in Africa, Ancient Greece and Rome and for comparative purposes Medieval Europe, China, etc.), many of them peasant societies, and

c. various modern societies. It is obvious that this distinction between primitive, historical and modern societies is mostly a descriptive and not an analytical distinction; yet it has some analytical assumptions. It relates in main to the extent of social differentiation and specialization, to the existence of special ruling classes and cultural elite, to the extent of universalistic value orientations. Throughout our analysis we shall apply to these various societies more sophisticated analytical distinctions, but for the time being for general descriptive purposes this tripartite distinction will suffice. The purpose of presenting these descriptions in this chapter is twofold. On the one hand, they will provide a concrete description of various age groups and will in this way facilitate the presentation of material in the following chapters of the book. On the other hand, they will already now show us what are the most significant differences between various types of age groups—differences for which we shall have to account in the forthcoming analysis.

Before presenting these descriptions and a detailed analysis of each type of age group, it is worth-while to indicate the main elements in the structure of age groups which should be analyzed and compared. We can discern some of these basic elements on the basis of our former discussion and analysis. Our main problem, we have noted, is the extent to which the criterion of age is a constitutive element in the formation of groups. Hence we are also interested in the internal arrangement and structure of these groups. Finally, we have postulated that age groups play some part in the social structure in general—although the exact nature of this part may differ. These are then the three main elements of comparative analysis—the criterion of membership of age groups, their internal structure and their place in the social structure. Each of them may be subdivided in the following way:

I. CRITERIA OF MEMBERSHIP

A. Extent to which age (homogeneity) constitutes an explicit criterion of membership

B. Extent to which membership in the age group system is universal and common within the society

C. Age span covered by membership within the age group system and how precisely defined and adhered to this age span is

D. The extent to which an age grade (or part of it) is organized in a specific age group.

II. INTERNAL STRUCTURE OF THE AGE GROUP SYSTEM

A. Internal differentiation of age groups and extent to which they form a part of one system

B. Types of relations existing between various groups of the system

1. Rights and duties vis-à-vis one another; Principles of allocation of roles within the system

2. General attitudes vis-à-vis one another (respect, competition, etc.)

3. Extent of authority of senior over junior sets

4. Order of passage of sets from one grade to another

5. Extent of autonomy and autocephaly of the whole age set system

C. Extent of formal and corporate organization of the particular age groups

D. Extent of society-wide corporate organization of the age groups

E. Internal structure of the particular age group

1. Mutual relations of members: solidarity, cleavages, intensity of attachment

2. Extent to which a group or generational ideology develops

3. Extent of autonomy of the group

4. Criteria of internal allocation of roles and authority within it.

III. THE PLACE OF THE AGE GROUP WITHIN THE SOCIAL SYSTEM

A. Extent to which the age groups regulate behavior and allocate roles to members of the social system (both their own members and other people)

B. Extent to which age group roles are fully accepted and legitimized in the society

C. Extent to which age groups are directed by various agents of the social system who are not themselves members of the age group (this criterion is related to the extent of age group autonomy)

D. Extent to which membership in age groups is a prerequisite for (and/or an indicator of) their members' social status

E. Extent to which age groups develop deviant behavior of any kind—either aggression or withdrawal

F. Extent to which age groups develop deviant ideology

In the following sections we shall describe the main types of age groups and will apply to them, in so far as the material available permits it, the criteria set out above.

A. Primitive Segmentary, Acephalous Tribes

The *Nuer*[1] are a pastoral Nilotic (Nilo-Hamitic) tribe of the Southern Sudan. Their age set system has been fully described by E. E. Evans-Pritchard.

The age set system provides the Nuer with social stratification on the basis of age, a stratification cutting across the whole tribe. From the point of view of the individual, the organization of age sets begins with initiation, with the passing from the age grade and the status of boyhood to that of manhood. Initiation involves not only a change from one age grade to another but also entrance into a set in which the individual remains for the rest of his life. The members of each set have a common name, similar status and patterns of behavior towards one another and towards members of senior and junior age sets.

All boys initiated for a number of successive years belong to a single age set (Ric). There usually is a four-year interval between the end of one such set and the commencement of the next. A certain "wut glick," "Man of the Cattle," is, in each tribe, responsible for opening and closing the initiation periods and thereby dividing the sets. He performs the appropriate rite in his district, and when the news goes round, other districts begin initiation. Ten years may be regarded as an average period between the commencement of one set and that of the next. The number of sets is not fixed (during the period of investigation the number was six, but there were very few survivors of the senior set), nor are the names, which are fortuitous, and not repeated ni a cyclical form. Each age set has two or three subdivisions (according to the years of initiation), but all the members of a set are known by the name of the first division. If brothers belong to the same age set they are usually in separate divisions.

The age set system of the Nuer does not constitute, as in other tribes, the military organization of the tribe, nor a corporate group with common activities. It is in more general social relations, chiefly of a domestic or kinship order, that behavior is specifically determined by the positions of persons in the age-set structure. When a boy passes into the grade of manhood his domestic duties and privileges are radically altered. From being everybody's servant and an inferior, he becomes an independent adult. This change of status is epitomized in the taboo on milking through which he becomes separated from women, with whom he was identified as a boy—a taboo which begins at his initiation and remains in effect throughout his life. The change of status is also expressed in other domestic tasks, in habits of eating, etc. At initiation the youth receives a spear from his father or uncle and becomes a warrior. He is also given an ox, from which he takes an ox-name, and becomes a herdsman. From that time onwards until he becomes a husband and father, his chief interests are dancing and love-making. He becomes a true "man" when he has fought in war (battle) and has not run away, has duelled with his age mates, has cultivated his gardens and has married.

The change in status from boyhood to manhood is sudden and great, but the modes of behavior peculiar to each do not distinguish one set from another; for the privileges of manhood are enjoyed by the members of all sets equally. The sets are, however, stratified by seniority and by well-defined relationships between them.

Within the age set system the position of every male Nuer is structurally defined in relation to every other male Nuer and his status to them is one of seniority, equality, or juniority. It is difficult to describe these statuses in terms of behavior, because the attitudes they impose are often of a very general nature. The following points may, however, be noted.

(1) There are certain ritual observances and avoidances, chiefly between members of the same set, but also between sets. The most important of these are the segregation of the sets at sacrificial feasts, and the stringent prohibition on members of a set burying an age mate or partaking of the meat of beasts sacrificed at his mortuary ceremony; but there are a number of other ritual injunctions.

(2) A man may not marry, or have sexual relations with, the daughter of an age mate, for she is his "daughter" and he is her "father." Also, while a man may always have sexual relations with the daughter of one of his father's age mates he ought not to marry her unless either his father, or her father, is dead, and then only after the parties to the marriage have exchanged beasts as atonement to the age set of the fathers.

(3) Members of the same age set are on terms of entire equality. A man does not stand on ceremony with his age mates, but jokes, plays, and eats with them on easy and natural terms. Age mates associate in work, war, and in all pursuits of leisure. They are expected to offer hospitality to one another and to share their possessions. Fighting is considered an appropriate mode of behavior between age mates, but a man ought not to fight a man of a senior set. The comradeship between age mates springs from a recognition of a mystical union between them, linking their fortunes, which derives from an almost physical bond, analogous to that of true kinship, for they have shed their blood together.

(4) Members of a set are expected to show respect to members of senior sets, and their deference to them can be seen in discussions, in etiquette, in division of food, and so forth. Whenever a question arises about the propriety of a speech or an action, the point is judged by reference to the relative positions of the persons concerned in the age set structure, if kinship status is not also involved.

The relations between the sets are defined in the idiom of family relationship. The members of a man's father's age set are his "fathers" and the members of his father's brothers' age sets are, in a less precise sense, also his "fathers." The sons of the members of a man's set are his "sons," and they may fall into several sets. The wives of members of a man's father's set are his "mothers," and the wives of members of his son's sets are his "daughters." All members of a man's own set are likewise "brothers," though here the analogy is seldom expressed because the comradeship between age mates is strongly affirmed in the idiom of the system, for they are all *ric*, age mates, to one another.

We see, then, that the age set organization of the Nuer greatly changes the behavior of its members after their initiation. It takes them out of the particularistic framework of the family and widens the scope of their relationships, extending it to all members of the tribe who are of similar age. It organizes the mutual relations of all members of the tribe, cutting across family and kinship units and extending the general relations of respect towards elders and equality among members of the same age set. In this tribe, which is organized, as we shall see, largely on universalistic bases, the age set system maintains and extends the asymmetrical relations between various age grades to the interaction of all members of the society.

We may now classify and elaborate the main characteristics of the Nuer age set system, according to the general criteria of comparison outlined above.

I.

A. Age constitutes here an explicit criterion of membership of a set, and the age span covered by the age sets extends from initiation until death. It is very strictly adhered to.

B. The various age grades are organized in different age sets, although no definite relation exists between various age grades and different sets. The age set system tends to emphasize sharply the difference between boy and adult status and enrollment in an age set is connected with initiation ceremonies, but there is no further correspondence between membership in an age set and passing an age grade.

C. Membership in the age set is universal in the society.

II.

The various age sets do not constitute corporate groups or a unified corporate hierarchy. A set gradually advances to positions of relative seniority as older ones die out and younger ones are initiated, but there are no special ceremonies of corporate transition.

Age groups set only the pattern of general behavior and attitudes among their own members and towards one another—attitudes which find their clearest expression on ritual occasions.

Among these patterns of behavior those stressing equality among age mates and attitude of respect towards elders are of special importance.

Age group relations constitute, to some extent, extensions of kinship relation both in terminology and in exogamous prohibitions.

III.

Membership in age groups is universal and regulates overall behavior of the society's members. The duties, roles and relations prescribed by age groups are fully recognized by all members of the society and fully legitimized. Membership in age sets is a basic indicator of one's social status and is a basic prerequisite for the attainment of full social status.

The activities of age groups conform with the values and norms of the society, and no deviant behavior or ideology are to be found there.

The cyclical age set system of the Nandi (Kenya). The Nandi are a segmentary tribe in Kenya.[2]

Among the Nandi every male belongs to one of the seven age sets. Each one was subdivided into four "fires," two senior and two junior ones. The sets contained two groups of boys, one of warriors and four of elders. The set of warriors was the ruling set which went out to war and enjoyed most privileges. The functions of the elder sets are of a more advisory and juridical nature. The warrior age set is responsible for the safety of the country and the welfare of its inhabitants.

The Nandi age set system is a cyclical one.

In the cyclical type a man is born into a set and remains in it throughout his life. This set is usually the next one below that of his father. There is a fixed number of sets, each of which has a definite name, and the sets succeed each other in a recurring cycle. Among the Nandi there are seven such ages with fixed names, running in a recurring cycle of about 105 years, which means that each age is the fighting age (i.e., provides the fighting men) once in a century. At intervals of about 15 years each fighting age hands over to the age next below it, the members of which have during the 15 years been qualifying themselves for warriorhood by circumcision. The members of the retiring age move up and become elders. The result is that every 15 years each age moves up one place.

These age-sets, which divide the tribe into seven groups, provide a source of manpower for military purposes and also an important means of regulating behavior. They are therefore an important part of the social system. All the men of any one age are equal vis-à-vis one another, but they treat men of senior and junior sets much as seniors and subordinates are treated in a modern army. And when a man's younger brother belongs to a set junior to his own, as often happens when there is a long interval between the birth of two sons, then instead of being social equals—as they would be if the kinship rules alone applied —the age set rules of subordination cut across the kinship rules, so that the younger brother has a definitely inferior status to that of his elder brother.

The transfer of government from one age set to another is effected at a special ceremony (the sowet) at which all the tribe participates. At the ceremony there usually is a symbolical show of force between the retiring and the new warrior age set, the retiring age set being unwilling to relinquish its privileges. (Among some other tribes of the Nandi group, and especially among the Kipsigis, there is real animosity between adjacent age sets, the set holding power being prepared to hand it over only after some real fights.) The elder sets alternate in performing their tasks of mediators between the adjacent ones.

The feeling of comradeship between age mates is very strong, leading even to a sharing of wives, but there is no extension of kinship terminology to them. Entrance into the warrior age set entailed various privileges not accorded to any other set, among them privileges in sexual matters. The warriors, after circumcision, enjoyed a great deal of sexual license, taking uninitiated girls for their sweethearts. A warrior did not marry his sweetheart, but could continue his relations with her after marriage (as long as he stayed in the warrior set). After retirement from warriorhood the men had to confine themselves to their wives. (This explains the incidence of jealousy between overlapping sets.) Action of corporate sets was confined mostly to the local divisions (provisions) and the warriors constituted the main fighting power of the regiments (porokiet). The exact relations between the age set regiments and the porokiet division among the Nandi are not, however, clear.

The division into age sets constituted the most important way of assigning status to an individual and belonging to a given age set was the most important index of a man's general status in the tribe.

Here we find that the age criterion was very important in the general allocation of roles and prestige in the tribe, and most of the important roles were allocated on the basis of age. Within the kinship units, which were also the main economic units, usually elder people held the most important positions. In the political, ritual and juridical spheres the main roles were allocated, as we have seen, to the age sets. Very few important roles existed which were not related to these criteria of allocation.

From the point of view of our main comparative criteria, the Nandi age groups evince the following characteristics:

I.

Age constitutes an explicit criterion of membership of groups and membership in age groups covers the whole lifetime—from birth to death, although active membership begins only after initiation. Membership in age groups is universal in the society. There exists a close correspondence between age grades and age groups and each age grade is usually organized in a group (or groups) of its own.

II.

There exists a unified, corporate, age group hierarchy and system, organized on a cyclical basis. Relations between the various age groups are regulated through the fixed specialization of functions and the transition of a set from one grade to another at fixed periods.

The age groups perform many important activities—educational, political, warfare, etc.—each of these being usually allocated to a special age group. These activities encompass most of the important activities of the tribe—with the exception of (a) those regulated by the family and (b) economic activities.

Age groups set the pattern of general behavior, emphasizing solidarity and equality between age mates and respect towards seniors.

Strong feelings of competition and animosity exist between adjacent sets—especially when the time for transmission of government function arrives—tempered by the mediation of the elder age sets.

The whole system is autonomous and autocephalous as are, to some extent, each of the particular age groups. But generally, the elder groups exercise some authority over the younger and divert their activities.

III.

Age groups regulate many aspects of the overall behavior of the members of the tribe and are fully accepted and institutionalized. Most of the important roles in the social system are allocated through the age groups. As already pointed out, age groups are directed by elder grades to which the main integrative tasks of the society are allocated.

Membership in the age groups is a basic prerequisite of social status and an important indicator of a person's status within the society.

The age groups are fully conformist and no deviant behavioral or ideological tendencies are developed.

The Plains Indian Age Societies.[3] Among five of the Plains Indian tribes—the Hidatsa, Mandan, Arapaho, Gros Ventre and Blackfoot—there are some common characteristics which we shall first describe briefly, and then give a more detailed account of one of them, the Hidatsa. Most of the societies incited or induced their members to distinguish themselves in war. Membership, or rather, ownership of each society is acquired by a group of age mates' purchasing the rights (which include mainly the rights to perform various ceremonial functions, dances, and the use of various ceremonial objects, such as pipes, etc.) in it collectively from an older group. The elders never buy societies from younger people. Buyers and sellers are regarded as standing ceremonially in the relation of "sons" and "fathers" respectively. The progression through these societies is regulated by age and the feeling of moving with the age group is strong. It is felt that a man should belong to the same age group as his age mate. But the direct basis of membership in the society is purchase, and not age. At times a given age group may remain without a ceremonial name, if it refuses to buy a title from the older group after selling its own name to a younger one. There need not be a fixed relation between a given ceremonial complex and a specific age.

The Hidatsa had a series of military organizations, many of which closely resembled those of the Crow, as might be expected from the partial identity of names. Thus, the Fox and the Lumpwood, Hammer and Dog societies are common to both tribes, and often the similarities are of the most detailed kind. The officers of the Crow Foxes reappear in the Hidatsa equivalent with precisely the same duties; and in both tribes the Dog men carry peculiar rattles of dewclaws tied to a stick, while certain officers wear slit sashes. But while corresponding clubs were fundamentally alike and doubtless served similar social needs of the members, the mode of entrance was wholly different.

The Hidatsa were not invited to join individually and gratuitously, nor were they tempted by desirable presents; they were obliged collectively to buy membership, which was henceforth renounced by the previous holders, so that the whole transaction was tantamount to a transfer of property rights.

But there was another basic difference between the two schemes in addition to the different modes of acquiring membership. The adult men's clubs of the Crow were co-ordinated organizations with which men were as a rule permanently associated. Among the Hidatsa the military societies formed a graded series, and in the course of their lives the men passed from one grade to another. With the Hidatsa advancement is uniformly collective, and the buyers are all age mates. In other words, the Hidatsa recognize a dual basis for membership, purchase *and* age. No group of persons can automatically become Foxes or Dogs when they have attained a certain age; they can only become members by paying the required fees. On the other hand, no man can become a Fox or a Dog as an individual but only in conjunction with a whole body of novices all about his own age.

In 1833 Prince Maximilian found all the male population, except for very young boys, grouped into ten societies. The youngest were the Stone Hammers, aged from ten to eleven; lads of fourteen or fifteen formed the Lumpwoods; youths of seventeen and eighteen owned the next higher society; and so it went on to the Raven club, which united the oldest men in the tribe. Strictly speaking, it is not true that the males of the tribe were divided into ten societies, but rather into ten *age classes*. The societies really correspond to degrees, and according to the Hidatsa scheme, which precluded automatic promotion, certain degrees would be vacant whenever an age class had sold its membership since its members might have to wait a long time before being able to buy the next higher degree. In other words, each age class was a permanent unit but it did not always possess a definite place in the series.

There was a somewhat amusing alliance between alternate Hidatsa age classes. When age-class 2 attempted to buy the membership then held by age-class 3, it could rely on the help of class 4, and of the other even-numbered classes, while a similar bond united the odd-numbered classes. The reason for this alternation may be sought in the mutual relations of adjoining classes. Between these there was necessarily a "class struggle" since the sellers would always extort the highest payments possible; hence alternate classes would be united by their common antagonism to the intermediate class, which was the prospective flayer of the lower group and the future victim of the higher one.

While the Crow women had no societies of their own, their Hidatsa sisters had a smaller but parallel series slightly enlarged by borrowings from the neighboring Mandan. The mode of purchase was identical with that of the men's club, and there was even a direct affiliation with the male series, inasmuch as certain groups of women aided the odd and even male classes, respectively. Naturally these organizations were not distinctively military, but indirect martial associations are recorded.

The societies usually performed different general duties within the tribe, especially at the periods when the whole tribe camped together. Thus among the Blackfoot the "All Comrades" were responsible for the safety of the camp while among the Arapaho a whole series of sets were under the guidance of the old men's grade.

The age societies were especially important in the ritual and, to some extent, the political field. Their importance was most evident in those periods when the various bands of the tribe camped together. When they were separated the importance of the age societies was much smaller.

The great emphasis which was laid on warriorship and on wealth within most of these societies necessarily diminished to some extent the importance of the age societies and age criteria in general in these societies. Many more spheres of social life were here, unlike among the Nuer and Nandi, directly related to the age group organization. From the point of view of our general criterion the Plains Indians' age groups evince the following characteristics:

I.

Age constitutes an explicit criterion of group membership, although the element of "purchase" enters as a subsidiary element in the definition of the group. The age groups extend from adolescence to death and the different definitions of age group are rather strictly adhered to, although some individual exceptions may sometimes occur. Membership in the age group is universal within the society.

II.

A. The age groups have a unified organization throughout the tribe regulating the behavior of all members vis-à-vis one another.

B. The age groups have corporate organizations and their activities are oriented towards the achievement of ceremonial status through purchase of ceremonial dances, performances.

C. There exists a definite hierarchy between various groups, interlocked through the purchase of ceremonial privileges from one another.

D. Relations between adjacent groups are competitive and semi-aggressive, while those between alternate ones are more friendly.

E. There exists some degree of extension of kinship terminology, but to a smaller degree than in formerly cited cases.

F. Age group activities foster general feelings of solidarity between age mates and respect for seniority.

G. Each of the various age groups has a large degree of autonomy, but sometimes their activities, such as police duties, etc., in the camp, are directed by chiefs.

III.

The age groups regulate many aspects of the behavior of their members, especially in regard to mutual attitudes of equality, seniority, etc. Their activities are fully accepted and institutionalized in the society, and membership in them is usually a prerequisite indicator of full social status. Cases of individual nonacceptance of age group roles, or of a temporary "failure" to buy the ceremonial bundles are exceptional. Otherwise there are no deviant tendencies within them.

B. *Conciliar* (*Acephalous*) *Primitive Villages*

The *Yako*[4] are a southeastern Nigerian people, living in five compact villages a few miles apart, each of which was formerly autonomous in its political as well as its ruling organization. Within these villages some degree of economic specialization and interdependence between the wider family units can be discerned. The most important centers of power and influence are various types of titled associations and special councils of ward and village heads which are not closely related either to the family kinship heads or to the age groups. They are mostly based on individual exertion and achievement. Most of these villages are divided territorially into wards with a population of from 1,500 to more than 3,500 in each. They have no fully centralized system of government. They and their age groups have been fully described by D. Forde.

Men's age sets (*nko*, sing. *eko*) are formed within each ward, and in Umor the formal establishment of a new age set from young men about to marry should in principle follow the four-yearly *Ligwomi* ritual. A new set is then called into existence by the Ward Head to whom it presents its chosen leader and his deputy. The large decorated wine jar of the new age set is prepared by them and set out in the ward square for the first time. The other sets bring out their jars, and the new set collects food offerings and palm wine to fill them. Before the drinking begins, the Ward Head, surrounded by the elders, sprinkles chalk on the new set's jar, blessing it and enjoining the members to be of good conduct. Although four years is regarded as the proper interval between the formation of two sets and, in the past, appears to have been generally observed, in recent years, owing to increase in population, the interval between calling for the leaders of one set and the next has tended to diminish.

At any one time there are about sixteen sets in existence in each ward and among them are distributed men ranging in age from 17 or 18 to over 70 years, but the numerical strength of the sets sharply diminishes after middle age with increasing seniority. The age sets in each ward are alternately labelled *okprike* and *agbiagban*, and each set is further identified by the name of its senior leaders, being known as the *okprike* or *agbiagban* of so-and-so. The sets of the different wards, although they are formed independently and there is no co-ordination of establishment ceremonies, are in practice equated. Thus a man of one ward in a village can name the sets in the other wards which correspond with his own, and are regarded as equivalent in age. In the same way, although it is less frequently needed, a man in one village can determine the age set of any ward in another village which is held to correspond in seniority with his own. Should an adult migrate, he will be accepted as a member of such a set in the ward of his new residence.

The principle of age grouping operates long before the formal recognition of a set and a man's age set membership has, in fact, been established in childhood. Gradually, during their childhood the boys of a ward sort themselves out into a series of groups of increasing seniority and as the members of each group reach the age of marriage, the group is formally established as an age set. If, however, a potential set is too large or too small in number in the opinion of the Ward Head, it can be split or joined to its next junior group at this time.

Age groups are similarly formed among the girls of a ward during childhood and the separate groups are distinguished in the ward dancing parties which take place especially during and after the New Yam festival. But women's age sets, similarly formed by combinations of the smaller groups are not formally established in a public ceremony like those of the men, although they choose leaders and, like those of the men, act corporately in performing tasks such as path weeding at the request of the Ward Head.

A male age set is further subdivided into a number of groups of closer friends or companions known as *liboma* (sing. *koboma*— finger). These groups of age mates are conceived as subgroups of the larger age set and an analogy with lineages of a clan is made: "We have *liboma* in *eko* just as we have *yeponoma* in *kepun*." But the age mate groups are not mutually exclusive and comprehensive subdivisions of an age set. A man may, although it is exceptional, belong to more than one *koboma* at the same time, so that the membership of the various groups overlaps to some extent. Furthermore even the ward boundaries of the age set system can be overstepped by accepting into an age mate group a man of an equivalent age set into another ward. An age set is concerned with the marriage or death of one of its members or of a member's close relatives, and the part played by the relevant age sets in the conduct of rites and feasts in which marital status is established is considerable. But the entire age set does not usually function as a corporate group on these occasions; the age mates of the member concerned are the main participants to whom may be added less intimate age set fellows who have other ties with him.

The age sets, however, have definite obligations to the ward as corporate groups, of which the most prominent is that of guarding the houses against fire during the dry season, when most people are away from the village during the day, clearing land and hoeing the ground for new farms. For this guard all men's age sets are expected to serve a day at a time in rotation, but the older sets, if they are very small in number, join together to form a single group.

In general an age set takes care of its own backsliders and exacts a penalty in food or palm wine from anyone who fails to do his share without a good reason; but a person or set which refused customary duties without good reason would be punished with a fine by the Ward Head.

Two or three times a year the age classes are also called out to cut the growth of vegetation choking the main paths leading through the farm lands of the *yepun* of the ward. A third task that is regularly assigned to the age classes is the maintenance of the main springs from which the domestic water supply of the ward is obtained. The clearing of springs is usually undertaken during the growing season in June or July by one or more of the junior classes under the direction of a few older men. In addition to these regular duties one or more of the Classes can be called upon to undertake a particular task in the ward, such as cutting a new bush path or, more occasionally, joining with classes from other wards at the request of the village leaders to do some work required for the village as a whole, such as the rebuilding or repairing of the Village Head's house.

The calling out of the age classes is one of the duties of the ward crier known as Edjukwa. Edjukwa has no independent authority, but merely summons persons or assemblies at the instance of the appropriate village or ward authorities, and the running of the age class system is largely in the hands of the members of the three or four senior classes who will usually include nearly all the prominent men in the ward. When any work has been decided upon, Edjukwa walks through the ward beating his drum and calling out the name of the group concerned and the time and nature of the work.

The Yako age classes evince markedly different characteristics from those of the Nuer, Nandi and Plains Indians. The main difference is in the smaller extent of overall social relations which are regulated by the societies and by criteria of age in general. This is mainly due to the great extent of social, political and, to some extent, also economic specializations and to the existence of many special associations in which most of these activities are centered.

From the point of view of our formal criteria, the Yako age groups evince the following characteristics:

I.

Age constitutes a clearly defined criterion of group membership and the age span covered by age groups extends from before initiation until later middle age. There is no formal final age for membership in age groups—they gradually cease to exist in later middle age. Until then the age criterion is fairly closely adhered to and membership in age groups is universal in the society. There is no relation between definite age grades and age groups, i.e., the various age groups may not cut across the main age grades.

II.

A. The age groups are organized and perform certain specific activities within the general society, at the behest of its officials.

B. The age group sets the patterns of mutual help (especially in relation to problems of marriage, etc.) among its members, maintains internal discipline and to a smaller extent also patterns some general attitudes of respect towards elders.

C. These general patterns of behavior among age mates are most clearly manifest at different "points de passage"—marriage, birth, death, etc., of members.

D. The age groups have a separate but parallel organization within the main territorial divisions of the society.

E. The various age groups do not form an autonomous unitary hierarchy, although the various sets are interconnected in a general way. There is no corporate transition from one grade to another—only gradual advance in seniority.

III.

The age group criterion does not dominate the behavior and attitudes of all members of society vis-à-vis one another, and the scope of the group's regulation of members' behavior is not as full as in the former instances (Nuer, Nandi).

The age group activities are, however, fully accepted and recognized within the society. The age groups do not form fully autonomous or autocephalous groups, as in most of their activities (with the exception of internal, recreational ones) they are directed by "outsiders," village officials, etc. Entrance into age groups is a basic prerequisite of full social status, but membership in more advanced stages of age groups is not a main indicator of social status. Membership in the various associations is here of much greater importance.

The age groups do not evince any deviant behavioral or ideological tendencies.

C. Primitive Centralized Chiefdoms and Monarchies

The *Swazi*,[5] of South Africa, constitute a primitive centralized monarchy, founded on conquest and amalgamation of the conquered tribes (clans) into one state based on direct allegiance to the king. They are mainly a pastoral people, numbering about 60-70,000 persons.

The age groups of the Swazi are organized in the army, forming "age regiments." They include all the adult males in the country and regulate their activities. The regimental system is developed on the basis of the physiological factor of age, which cuts across local boundaries. Initiation into a regiment had formerly been dependent on circumcision, but this old custom was abandoned by one of the kings.

It is the king who forms new regiments and exercises ultimate control. There is no regular period between regiments, but the average period is usually five to six years. The number of years varies with the conditions of the day, but a new group must be formed when the one ahead of it is ripe for marriage—for which permission must be given by the king. If there are great differences in age within a regiment, it may be subdivided into older and younger sections. The announcement of the new regiment is made to a representative gathering on some suitable occasion in the cattle kraal of the capital. It is the duty of each chief to make this known to all the young boys in his area, who later can summon the youngsters to his village. At the inauguration only a nucleus composed of youths living in the capital is present.

The army is composed of central royal regiments serving permanently at the capital, local contingents under local chiefs, and regiments which are only on temporary service at the capital, or who may be called for such temporary service. The royal soldiers have an especially high status unequalled by any other soldiers. The royal regiments are composed of special volunteers for this position, striving for the higher social status attached to it. (For example, whenever a royal soldier-messenger is sent, all possible assistance is given him and a beast must be killed at each village in which he spends the night.)

At the head of all the regiments of the country is an *induna yemabutvo*, commander-in-chief of the regiments, who is officially appointed by the king. He must lead the army in any national expedition and assumes control of all local companies. He arranges for their accommodation and sees to it that their presence is made known to the rulers. He is chosen from among the commoners for his ability to maintain discipline, his knowledge of military organization, and his trustworthiness and loyalty. The commander-in-chief works in co-ordination with a prince appointed by the king as his representative.

The king, together with these two officials, selects assistant officers (*emapini*) out of any clan, who are valuable in supervising labor and executing the king's commands. In addition, individuals with personal ability who have been of valuable service become known as "*itilomo*" (cp. *umlomo*, a mouth), and hold positions of honor, their opinions being sought on matters affecting the regiments. Finally, in order to keep traditional knowledge alive, the king selects at least one "old person" (*umuntu lomdzala*) to act as exemplar and tutor of the young. Respectful behavior is taught to the regiments and respect (*inhlonipo*) is demanded by all members of an older group from those of a younger one. Every representative of civil authority is a member of a regiment and is usually on the staff. The staff of each regiment is a weak reflection of the staff of the whole army. The official personnel is not so clearly defined, but there is usually an officer or *induna* of common birth and a prince, as well as a few trusted men who are responsible for the execution of any tasks allotted to their group. A similarly constituted staff organizes the activities of local contingents, but where a chief holds hereditary territorial jurisdiction he appoints, instead of a prince of the ruling clan, a member of his own clan.

Members of a local group perform most of their work for their own chief. When they are summoned to the capital they come under an officer who immediately becomes subordinate to the *induna yemabutvo*. Important chiefs with large districts might summon a single regiment of their local contingent. Their men will obey a call to the capital in regimental formation. Participation in sporadic national work, however, does not raise a member of the local group to the status of *umbutvo*.

The regiment is composed of platoons, which own central meeting-huts of their own which serve also as general hostels for strangers. A platoon may be composed of any number of squads, groups of 8-20 boys each who are in one line for drilling and dancing, though they do not necessarily share one hut. The smallest unit is a group of close friends sharing the same living accommodations, but the squad is not necessarily composed of people living in the same huts.

Incorporation into a regiment is a continuation of the more informal childhood education and constitutes the first steps of transition into adulthood, from one age grade to another. While within the barracks, the soldier may enjoy unprocreative sexual relations, which are under strict supervision so as to avoid license. No married women are allowed into the barracks. The soldiers are not allowed to marry until the king gives formal permission to an entire regiment, thus giving them the status of full adults, which lasts until they become old grandfathers. In this way social recognition and definition of age stages was effected.

The regiments' main activities are national war-making and, in times of peace, public works throughout the country, initiated by the king, the queen mother or local chiefs. When not engaged in any work the soldiers in the capital attend at the royal courts, listening to discussions and learning the tribal lore.

Each regiment has a strong corporate life and is distinct from other regiments. But within each the tie is closest between contemporaries coming from the same locality, and particularly between those who are more or less permanently together in the barracks.

Despite the general inculcation of respect for seniority, there is often rivalry and resentment between various age classes. A senior regiment has priorities in the distribution of food, has first right to the women and leads in ritual. The younger men do not accept subordination willingly, and may take up arms in rebellion. They are, however, usually restrained by loyalty to the same chief and by local solidarity.

Within the age classes, the political leaders whose rank is determined by birth, continue as the elite. Their position is not challenged by the plebeians, who attain recognition within the age classes and whose prospects of advancement are dependent on the will of the established (royal) aristocracy.

The Swazi age groups evince the following characteristics:

I.

Age is an explicit criterion of group membership, membership being universal in the society. The age span covered by the age groups extends from initiation until the beginning of middle age. Afterwards there is but little active participation in them. There is no strict relation between age grades and age groups.

II.

A. The age groups have a corporate organization in regiments. Their functions are mainly military, and they also serve as the king's labor force on "public works."

B. The age groups emphasize military virtues and behavior, the maintenance of strong solidarity among age mates and general patterns of respect for elders. There exists, however, a strong spirit of competition between the various age-regiments.

C. The age groups constitute a unified hierarchical system organized and directed by the king, who allots specific roles to each regiment, with a small degree of internal (age-set) autonomy. There is no corporate transition of regiments from one grade to another but only gradual advancement.

III.

Age group life influences many aspects of life except that of family life, and stands in strong opposition to the latter, as manifested in the ban on marriage affecting the most active warriors.

Their activities are fully accepted and institutionalized in the social system. They have but small autonomy—as they are mostly directed by the king's officers. Membership in an age regiment is a basic prerequisite of social status and service in regiments constitutes one of the main channels of social mobility for the commoners. The age groups do not evince any deviant tendencies.

The Nupe.[6] The Nupe are a semi-feudal kingdom in Nigeria, based on conquest by the Fulani clan. They are a relatively highly differentiated society, with great differences between country (mostly villages) and town, in which the ruling class concentrated and in which we find handicraft guilds, merchants, etc. The official religion is Islam, which plays a very prominent part in the social life of the state.

The age set system is typical of the whole country and plays a prominent part in its social and political life. It is not, however, a unified, centralized system uniformly enforced throughout the country. It consists of many different age sets in villages and towns, which though organized in similar ways do not constitute a centralized social system. One should differentiate particularly between age sets in the villages and those in the capital (Bida).

The majority of villages have three age grades: grade I is

called *ena dzakengizi*, "society of children" (aged 10-15); grade II, *ena gbarufuzi*, "society of young men" (aged 15-20); and grade III, *ena nuzazi*, "society of old ones" (aged 20-30 and mostly already married). The boys below the age of admission to the first grade are known as *wawagizi*, "little ones," and may form similar groups of their own, which are not, however, officially recognized and are spoken of as being "only for fun." The men who leave the highest grade, though they no longer corporately share in the age grade activities, continue to recognize their one-time membership throughout life and are expected to help each other as friends would do, to attend each other's family feasts, and to take an interest in each other's political careers. Above all, they keep the titles which they acquired in the senior grade. This acquisition of titles, which are accompanied by definite rights and obligations, is of paramount importance in age grade life. Each member of an age grade bears a title bestowed upon him by his fellows. In each grade the titles are arranged in a rigid hierarchy, election to a particular title depending on the success and popularity the individual youth is able to gain in his age set. The hierarchy of titles, the corresponding differentiation in duties and privileges, and equally the constant by-play of ambition and rivalry are all faithfully modelled on the rank system of the adults, which is in turn the most salient feature of Nupe political life. The age grade responsibilities can thus be regarded as a planned anticipation of adult responsibilities or as a typical "education for citizenship."

Grade I is made up of all the boys of suitable age who join together (only cripples and backward children being excluded), elect their leader, and distribute the various titles. To be more precise, each grade has two leaders: one, called *etsu* or "king," belongs to the respective age group and is elected by it; the other, called *ndakotsu*, "grandfather of the king," belongs to the next higher grade, in which he must hold a high rank. In grade III the *ndakotsu* is a man who has already left the age grades. Each *ndakotsu* holds office for one term only, and before relinquishing his office appoints his own successors from among the group whose leader he had been. The leaders organize all age grade activities and maintain internal discipline. Parents, incidentally, are allowed no influence in the running of the age grades or in the selection of boys for the first grade. During the *ganni* ritual anxious fathers or mothers are seen trying to protect their children from the cruel discipline all too rigidly enforced on this occasion, but their attempts at interference do not succeed. Although a father or elder brother will always help a boy to fulfill the various duties of hostility towards his age mates which are expected of him, the age grades remain a fully autonomous organization of the adolescents. Those adults who play a part in age grade life do so only in their capacity of retired, high-ranking members of the senior grade.

In most villages the age grades are subdivided according to locality, each village ward having its own local age grade associations, whose average membership is 15-20. In the villages here considered (the rule varies slightly) each age grade lasts six years, and is reconstituted in the seventh. On that occasion a new grade I is formed and the members of the existing grades I and II are promoted *en bloc* to the next higher grade, while the members of grade III retire from age grade life. This corporate promotion does not mean that everybody keeps the rank held previously; the ranks are reshuffled, some members rising and others declining in rank. No public ceremony is connected with this event, nor is its date rigidly fixed. The reconstitution of the age grades takes place privately in the house of the retiring *ndakotsu* usually towards the beginning of the rains. Moreover, the promotions in grade and rank are purely private affairs in which no one outside the age grades takes any interest.

Within the capital enlistment is not universal; it is carried out separately within the various quarters and is based more on voluntary enrollment, canvassing and attachment to a freely chosen leader of a local political faction.

Age grade ranks are largely copied from the political rank-system obtaining in the community to which the *ena* belongs. The system is not duplicated exactly, although the *ena* tends to arrange its ranks according to the order of precedence which they follow in the political hierarchy. In Bida the distinctions between the different classes of political ranks are not observed, and military and civil ranks, office titles and titles of the royal nobility are bestowed indiscriminately. The village *ena* remains more faithful to the rank-system of the community, and would, for example, adopt its typical, possibly uncommon, titles of elders. But as the membership of the *ena*—especially of the junior grades—may be considerably larger than the number of titled village elders, ranks from outside the traditional rank system may have to be introduced, preferably from the rank system of the capital. The younger generation is indeed always ready and eager to adopt such innovations. Rank systems of heterogeneous nature and rather arbitrary precedence are the result. However, we must not forget that the rank systems of many villages are themselves similarly heterogeneous and arbitrary, including Bida titles among their traditional village ranks.

The integrative tendencies in the *ena* are expressed in every one of the typical age grade activities. In the village they revolve round the three centers of social life: work, recreation, religion. In the Bida *ena* the first is reduced to insignificant dimensions; the second is raised to almost paramount importance; the third remains on the whole unchanged, being only transferred to a different plane—Mohammedan religion.

Some of the characteristics of the Nupe age set system differentiate it from those hitherto discussed. Most important of these are the following:

I.

Age is an important criterion in the formation of groups and is more or less adhered to by the members of the society. Age group membership covers the span of life from early adolescence until early adult life. Membership in the age groups is voluntary, but in the villages it is almost universal. There is no correspondence between age grades and age groups.

II.

A. There exists no central organization throughout the country, but each locality develops its own set. Those sets, although similar in many respects, are not exactly equivalent to one another (as for instance in the case of the Yako).

B. The age groups have corporate organization within the

group with detailed activities, in the villages centering mainly
on work and recreation while in the towns mainly on recreation.

C. Within each locality there exists a hierarchy of sets, with
corporate and almost automatic advance of the age groups from
one grade to another, and complete autonomy of the sets (especially in the towns). This autonomy and independence is particularly stressed in relation to the family. Interrelation among
the sets is effected through members of older sets performing
functions of sponsorship and patronage with regard to the junior
sets.

D. The age group activities are patterned mainly as an imitation of the status system of the adult society—especially from the
point of view of their internal system of ranks and titles. They
pattern the general role disposition important for the assimilation of the values of the general society, and at the same time
foster strong group solidarity among their members and emphasize relations of respect towards seniors.

III.

The age groups are reorganized within the society, but they
perform preparatory and educational activities and almost no
fully institutionalized tasks (especially in the towns). They do
participate, however, in some of the main festivals of the society.
They regulate mainly the internal activities of their members
and not their overall behavior or the behavior of other members
of the society.

Membership in age groups is an important, although not the
main, prerequisite for full membership in society. Status within
age groups influences one's position in adult life to a small extent.

Age groups do not evince any specific deviant tendencies.

The Nyakyusa Age Villages.[7] The Nyakyusa are a Bantu-
speaking people living at the northern end of Lake Nyasa. They
are cattle owners and cultivators. Their most peculiar and unique
institution is that of the "age villages." Kinsmen do not live together. A village consists of a group of age mates with their wives
and young children, while men of one lineage are scattered

throughout the chiefdom, and may even live in different chiefdoms.

The age village starts when a number of herd-boys, about 10 or 11 years old, build together at the edge of their fathers' village. They had been practicing building huts for some time, as small boys in other cultures do also, but when they reach the age of 10 or 11 they actually go to live in their huts, sleeping and spending their spare time in them, though still going to their mothers' huts for meals. A boy should not and does not eat alone, but a group of friends eat together, visiting the mother of each member of their gang in turn. This system is regarded not only as being congenial to small boys (as with us) but also as moral. For the Nyakyusa, eating with age mates is a cornerstone of morality, and a boy who often comes home alone to eat is severely scolded.

Moving out of the parents' village to sleep is directly connected by the Nyakyusa with decency. They say that a growing boy should not be aware of the sex activities of his parents, *and therefore* he must not sleep at home, even in a separate hut, but in a different village altogether. As they put it, "the night is full of lewd talk" and that is all right between equals, but not in the presence of people of another generation. Their idea of "mixed company" is not male and female, but fathers and sons.

A boys' village starts quite small, with perhaps not more than ten or a dozen members, but it grows as young boys from the fathers' village, or from other villages in the neighborhood, become old enough to join it. When the original members are fifteen or sixteen years old the village is usually closed to any further ten-year-olds, who must then start a new village on their own. Conditions vary with the density of population in the neighborhood and other factors, but generally the age span within a village is not more than about five years, and a village numbers between 20 and 50 members.

The boys who thus establish a village continue to live together through life. When they marry they bring their wives to the village, and, when the last of them die, the village dies. As their sons grow up they move out to build villages of their own. Daughters often move out, too, marrying men in other villages, but they may, and quite often do, marry an age mate of their father and remain in the village. A village (*ikipanga*) consists of a group of male contemporaries with their dependants, not in a site, and it retains its identity no matter how it moves.

The men of a village are all of similar age and are bound together by a common life shared from early youth, but the women in any village are of diverse age and experience. Men usually marry as their first wives girls about ten years younger than themselves, but not all the men of a village marry at the same time, and as they grow older they continue to marry young girls as junior wives. Often the junior wife is a niece—a brother's daughter—of the senior. Moreover, wives are inherited from elder brothers and fathers, so that a man may have some wives older than himself and others who are very much younger.

Once in each generation there is a great ceremony at which administrative power and military leadership are handed over by the older generation to the younger. At this ceremony there is a new deal in land. The men of the retiring generation move to one side to make room for the expanding villages of the younger generation, but it is not simply a transfer of land from one village of fathers to one of sons; the boundaries within the chiefdom are all redrawn, and the old men move even when there is unoccupied land available for their sons. The only lands excluded from the new deal are the very valuable fields made in the craters of extinct volcanoes, and these are inherited, like cattle, within lineages.

At this ceremony, which is called *ubusoka*, "the coming out," each village of young men is formally established on its own land. One of its members is appointed as headman, and its relative status in the hierarchy of villages in the chiefdom is demonstrated. At the same time the two senior sons of the retiring chief are recognized as chiefs, and the old chief's country divided between them.

Village headmen are always commoners. Sons of chiefs and sons of village headmen of the previous generation are not eligible, for, the Nyakyusa say, if a son of a headman were chosen each generation he would become a chief. The headmen are the leaders of the people, the *commons*, and a contrast is constantly being made between chiefs (*abanyafyale*), on the one hand, and commoners (*amafumu*) on the other. The village headmen are the *amafumu par excellence*: that is, the "great commoners."

At any one time there are are three age grades: that of the old men who are retired from administration but whose leaders have certain ritual functions to perform; that of the ruling generation which is responsible for defense and administration; and that of the young men and boys who have not yet "come out," but who fight when necessary under the leadership of men of their fathers' generation, though in their own age units.

Within each grade there are a varying number of villages each composed of near contemporaries. The ages of the men in each grade vary, of course, with the date of the last "coming out" ceremony. Just before such a ceremony the old retired men will all be over 65, while the ruling generation includes those between about 35 and 65; just after such a ceremony everyone over 35 is retired, and those from about 10 to 35 are in office. The youngest members of a generation taking office have at first very little share in public life, but individuals may gain power later through inheriting the position of an older brother.

The age grouping is somewhat modified by the system of inheritance, under which a man's heir, who is his next younger full brother or, under certain circumstances, a half-brother, or his senior son, may take over his homestead and his social personality. An heir, though he is much younger than other men of the village, is treated as one of them.

The Nyakyusa pattern of age villages is unique within the known range of human societies, and therefore some of its characteristics are also unique. We shall dwell here only on some of the more general characteristics:

I.

A. The criterion of relative age (mostly place in the generations system of the family) constitutes a criterion of membership which is adhered to, with some minor exceptions.

B. Age groups begin before adolescence and become particularly stressed during sexual maturation and the transition period to marriage and continue throughout life.

II.

A. Age groups are separately established in each village and create new villages of their own. They are unified throughout the country on a generation pattern, with similar principles of organization.

B. Strong solidarity and attachment among age mates constitutes one of the main values of society.

C. There does not exist an overall hierarchy and organization of the age villages as such. They are co-ordinated by the chiefs and the major political institutions of the tribe.

III.

A. The age groups form the main territorial units of the tribe —the villages—and because of this they encompass all the social life of their members. But there does not exist any additional, specific, organization of the *age group* as such.

B. There exists strong ideological emphasis on the antagonism between ages within the family, especially in sexual matters.

D. Peasant Villages: Age Groups Among Irish Peasants[8]

The behavior of the different age groups is of the most intimate everyday kind, and consequently reflects those differentiations of status which are given formal and explicit recognition at marriage. Felt to be too natural a part of daily life to require explanation on the part of the Irish farmers themselves, their behavior, nevertheless, is very easily remarked by the observer. In the ordinary countryman's house, for example, the man of the house and whatever older men may be present occupy chairs drawn up before the hearth. The hob by the fire belongs to the old couple by right. The younger people, the sons and daughters, sit behind them round the room on other chairs or on the window seats of the rectangular kitchen, which is the principal room of the usual small farmer's house. This arrangement shows itself best in the *cuaird* or visit, where the old men of the district drop in on neighbors and "friends" to sit around the hearth together passing the winter evenings in conversation, singing, discussing the news, and telling old tales, legends and folklore. Younger men and women, if they attend the *cuaird*, sit behind, usually leaving the center of the stage to the old men, and the children stand up behind in silent admiration. The younger men have their own pursuits, of course, though at present the divergence may be more marked than formerly. Lately, in Clare at least, they have taken to card playing for stakes of small livestock in the country districts.

When the whole population of a country district is on the move on Sunday, the groupings are especially interesting. There are occasional family groups driving in the jaunty car, but generally the older men walk in a group of their own; the older women in another. The young men walk together by themselves and the young women by themselves. On Sunday afternoons the young men can be seen at the nearest crossroads standing together in groups of ten to thirty, while the older men keep more to their houses or visit one another. Before mass, when the weather permits, the men congregate outside the church and do not move in until all the women have entered and the priest has arrived. As the groups stand outside waiting for the mass to begin and engage in gossip, the older men stand off together and the younger men keep to themselves. In wakes, weddings, christenings, the same age groupings are observed.

There is, of course, no formal prescription of such behavior nor formal taboo against its infringement; the conduct springs rather from the divisions of the family and the solidarity of the individuals occupying similar status as these forces operate in everyday life. It is evident how close a connection exists between age grading and marital status.

If behavior of this type reflects the age grading within the family and the transitions between age grades which are part of the transformation of the family at marriage, the interior arrangement of the house does likewise.

But within a system of values in which the old represent the nexus of kinship and are honored within the community, the young people do not see the issue so clearly. There is as much respect as there is antagonism in their verbal assessment of the older men and women. The young people recognize themselves as forming a distinct group with interests and sentiments of their own, opposed to the elders in the scheme of rural life. They use the word "we" and oppose its use to "them," meaning the old. They recognize places, pursuits and forms of activity as their own and find much more interest in them than in those of the other group. The suggestion that they should take their place in the gatherings of old men is greeted by the young ones with a derision reminiscent of the tone which they reserve for women. But the rivalry in their sentiments between respect and ego-centric feeling, like the controls imposed by their parents to keep them respectfully silent in the presence of their elders, imposes a silence upon them. Consequently, one cannot find among them the voluble expression of attitudes based upon one's belonging to a certain relative age. One must look for it rather in particular expressions of annoyance, boredom and chafing against restraint.

Expressions of sentiment about age are the products of a system of values in which the individual makes the valuation within the place he occupies. They express not only a grouping of individuals of similar age but a mutuality of sentiment. And, too, they form a set of categories in which each person takes his relative place.

Gambling and dancing do not, of course, exhaust the list of the young men's activities. They have other activities, games, sports, contests, and playful roles on solemn occasions, such as acting as strawboys (mummers) at weddings. But all these activities, in which the old members of the community do not directly participate, are alike in that they play no great part in organizing elements in the community other than the young people themselves. They serve other functions.

All these activities bind the young men, the young people, together in common interests. They provide them with a scope of action in which they are comparatively free, but which keeps them divorced from the seats of power over community life, which is denied them. In this sphere they may develop complex norms, valuations and conducts.

But such developments do not serve primarily to knit the community more firmly as a whole. They are associated with the lesser prestige of the young people. Consequently, the old men's house, in contrast, derives a double function. It unites the old men in much the same way as gambling and dancing unites the young men; in fact, even more strongly. But it does so in terms of the old men's common position as recipients of the respect of the community and in terms of their individual positions as integrators of their families. The difference is structural. The activities of young men unite them across family and clique lines even from one community to the next. But those of the old men do more; they unite young and old as well. The integration of the young men is a looser and less inclusive one, even though the numbers ephemerally joined in gambling and dancing may be greater.

The main characteristics of the Irish age groups are the following:

I.

The age criterion is not the sole criterion of formation of age groups and cliques. They are also determined by progression in marital and family status. Therefore the criterion is not very consistent and not always very rigidly adhered to. Membership in the age cliques goes on from adolescence until attainment of headship of the family.

II.

A. The groups are organized into cliques, with varying degrees of cohesion and stability, whose main activities are "social" and recreational.

B. No consensual hierarchy of different age groups: dissensual among various age groups.

III.

A. The age groups are not fully institutionalized and there exist strong elements of antagonism between age groups, especially between youth and the age group of old people, with different emphases on common values and on various patterns of behavior.

B. Membership in an age group is a significant determinant of social status, but not preponderant; full status is achieved only in old age.

In the foregoing pages we have described and analyzed some types of age groups, which seemed to us to be, in broad lines, representative of the age groups found in various primitive and peasant societies. While it is obvious that each type of age group described has many detailed characteristics of its own some of its most important features are similar to those of other age group systems. We shall therefore indicate here briefly in what tribes we find age group systems which are, *in broad outlines*, similar to those we described in the foregoing pages. Throughout the discussion in the following chapters we shall indicate the most significant differences between them .

The type of age group system that exists among the Nuer, is found also, in broad outlines among:

The Bantu Kavirondo, the Gusii, the Topotha, the Latuka and other Nilotic tribes; the Turkana and other tribes of the Karamajong cluster.

The type of age group system that exists among the Nandi, is found also among:

The Suk, the Kipsigis, the Meru, the Murle, the Dorobo, the Kamba, the Kikuyu, the Galla, the Pokomo, the Masai, and some other neighboring tribes.

The main difference here is, however, that not in all of these tribes (especially not among the Masai) is the age group system a cyclical one, but is a lineal one.

The type of age group system that exists among the Yako is to be found also in various Ibo and Ibibio and Ika groups, among some of the Yoruba tribes and in several other African peasant communities.

The type of age group system that exists among the Plains Indians, seems also to be found among some other tribes in South

America, although the information about them is not full enough (see App. to ch. III).

The type of age group system that exists among the Swazi can be found also among the Zulu, in various Tswana groups: it seems to have existed at one time among the Lovedu and to some extent also among the ancient Spartans. Probably they existed also in the ancient Inca and Aztec empires.

The type of age groups that exist among the Nupe, seemingly can also be found among the Bamileke tribes and some of the Berber tribes settled in town in North Africa.

The type of age group system that exists among the Nyakyusa can be found, with an important difference—*the lack of age villages*—among the Tiv.

The type of age groups that exist among the Irish peasants seemingly can be found, with some differences, among various tribes in India, where the institution of youth houses and youth dormitories is very prevalent. (On the two last types see, in greater detail, the discussion of ch. V of this book.)*

E. Modern Societies

In the following pages we shall give brief descriptions of various types of youth groups, organizations and movements existing within various sectors of modern societies. We shall, first, describe, very briefly, some types of more informal youth groups —types that are very well known in the relevant literature. We shall then proceed to describe, in somewhat greater detail, some examples of the more organized youth movements.

Informal Youth Groups in Various Sectors of Modern Societies. The informal or semiformal youth group is very widespread in most sectors of modern societies, and is to be found in all European countries, in the U.S., etc.[9] Despite many local differences some general types can be discerned. Such groups are usually formed within a given neighborhood, or near a school or a place of work. They consist of boys (and sometimes girls), of a given age group. There usually is a difference between preadolescent and adolescent groups. The former may be more heterosexual, while the latter are mostly composed only of mem-

---

* For the literature on these and related societies, see Notes to ch. III.

bers of one sex, although they may engage, as a group, in various activities with a parallel group of the other sex.[10] These groups may develop a strong, although informal, organization of their own, with various "secret rites," with special officers, etc. Such a development is most conspicuous in various fraternities and sororities; but it exists also, even if in an embryonic form, in other groups of such kind.[11] Such youth groups may, in some instances, be affiliated with a certain formal organization—either a school or some youth organization or movement: Scouts, a youth organization of a political party or religious organization, a sports organization, etc. In that case the various small local or neighborhood groups are interwoven into a wider framework. In that case they evince some of the organizational characteristics of the more organized youth movements to be described later. But even in these cases the small youth group has a very strong autonomy and solidarity of its own and does not always fully accept the directives of officials of the central organization. This is especially evident in the strong adherence to its informal leadership as opposed to the "official" leadership set up from above. But the latter do play, nevertheless, an important role in the life of the group—even if not always fully accepted. The extent of organization, and especially the values of these groups vary greatly according to the class and ethnic composition of the group. It is interesting to note that most of such informal groups are usually homogeneous from the point of view of class and ethnic affiliations.[12]

Thus, for instance, in one of the studies dealing with middle-class youth-groups the following were found to be its most important values:

"The principal values of the adolescent peer culture were social participation, group loyalty, and individual achievement and responsibility. As a means of social participation, such social skills as dancing are desirable, as well as a supply of spending money and good clothes. Group loyalty took the form principally of loyalty to the high school and its activities, but church youth groups and the informal cliques of the adolescent social world also commanded loyalty. Individual achievement and responsibility meant, for most young people, doing well in school, getting a part-time job, and being a responsible member of several clubs or other organizations.

"The high school was the principal locus of the adolescent peer culture. School dances, athletic contests, hay rides, and club activities, as well as study halls and classrooms, are the places where boys and girls learn how to behave socially and morally as young men and women.

"Thus the two most powerful groups in the school, the teachers and the leading clique among the adolescents, worked pretty much together in setting standards. Most of the students followed their lead. Only in the sphere of relations between boys and girls was there any considerable conflict between teachers and parents, on the one hand, and adolescents, on the other hand. . . .

"To achieve success in the adolescent peer culture, a boy or girl must stay in school, be a reasonably good student, take part in school activities, and go to the school dances and parties. In the process of adjusting successfully in these ways, he would be learning middle-class morality. The majority of young people attempted to fit themselves into this situation."[13]

While the organizational framework of the group and the values of various upper- and middle-class youth may differ from place to place, and from country to country, yet their main values and orientations seem similar. In some places there may be a greater emphasis on "sports" and "games," and a very strongly organized hierarchical self-government of the boys (like in the English public schools)—while in others there may be a stronger emphasis on various collective values and political, religious and community-oriented activity may be found.

Despite the close relation between the values of the youth group and youth culture and those of the strata to which they belong, there usually exists also a very strong difference in emphasis between the two. Although the extent of the difference may vary greatly from place to place, to some extent it exists everywhere. It is perhaps most pronounced in certain groups of American youth, among whom a distinctive youth culture has developed which has been analyzed in the following way by T. Parsons:[14]

"By contrast with the emphasis on responsibility in the adult role the orientation of the youth culture is more or less specifically irresponsbile. One of its dominant notes is 'having a good time' in relation to which there is a particularly strong emphasis on social activities in company with the opposite sex. A second predominant characteristic on the male side lies in the prominence of athletics, which is an avenue of achievement and competition which stands in sharp contrast to the primary standards of adult achievement in professional and executive capacities. Negatively, there is a strong tendency to repudiate interest in adult things and to feel at least a certain recalcitrance to the pressure of adult expectations and discipline. In addition to, but including, athletic prowess the typical pattern of the male youth culture seems to lay emphasis on the value of certain qualities of attractiveness, especially in relation to the opposite sex. It is very definitely a rounded humanistic pattern rather than one of competence in the performance of specified functions. Such stereotypes as the 'swell guy' are significant of this. On the feminine side there is correspondingly a strong tendency to accentuate sexual attractiveness in terms of various versions of what may be called the 'glamor girl' pattern. Although these patterns defining roles tend to polarize sexually—for instance, as between star athlete and socially popular girl—yet on a certain level they are complementary, both emphasizing certain features of a total personality in terms of the direct expression of certain values rather than of instrumental significance."

While such a strong difference in emphasis may be perhaps found only in very specific groups, the general emphasis on diffuse and solidary relations, on ascribed mutual acceptance of the members, and a concomitant somewhat ambivalent attitude towards the adult world can be found in most such youth groups. In some cases which will yet be analyzed in greater detail, this ambivalent attitude may express itself in an intensification of political activity.

The pattern of youth groups among skilled workers, etc., differs mainly from the former in the following points:

The life span which these groups cover is usually somewhat shorter (as the marrying age is lower), there is a stronger emphasis on the instrumental aspects of school life (e.g., vocational education), a smaller extent of organization in cliques, clubs, etc., a smaller emphasis on athletics and organized sports (although there exists a very strong evaluation of physical prowess and skill), and a relatively weaker attachment to youth organizations and movements, to political organizations, etc.—unless these are specific working youth movements. We do also find among them a greater emphasis on attendance at movies, some drinking parties, etc.—and a relatively high evaluation of various leisure-time activities which render direct expressive satisfaction.

The picture of youth groups within lower sectors of society, which tend, especially in the U.S., to coincide with specific ethnic groups, is somewhat different.[16] The main differences may perhaps be summarized, very generally, in the following way. Lower-class boys and girls, especially among children of un-skilled workers, spend a much greater part of their time outside of the home than do middle-class adolescents. The activities of the group encompass many more aspects and spheres of life, and home is more of a hotel-and-eating-place. These groups are usually affiliated to a lesser degree with either adult-sponsored organizations (Boy Scouts, clubs, etc.) or established institutional fields of activities (such as the school, etc.); and are much more separated from the sphere of official organization. On the other hand, paradoxically enough, the tension between adults and children of the lower classes is smaller—or at least of a different kind —than that evinced in the middle-class youth groups and youth culture. While there exist many concrete tensions between parents and children, even giving rise to running away from home, etc., these tensions do not necessarily involve an ambivalent attitude towards the whole cultural world of the parents as adults, and does not necessarily define the life of youth and adolescents as entirely different from those of the adults. In many ways the pattern of behavior prevalent in these groups—emphasis on drinking, some gambling, various types of unorganized recreation, unplanned spending of money, earlier sexual experience and sometimes perhaps some extent of promiscuity, great extent of aggressiveness, etc.—is to some extent a continuation of the pattern of adult life within these sectors; or at least there is a stronger emphasis on some of the patterns of behavior accepted in the adult group, and not a distinctive opposition to it.

Another very important and prevalent type of youth group, in America and in many other countries, is the group of juvenile delinquents, the "gang."[17] Since it has been described so often there is no need to give any details here, and some general characteristics will suffice at this point. The "gang" may originate either within the framework of ambivalent "youth cultures," or within some of the lower-class groups. Its main characteristics are the following:

The activities of its members are usually directed towards the open violation of the mores and norms of the society in which they live—stealing, pilfering, various types of aggressive behavior, whether group or individual—acts which may be directed towards adults as persons or towards social and cultural norms and symbols. We may distinguish several types of such groups, especially from the point of view of their relations with the adult world:[18]

(a) Those groups which are more or less connected with deviant adult organized groups—crime syndicates, etc.—and who are highly organized, possess a strong internal status symbol hierarchy and status differentiation patterned after that of the adult criminal sector.

(b) Those who are more in touch with the law-abiding adult world, and live, as it were, in a state of constant tension and dual norms. Within these groups membership fluctuates considerably between the delinquent and nondelinquent spheres, and the degrees of internal organization and structure.

(c) Those groups of delinquents who are out of touch with any section of the adult world and outside adult control, and which, consequently, evince the maximum degree of internal aggression and other deviant traits.

A sociologically important characteristic of these groups is that their deviancy is oriented more towards the normative means of the societies than to their ends, which they seek to attain by uninstitutional means. This tendency is usually coupled with a strong ideological emphasis on the distinct characteristics of the youth and the "strong man" which differentiate him from the established, conforming values of the adult world. It seems that in this ideological emphasis these groups are in some respects more akin to the middle-class "youth culture" than to some parts of the working- or lower-class youth group. The same may be said, in broad lines, of their internal structure; these groups—as do the middle-class "youth culture" groups—usually evolve a status system of their own, which allocates prestige according to their own specific goals and value emphasis.

The foregoing discussion of the various informal and semi-formal youth groups and youth culture has been very brief and cursory, as the facts are rather well known. Throughout our discussion in the following chapters we shall analyze many additional details, but at the present stage the description given above will suffice.

Israel's Voluntary Youth Movements.[19] A large part of the adolescent population in Israel participates in special youth organizations and youth movements. These groups begin to recruit children at a relatively early age—nine to ten years—but their activities reach their peak in the adolescent period. It has been estimated that about 30 per cent of the adolescents in the country are organized into these movements; but the number of those who have passed through them is much greater, and they touch, in one way or another, upon the social life of almost every boy and girl. Three main types may be discerned: (a) The pioneering type, which emphasizes Zionist and social ideals and whose manifest aim is to make its members into members of agricultural communal and co-operative settlements; (b) the "working youth" movement, whose main aim is the educational and occupational advancement of its members; and (c) a chiefly recreational type with strong emphasis on sport and leisure-time activities. There are, altogether, about nine to ten movements. Enrollment in them is voluntary, being effected through canvassing, informal social influences (whole groups of friends joining the same movement, etc.), membership shifting with a strong persistent nucleus.

The most distinctive type of all is the "pioneering" type, which is historically connected with Zionist youth movements in the Diaspora.

All of the pioneering movements have central organizations,

affiliated either with political parties or in a more general way with the General Federation of Labor. The central staff, which is composed of young adults, comprises members of agricultural settlements who either volunteer for or are assigned this duty, and a more urban nucleus. Both groups are paid some salary or emolument. Sometimes the chief instructors live in a "commune" in town as a sort of preparation for settlement work, and at the same time perform their duties as instructors (*madrichim*). This, however, holds true mainly of the central and older instructors, while instructors of young groups are themselves usually members of older groups and are still in school.

The members of the movement are organized into small, local groups composed of 20-30 members, several of these groups into a "regiment," and these finally into a "stratum," according to age groups. Each small group has its own organization—an instructor, secretary, treasurer, etc.—and the same applies at the higher level, though with a much greater degree of formal organization.

The final age group of organization is the *garin hachshara* (training nucleus), the small group (usually composed of school-age adolescents) which actively prepares itself for life in the settlement. The membership of these groups is, however, very small in proportion to the total membership of any of the movements, as only a few members are actually prepared to go out and be "pioneers," a great majority of them dropping out on the way.

The main activities of the members are: (1) social and sport (excursions); (2) cultural; and (3) inculcation of the pioneering and social ideology of their specific movement. They also perform some more general functions, such as fund-collecting for the National Funds, etc., and, in the days of the Mandate, para-military and political functions such as helping the *Haganah* (Defense Army), etc. While most of their time is actually spent in social and cultural activities, dancing, etc., they emphasize strongly their negative attitude towards mere "recreation," and particularly that of the "salon" type. Thus they put greater emphasis on folk dances, unsophisticated relations between the sexes, etc., and have a definite ascetic aversion to smoking, gambling, fancy dress, etc. (Khaki shorts are a typical part of their dress.) Their entire ideology emphasizes that they, as youth, have more opportunities—and the consequent duty—to realize the basic pioneering values, etc., than the adults, who have already been contaminated by their worldly pursuits (all these emphases differ, of course, among the various movements). Within the more recreational types of youth movements and within the "border type," the Scouts, the development of individual character, of manly and civic virtues, is particularly emphasized. Within the more pioneering types these values are inseparably interwoven with more social goals: serving the country, realizing the distinctive common goals of the Zionist movement and its various parts (especially pioneering values), and the belief that youth is more apt to realize these values than adults. Because of this they are not usually over-enthusiastic about direct leadership by adults. Even when thoroughly loyal to the political cause of a given party, they regard the adult leadership distantly, without attempting effective, primary communication towards the rank and file of the youth. They are led mainly by slightly older coevals of their organization. The success of a given group, stratum, etc., is to a very large extent dependent on the existence of a gifted leader-instructor who can directly and personally appeal to the youth. Official status is not enough; "personality" is what counts most, with a strong leaning towards a charismatic type. Such a leader should "practice what he preaches," and it should be known that he intends to go out pioneering. Otherwise half his attraction is lost, whatever his official status within the overall organization.

This fact constitutes one of the main difficulties and permanent critical points of the movements. As the members advance in age, more and more feel disinclined to become pioneers, while at the same time they still perform various tasks in the movement and are socially strongly attached thereto. There are never enough pioneer-instructors to lead in pioneering, and after the peak of activity in middle adolescence the enthusiasm for the instructor fades a bit, as they approach maturity and enter upon the threshold of adult life and occupational achievement.

While membership in youth movements usually ceases in the

first stages of adulthood—except for a small band of officials, etc.
—the comradeship established in them is of longer standing, continuing into adult life and sometimes forming the basis for adult cliques in various spheres of life.

Within the organization there is strong emphasis on common rituals, and particularly on those of passage from one stratum to another, from one age grade to another. But the strongest cohesion is usually that of the smaller group or at the most of the entire "regiment," the country-wide groups meeting only on special occasions, excursions, festivities, etc.

The Free German Youth Movement. Among the various types of age and youth groups of modern society, the German youth movements have occupied a prominent and special place, serving in a way as a prototype of rebellious youth, of a specifically juvenile social movement. It is difficult to give a clear, brief picture of these movements, because they varied in detail and changed greatly in the course of their development. We shall, then, give here a mere outline of some of the most important features of the movements in a very cursory way. In further chapters we shall extend and elaborate this description.

The first German youth movement, which later developed into the *Wandervogel*, began at the end of the 19th century in one of the new industrial centers of Prussia-Steglitz. It started as a camp of school youths, led by a young leader, who sought to free themselves from the "suffocating" atmosphere of the bureaucratic formal school structure and of the home. At first its activities were concentrated mainly on going on excursions in the country, behaving generally in a way contrary to the prevailing mores of bourgeois life, such as going on these excursons on Sunday mornings, wearing light, sports clothes, spending the whole day in the country among "haystacks," singing folk songs, and generally disengaging themselves from the atmosphere of home and school life. Soon many such groups were formed in different parts of Prussia and Germany, showing that there existed some general tension and some preconditions for their emergence. At first their numbers were not large, and a contact based to a very large extent on the personality of their leader and his driving force was established between the various groups. At first the movement did not have any aims which could specifically define the scope of its activities. There were no definite activities, but all the activities of the members were directed towards the achievement of a new way of life, the development of a new type of person who could shake off all the trimmings of contemporary society, emphasizing only the inner nature of man, his innermost self. Although these attitudes were mainly individualistic, preparing, as it were, an individualistic escape within a small circle of friends, they slowly acquired a more community-oriented, nationalistic meaning and emphasis. The escape to nature, the emphasis on asceticism (abstention from drinking, smoking, etc.), the "roaming about" (hence the famous name of "Roamers," the "Wandervogel") slowly acquired a folkist, nationalistic meaning and became a yearning for the establishment of a true national community (*Gemeinschaft*), in place of the artificial one existing at that time. The entire ideology —or ideologies—of the movement were greatly influenced by the romantic movement, and the similarities between the two are obvious. The whole attitude of the movement towards the established social order was very ambivalent: On the one hand, an attempt to separate its members from society and a negative attitude towards its values and norms; on the other, an attempt to recreate society and a utopian emphasis on common values and spirit. "It (the youth movement) was purely secular but was colored by religious or mystic enthusiasm. . . . It sought to create true and free individuals but at the same time was agitated by a longing for a new and true country, a *Gemeinschaft*, which should be both a symbol of the rebirth of the nation and the only place where such freedom could be made universal. It fought against all established authority but it longed for a new authority, for a real *Fuehrer* instead of established bureaucratic leadership." The revolt against authority—parents, teachers, officials—gradually gave rise to an ideology in which youth was set apart as a separate distinct type of human being, the only type within which this full realization of humanity can be achieved. Through various stages it developed into an ideology of "youth culture" ("*Jugendkultur*"), as a distinct type of social and cultural life. The first full declaration of youth's distinctiveness and its right to shape its own destiny was made at the Hohe Meissner rally in 1913, where it was declared that: "Free German Youth, on their own initiative, under their own responsibility, and with deep sincerity, are determined independently to shape their own lives. For the sake of this inner freedom they will under any and all circumstances take united action."

Despite some common basic characteristics, the German youth movement never acquired nationwide comprehensive unity of organization. Developing slowly from small bands of "roamers" into a wider movement, it was riven by various schisms and quarrels which undermined its unity. These rifts were caused mainly by dissension from the charismatic qualities of its first leadership, the rise of new leaders, and constant quarrels among them. Numerous attempts to unify the different parts of the movement were never totally successful and internal dissension continued throughout the history of the movement. Behind these quarrels were hidden, however, some crucial issues which faced the movement. The first was involved in the movement's attitude towards its contemporary social order. The early sectarianism involved a complete separation from society—a separation which became more difficult with the advancing age of the members. At the same time the religious zeal of the movement necessarily involved a "missionary" trend—a wish to instil the spirit of the movement into all spheres of life; into the fields of politics, social movements and education. This dilemma between withdrawal and alienation aiming at the domination and transformation of social life became particularly acute with the passage of time, as many institutions sponsored by the youth movements—youth hostels, etc.—were adopted by various youth welfare organizations, schools, etc. From the political point of view the problem became more acute after World War I and the Revolution. The second main issue which faced the movement was caused by the growing up of members and by the relative bureaucratization of the movement, which necessarily meant a loss of the primary élan and charismatic identification with a leader and within the group.

Dissension within the movement developed to an even larger extent after World War I, as political activity and interest in politics increased, and political parties began to encroach more and more on the sphere of youth movements. The internal tension and ambivalence of the youth movements' ideology and attitudes was not resolved, becoming accentuated by postwar disillusionment, until the movements were abolished, and, in a way, absorbed by the Nazi youth movement.

The Kibbutz. We shall now describe the patterns of group-life existing among the children in a Kibbutz. As we have already indicated above, they live most of their life apart from the adults. They sleep and eat and study in houses of their own. Their life is organized in definite groups which are usually constituted on the basis of *age differences* instead of "ages," because the absolute age level may not be fixed and varies according to circumstances to the number of children of a given age now living in a Kibbutz, etc. The relative difference of ages (younger—older) is, however, almost always maintained. Each group leads its own life in school and at home and has its own autonomous arrangements and institutions. Usually it has its own living rooms, dining room and services, its own instructors and sometimes even teachers. (In one Kibbutz, for instance, the distribution of age groups has been as follows: five groups, corresponding to the school grades, each comprising children with two years' difference in age, from six-and-one-half up to sixteen-and-one-half.) The basic principles and framework of the children's work, studies and life are set up by the General Assembly on the recommendation of the educational committee, to be implemented by the teachers, instructors, etc. The working out of these principles and their application to daily routine and problems are left to them and to the "autonomous" institutions of the age group. The life of the age group as an entity is centered around three poles: (a) School—education, comprising most of the usual subjects with strong emphasis on agricultural and technical education and on the ideological basis of the pioneering Zionist movement. Here they are taught by teachers who quite often divide their time between different age groups, according to their special professional qualifications. In the younger age groups, however, it is usually so arranged that one *main* teacher is assigned to a class, with only a small degree of outside help for some special subjects. (b) Work—usually every group (or two groups together) has some small plot of land allotted to it for cultivation, and the elder groups also usually participate, to different degrees, in the work of the various economic branches of the settlement. In these matters every age group has its own committee, which arranges the division of labor, the allotment of different tasks to different children, etc. This committee is usually guided by the group's own instructor (*madrich*), who also acts as an intermediary with the heads of the different economic branches of the settlement. On its own plot of land the group is usually advised by its instructor and by the various experts or teachers of different agricultural subjects. (c) The social and cultural life of the group—the most important of them are: library and newspaper distribution, editing of own newspaper, arrangement of games and festivals (it is very important and interesting to note that on almost all festive occasions—Sabbath, the various holidays, etc.—the children do not participate in the general festival but arrange special festivals for themselves, in which the adults participate at most as spectators, the only notable exception being the Passover "Seder," the culminating feast of the year, in which children and adults participate together), various discussions, disposition of their communal property and various scouting activities. (These usually form part of the youth movement to which all the children officially belong.) All these activities are organized by the children themselves, guided and advised by their instructors (sometimes children of older age groups). Almost every activity is organized and supervised by an elected committee of the children, and the number of committees is usually large so as to enable the greatest number of children to participate. (In some Kibbutzim the number of committee members among the children comprises more than half of the total number of children.) Parallel to life in the adult section, the supreme authority here is the assembly of all of the children. Assembly meetings are very frequent. Almost all members take part in all of the activities carried on by the age group. The whole group is quite often summoned by the instructors to discuss various problems arising out of their common life. This is utilized as a very important educational means, especially for the inculcating of the various ideological foundations and practical norms of Kibbutz life. The main pedagogical means is the open explanation and discussion, skillfully guided by the instructor or teacher. In this way the acceptance of various behavioral norms is based on active group participation, and carries with it the whole weight of group approval. It is thus quite natural that one of the most important occasions for a meeting of the whole group and a full discussion is the unruly and undisciplined behavior of one of its members, a quarrel with a teacher or an instructor. Such quarrels may give rise to various tensions, especially as the children are wont to complain of unjustified disciplinary measures, scolding or harsh words from the teachers, etc. If such a matter cannot be settled by one of the older children, more influential committee members, etc., or the instructor, then a general meeting of the whole group is called and both parties lay their case before it and a full-fledged discussion arises. This discussion, however, is guided by the teacher or instructor so as to lead at least to the full explanation of the behavior of both parties and to the resumption of the approved group behavior. Quite often the adult member involved in the case may be censured for deviating from the proper and ascribed modes of behavior. Whatever the exact outcome of such a discussion may be, it is always intended to serve as an occasion for catharsis on the one hand, and as a guide to the inculcation of group norms on the other.

A very important feature of the children's life is the transition from one age group to another. It does not, however, involve a change of personnel, as it is the whole group that changes its status. The identity of the group is usually preserved throughout the children's life span (as children).

Almost every group has its own name (usually a name of an animal, plant or tree; sometimes a name designating an activity, such as fishing, singing, etc.). This name does *not* change while the group passes from one grade to another, and so the group's preservation of its identity receives a definite symbolic expression. The exact age grades may differ from Kibbutz to Kibbutz, but the main outlines exist in almost all Kibbutzim; they comprise about four or five age grades, varying according to school-age, scouting performance, relative age, etc. The transition of a group from one grade to another is quite often a festive occasion, organized in a rather ceremonial fashion, in which all other age groups and the adults participate as onlookers. The transition from one age group to another, which is in many places linked together with transition from one school grade to another—although usually almost automatic—is dependent on various performances and achievements of the group, either in the school, in work or in scouting activities. Almost all the activities of the group during the preceding months are directed towards the successful performance of these activities. Thus the transition ceremony comes as a culminating point of a long period of rather hectic activity. The most important of the ceremonies is the graduating ceremony, when the children acquire the status of pre-adults (candidates for full membership in the Kibbutz), or immediately to full adult status. (There exists no fixed and ascribed norm in all the settlements in regard to this matter. Some insist on a transitory period of "candidacy," while others do not.) The degree and intensity of ceremony on these occasions varies in different Kibbutzim. Some of them have different graduation ceremonies and ceremonies for acceptance as full members, and some do not. In other words, in some places the young men and women are accepted as a *group* of new members, while in others this acceptance bears a more individual character. The element of ceremony and festivity exists, however, in almost all settlements.

There is one more aspect of the age group that should be emphasized, and that is that boys and girls participate equally in the same groups. There are no separate groups for the sexes. They also live in the same buildings, although usually in separate rooms. This characteristic also stems from the ideological bases of the pioneering movement, but its full understanding can be achieved only through the analysis of its place in the social structure.

The Komsomol. The Komsomol is the overall official children's and youth organization of the U.S.S.R., organized by the Government and the Communist Party.

The process of official, semi-political training starts in the kindergarten, where play, singing and story-telling are used for the inculcation of patriotic feeling. The child is first enrolled in the "Little Octobrists," where his education in civic responsibilities begins. At the age of nine he becomes eligible for membership in the "Young Pioneers," where his political education begins to assume more significant proportions. Membership in the Young Pioneers is virtually universal in the eligible age group (nine to fifteen). The drive to affiliate is so great in the early, impressionable years that the threat of exclusion is frequently a sufficient sanction to discipline the most unruly. Entrance into the Pioneers is the occasion for an impressive initiation ceremony replete with symbolism.

Once enrolled in the Pioneers, the new member becomes part of a "link" of eight to twelve youngsters who elect their own leader. The "links" are united in a "brigade" with approximately forty members in the same or adjoining classes. Each brigade chooses its "council" of five to represent it and functions under a Komsomol leader who is designated to supervise and direct brigade activities. These activities vary with the age level of the Pioneers. In the younger classes, political indoctrination at meetings largely takes the form of tales of the childhood of Lenin or Stalin or stories of heroism on the part of young Pioneers in the war against the Nazis. With older children, political instruction becomes more pointed.

Political instruction in the narrow sense, however, is only one part of the Pioneer program. There are also a variety of organized activities such as excursions for nature study, to museums and points of historical interest, athletic competitions, literary, dramatic and musical evenings, and opportunities to pursue hobbies at school or at the so-called Houses of Pioneers, which are set aside as centers of Pioneer extra-curricular programs. There is the requirement to engage in socially useful work, which may embrace such diverse activities as helping to edit a wall newspaper for Pioneers, gathering scrap, working in the school garden or on a neighboring Kolkhoz, or even helping combat "religious prejudices" in the home. The tendency of these extra-curricular activities to compete with and even interfere with school programs has led to periodic protests by Soviet school authorities against overburdening the child with outside activities. The present tendency is to integrate Pioneer activities as closely as possible with the school, to emphasize classroom obligations as the first responsibility of the Pioneer, and to arrange the Pioneer program so that it supports, rather than comes into conflict with, the school curriculum.

At the age of fourteen the child becomes eligible for membership in the Komsomols, provided, of course, that he can fulfil the conditions for admission. These conditions include recommendation by one member of the Communist Party or two Komsomols who have themselves been members of the organization for at least one year. Recommendation by the council of a Pioneer brigade counts as the equivalent of one recommendation by a Komsomol member.

Enrollment in the Komsomols is thus a much more selective process than membership in the Pioneers. Whereas the Pioneers operate as a virtually universal organization for all children in the eligible age group, not more than half of the students in the upper three classes of the ten-year school ordinarily join the Komsomols, and only about a quarter of those in the eligible age group (fourteen to twenty-six) become Komsomol members. The Komsomol is the reservoir from which Party members will be recruited; and in the eyes of the Party leadership at least, this is the period of tutelage when qualifications and political ardor can be tested.

The organization of the Komsomols is closely modeled on the hierarchical pattern of the big brother, the Party. At the bottom of the pyramid are the primary organizations in factories, collective farms, state farms, educational and other state institutions. Each primary organization must have at least three members and is established with the consent of the district or town committee which supervises it. Where the primary organization consists of more than a hundred members, it may be broken down into subgroups in shops of a factory, different faculties of a university, etc. Where the group has less than ten members, a secretary is selected to provide leadership. In larger groups a committee or bureau as well as a secretary serves as the directing nucleus. Both perform their Komsomol duties in addition to their regular employment. Full-time Komsomol secretaries are ordinarily assigned by the central apparatus only to important enterprises or institutions where there is a substantial membership and a program of work requiring the exclusive attention of a Komsomol functionary. In most cases the primary Komsomol organizations operate under the control of the district or town Komsomol committees and their secretaries; but in the armed forces and in institutions where special political sections have been established, the line of responsibility leads directly to the head of the political section, or his assistant in charge of Komsomol activity.

At the district or town level, supervisory power is concentrated in a committee which in turn elects a bureau and a number of secretaries. The next higher levels in the Komsomol hierarchy are the regional and republic organizations. Here the basic pattern of organization is essentially the same as below. At this level secretaries are required to be Party members with at least three years' experience in the Komsomol. Operating under them are substantial staffs of full-time Komsomol functionaries with specific responsibilities running the gamut of the organization's activities.

The central administrative organization of the Komsomol consisted in 1949 of a Central Committee of 103 members and 47 candidates, a control commission of 31 members, a bureau of 11 members, five secretaries, and a large secretariat, all of whom operate under the general direction of the First Secretary. Theoretically, the highest organ in the Komsomol is the All-Union Congress, which, according to the Rules, is required to meet at least once every three years. Until the Tenth Congress in 1936, meetings were held with reasonable regularity.

While the responsibilities of the Komsomol organization embrace a wide range of diversified activities, the emphasis, in contrast to the Pioneers, is much more heavily on politics. These activities include:

(1) Political instruction of Komsomol members;

(2) Political instruction and leadership supplied by the Komsomols to the Pioneers, to non-affiliated youth, and to other groups;

(3) Military and para-military training and physical culture and sports;

(4) Leadership and assistance in carrying out governmental and Party programs;

(5) Social and cultural activity.

The political indoctrination of all Komsomol members is a central concern of the Party. As has already been observed, it begins seriously with the Pioneers and increases in scope and intensity as children grow older.

The various age groups existing in modern societies have some basic characteristics in common:

I.

Age is here a criterion of group membership, although it is not very strictly defined or adhered to. Youth groups extend usually through adolescence and very early adulthood only and membership in them is not universal, nor equally distributed in all sectors of the society.

II.

Within all modern youth groups, the small primary groups forms the basic nucleus of the organization—a nucleus which may or may not be incorporated in wider formal organizations.

III.

All modern youth groups perform mostly preparatory tasks and concentrate on recreational and cultural activities of their members. They regulate only the internal relations of their members and their behavior, but not their overall behavior nor that of other members of the society.

In addition to these common characteristics, each of the types presented evinces some characteristics of its own. The most important of these are:

The Informal and Semi-Formal Youth Groups and Youth Culture:

1. Small extent of institutionalization, although most of their ac-

tivities are legitimate. (This does not, of course, hold true with reference to the juvenile delinquents group.)

2. No unified organization, although similar development in many parts of the country. A formal, unified hierarchy may exist in the case of youth organizations and movements. Groups based mostly on membership usually homogeneous from the point of view of class and ethnic group affiliation.

3. Corporate organization into small groups and cliques with various organization and informal status systems of their own. Differing extents of cohesion and stability.

4. Large extent of autonomy, tempered by some very general adult supervision.

5. Most activities centered on recreation, heterosexual relations (in the later stages of adolescence) and general emulation of certain aspects of adult culture.

6. Ambivalent attitude towards adult culture, strong emphasis on overall, diffuse humane characteristics in opposition to more specific achievements, and on physical prowess, early maturity. Despite this there exists, in most cases, ultimate acceptance of adult values (with the exception, of course, of the gangs, etc.).

The German Youth Movement.

1. Lack of institutionalization and a strong element of deviancy, rebellion against established social order.

2. Corporate groups, but without unitary organization; parallel developments in different parts of the country.

3. Close relations between various groups, but no full unification; continual rifts and schisms.

4. Organization into close, sectarian groups with high degree of internal solidarity and identification, strong identification with a charismatic leader. Complete autonomy; group led by the leader, with a strong element of homosexual identification.

5. Manifold activities—mainly recreation, cultural and educational.

6. Completely negative attitude towards existing patterns of authority, and a specific romantic youth ideology which sets youth up as a different—and the only complete—free human being.

7. Despite these attitudes, a strong yearning towards an authori-

tative charismatic leadership, national folk community and strong community orientation.

8. Movement originated among adolescents but slowly developed into a more adult group, thus facing its perpetual crisis because of its adherence to and emphasis on "youth ideology."

In comparison with these characteristics, we find among the *Israeli Youth Movements*:

1. Institutionalization and legitimacy.

2. Country-wide organization, but with smaller groups constituting the main foci of social life and solidarity.

3. Organizational hierarchy and collective passage of group from one grade to another.

4. General principles and programs of activities drawn up by the (mostly adult) leaders of the various movements, which are affiliated with political parties, social movements, etc. Despite this, great extent of social autonomy of the smaller groups.

5. Relation between adult leaders and rank and file constitutes one of the main points of tension in the movements.

6. Values of the movements do not constitute a negation of those of adult society, but rather an emphasis of them.

7. The movements develop a general ideology of youth as the potentially better realizers of the basic values of the society.

The Komsomols and the Kibbutz youth groups show these different characteristics:

1. Overall, unified, country- (or community-) wide organization.

2. Organizational hierarchy and collective passage of groups from one grade to another, directed by the adult society, with different degrees of internal social autonomy (greater in the Kibbutz).

3. Identity of values with those of the adult society, age group life constituting mainly preparation for full membership in adult society.

4. Particularly strong emphasis on the collective, common values of the society.

The foregoing descriptions have given an overall picture of the main types of age groups and of some of their basic differences. While all of them have some basic common characteristics —the age criterion, the basic nucleus of a primary group, some general attitudes to the social structure in which they are formed, etc.—yet there are many outstanding differences between them. We have seen that they differ in the extent of the explicitness of the age criterion, in the extent to which they are universal in any given society, in the age spans they cover. They differ in their internal structure, in the extent of existence of a unitary hierarchy of age groups, of corporate organizations; in their relations to other age groups and generations and in the extent of their autonomy and autocephaly. They differ in the type of tasks which are allocated to them, in the extent to which they regulate the behavior of their own members and of other members of the society and in the extent to which they are conformists to the main values of society, or deviate from them.

In the following chapters we shall have to explain and analyze in greater detail both the common characteristics of age groups and their main differences, as well as the social conditions which account for them. We shall have to see to what extent this analysis can be done within the framework of our basic hypothesis.

CHAPTER III

Age Groups in Nonkinship (Universalistic) Societies

A. In this chapter we shall try to validate the first part
I   of our hypothesis: namely, that age groups tend to arise
in those societies whose main integrative principles are
different from the particularistic principles governing family and
kinship relations, i.e., in societies whose integrative principles are
mainly "universalistic." We shall first explain in somewhat greater
detail the exact meaning of nonkinship, universalistic criteria
for the *allocation of roles* within the main institutional spheres
of the social system. Secondly, we shall present our material, or
rather those parts and aspects of it which have a more or less
direct bearing on the part of our hypothesis. The material presented will include both comparisons between kinship and nonkinship societies and internal comparisons within the framework
of nonkinship, universalistic societies. With regard to the first,
we shall attempt to give more or less detailed comparisons between societies not too dissimilar in their general cultural milieu
and social characteristics, so as to minimize as far as possible the
introduction of factors unaccounted for;[1] then we shall give comparisons of a wider range. As to the second type of comparison, its purpose will be both to elaborate our hypothesis and
to account for at least some of the structural variations in the
composition of age groups. In both cases we shall concentrate on
the analysis of those societies which have been more or less fully
and adequately described, and shall allude only briefly to other
societies about which no such adequate descriptions exist.

Thirdly, we shall describe the composition, activities, authority structure, etc., of age groups arising under these conditions, and, in very broad lines, their place both in the individual's life and within the social structure. We shall attempt to show that their nature and organization are very closely related to the needs postulated in our basic hypothesis. Throughout this description the fact, already seen and stressed in the previous chapter, namely, that there exists a great variety of such groups, with many differences in their composition and structure, will be emphasized once more; although some basic common characteristics will be easily discernible. In this chapter we shall analyze and explain only a few of these differences. A full explanation or analysis of the conditions under which different types of age groups arise will be possible only when some other criteria, in addition to those of particularism-universalism, are taken into account. These additional variables will be analyzed in subsequent chapters. Thus the material presented in this chapter does not constitute a full "functional" analysis of age groups, but purports only to validate the first part of the basic hypothesis; and to analyze, partly on the basis of the descriptions given in the previous chapter, the general characteristics of age groups, the variations of which will be analyzed only subsequently.

B. What is the exact meaning of nonkinship, universalistic principles of allocation of roles within the most important institutional spheres of the social system? The following are proposed as the most important institutional derivatives of these criteria:

A. The existence within the social system of many roles the incumbents of which act towards other persons without regard to the familial, kinship, lineage, ethnic, or hierarchical properties of those individuals in relation to their own. In these roles incumbents act in accordance with general rules of expectations referring to the other individuals, and without regard to them as incumbents of various classificatory or group-membership properties.

B. Membership in the total society (i.e., citizenship) is not defined in terms of belonging to any particularistic subgroup, nor is it mediated by such submembership. Membership in the total society entails the performance of some roles which are not incorporated in any such group and whose incumbents act towards one another in accordance with general roles of expectations.

(1) Within the political field this means that the family, descent group or any other particularistic group (e.g., caste) is not the basic autonomous group to which political tasks are allocated, and that such tasks are allocated to members and groups which are not based on kinship and other particularistic criteria.

(2) Within the field of values and ritual this means that the family and kin groups (or other particularistic groups) are not the exclusive bearers of the ultimate values of the society: i.e., the symbolic expressions of these values are not incorporated solely or mainly within these groups, but can be attained in role clusters outside the realm of these groups.

(3) The economic division of labor is not based on the family or kin unit as an almost completely autonomous and self-sufficient unit and/or the main unit of economic specialization.

(4) From the point of view of status criteria, a nonkinship and nonparticularistic, universalistic allocation of roles entails either (a) that status differentiation and stratification within a society depend on occupational roles, political power, wealth and personal properties, and not on kinship connections, ethnic ties or personal relations; or (b) an individualistic achievement orientation, i.e., one in which deference is given for individual achievement and not in recognition of family or personal or ethnic connections or achievements of the group (as, for instance, the famous potlach of the North American Indians).

(5) As far as territorial and ecological settlements are concerned, such a division of labor means that the rights of residence in any territory are not vested in any kinship, ethnic, etc., groups, but are to a large extent open to all members of the society who can qualify according to some universalistic criteria (e.g., payment of a given amount of rent, etc.).

It should, of course, be emphasized that no society can be entirely and wholly universalistic. Even in those societies to which the foregoing criteria most clearly apply there are many subgroups and sectors in which particularistic criteria and relations prevail. Family and neighborhood relations, friendships and various primary groups, sometimes even certain parts of the economic structure, and always some parts of the system of stratification, are necessarily governed by particularistic criteria. We have already seen in the preceding chapters of this book that different sectors of any society are usually organized according to different criteria. Here we have been interested only in the principles of overall integration of societies and in the criteria which organize the membership in a total society, and the overall interrelations between the various subsectors of the society, which in themselves may yet be particularistic. The various institutional derivatives are here related only to the basic difference between universalistic and particularistic criteria. Some of the other pattern variables (especially ascription-achievement) are mentioned, but only in so far as they are related to universalism, etc., and not as fully independent variables.

We have not differentiated here between kinship groups and other particularistic groups and relations because the differentiation is immaterial for this part of our hypothesis. It will become important when we discuss the integration of societies on the basis of particularistic nonkinship criteria and their relation to our problem. It is our contention that every such integration involves the definition of the family or kin group as at least one of the basic units of role allocation and division of labor, although it may entail a transition from the family group and other particularistic groups and a consequent break or tension.[2] Therefore, as far as the emergence of age groups under conditions of nonkinship integration of the social system is concerned, this distinction is not as yet important.

These various criteria of universalistic role allocation, although clearly interrelated, do not always have to co-exist, and it may well happen that the strength of universalistic criteria will be greater in one institutional sphere than in another. As we shall see, this may influence the structure of age groups in various ways.

The above-enumerated derivations of the universalistic, nonkinship allocation of roles are necessarily rather general. They may, however, serve as a starting point for our comparative analysis, and their details may become clearer through that analysis.

II   In the following comparative analysis we shall present the material in order of complexity, beginning with the "simpler," less differentiated social systems and gradually advancing to the more complex ones. We shall begin, therefore, with the so-called segmentary tribes, i.e., those which have no central authority, administrative organs of government or constituted judicial institutions. The best material on age groups in these tribes is available from Africa, and was exemplified in the second chapter of this book by the Nuer and the Nandi, and also to some extent by the Plains Indian age groups. Information on age groups among the African segmentary tribes concerns some of the Nilo-Hamitic group (Nuer, Topotha, Turkana, Bari, Lango, Shilluk);[3] the Karmajong cluster of that group (Turkana, Jie, Topota);[4] the Nandi-speaking group (Nandi, Pokot [Suk] Kipsigis);[5] the Masai;[6] the Meru, Kamba, Kikuyu group;[7] the Galla;[8] the Murle;[9] the Chagga;[10] the Bantu Kavirondo;[11] the Gusii;[12] the Dorobo, the Pokomo, Nyika and Teita;[13] and tribes of the Nuba group.[14]

The first step in such a comparison should be the derivation, from our basic institutional criteria, of concrete indices applying to segmentary tribes. Within these tribes (as also among most primitive tribes that will be discussed here) the family or kinship and descent unit usually constitutes the main type of particularistic group, and is always one of the most important social groups in the society. Therefore all indices relating to particularistic-universalistic criteria of role allocation will be couched in terms of family and kinship groups. This should not, however, be taken to mean that in principle these are the only types of particularistic groups. Whenever another type of particularistic group appears in these societies, the fact will be especially noted.

The main criteria of comparison are the following:

(a) The extent to which lineages and clans organized in corporate units are the main bearers of the political tasks of the society and the main channels of political activities of the people;

(b) The extent to which the clans, subclans or lineages are territorial units;

(c) The extent to which there exists fixed institutional machinery for the adjustment of interclan (etc.) quarrels and the extent to which these roles are incorporated within the kin units;

(d) The extent to which the most important ritual, political and prestige-bearing offices and positions are vested in members of lineages and kin units by virtue of their roles in these units;

(e) The extent to which social relations not confined to the corporate groups are, within the limits of the tribe, regulated by distinct kinship criteria.

On the basis of these criteria we may differentiate between two types of segmentary tribes. The first type consists of those tribes in which the various family and lineage groups are more or less self-sufficient and self-supporting in their social life, and in which there exists only minimal interaction between the various family groups. The second type consists of those tribes in which the extent of such interaction is great.

Within segmentary societies it may occur that a family or kin group (extended family, household), etc., is an almost self-sufficient social unit (except, of course, in the matter of intermarriage, which in these cases is always regulated according to kinship criteria). Its relations with other such units are superficial, of small significance for the stability and maintenance of the group, and when they occur are regulated by kinship criteria (through kinship extension). According to our analysis, no age groups should, of course, arise in such cases. Such societies may be found in many regions of the world, the best examples being the Eskimo[15] and some Australian and Brazilian tribes.[16] In all these cases the extent of self-sufficiency of the family units is maximal, and that of social specialization and interdependence between various households is minimal and usually seasonal only. While in most of these societies age differences play an important role in the allocation of status within family and kin groups, and are also of general importance in the social relations—e.g., elder people are treated with deference and respect and have some general juridical status and authority—in none of these societies do we find any trace of organized or semi-organized age groups. The individual's life in these societies is encompassed within the fold of his family and kin group, in which he acquires not only the most general role dispositions necessary for the acquisition of social status, but also most of his concrete roles.[17] Among African tribes some extent of self-sufficiency of small units is found among the Tonga, whose clusters of hamlets and villages are relatively self-sufficient units (mainly from the economic point of view), most of their wider relations being ritual and jural ones, based on kinship and clanship relations.[18]

This type of self-sufficiency is a rather extreme case, however, and, beyond certain very narrow limits, obviously a matter of degree. A most characteristic case from this point of view is that of the Turkana (and probably other tribes of the Karamajong cluster) in Africa.[19] Among the nomadic Turkana the nuclear and extended families are the most stable and continuous groups, with a relatively great degree of social and economic self-sufficiency. The relations with other such clusters are mainly seasonal (in the rainy season, making possible a greater concentration of people), and largely concerned with intermarriage and general social and ritual intercourse. While the widest spheres of relations and roles are not kinship-structured and definitely involve interacting outside the scope of kinship relations, the importance of these sectional and tribal interrelations from the point of view of both the individual and the total society is relatively small; the individual's status is not defined in terms of total tribal membership and the section and tribe do not act in any corporate capacity. The Turkana have age sets, in which membership is for life; these sets are important for the patterning of tribal relations (seen especially in different ritual arrangements at feasts), but both their scope and organization are of small importance in the social structure of the tribe. The age sets function only seasonally, and do not constitute permanent corporate structures or relations. Although they continue throughout life, they are most important after initiation, and membership in them does not confer full social status on the individual; this is achieved only through marriage and the establishment of a household. The sets do not constitute a series or a unitary hierarchy, and there are not direct relations between the various sets, but only the most general considerations of relative seniority. The single set, or even a smaller part of it which consists of initiates of the same camp, is the most solidary group. Thus these age groups, far from evincing a strong corporate organization, do not even definitely pattern the relations of all tribesmen vis-à-vis one another. (There exists no kinship terminology extension among them.) Here, as in the former cases, age differences play an important although not exclusive role in the status-system of the community. Old people are treated with deference and respect and wield great influence within their families, lineages and territorial groups. But these age relations are not organized within the corporate age groups, the importance of which weakens after marriage. This weakness in the organization of the age sets is clearly related (as can be seen in the relatively unimportant part they play in status-attainment, etc.) to the small scope of roles and interrelations which exist outside the scope of the single extended family unit.[20]

A more detailed and fruitful analysis relates to those societies among which there is a high extent of interaction between "isolated" family units. Almost all of the above-mentioned societies (with the exception of the Turkana, etc.) are of this kind, the interrelation being mostly in the political, judicial and ritual fields and also, although to only a very small extent, in the economic field. In all these cases an integrative mechanism of some sort is necessary in order to regulate these interactions and relations.

In order to study these mechanisms we may first compare one of the best-studied segmentary tribes having no age sets at all, the Tallensi,[21] with all the others. Although it is a segmentary tribe, the Tallensi social organization is complex, the most important units being defined in terms of common ancestry and descent. This applies not only to the nuclear family units, but also, and mainly, to the wider and more formally organized relations. The main unit of political activity and specialization among them is the lineage, i.e., a segment of the clan in which the members are genealogically related to one another. The lineages may be of various generation depths, and after some generations may split off; but the common identification expressed in terms of common ancestry persists. The different lineages and clans are usually localized groups, with a strong corporate organization. Their interrelations are defined in corporate terms, and the most important political, judicial and ritual interaction of their members is carried on in the name of the corporate units, the lineages, the individual members acting as their representatives. The same applies to a large extent within the maximal lineage, in the mutual relationships of its segments. The ideological framework of the lineages is the ancestor cult, and that of the locality is the cult of the Earth, the two being interrelated through the corporate activities of lineage heads. The mutual specialization and interdependence of corporate lineages and clans is most manifest in the two types of chiefdoms, the *na'am* and the ritual *tendaam* (custodian of the Earth), the first related to Earth and the second endowed with rain-making powers, which are permanently vested in certain clans, and which assure their interdependent functioning and the existence of ritual mediating factors in cases of quarrels, feuds, etc. The main factor which counteracts the possible separatist tendencies of these lineage groups are extended kinship relations, which cut across the lineage groups and yet bind their members together. The Tallensi constitute an excellent example of a segmentary tribe entirely organized in complementary and "specialized" lineage groups, the interrelation between its members being wholly regulated by these relations. Accordingly, the individual's life is entirely encompassed by these kin groups and relations, and it is through identification with the adult members of his lineage that a child gradually attains complete social maturity. Thus, except for very informal and unstable groups of young children, no institutions or formalized age groups are to be found among the Tallensi.

In other parts of the world we may also find similarly organized tribes whose structure is regulated by criteria of kinship and lineage. To list all of these tribes would be superfluous here; it is enough to mention those which have been studied most intensively and have become classic cases of anthropological research. The Trobiands, the Tikopia, the Pueblos, various Indian tribes, several Polynesian societies—all these, despite many differences between them, evince the same broad characteristics described above. They are all regulated by various particularistic criteria and value orientations, mostly kinship criteria, and accordingly in none of them do we find organized age groups.[22] In most of these cases the principle of seniority plays a very important role in the regulation of behavior, both within clans and in their interrelationships, thus stressing the importance of age-heterogeneous relations.[23] The case of the Tallensi is more relevant, however, because it is relatively easy to compare them with other African tribes which have an age set organization. In none of these tribes do we find such complete specialization and complementariness of lineage and clan groups as among the Tallensi. But the operation of this kinship regulation of the social system is a matter of degree, and a comparison of these different degrees is very helpful in explaining the distribution of various types of age groups.

We may now analyze the various segmentary tribes in which interaction and integration of the tribal society is not effected through family and kinship units, and compare them according to the extent of the prevalence of such kinship criteria.

Measured by such criteria, the Bantu Kavirondo, Gusii and afterwards the Nuer and other Nilotic tribes should range at one end of the scale, with the Nandi group, Murle and Masai at the other. The first group is characterized by a smaller extent of nonkinship regulation than the second. Among the Nuer there still exists a definite relation between lineage and not to the though this applies only to the dominant lineage and not to the nonaristocratic ones; and there exists a greater dispersal of lineages among various territorial tribal units than among the Tallensi. The lineage exists among the Nuer as a corporate unit, although not all interaction between members of the tribe is mediated through the lineages' corporate activity or through complementary kinship relations alone. Neither are any fixed mediating and complementary offices vested in the lineages. Accordingly, unsettled strife and quarrels and self-redress are more frequent here. At the same time, ritual and prestige-bearing offices are not necessarily vested in members of different lineages, and are, on the one hand, of a more accidental personal nature, while, on the other, they are of no great political importance.[24]

Among the Bantu Kavirondo and the Gusii, co-ordination between clan and territorial, political and ritual institutions is still very strong, since overall dispersion of descent groups is smaller in extent, and the clan (or maximal lineage) is still the main corporate political and ritual unit. Even among them, however, and especially among the Bantu Kavirondo, not all intratribal relations are organized according to kinship principles, and certain spheres are reserved for individual achievement (wealth and prowess) and relations based on it.[25]

The picture among the Nandi group, the Masai, the Kikuyu, etc., is entirely different. There are no corporate lineages, the clans and subclans are not territorial units and do not serve as coordinate principles of territorial organization, while the territorial groups are composed of kin and family heterogeneous elements. Interaction between the various subunits of these tribes is regulated by a purely local and territorial hierarchy, emanating from the smallest units and extending up towards the wider and more "inclusive" ones. This is also the way in which the judicial system is organized among these people: quarrels which cannot be settled within a small local unit or in which several such units are involved are settled by representatives of larger territorial units; but nowhere are these judiciary offices vested in representatives of lineages, clans or other kin groups. The same holds true of ritual offices. The military system is often based on purely territorial units (if not—as is sometimes the case —on the age set system itself). While the literature on the Pokomo, Teita, Kikuyu-Meru-Kamba group and the Gallas is not as adequate as that on the Nandi group, the Masai, etc., among these tribes, too, the lack of co-ordination between territorial organization and clanship, the relative absence of corporate lineages with political functions, and to some extent also the relatively small importance of these groups for ritual offices, are always stressed.[26] Some recent interpretations tend, however, to emphasize the fact that senior members of extended families do perform political functions which, as we shall see, have tempered the purity of the age set system. The lack of co-ordination between lineage and the territorial system among the Murle is also emphasized.[27]

The differences between these types of segmentary tribes are closely related to the organization of their age groups. This relation may, in most general terms, be stated as follows: The extent of corporate organization of age groups and of an age group hierarchy, the age span over which age group relations are effective, and the extent of regulation of behavior by age groups are greater in those tribes in which kinship groups do not perform basic political and ritual tasks and in which territorial rights are not vested in such groups. The greater the extent to which these tasks are performed outside kinship groups and the greater their independence of them, the greater the scope of social relations which are regulated by age groups. Among the Nuer, the Bantu Kavirondo and the Dorobo, the age groups are not corporate groups and only influence and organize the general attitudes and behavior of their members in their relations with one another, finding their clearest expression on tribal occasions, in ceremonial deference, and generally in emphasizing the patterns of respect for seniority and for equality among age mates. In these tribes the mutual attitudes of members of different age groups—attitudes of respect, deference to older people, etc.—seem to be an extension to the whole society of the patterns of authority within the family and kinship groups. Within these groups status and power are very largely determined by age differences, and are mostly vested in elders. The age groups transfer these attitudes to all members of the tribe. In this way the status contingent on age becomes, to some extent, independent of family position and valid for the whole society. The age groups do not, however, constitute here a corporate hierarchy of age groups, and no specific tasks are allocated to each of them. Neither do we find among them a close correspondence between definite age grades in the life of the men and the organization of age sets (except for the transition from boyhood to adulthood). Among the Gusii the importance of age set relations diminishes with advancing age, when the individual's roles and relations are again included within the lineage and kinship relations.[28] The reverse is true of the Nandi group, Masai and Murle, and to some extent also of the Kikuyu-Kamba-Meru group. Here the age groups are corporate groups, which not only possess a general organization of behavior and attitudes similar to that in the former group, but also perform specific tasks. Various tasks of extreme importance from the point of view of the integration of the social system—such as warriorship, government, judiciary functions—are allocated to them. They form an interlocked hierarchy, each grade within it usually corresponding to an age grade, and attained in turn by each group upon reaching the appropriate stage. The close interlocking of the whole system is most clearly evinced in the cyclical arrangements of the Nandi group and in the ubiquitous ceremonies of handing over the government, warriorship, etc., from one age group to another. Thus we see here that the articulation of age grading and age grouping into a corporate, integrated hierarchical organization is inversely correlated with the extent to which kinship principles and groups serve as focal points of social integration. This seems also to apply, in a different way, to the Kikuyu and Kamba, if the above-mentioned interpretation of the data is accepted. It seems that among them the highest governmental grades of elders are not given equally to all members of the elder age grade, but only to some of them, usually the heads of family groups. It is thus clear that the two integrative principles, the one based on age and the other on family seniority, are incompatible, one negating the other.

A similar comparison may be drawn between two of the tribes of the Nuba group—the Moro and the Tira.[29] The Tira, like some other tribes of the group (the Otoro), have a very formalized and corporate age group system covering the ages of fifteen to approximately twenty-six, comprising four grades. The Moro, on the other hand, have only a fluid recognition of age groups, with no formalized groups or systems and no promotion ceremonies, etc. Although no exact structural comparisons can be made on the basis of the available material, some broad lines may be suggested.

Among the Moro the clans are concentrated locally within their hill communities to a much larger extent than among the Tira, where they are more dispersed. Among the Moro each of these hill communities is more socially self-sufficient than among the Tira, and relations between the various Moro hill communities are vague and unstable. Even among the Moro, no one hill community is limited to one clan. The interrelation between these clans, however, is of what Nadel calls a "symbiotic" character,[30] i.e., they perform, as clans, mutually complementary functions, particularly in the ritual field. Here, then, our hypothesis is once more validated.

III We shall now turn to the so-called uncentralized, primitive village communities, which were exemplified in Chapter II by the Yako, and to which in a general way some Ibo, Ika, and Ibibio groups and many other African peasant communities also belong. For the same of comparison, we shall analyze some Yoruba tribes.[31] The degree of functional independence of territorial, political, judicial and ritual organization from kin groups among these tribes is even more extreme than among the segmentary tribes. Among the Yako, the most fully described of these peoples, the village (or town) is divided into several wards which form the basic administrative units of the society. Within these wards several family groups and patri-clans live together, while other members of the patri-clans may be found in other wards. Except on the lower, family unit level, the organization of the ward is not based on the corporate interaction of the family and kin groups. The patri-clan has some corporate functions and its heads perform both ritual and judiciary roles; but only with respect to their own internal affairs, and not in relation to members of other patri-clans, to members of a ward or to the common economic enterprises and ritual observances which bind the whole village together. The common affairs of the ward are supervised by various officers. These officers—who, as we have seen, supervise the activities of the age sets—are not elected on the basis of kin affiliation or membership, but on the basis of wealth, age, wisdom, and various other personal qualities and attainments. The organization of village-wide activities in various associations is even less related to any kinship or family criteria. The same holds true of most of the Ika, Ibo and Ibibio settlements.[32] Although here we do find lineages of relatively small depth acting as corporate groups, sometimes defining the boundaries of a settlement, etc., the lineage's importance is not great in defining either the territorial units or the wider interaction of the society's members. Although many settlements may have a nucleus or a given lineage group, this nucleus does not necessarily define the limits of the group and does not constitute a dominant element, as, for instance, the "aristocratic" Nuer lineage in a given locality. Through incessant division, accretion, etc., the locality, the village and the village group are composed of many various lineage groups, and regulated, as among the Yako, by entirely autonomous criteria according to which one's attitude towards a fellow villager is not determined by his being a member of a given particularistic kin group, but through an application of the universalistic criteria of a member of the ward, village, etc., to him. In so far as the evidence allows any detailed and accurate interpretation, the same holds true of many other African peasant villages.[33]

Within these villages we witness, however, a development distinct from that of the segmentary tribes. First, we find here a growth of economic specialization and a breakdown of the economic self-sufficiency of the family unit. This is, of course, a matter of degree, but in broad comparative terms it is true of all of them. The labor power of a household is not sufficient, particularly during certain seasons, to cope with its productive problems. Secondly, the economic system requires a larger amount of co-operative work to be done by all of the villagers—clearing paths, organizing the water supply, etc. Thirdly, more specialized activities, such as hunting, etc., emerge, although still in a very embryonic form.[34] This development necessarily influences the structure of age groups within these villages. First, they are usually corporate groups with definite tasks and functions allocated to them. The various groups are organized in one set, although not on a successive pattern; they do not succeed each other as among the Nandi, etc. These characteristics are related, as we have seen, to the relatively smaller importance of kinship units and criteria as integrative forces within the society. Secondly, the tasks allotted to them are clearly connected with these necessities of economic co-operation—clearing the bushes, cooperative farming, keeping public order, organizing the water supply, cleaning the village, etc. It should be remembered here that these villages are relatively densely populated units, thus necessitating all these regulations. Thirdly, the greater economic specialization entails certain risks, such as loss, etc., and the age groups often perform the functions of mutual aid societies. Fourthly, the specialization mentioned above gives rise to specific integrative agencies—associations, councils of elders, etc.—based to a large extent on achievement criteria. These associations, as we shall see in the following chapter, curtail the scope of age group activities and their autonomy.

It is somewhat difficult to find fully adequate data for comparison with these villages, i.e., to find similar social organizations in which kinship units are of greater importance as foci of social integration than among the Yako, Ibo, etc. The nearest example may be found among the Yoruba, inadequate as the literature about them may be.[35] It seems that four main points should be stressed in this connection:

(a) Among some of Yoruba, the territorial community seems to be more closely confined to kinship units than among the Yako and the Ibo.

(b) The political co-ordination of the various territorial units is effected, in some places at least, through corporate interlinking of such units and through offices which tend to be hereditarily vested in different families and kin groups.

(c) Membership in associations, religious cults, etc., tends here to be limited to members of kin groups much more than among the Yako and Ibo, and consequently social stratification is hereditary within these groups.[36]

(d) Within the kin structure of the Yoruba the principle of seniority is stressed to a maximum degree.[37]

With regard to the problem of the integrative principles regulating the structure of a society within which specialization manifests itself in group associations, etc., it is perhaps worth-while to draw attention here to the Mende of Sierra Leone and Liberia tribes (which will be dealt with in greater detail in the following chapter), in which these associations perform integrative functions and which are ruled hereditarily.[38] Neither among many sectors of the Yoruba nor among the Mende, etc., do we find any articulate age groups, except for informal children's groups.[39] Within the framework of our comparative analysis an additional variable of our hypothesis has been validated here—even if only in the first stage—namely, the relation between types of social stratification and age sets: the positive relation between the emergence of age groups and individualistic achievement-oriented stratification as opposed to that confined to hereditary kin and other particularistic groups. It has been shown that age groups arise in those societies in which, as among the Yako, the Ibo, etc., social status depends, to some extent at least, on individual achievement, and is not entirely based on membership in kinship or other hereditary groups, as among the Mende, some of the Yoruba tribes, etc.

IV   We may now turn to a very brief comparative analysis of the Plains Indian age groups, and attempt to analyze the reasons for the existence of these age groups and age systems among only five of the many tribes, and to see if this can also be mastered by our hypothesis. Unfortunately the available data are insufficient for as full an analysis of this aspect of the problem as the African data permitted. A broad comparison may, however, clearly bring out some very significant data. Plains Indian society is characterized by the importance of various societies and associations which perform very vital ceremonial, military and police functions. Each tribe consists of several such associations, each of which usually functions at a given period of the year. These associations are also of great importance from the point of view of the individual's life history, as it is within this framework that he can attain his status and social distinctions. The various ceremonial privileges and the honors of warriorhood, etc., more or less concomitant with membership in the associations, have to be achieved by the individual (he has to prove himself) and by the group, and are not purely ascriptive. The element of "purchase" of the ceremonial bundles and rights seen in the previous description of age societies is a clear indication of this. The great number and variety of the associations emphasizes the element of social specialization existing within these tribes, as does the consequent existence of differential status expressed in wealth, warrior prestige, possession of supernatural powers, political authority, etc. A broad comparison between these tribes, whether containing age groups or not, reveals striking differenes in (a) the degree of their status differentiation; and (b) the nature, criteria and organization of these differences. As to the first, it seems that the extent of status differentiation based on wealth acquired through raiding and breeding of horses is of greater importance among the Kiowa and the Crow (non-age-graded societies) than among those of the age-graded type.[40] Secondly, and this is probably more important, the patterning of these status differences among the two types of tribes is essentially dissimilar. Among the non-graded tribes, membership in associations (and concomitant status differences) is to a very large extent bound up with specific family and kin groups, membership being either formally or at least practically hereditary through the help that a young man receives from his kin in acquiring the necessary honors and privileges. This can be seen most clearly as regards those honors which are dependent on warlike activities based on horse raids, where ownership of great herds of horses is essential in view of the risks involved. Within the non-graded societies the chief tribal offices, too, tend to be hereditary in families and lineages much more than among the graded ones, where it is more dispersed.[41] As the various associations in both age-graded and nongraded tribes perform more or less similar functions and are even historically interconnected,[42] the sharp difference between those associations based on family and kin principles and those based on age is here clearest, particularly from the point of view of different ways of articulating status differences.

Another point concerning the importance of the degree of interconnection between self-sufficient family groups may be briefly mentioned here. The age associations (especially in tribes such as the Arapaho) usually function at those periods during which all the various bands composing the tribe relinquish their autonomous, relatively self-sufficient existence.[43]

The integration of tribes on the basis of ceremonial association and principles, vested in a complementary way in various descent groups composing the tribe, is characteristic of the Pueblos,[44] while strong status differentiation based on competitive achievement between families, households, etc., acting as corporate groups, represented by some of their individual members, and not oriented only towards individualistic achievement, may be found among the Kwakiutl and other Coastal Indian tribes with their former Potlatch institution.[45] Neither of these has any age groups.[46]

V   Hitherto we have dealt (except for needs of comparison) principally with societies devoid of central authority and administrative machinery. In this section our comparative analysis will deal with some centralized primitive kingdoms, i.e., tribes with a chief wielding supreme power at the head of a political and sometimes even an administrative hierarchy. In most of these African kingdoms the extent of economic specialization and differentiation in standards of living is small, and although there exist differences in wealth they do not greatly influence the actual modes of living of the people. Among these kingdoms some have very articulated age-grading systems, of the type of the Swazi age regiments, while others do not. To the first belong the Swazi,[47] the Zulu,[48] the various Tswana groups,[49] the Baxaefele;[50] to the other belong the Ashanti,[51] the Bemba,[52] the Pondo,[53] some of the Khosa groups,[54] and the Lozi.[55] The Lobedu[56] and the Basuto[57] may serve as a borderline type, while the comparison between the Heiban and Otoro of the Nuba group is also of great interest here.[58] (The more complexly organized kingdom of Dahomey[59] may perhaps also be used in comparison.)

Within all these kingdoms the political sphere is distinct from that of lineage and of kinship relations, and political positions acquire a certain degree of autonomy. In almost all of them the relative importance of corporate descent groups, lineages, clans, etc., for the definition of the territorial units of society and for the general political life of the tribe is smaller than among the various segmentary tribes, with the possible exception of the Ashanti. Most of the kingdoms were founded through amalgamation, conquest, or federation of clans and smaller tribes; and necessarily the importance of corporate descent groups, particularly in relation to territorial groups, has somewhat diminished. Yet the diminution of this importance is relative, as in all these kingdoms the clans, and especially the royal clan, are still important in the regulation of various aspects of social life. Yet the diminishing importance of the corporate descent group does not necessarily mean that a nonparticularistic group develops as the main group in the society. The local territorial group itself may be composed of family and household groups held together by common allegiance to a chief or headsman, whose office is hereditarily vested in a family or lineage. To some extent this type of local unit exists in all of these kingdoms. But as the political sphere becomes more autonomous it is within the framework of the relative importance of social units (whether corporate descent groups or local family units) for political coordination that our comparison must be made. We shall, then, propose concrete specific indices for kinship and nonkinship, universalistic criteria of role allocation within these chieftainships. These indices necessarily differ from those for the segmentary tribes; but they are similarly derived from the general criteria set out at the beginning of this chapter.

The following are the main indices:

(1) The extent to which membership in the tribe (kingdom) is attained through direct allegiance to the supreme chief; or, conversely, the extent to which it is mediated by local chiefs, heads of clans, etc., and conditioned by membership in these units.

(2) The extent to which the administrative hierarchy, whose apex is the king, is or may be in direct touch with all members of the tribe in their different localities; or, conversely, the extent to which it has to be mediated by various hereditary chiefs, who monopolize it to a greater or smaller extent.

(3) The extent to which political positions (and especially membership in the king's council) are vested in representatives or heads of various clans, lineages, and local kinship groups; or, conversely, the extent to which the king may freely fill these positions and appoint the members of his council and various officers of state without respect to their descent. This difference is important in the judicial sphere, and also as regards the exaction of tribute and mobilization.

(4) The extent to which status positions are determined by

membership in kin and descent groups; or, conversely, the extent to which there exists an element of free, individual mobility, based mostly on services performed for the chief.

(5) The extent to which the king is the main legitimate expression and embodiment of the ultimate ritual values of the tribe, or the extent to which these values may also be expressed in rituals enacted within other corporate groups.*

In broad general lines, the difference between the two types of "primitive" kingdoms may be said to be a difference in the extent to which the political sphere is organized on a different level from the local kin and economic spheres. In all these kingdoms the family and descent groups still constitute basic units of the economic division of labor, and it is with regard to the political sphere that the main difference emerges.

If we compare the two groups of tribes according to these criteria, the broad differences are striking, even if in some details (such as the composition of the king's council, etc.) they may be only matters of degree. Among the Swazi, Zulu and Tswana, universal membership in the tribe through direct allegiance to the king is most striking. This allegiance has been established mainly through conquest which resulted in a deliberate policy aimed at destroying the political solidarity of the various clans and small tribes. Even in those cases where the policy of the conquerors was to maintain the loyalty of a given clan by leaving its chiefs with some authority, this authority was expressly derived from the king even if afterwards it was obviously necessary to employ heads of various kin groups as administrative supervisors of small units. Their authority (which at any rate was effective only within a limited local sphere—the wards, etc.[60]) was conditioned on that of the king. Even if the king's relation to all his subjects was couched in kinship terms (as seen most manifestly in the national royal ritual) and based on direct, relations towards him and the royal family and clan, this relation was, from the point of view of membership, definitely universalistic, i.e., open to anyone who would swear allegiance and attach himself to the chief; this membership was not

---

* Because of the relative lack of economic differentiation within these kingdoms, no indices relating to these are presented here.

necessarily conditioned by membership in any intermediary group. The opposite is true of the second group of kingdoms, which usually constitutes federations or amalgamations of lineages, clans or local kin groups which were incorporated as *groups* within the total social unit, membership in which could be attained only through these subunits. The nearest example of this kind is the Ashanti Union (Federation), which constitutes a federation of semi-autonomous lineages and lineage clusters; a parallel case exists among the Bemba kingdom, composed of various hereditary kin and territorial groups in which the main political positions are hereditarily vested.

The same difference applies to the administrative hierarchy of the two types. Among the first there always exists a possibility of direct approach by the king and the royal clan to all his subjects, in judicial matters and especially in the exaction of tribute, in calling up the army for either military exigencies or "public works," and in the king's overall ultimate authority over the various heads, chiefs, etc. In the second type the ultimate legitimate dependence of the king on the lesser chiefs and on the organized, corporate activities of these groups is most clearly evident among the Ashanti; somewhat less so among the Khoze group, Bemba and Pondo. The composition of the king's council is more a matter of degree, although even here the differences— at least in emphasis—are clear-cut. Everywhere the council is composed of some members of the royal clan (family), some heads of the leading clans and families, and some personal favorites of the king. The relative importance of these elements, especially of the last two, does, however, vary to a very large extent. Among the Swazi, Zulu, etc., the common advisers are not merely private advisers and favorites of the kings, but full legitimate members of the council (sometimes even having a monopoly of it), holding central offices. Among the Pondo, Bemba, etc., they act in a much more private capacity, while among the Ashanti they are almost nonexistent.[61] In these societies the council is composed mostly of heads of different territorial units, clans, lineages, etc., who have a basic right to belong to it, and without whom it cannot properly act. The place of such hereditary councillors among the Swazi and Zulu, although important, is not as fully independent of the king's will as among the Bemba, etc. Sometimes the council as such does not even function as a very important body, but the king deals separately with every chief (among the Bemba). The same difference also applies to the juridical system, so that smaller chiefs and units may possess juridical autonomy. Among the Pondo and the Ashanti (and probably also among the Bemba) the smaller chiefs (units) could almost legitimately sever their relationships with the paramount chief.[62] The composition of the chief's council and the importance of the king's personal favorites in the body politic also constitute in these tribes the main index of status mobility; as it is mainly through service to the chief that an individual can distinguish himself, since the king constitutes the only "fountain of honor."

The most interesting manifestation of the direct, unmediated relation between the chief (king) and his people is the institution of the tribal assembly, the famous Kgotla of the Tswana,[63] which is called by the chief to discuss important tribal matters, must be attended by all full adult members, and constitutes the supreme authority of the tribe. While the possibility of an individual member's attendance at the council meetings exists in many kingdoms, such a full institutionalization of universal political membership and allegiance as manifested in the Kgotla is to be found among the Tswana, Zulu, and to some extent among the Swazi. (Among the latter two its effectiveness is somewhat limited by obvious ecological considerations.) This is paralleled by the universal ritual importance of the king to the welfare of his tribe.

We find an entirely different type of political integration based on particularistic principles among the Lozi. Here the political organization is based on a series of titles carrying with them political office and ritual symbols, to which rights, jurisdictions and people are attached and which are the main status positions of the society. Every title is vested in a specific official, mostly on a hereditary basis. Every person in the kingdom is bound, not to one, but to several such titles for different juridical, social and political purposes. Only kingship is a unitary, overall allegiance. Consequently there are no age groups among the Lozi.[64]

Thus we see here once more the universal correlation between nonkinship, universalistic allocation of roles and the emergence of age groups. Universalistic criteria for membership in the total community can be seen here, in these kingdoms, even more clearly than in the segmentary tribes. From the point of view of our problem it seems worth while to juxtapose these two types of kingdoms and to compare the execution of those functions which among the Swazi, Zulu and Tswana are allocated to the age regiments, namely, the military functions and the performance of public works on behalf of the king and the local chiefs. Among the "kinship" states those functions are allocated to the territorial-kinship units; the exacting of tribute and of work is almost purely an internal matter, while the army has been organized on a purely territorial basis, each chief raising his own contingent and leading it through battle. Among the Swazi, Zulu, etc., only the smallest units of the army are based on locality, and, within the general framework, are unified in non territorial, country-wide, universalistic units. Such amalgamation never took place among the Pondo, Bemba, Ashanti, etc., and the army itself is co-ordinated on the basis of principles of clanship. The naturally exclusive possibilities of universalistic and particularistic principles of integration and their relation to age groups may be clearly seen here. This mutual exclusiveness may also be clearly seen within the composition of the age regiments themselves. The criterion of age homogeneity holds good everywhere, except in those positions of command which are allocated by hereditary right to members of the royal clan, the only clan which remains fully effective within these kingdoms. They are the only exceptions to the universality of the age criterion. Otherwise the age group criterion cuts everywhere across the various kin and descent groups.

From the point of view of this comparison the Lobedu may serve as an interesting "experimental" case.[65] According to the ethnographers' records, two historical phases may be distinguished. The first stage, that of political unification cutting across existing families, lineages, etc., has witnessed the emergence of age grades of a distinctively tribal-military character. In the second stage a process of gradual pacification and new integration took place in which political power devolved on representatives of kinship and local units. At this stage the age sets lose much of their importance and slowly disintegrate.

Another relevant comparison is that between Heiban and Otoro, two tribes of the Nuba group, the first a noncentralized tribe without age groups, and the second a chiefdom whose centralization is still a matter of historical ceremony. One of the main problems of centralization was to weaken the political importance of the local clans and to establish direct allegiance to the chief; this has been effected through the formation of (or utilization and formalization of) age grades under the direction of the chief, performing economic, and also to some extent military duties.[66]

The Inca and the Aztec empires[67] are another example of the weakening of local clans and kinship by a conquering power and consequent universal regimentation of the conquered population on the basis of age.

Some of the more salient characteristics of age regiments within the general framework of the typology of age groups may, even at this point of our discussion, be definitely connected with the regiments' complete subordination to the king, their service under him and his allocation of various functions to them. Their corporate nature is an important factor for the integration of the tribe. This corporate, formal organization does not, however, make them a unitary, autocephalous self-regulating hierarchy with autonomous promotion, succession of grades, etc. The various regiments are not connected by means of interlocking, but mainly by the king's person and officers. Similarly, they are not allocated totally different functions, but only different degrees of the same, mainly military, functions; governing power being vested solely in the king, the royal family, etc.

VI   The existence of the somewhat special type of age groups in the kingdom of Nupe[67a] is also clearly related to a nonfamilial, nonkinship allocation of roles on the basis of ascriptive criteria. The Nupe age group can be analyzed on two distinct levels: that of the individual village and that of the entire kingdom. In the villages the case is not very distinct from other African peasant villages (such as the Ibo, etc., Yoruba, etc.). The various economic tasks which have to be performed usually necessitate a larger labor force than can be mustered by the individual (extended) family. The political offices of the village (chiefdom, membership in council, and incumbence of various graded positions on the council) are not completely vested in extended families and lineages, and are to some extent allocated according to individual achievement, according to universalistic criteria of competence. Thus in both these fields, the economic and the political, we find, on the village level, some distinct indices of a nonkinship division of labor; the structure and tasks of the age groups are clearly related to it, especially in the economic field, and also in their general fostering of village solidarity.

On the level of the total society we encounter a somewhat more complicated picture. From a certain point of view Nupe society may be seen as having a particularistic bent; it is rather rigidly stratified into castes based on conquest, and its political organization is a semi-feudal one, headed by a hereditary caste and a caste of civil and military officials. The economic division of labor is, to a great extent, geared to this stratification, and economic specialization in the towns, in various crafts, is organized into various guilds with a semi-hereditary basis, and in any case based on mainly personal, particularistic relations. Yet there are two important factors which modify this "particularistic" structure and which are of overwhelming structural importance: First, there exists a very important element of mobility and achievement orientation within this society: the class of civil and military officials is recruited mostly from the conquered people and is not identical with the conquering caste, and a very important stratum in the society is formed by the Moslem "*maalams*" (teachers), a profession which is open to everyone and enjoys high prestige. (In the economic field there also exists a "free" competitive sphere, albeit a rather narrow one.) What is of special importance here is the fact that this mobility and achievement orientation is universalistic: first, open to everyone; second (particularly in the case of the *maalams*), not organized on any particularistic or hereditary basis; finally, based on universal participation in the common, ultimate values of the society. Also, the criteria of achievement are here universalistic, i.e., one is judged by certain properties, knowledge, etc., which he acquires, and not by any relations he may have to any group. This constitutes the second main universalistic element in the social structure of the Nupe, which outweighs the relatively small extent of its social mobility. No particularistic unit (family, guild, caste) fully embodies the ultimate values of Nupe society, especially those connected with the Mohammedan religion. These values and common participation in the history of the society are embodied only in the total community, and are equally approachable by all. Even the social stratification is seen, to some extent, as an embodiment of these common values.[67b].

The Nupe age groups are clearly related to these universalistic elements in the social structure. Their organization is oriented towards this general "education for citizenship" and the general values of the society, and their title system is an emulation of the stratification system of the society. The age groups operate in these institutional fields, and not, for instance, in the more particularistically structured economic field (except on the village level).

In some respects these age groups differ greatly from those discussed so far. The main difference lies in the fact that they do not form a unitary organization and an agency for allocation of roles throughout the society. In this way they form a transitional link between the former, primitive age groups and those of modern societies to be discussed now. The full analysis of the age groups must, however, be postponed to the next chapter.

In our material the Nupe age group constitutes a unique type; there are only very few, inadequate indications of a somewhat similar type in other African tribes,[67c] and some indications that they existed also among some of the Arab and Berber tribes.[67d]

VII   The development of different types of age groups in Ancient Greece is also clearly connected with the emergence of a social and political organization not based on kinship units and criteria. Here we find societies in which the degree of internal differentiation of the main social spheres and units is greater than in the various societies hitherto analyzed.

The most outstanding example of this development is, of course, Sparta after the Lycurgean reforms.[68] These reforms (whether really introduced by one man or developed only gradually) established a political and social system which was a peculiar combination of monarchy, oligarchy and democracy. There were two hereditary kings in Sparta, but their importance was very small and was confined mainly to the performance of various ritual duties, on the one hand, and to (sometimes nominal) leadership in wartime, on the other. The effective rulers were the *ephors*, five in number, who were officials elected by the people at large, without any special ascriptive qualifications such as belonging to a given family, clan, etc. Side by side with them was the *Gerusia*—the Senate—a Council of 28 elders, together with the two Kings elected for life by lot or acclamation from all men above the age of 60. It seems that the *ephors* and the *Gerusia* were principally active in initiating government measures and legislation, which were then brought before the General Assembly—the *Apella*—of all Spartan citizens (or peers). All these political and social arrangements were based on an internally universalistic allocation of roles. Within the group of citizens no special place was given to the family or kinship unit. There is reason to suppose that this order developed out of a more tribal or familial social organization, and the Spartan age groups developed together with this nonfamilial organization. It should, of course, be emphasized that these universalistic and "democratic" political arrangements were operative within a rather restricted social stratum—that of the full citizens of Sparta, who constituted in themselves a rather closed oligarchy in relation to other elements of the population (the Perioeci, Helots, etc.).

The scope of the family in Sparta was also restricted in several other spheres. The educational functions of the family, which kept the sons at home only until the age of six, were limited. Afterwards the boys were enlisted in formal age groups. In later, married life the men did not fully participate in the internal life of the family; the main meals were eaten by them not at home, but in men's clubs—the *syssitia*—which constituted, to some degree, an extension of their age groups. The wider family group—clan, tribe, etc.—seems to have played no important roles in pub-

lic life, save in some ritual affairs. In the economic sphere the
family unit was much more important, as it constituted the main
unit of (agricultural) production, and the family farm was the
most important economic unit among full Spartan citizens. Some
other, secondary economic units were organized in hereditary
guilds—such as that of the bakers and cooks—to which people
who were not full citizens belonged. Although among the full
citizens of Sparta there was little economic specialization, a continuous process of economic development, of upward and down-
ward mobility, of development of larger farm units and lati-
fundia of various types, went on, especially in the fifth and
fourth centuries B.C. Thus, despite the importance of the family
unit in the economic sphere, even here family status and positions
were not fixed.

The structure and organization of Spartan age groups is closely
connected with this nonkinship social and political organization.
The Spartan age groups extended, as we have seen, from the
age of six to thirty. These age groups were formally organized
by the State; they constituted unitary organizations controlled
by adults. At the ages of six to approximately 18, the age groups
were the most important educational and training agency. From
18 to 30, they performed various para-military and military tasks
and were the backbone of the Spartan army. Throughout most
of this period, with the partial exception of the earlier age groups,
the young Spartan lived in barracks, under the supervision and
tutelage of special supervisors and the adult community in general, and was not allowed to live with his family. It seems that
the various age groups and age regiments were organized on a
yearly basis, and each yearly age grade had a specific name;
although modern historians do not entirely agree on the exact
names of each group. After the age of thirty, when he received
full citizenship and became a member of the *Apella*, the Spartan
was allowed to live at home, taking most of his meals in his *syssitia*, and being a member of his regiment in the army. At the age
of sixty, he became a member of the oldest age group, from which
the members of the *Gerusia* were chosen.

It is not our concern to enter here into the well-known details
of Spartan discipline and education. Suffice it for our purpose to

show that in the societies hitherto analyzed, the development and maintenance of an age group organization is closely connected with the existence of universalistic principles of division of labor and allocation of roles.[69]

A parallel development—although differing greatly in details—can be traced in Athens.[70] There the transition from a tribal, particularistic and aristocratic society and political organization to a more universalistic and democratic society can be traced. It is connected mostly with the reform of Cleisthenes in 508 B.C. In the place of the old system of voting according to the division of the state into four primitive kin tribes, these reforms substituted an artificial division into ten units, still called tribes. Despite the retention of the name and concept of the tribe, this change denotes the passing of systematized voting on the basis of kinship and clan solidarity. Membership in the ten new tribes was geographic, but under a system in which three separate and noncontiguous territorial areas were combined in each so-called tribe. In this process the actual clans and phratries were not destroyed, but continued to exist only as religious and social organizations. Similarly the main political offices, those of the councillors (members of the Council—*Boule*), the *prytaneis* (members of the directing committee of the Council) and the magistrates were no longer tied to the kinship units, but were distributed either by election or by lot, divided between the representatives of the territorial divisions, which were not based on kinship ties. Membership in the general assembly of the people was compulsory for all citizens without distinction of family or kinship unit, although citizenship itself was largely hereditary. Here, as in Sparta—although to a smaller extent—we find a rather ascriptive and particularistic group, within which the internal allocation of roles was largely universalistic. The economic functions of the family were here much more restricted than in Sparta, owing to the greater extent of specialization, of diversity of trades and occupations, greater economic differences and a greater mobility.

We also find here a very strong development of age and youth groups. But unlike Spartan groups, these youth and age groups did not have a unitary organization and uniform characteristics.

We find here two or three distinct types of age groups and organizations. On the one hand, there were various types of schools, while on the other hand, there was the more strictly organized group of *epheboi* (aged 18-20).[71] It is usual to distinguish between the various types of schools: First, there were the so-called primary schools, in which the rudiments of writing, arithmetic, etc., were taught to boys between the ages of six and 14. It is presumed that most Athenian children attended these schools. Then there were secondary schools, attended only by members of the wealthiest classes, aged 14-18, approximately. All these schools were private, with a minimal degree of state supervision. They seem to have developed in the fifth century, side by side with the democratic reforms, and to have replaced a more family-bound system of training and education. Third, there were the pilaestrae and gymnasia, schools of sports and athletics, the latter supported by the State, open to all, and drawing their attendance from elder age groups as well.

At the age of 18, the young Athenian became an *ephebos* and was enrolled in the group of *epheboi* until the age of 20. In this group, formally organized by the State, he received military training and performed, from the age of 19, various military duties. At the age of 20 he became a full citizen, receiving his shield from the State and swearing the oath of allegiance. At one time the *epheboi* were organized in a complete *ephebia* system, in which the youth received not only military and perhaps general training in citizenship, but was also taught philosophy, the basic laws of the State, etc. Certain historians think that this system was an ancient one; others maintain that it was introduced only in the late fourth century B.C. as a last attempt to revive the patriotic spirit in Athens. But the existence of the *epheboi* as such is beyond doubt; although it has not been proved that they were but a transformation of tribal initiation ceremonies, the functions they performed were, to some extent, similar. With the decline of Athens, the system of *epheboi* as universal training for citizenship declined as well, and only members of the upper classes participated in it.

Here we find, then, a much more complex development of age group structure than in Sparta. The official, formal, unitary organization of age groups is to be found only in the case of the *epheboi*, at the ages of 18-20.[72] Below that age there were no uniformly organized age groups. First, the various schools, although usually very similar in their curriculum, were not uniform or connected with each other. There are some indications that there were "better" and "worse" schools, to which members of different classes sent their children. Secondly, not all children attended schools for the same number of years, and only the sons of the wealthier families attended all of them. Thirdly, the gymnasia provided yet another framework for youth activities, and there was also quite a lot of spontaneous youth life. In all these respects the situation in Athens may be seen as a forerunner of developments in modern societies—together with some emphasis on youth ideology and identification.

A similar situation developed in most of the Greek and Hellenistic cities.[73] With the spread of the *polis* we see also the spread of school, gymnasia and the systems of *ephebia*—albeit not as universal groups of citizens, but more as organizations of the wealthier classes. But the system itself was one of the main symbols of Hellenistic culture and society.

A brief glimpse at the development of youth groups and education in Ancient Rome will be in order here, and will make possible some wider comparisons with Ancient Greece. The political and social order of Republican Rome was based on family, kinship and particularistic criteria of stratification to a much larger extent than in Greece. The Senate and the Consulate were mostly "patrician" bodies and offices, membership in which was more or less confined to sons of aristocratic families. There existed also more popular assemblies, with their special officers, the tribunes, albeit selected from the aristocracy, which had a great influence on the outcome of elections; but this influence was exercised mostly through the various channels of "patronage."[74] Moreover, the power of the popular assemblies themselves was in practice very restricted.

The picture of education in ancient Republican Rome is closely related to this social organization.[75] Among the upper classes the burden of education fell on the family. The child was first educated by the mother, then by the father, perhaps with the help of a domestic slave or tutor. Even at a later stage, when the boy of a good family would begin an apprenticeship in public life, this apprenticeship was usually supervised by a personal friend or patron of the family. The initiation rites of the Romans—the investment with the *toga virilis*—were also to a very great extent a family affair. It was this type of traditional education that was extolled at the end of the Republic by Cato and Cicero, as contrasted with the new Hellenistic trends.

A new development took place during the last century and a half of the Republic and the Empire. Political developments, on the one hand, and the influence of Greek culture, on the other, had greatly changed the manner of life of the Roman upper classes. First, there developed somewhat greater specialization within these classes. The scope of the family diminished to some extent, and the various universalistic values of Greek culture became more and more predominant. The extension of Roman citizenship, although not very effective in daily political practice, also exerted its influence in the same direction. All these developments did not create a universalistic, democratic social structure, as they did in Greece. The social structure continued to be organized hierarchically, divided into particularistically defined strata. But the internal organization of the upper strata did change to some extent in the directions outlined above. This gave rise to a marked change in the educational system—a rapid development of formal schools on the Greek and Hellenistic pattern, development of special *collegia invenum* sponsored, at first, by Augustus, etc. While the existence of schools of various sorts is known of already in the earlier period of the Republic, they seemed to be but subsidiary to the familial education. It was only in the later period that they developed into autonomous structures; although disputes as to the relative advantage of familial vs. school education continued in Rome for a very long period.[76]

The development of these schools did not change the socially restricted nature of this type of education and its restriction within the limits of the higher classes of Roman society—as was also the case in the various Hellenistic cities. These schools were similar to many other systems in particularistic societies and strata, which will be discussed in the next chapter. But within these limits, both the internal development of Roman education and its comparison with that of Ancient Greece fully substantiate our hypothesis.

VIII   The material presented above provides a full validation of our hypothesis within the limits of primitive and historical societies and kingdoms. We have tried to find complete conformation in so far as it was available. Within all of those tribes and societies about which there exist more or less full descriptions and data, the structural correlations we have postulated as derivatives of our basic hypothesis have been fully validated, without exception. Among those societies about which the material is not so adequate, the broad contours suggest a parallel validation; at any rate no exception has been found.

All this, however, is insufficient for the full elucidation of the problem. In order to make these various structural correlations more meaningful in terms of our basic assumptions, we must analyze more fully the activities and functions of the age groups within those societies where they exist, and compare some of these activities with non-age-graded societies. The description will at this point be mainly concerned with the various primitive societies; and only at a later stage shall we proceed to a parallel description of other types of social systems. In this chapter some of the basic characteristics of age groups will be presented, while a fuller analysis of differences among them and of the conditions under which they occur will be given in subsequent chapters.

The most general facts in relation to the activities of these groups are that they are all built on more informal and embryonic groups of children, which may or may not be confined to kinship units; that the scope of their activities is always beyond that of the family and kin unit (and often opposed to it); and that they all involve, at a certain point in their organization, a change of status and of personality evaluation of the individual.

Informal groupings of children exist, in different degrees, within any society, and their importance for the process of socialization has often been stressed. In all our cases we find that formalized age groups, age sets, age regiments, etc., are built on the basis provided by these informal groupings, and that they provide extension and continuation of these groups—an extension and continuation which does not exist within the "kin societies." This extension is not, however, merely quantitative or temporary; it entails a definite change in the quality of these groups. This change can best be understood—from the point of view of the individual—in relation to the acquisition of new status and, as it were, a new personality, a new identity. The point at which these groups are given formal recognition within the society always serves as the starting point for a new phase of life, the entrance into a new age grade. This entrance, connected in most cases with initiation, includes all the various elements of initiation analyzed in Chapter I.[77] From the point of view of the individual it means the acquisition of a new identity (often occasioned by the taking on of a new name, specially connected with the ceremony), usually the first and main step in the attainment of full social status. This transition is closely related with the annulment of old restraints and the imposition of new ones. These new restraints emphasize the individual's bodily prowess, the necessity for its full and autonomous regulation—in sexual matters and in military and physical performance—and the necessity of its being geared to socially accepted goals. The most crucial fact about this transition, within age-grouped societies, is connected with a definite "going out" of the family. This "going out" is not merely of a temporary and symbolic nature, as in all initiation ceremonies, which in reality involve only the redefinition of the individual's role within the family. Here it is of a much more real nature, involving not only a temporary and symbolic association with co-initiates, but a more permanent and general one. The full redefinition of one's status is not fully effected so long as it is not connected with the formation of a formalized group and the individual's participation within it. The individual's new identity is inseparably connected with membership in the group of age mates, and with the collective identity of the group. This point is first manifested in the children's and adolescents' eagerness to form such groups. This eagerness is not oriented—as among the informal children's group—only towards the mutual play and interaction of the group; it is clearly oriented towards the formal establishment of the group and the establishment of its identity. This eagerness quite often brings the children into opposition to their parents and other members of the family, who may sometimes wish to postpone the formation of the group. Secondly, the importance for the individual of the establishment of these groups may be seen in the cases of those boys who are, for one reason or another, left behind and not incorporated into the group. They lose their self-respect as well as any possibility of attaining social recognition; their physical maturity is not matched by social maturity, and they are involved in a contradictory and, for them, undefined situation.[78] A very important and crucial example of the importance of such full incorporation within the group may be found among the Zulu, Swazi, etc. Here the first stage of initiation is a family, or at most a purely local, affair. This stage does not, however, confer full social status on the individual: that can be attained only through incorporation within a (royal) regiment. Hence the boys' eagerness to join these regiments, to leave their homesteads on royal service sometimes even before the official call-up.[79] In the first stages of age group life, in which the spontaneous group prevails, we usually find the adolescents still playing at various roles without undertaking any definite tasks. In this they are very much like children's groups, in which the members acquire somewhat wider orientations to general norms in the society. This stage usually lasts until the end of the initiation ceremonies. After that we find, unlike children's groups in particularistic societies, that the age groups become more and more formalized and various definite tasks are allocated to them.

The new group life means an extension of the individual's social sphere and relations, in which he meets people from wider groups than his family and kinship, in which new tasks are demanded of him, and which serves as a good basis for education in new techniques and transmission of new knowledge (tribal lore and various practical information, etc.)[80] The new group life also involves, as we shall see, various restrictions, new patterns of obedience, behavior, etc. These restrictions and patterns of behavior are, however, always seen and felt as being different from those imposed within family life, and sometimes openly opposed to them. Where the authority of the group begins, that of the

father and the family stops. Their spheres of action are distinct
from one another (with perhaps some very partial exceptions in
the more gerontocratically structured age groups of the Kambo
and Kikuyu type), and enrollment in the age group usually
constitutes acknowledged and legitimate emancipation from the
authority of the family. The mutual exclusiveness of family and
age group spheres is manifested in different ways in the various
societies: In some (Meru, Nandi, etc.) we find the definite postponement of settled married life until the period of most active
participation in age groups (mostly as warriors) is over, with a
strong distinction between sexual relations with "sweethearts"
and procreative sexual intercourse with legitimate wives. Among
the Meru, for instance, that period of a man's life when he is
most occupied in building up a family is his most passive period
—either as a warrior or as an "elder"—in the age group system.[81]
Among most of these tribes the age groups of the women are less
organized than those of the men, and more or less cease to function autonomously after women's marriage, when they are affiliated with their husbands' groups.[82] Among the Yako, and especially among some of the Yoruba and Ibo tribes, a boy's enrollment in an age group is concomitant with his gradual—eventually
complete—economic emancipation from dependence on his father
(getting a holding of his own, etc.).[83] This separation between
family and age group life may be defined in terms of mere
separation (as among the Nuer, Gusii, Nupe, et al.), or of distinct, formal opposition (as among the Nandi, Masai, Kipsigi,
et al.). We shall later explain the reasons for this difference, but
here the general fact itself is of importance.

This difference between family and kinship behavior and age
group life is not, however, confined merely to the content of
roles, restrictions, etc., important as it is. This difference becomes of crucial importance mainly through the different organization of the roles and attitudes involved in age group
membership. These roles entail a definite transition from one
type of relations to another. The age group is constituted according to criteria which cut across family and kin groups and
which apply to all the members of a tribe. In cases of formation
of definite corporate organizations, this may be seen in the nature

of the enrollment; the boy may leave his family household to join a group most of whose members may come from distant places and thus be entirely unknown to him. Their common bonds are the commonly shared qualities of belonging to a certain general classificatory age category, but not their personal relations to one another. It is worth while to note here that age group solidarity is different from, and sometimes even opposed to, a particularistic personal relationship existing in many tribes—that of a "best friend."[84] Among the Gusii there exists a sharp difference between the respect relations the individual owes to senior kin members and to members of senior age sets. The former are based on mutuality and complementarity, while the latter are more of a one-sided privilege which emphasizes the absoluteness of age distinctions.[85] This difference between kinship and age group relations can also be seen in the general patterning of role expectations and role performance inculcated through this membership. This may be seen in both noncorporate age groups (or perhaps even more pronouncedly among them, such as the Nuer, the Dorobo, the Bantu Kavirondo) and the various types of corporate groups. As we have seen, the most general attitude inculcated in these groups is that of equality and solidarity among age mates and respect towards members of senior age groups. These attitudes are divested of any specific and personal connotation, and are given a completely impersonal meaning. These attitudes or patterns of behavior must be expressed towards any member of the ascriptive age category or age group, without reference to any previous personal relations. The clearest example of this is the transformation of kinship terminology with regard to age mates and age seniors(juniors), an extension that we find among the Nuer, Bantu Kavirondo, Kipsigi, etc., and among the Plains Indians. Here all age mates are called "brothers," or seniors, "fathers" (juniors, "sons"), and many of the rules of exogamy apply to them. And yet this extension of kinship terminology is different from the usual kind. It loses its special kinship relation to ego, its linking with ego's specific biological relations towards parents and siblings. Kinship terms here become a more general connotation appropriate to any member of the society within the same age category.

Through this extension the kinship connotation becomes to some extent depersonalized, divorced from the limitations of personal and face-to-face relations. The transfer of identification involved in this extension necessarily involves a severance of the specifically personal attachment to the bearers of these kinship terms (parents, siblings, etc.), instead of a smooth personal extension.

Besides this difference between the kinship groups and age groups, there is another important difference in the *internal* organization of each age group (or set). While the general criteria of membership in age groups and relations between age groups are necessarily particularistic, as they relate to certain qualities (age) which people have in relation to other people, the internal allocation of roles is different. In most of the societies hitherto analyzed, the internal allocation of roles and tasks within the formal age groups is mostly universalistic, and sometimes, although usually to a very limited extent, also achievement-oriented. Most of the tasks within them are allocated either indiscriminately to every member or according to universalistic criteria of competence. While the small group of children and adolescents which forms the nucleus of the total age group is, like any other primary group, strongly particularistically oriented, the overall internal allocation of roles within the age group is mostly universalistic. In this respect the age group also differs from the family and kin group, and membership in it involves a transition from the latter type of groups.

This transition, connected as it may be with severance of personal relations, is effected through strong emphasis on the solidarity of the age groups and through identification with it. All age groups stress and organize such solidarity, firmly emphasizing the priority of the group's collective goals and limiting the sphere of enjoyment of individual goals. The mutual obligations of the members are usually manifold, and claim priority—whether it is a matter of help, hospitality (even, in extreme cases, lending of wives, as among the Nandi), loyalty, or upholding the honor and name of the group in various group activities, such as warfare, public works, etc. Where the age groups are not organized corporatively, this solidarity and loyalty manifest themselves in various ritual observances, during ceremonies and the ceremonial partaking of meals (each grade receives a specified portion of the food), at which the cohesiveness of the group and its distinctness from other age groups are expressed.[86]

This solidarity is expressed, first, through the primacy of diffuse and expressive roles in relations between age mates. These relations, in almost every type of primitive age groups, necessarily involve many specific and instrumental orientations and activities, such as help in various tasks, assistance on certain specified occasions, etc. These instrumental and specific roles are not, however, given primacy within the age groups. They are usually symbolic expressions or concrete manifestations of an overall attitude, which defines most general mutual obligations and which provides expressive gratifications. The individual strives for the response of his age mate because of the totality of experience it involves, because such a response, being an expression of full social acceptance, strengthens his self-identity, and not because of any specific, instrumental gain. Mutual identification with age mates gratifies the individual's need for acceptance, and for continuity of attachment. This is most clearly manifested in the case of extension of kinship terminology to age relations, but can also be discerned in all the other types of age groups—in the broad definition of mutual help and assistance and in the life-long bond that is usually maintained between the age mates—whether institutionalized in corporate progression from one grade to another or patterned in less formal ways.[87]

Secondly, then, the solidarity of the age groups is strongly emphasized by becoming a condition for the development of the individual's full identity and for his personality integration. The various symbols of status, of participation in a new situation, are here, as we have seen, conditioned on participation in the group. This connection is most evident in another universal trait of all age groups, namely, self-discipline. Whatever the ultimate degree of age group autonomy at the small group level, self-discipline and corporate responsibility are always maintained.[88] This self-discipline is of crucial importance for the development of self-evaluation and ego identity, as it relates the personal experiences of the individual to the goals and values of the community, and helps him (and the group) internalize them.

Thus, age groups are everywhere composed of clusters of primary groups with a strong degree of solidarity, cohesion and mutual identification. Even when the whole age group system is very formalized, as among the Nandi group, the Galla, the Masai, and among the age regiments of the Swazi, Zulu and Tswana, the small solidary group forms its essential nucleus and the solidarity of the whole system is based on an extension of the identification engendered in this small group.[89]

All these characteristics of age groups are obviously related to our main hypothesis, and show the importance of these groups for the development of the individual's identity and personality integration, and its relation to the inadequacy of the family and kinship structure, with its basic age-heterogeneous relations. A brief comparison with kinship-regulated societies will throw these functions of the age groups into sharp relief. Within these societies the embryonic children's groups, with their emphasis on co-operation and their sometimes preparatory character in relation to adult life, do not become formalized and articulated into special cohesive groups. They are of secondary importance for the development of the individual's personality and identity. They are important in so far as they broaden, to some extent, the scope of the individual's relations, and teach him some of the basic moral rules of behavior and cooperation. But they do not serve as frameworks for the formation of his identity, which is attained through basic identification with the kin groups. Even if continuous relations with parents are strained, or temporarily changed, during the period of initiation, eventually the individual returns to his family and there attains full maturity. It is as a member of his family group that he performs various role vis-à-vis other units of the society and becomes integrated within its bounds. Whether he is a member and representative of a "primitive" lineage[90] or of a traditional peasant society,[91] his full identity is achieved only through interaction within his family (kin) unit and gradual progress through the age scale, in which he interacts mainly with people of other age grades and gradually incorporates their role dispositions into his own personality.

Here we may inquire what happens to the basic complementariness of age images in age-grouped societies. We have postulated this complementariness as a basic factor for the maintenance of the continuity and stability of the social system. It has already been emphasized that age grouping itself presupposes the existence of several age groups and age differences. These differences are, however, structured in a special way in age-grouped societies. Although the details vary, of course, from one place to another, some general, broad contours may be discerned. First, there is a stronger emphasis on the differences and discontinuities between various age grades. This may also be seen in the stronger dichotomizing of sexual relations and attitudes, as mentioned earlier in relation to family life. Thus the transition from one age grade to another becomes articulated in special *"rites de passage" which are performed among the total membership of the given generations, or their representatives,* and not among the representatives of these generations within particularistic family units. The transition is not dispersed over many units (groups), and consequently over a highly irregular period of time, but is articulated at certain intermittent, periodic moments which are common to the whole society. The succession of one age group by another, generally concomitant with the interchange of generations, becomes a universal ceremony including all the members of the society, juxtaposing the different generations by their mutual relations. This affects the whole gamut of relations between different generations in these societies. These relations are not confined within the scope of family and kinship units, but extend over the whole population of the tribe. They entail a combination of respect towards the elder generation, in the hands of which authority and power are concentrated, with a strong potential hostility to it. This hostility, which is connected with the strong emphasis on the differences between various age grades, becomes more acute when the time comes for one generation (age group) to succeed another in the positions of authority and power. This can be found among the Nandi, Kipsigi, Masai, etc.

Within most of these societies this element of hostility is, however, fully sanctioned and legitimized by the usages of society. The complementarity of age differences and of age images and the passage of generations is thus enacted, combining the possibility of individual catharsis with legitimate allocation of roles and legitimate ideological contrast. In a way this hostility performs a function similar to the "joking relationships," albeit a more important one. The similarity, although it should not be carried too far, is sometimes strongly manifested when relations between nonadjacent age groups are patterned after relations between grandfathers and grandchildren—one of the most widespread types of joking relations.[92] In this way the individual's transition from one generation to another is smoothly effected. In the various ceremonies connected with this transition the individuals transform their identity and assume the new age image; they begin to behave towards the age group below them in the same way that the older age group behaved towards them. In this way the complementariness of age images is articulated in the relations between generations and symbolizes their smooth interaction, and the basic attitudes of respect towards elder groups and the acceptance of their authority are also, in a general way, maintained in these societies.

This brings us to a point which is of crucial importance for the analysis of age groups in the hitherto discussed primitive societies. In these societies, with a partial exception of Athens in the fourth century B.C., the importance of age groups from the point of view of the individual's personality development is matched by their complete institutionalization within the social system, and their function as bases for institutional allocation of roles and for the maintenance of the solidarity of the social system. This can be seen in the way in which the small primary group of adolescents is interwoven within the formalized age group hierarchy. In this way the age groups serve as meeting points between the personality systems of their members and the social system, being articulated in terms of one another. In so far as we can judge from the literature, the compatibility of the two is almost complete.[93] This may first be seen in the fact that the overall, tribal definition of membership in them was not only a tendency, inherent in the need dispositions of the individual members for the attainment of their identities; but effectively binding on all members of the society, unifying within their fold all of the appropriate (ascriptively categorized) people, and cutting across all "parochial" kinship, local, etc., units. Secondly, these groups and criteria serve as foci of mutual categorization of people, and thus as one of the most important mechanisms of allocation of roles and rewards; i.e., also as integrative mechanisms. The fully institutionalized allocation of roles has been frequently mentioned and exemplified above. It assumes different manifestations in various societies, but the general picture is similar: definite roles of highest importance from the point of view of the social system and the concomitant rewards of prestige, authority, etc., with them, are ascribed to members of various age groups. Thus age group membership both regulates the flow of facilities available to any individual, and at the same time, through the distribution of rewards, gears his action to precisely ascribed roles. The solidarity of the age group system in these societies is not a purely internal affair; it forms a basis for the solidarity of the entire social system. Through these allocative processes the primacy of collectivity orientation is extended to the entire social system. This may be achieved either through making age group relations regulate the whole scope of social relations, or through making the age groups of smaller social scope (as among the Ibo, Yako) identify themselves with community-oriented goals and perform various communal tasks.

The importance of age groups for the maintenance of the solidarity of the society can be clearly seen both in some of their educational functions and in the important part they always play in tribal ceremonies. From the educational point of view it should be stressed that the different age groups, age regiments, etc., serve not only as transmitters of knowledge and tribal lore, but also as channels of social communication, through which members of the tribe meet with its chiefs, and participate, whether actively or as spectators, in tribal discussions, judgments, etc.[94] As for the ceremonies, in some cases, e.g., among the Nuba and the Nandi groups, the age groups are the most important participants, while among the Yako they also constitute important elements in these ceremonies. In all of these tribes the inauguration of an age set (or the transfer of government to a given age set) takes place in a "tribe-wide" ceremony.[95] These variations depend, as we shall see, on the extent to which other integrative mechanisms exist within the social system, and will be analyzed in subsequent chapters. But these variations do not affect the basic integrative role of age groups within these societies, an integrative role which has always been successfully juxtaposed with that of the family and kin group in kin societies.

This description of the functions of age groups both in the development of the individual and in the cohesion of the social system does not explain the conditions under which they occur. This explanation, which alone can furnish a full functional analysis, will be attempted in the last chapters of this book.

IX   We shall now turn to a systematic analysis of the emergence of age groups within the framework of various modern societies. "Modern society,"[96] which as we have already pointed out is only a synonym for highly differentiated societies, constitutes the fullest example of a universalistically regulated society. It is within the institutional framework of modern societies that the fullest implications of universalistic criteria for allocation of roles and of universalistic value orientations have been worked out institutionally. Consequently, it is also within the framework of modern societies that the great variety and complexity of age and youth groups can be discerned and analyzed—a variety and complexity which are both similar to and different from that of the hitherto discussed primitive societies.

Our task will, then, be to analyze in broad lines the relation between these institutional arrangements of modern societies and the various types of age and youth groups. It should, however, be obvious that the term "modern society" (with its institutional implications) denotes but an "ideal type," constructed out of various elements the distribution of which varies to a very great extent in various concrete cases.[97]

We shall first analyze, in general terms, those aspects of modern societies which are most relevant to our problem and hypothesis; and, secondly, the relative distribution of these significant aspects within various sectors of modern societies and their relation to the emergence of age and youth groups.

Almost all of the main criteria of a universalistically regulated society enumerated at the beginning of this chapter hold true in modern societies, and find their fullest realization within various modern societies. Their inclusive membership is usually based on universalistic criteria of "citizenship," and not conditioned by membership in any kin or particularistic group (except, of course, in so far as loyalty to a given total community as such constitutes a definitely particularistic value[98]). The family or kin unit does not constitute a basic unit of political and/or ritual activities. Economic specialization is organized in universalistically governed groups, and not, as for instance in the caste regime of India, within particularistic groups wider than the family. The family does not constitute a basic unit of the economic division of labor, especially not in production and distribution, and even in consumption to a lesser extent than in other societies. Moreover, the general scope of the family's activities is constantly diminishing, and various specialized agencies are, to some extent at least, taking over its function in the fields of education, nursing, recreation, etc.[99] The extent and scope of relations which are regulated according to kinship criteria is very small and, to a very large extent, not clearly defined.[100]

It should, of course, be emphasized that even in modern societies not all the sectors of society are regulated according to universalistic criteria. Here also many spheres—neighborhood, friendship, informal associations, some class relations and participation in a common style of life, ethnic and community relations—may be and are regulated according to various particularistic criteria. But the scope of these relations is, in these societies, more limited than in many others, and in the main institutional spheres of society universalistic criteria are much more prevalent. It should also be mentioned, as we shall see in greater detail later, that the extent to which universalistic criteria prevail differs from one sector of modern society to another. On the whole, however, modern societies are the purest type of nonkinship, universalistically organized societies.

The extremity of the nonkinship allocation of roles and institutional regulation within the modern (especially urban) society gives rise to a distinct segregation of family life (especially in its age-heterogeneous, parents-children relations) from other institutional spheres. The parent-children (and adolescents) roles enacted within the modern family are not only, as in other nonkinship societies, different in their general value orientations and organizational patterns from those of the other institutional spheres of the social system. They are also segregated to a very large extent from any roles enacted in the main institutional spheres of the adult society. The parents enact roles vis-à-vis their children which differ largely from those that they (and especially the father) perform in other institutional spheres. The discontinuity between the world of children and that of the adults may become sharpened and emphasized by this type of role organization.[101]

Accordingly, the difference between the particularistic family structure and the universalistic (and achievement-oriented) occupational and other nonfamilial spheres is also sharpened, and becomes very strong and complex, although it differs greatly in various sectors of modern societies. Owing to the limitation of the social spheres of the family and to the main value orientations of significant sectors of modern societies (particularly the "middle-class" achievement and individualistically oriented sectors) relations within the family are charged with deep emotion and characterized by strong emotional interdependence, with a very strong element of internalization of the parents' images. It is this strong internalization of the parents' images that may serve for the children as the first bridge to adult society. Through it the child may identify itself, in a general way, not only with the concrete roles of his parents in the family, but also with their general disposition and roles in other spheres. While such an internalization does not, in itself, diminish the segregation of the family from other spheres, it may, if successful, provide the first basis for an orientation and transition to these spheres.

All these characteristics of modern families and societies have given rise to various kinds of youth- (age-) oriented groups and agencies. These agencies and groups have grown with the development of modern economic and political systems, a development which was gradual and uneven in various societies and their sectors.

Unlike, however, in all the primitive and most of the historical (with the exception of Athens and the Hellenistic cities) societies, no one unitary organization of age groups can be found in modern societies. We may distinguish between three main types of such groups and agencies which develop within modern societies. The first is the educational school system, the second are various adult-sponsored youth agencies and the third are spontaneous youth groups. These three types usually develop concurrently, although in some cases they (especially the second type) may be absent. All of them develop in connection with the various problems stemming from the development of modern economic and political, etc., systems and their repercussions on family and youth life. From that point of view they may be seen as one system. But at the same time there exists a significant differentiation between them. Some are organized by adults, and aim at the preparation of children for their adult roles and the smooth transference of the social heritage; others are more spontaneously developed by the children themselves to satisfy their own needs. While there is a constant interaction and interdependence between these various types of youth groups and agencies, there does not always exist a full complementarity and harmony between them. It is highly significant that in modern societies, unlike even in the historical societies, there is a great dissociation between the educational system and other forms of youth groups and agencies. The analysis of the relations between them, and the factors which influence these relations—and foremost among them the family—is one of our main concerns in this section, as well as in other places in the book.

This transition to the universalistic sphere of adult society is, however, here much more difficult and complicated than in other societies. These difficulties are inherent in the structure of family relations and may often be accentuated because this transition involves, in particular, severance from the mother and her image—attachment to whom has necessarily been very strong, albeit at the same time ambivalent—because of her relative confinement to the family sphere and formally lower position in the authority structure.[102]

X   *The school system.* Economic and professional specialization in modern societies is based on an accumulation of technical knowledge, the transmission of which lies beyond the powers of any family, and also necessitates a period of learning and preparation, the length of which is usually directly related to the extent of specialization. This also holds true of many aspects of ideological, philosophical and religious knowledge, the acquisition of which constitutes a necessary prerequisite for the performance of many roles and for the attainment of full membership and status within the total society. The transmission of this knowledge is effected in special, institutionalized, educational organizations—the schools. While various types of professional and educational schools exist in many societies, it is only in modern societies (and perhaps to some extent in certain sectors of the societies of classical antiquity[103]) that they have gradually become an almost universal institutional device for the transmission of knowledge necessary for the attainment of full social status. Their first distinct characteristic is that, unlike the so-called initiation schools of the primitives, they organize the life of children for a long period of time, usually for several years. The second basic characteristic is their very strong technical-preparatory emphasis.

Their universal institutional importance clearly bears witness to the shrinkage of the family's scope of activities, and to the inadequacy of the family as the sole educational agency. In other words, they arise because family and kinship age-heterogeneous relations cannot ensure the smooth and continuous transmission of knowledge and role dispositions. The social structure and the sphere of the school is obviously distinct from that of the family, and necessarily involves a different way of organizing relations between the various generations. The school society, becoming more formalized, is organized on the basis of age-homogeneous groups, which interact with each other and particularly with representatives of the adult society (teachers) more or less corporately, in an organized way. The world of the school is a world of clearly defined age groups (grades, classes) which form a unitary heterocephalous hierarchy directed and oriented by specialized representatives of the adult world. Thus age grading within the school has, as it were, a dual differentiation. There is, first, the internal differentiation between different classes within the total hierarchy, and secondly, juxtaposition of the total organization of children and adolescents with adult society and its representatives who are the bearers of power and authority within the system.[104]

The internal age differentiation of the school society is primarily due to the exigencies of adapting the psychological (and to some extent also physiological) learning potential of the child to the various skills and knowledges which must be acquired by him.[105] The formal, official differentiation of school grades and classes is defined mostly in terms of advanced skills and knowledge: The overall juxtaposition of school life with adult society is defined in modern societies, more emphatically than in any other society, in terms of "preparation" for adulthood. The roles which are institutionally allocated to school children of various grades and ages are definitely preparatory; i.e., they are evaluated mainly in terms of their contribution to some future status, and do not constitute ends in themselves, or manifestations of full status and membership in the community. Age-heretogeneous relations within the school, between teacher and pupils, tend to emphasize the basic discontinuity between the social sphere of children and that of adults and the great difference in power and authority that exists between them. This preparation has both symbolical and technical aspects, and in so far as the symbolical aspects prevail, it entails a great extent of segregation—from the adult world. (In so far as purely technical aspects prevail, as for instance, in various technical schools, the exclusion from adult society is usually less marked.) In this respect the formalized age grouping of the modern school differs from formalized age grouping in any other society.

That is why the relation of the school to the family and to the total society is a very peculiar one. On the one hand, it constitutes the first stage of transition from family life to a universalistically regulated society. The school's universalistic orientation is obvious, and finds its fullest expression in bringing children of various separate families together. Within its basically age-ascriptive framework it also develops—to some extent parallel to the family, but much more intensively—within the children role dispositions for achievement orientation and for identification with universalistic values and symbols of identification. Through the persons of the teachers it also extends, in some measure, the children's identification with a wider cluster of adults, and gradually changes the nature of this identification from a very particularistic and personal one to a more universalistic and impersonal one.[106] On the other hand, however, it constitutes, together with the family, a children's world, segregated from that of the adults. This situation is explained by the fact that the adults who participate in this world enact roles which are specifically oriented towards it, and distinct from other roles in adult society. They specialize in dealing with children. And the very strong emphasis on "preparation" towards the adult world only emphasizes the segregation from this world.

This emphasis on preparation entails yet another problem. It usually involves the postponement of social maturity beyond the attainment of physiological and sexual maturity. The longer the period of preparation necessary for the achievement of any specialized task, the longer the corollary postponement of the establishment of a new family of procreation. Owing to the great stress on preparation for specialization and learning of various skills, the fact of sexual maturation does not receive as much symbolical recognition and ideological evaluation within the formal age culture of the school as it receives within most primitive age groups. It is usually vaguely defined and does not find prominent expression in the value system of the school.

This situation, of course, constitutes yet another difficulty in the transfer of identification from the family to the total society through the school, and in the development of the adolescent child's identity.[107] Because of all these factors, the age grading and culture of the school, the goals set up by it and the roles enacted within it do not usually constitute—within modern societies or within certain of their sectors—adequate objects for those needs which arise within the child's and adolescent's personality at the period of transition from the family to the total society. For this reason the child and adolescent always develops, although to various degrees, the predisposition to join in age groups in which the dignity of his current dispositions and values will be affirmed, within which a greater spontaneity of activities will be permitted, and which in some cases will also have a more direct relation to the symbols of identification of a total society, either the existing one or a new one to which he would like to develop. However varied the different age groups, peer groups, youth movements, etc., of various modern societies may be in their composition, organization, values, etc., the first two above-mentioned features are always characteristic of them, and, in certain cases, also the third. Even if they are concretely connected with the school, they are always somewhat distinct from it.[108] It is very interesting to note here that even in those societies which have established overall, institutionalized youth organizations (e.g., the U.S.S.R. and Nazi Germany), these youth movements are distinct from the school, however much they may be related to it in practice. Only under very specific conditions does the school system succeed in organizing all, or most of the life, of the children and youth, within the scope of the school. One such instance with which we shall deal in great detail later on, is the "classical" English Public Schools.[109] Another example can be found in the various "progressive" trends of education where there has been an attempt to encompass the whole of the children's life by establishing "children's republics." In all these cases, however, school life is infused with elements and relations which differ from those oriented to the distinct preparatory and specializing educational activities of the school system.

XI   The inadequacy of an educational system relying on the school as the sole instrument for dealing with *all* of the problems of youth gave rise to the second main type of youth organizations—the youth-oriented agency. This type includes various specialized agencies, sponsored by the institutional official representatives of the society to deal with youth and its problem.

The number and variety of the adult-sponsored youth organizations and agencies is legion, and there is no need to give a full list here. It will be enough here to give a very brief and general classification. First, we find various youth organizations and groups whose main aim is to find an outlet for the energies of youth by channeling them into various recreative and cultural activities, ranging from special recreational clubs to groups like the Scouts, Girl Guides, etc. All these groups, in addition to providing various recreative facilities, aim at molding the general character development of youth, at instilling various civic virtues in order to deepen their social consciousness and widen their social and cultural horizon. The most outstanding examples of this type are the YMCA, the Youth Brigades organized in England by W. Smith, Country Clubs and other types of youth clubs in cities, many of which are connected with religious and political groups, the Boy Scouts, the Jousters in France, the various types of community organizations and hostels of vocational guidance centers, etc. Secondly, there are many such organizations sponsored by specific political and religious organizations which, in addition to providing the above-mentioned facilities and instilling general virtues into the new generation, aim also at binding them to their own specific goals, at either maintaining or developing their loyalty to the specific party or group.[110] In short, in European countries, as well as in various colonial countries and in Israel, we find that most of the political parties and religious organizations attempt to organize various youth clubs and movements. Thirdly, there are agencies which deal with "problem children" of various kinds—delinquents, underdeveloped and underprivileged children—provide them with various facilities for adjusting themselves to what is supposed to be the normal condition of children within their specific societies.[111]

One may perhaps add, as a borderline case, between the second and the third type, the various vocational agencies and organizations whose aim it is to help children and adolescents, particularly those coming from underprivileged economic sectors, to advance professionally. The working-youth movements of Continental Europe (especially Germany) and of Israel constitute part of this category.[112]

All these organizations have in common the assumption that the complete integration of youth into society, the successful transition within the scope of the family from childhood to full, adequate citizenship and participation in community life can be effected only through allocating specific roles to youth and to adolescents, stressing their common youth-adolescent identity, and bringing them together in common life experiences. At the same time they stress the importance of expressive activities in the attainment of these goals and the importance of emphasis on orientations to common, ultimate values of the community.*[113]

The following excerpt from W. Smith's Manifesto about his Youth Brigades put before Church authorities is very typical:

He laid before the Mission authorities his scheme for banding together the boys of school above the age of twelve into a "Brigade," in which they would be taught elementary drill, physical exercises, obedience to the word of command, punctuality, and cleanliness. It would be something they could regard as distinctively their own, to which they would become attached, and of which they would be so proud that they would be ashamed to do anything that might bring discredit upon it. Thus would be engendered that *esprit de corps* which public-school boys acquire as a matter of course, but which was almost entirely lacking in elementary schoolboys. Organized games would follow, and he believed that the outcome would be discipline and order in the Sunday School, the retention of the older boys (who in the ordinary course would cease to attend as soon as they became wage-earners), and increased interest in school and church. . . .

Different clubs and youth organizations laid different emphases on the various aspects of youth life and activities. Some—like the Brigades, various para-military organizations, Cadets, etc.—laid great emphasis on physical training, others on "spiritual" religious, etc., values, still others on conviviality, on sports, excursions, etc. But all of them paid some attention to most of the aspects mentioned, and wanted to provide full facilities for their realization. It was in this way that they thought to supplement formal education and to imbue youth with civic consciousness.

---

* A full list of such youth groups and organizations can be found in the various publications cited in references 112, 113 and 114 of this chapter. among working-class youth usually cover a shorter period of life, and become one of the mechanisms of secondary institutionalization.

The development of all these agencies and organizations is historically connected with the growing impact of industrialization and urbanization, with the so-called later stages of the Industrial Revolution, when very wide strata of population became involved in these processes.[114] Some developed as agencies for working and slum youth (various clubs and settlement houses), some—like the YMCA, etc.—in answer to various needs of the growing middle classes. In the United States the development of these agencies was connected with the continuous influx of immigrants, the evolution of metropolitan centers, etc.—in other words, all those processes which indicate the expansion of universalistic criteria and the diminution of the family's sphere of life.

Side by side with the development of special youth agencies we witness also a development of the conception of a special "youth problem" in the main spheres of cultural activity in Europe and the United States—in literature, art, educational thought, etc. The beginning of these developments may be traced perhaps to Rousseau, to the main trends of European, and especially German, Romanticism.[115] The consciousness of youth vs. old age and of the whole problem of generations could be traced in most literary and artistic movements, and in the great plethora of new trends and schools. The problems of youth, its place in life, its being the fullest expression of vitality—or decadence— the problems of strife between generations were evident in most of the main literary trends of the nineteenth and twentieth centuries, and even special types of literary works were developed to deal with it.

In educational thought the problem of adolescence and youth was developed and stressed in the works of Stanley Hall and his numerous followers. In social thought—especially in France and Germany—the problem of relations between generations and of their educational and moral repercussions was widely discussed, finding its apogee in K. Mannheim's brilliant essay.[116]

In most cases all these developments were very closely connected with periods of social upheaval, rapid change and spread of universalistic orientations and organizations.

Side by side with the development of these various adult-
XII   sponsored youth agencies, a great development and intensification of spontaneous youth life and spontaneous
youth groups takes place. These are not in themselves, of course,
entirely new developments. Children's groups, play groups, etc.,
which are universal in all human societies were also abundant in
rural and urban Europe before the rise of industrialism, as all
the chronicles of the past tell us most clearly. They performed
also those general functions which we have analyzed before.

But with the development of industrialism and of modern
political systems, and with the growing limitation of the scope
of the family, their scope and vitality are intensified. They become more numerous; they extend over a much longer period
of time—till late adolescence; they become much more solidary
and self-conscious; they become more and more important in
the lives of their members and of the community as a whole.
They exhibit a great variety, and we shall not dwell on them
here in any great detail. Some of their most pertinent characteristics have been described in Chapter II.

We have seen various forms of organizations—informal play
groups, juvenile gangs, autonomous recreaitonal groups, student
organizations, organized rebellious youth movements of the
German and Continental type. Within all these groups, as we
shall see in greater detail below, common youth consciousness
and the importance of expressive activities, are heavily stressed.
A strong predisposition for orientation to common values, and
generally also a demand for a specific allocation of roles on the
basis of age homogeneity and community of experiences, are
also noticeable.

These various youth groups may be roughly classified according to the following criteria, indicating their relative importance
both for the individual and for the society: (a) The scope of
activities they cover; (b) the extent of their internal cohesion
and corporate organization; (c) the extent of conformity with
institutional roles or of deviancy from them; (d) the extent of
ideological conformity or rebellion and (e) the extent to which
adults or elder adolescents participate in them.

The interlinking of these spontaneous role expectations on the part of youth with those allocated to them by the adult-sponsored agencies is not, in modern societies, a simple and harmonious process. Such interlinking may take place and succeed in various sectors of modern society, and the goals and activities set up by the educational system authority and the adult-sponsored organization may be found adequate for the need dispositions of the youth. And yet, because of all the above-enumerated reasons (and particularly the emphasis on preparation in many of these organizations), the mutual compatibility between the adolescents' attitudes and the roles allocated to them by the adult-sponsored organizations is not automatically effected, and constitutes one of the main problems of modern societies. Because of this also (as well as for some other reasons), it is within the orbit of modern society that the deviant tendencies and orientations of age groups may attain such scope. All these problems will be systematically investigated in the coming chapters. Here we only intended to show the general relation between the development of modern universalistic societies and the various types of youth groups.

XIII   The connection between the development of "modern" social systems and the emergence of age groups can be seen in many instances. First, this connection can be seen in European society's transition from feudalism and absolutism to the modern universalistic and industrialized society. All the historical data show us how new, universalistic, educational systems and agencies and spontaneous youth groups developed during this transition. This can be seen in the rapid educational development in England in the 19th century, and in parallel developments in other European countries.[117] It can also be seen in the development of various spontaneous youth groups, in Students' Movements, in various ideological and semi-political movements and youth rebellions connected with the Romantic Movement in Europe and especially in Germany. The various social and national movements of the 19th and 20th centuries also gave rise to various types of youth organizations, youth consciousness, etc., as evidenced in such movements as Mazzini's "Young Europe," etc.

The same applies to the emergence of the German youth movement following the rapid transformation which took place during the post-Bismarckian era.[118]

Of special interest from the point of view of our analysis, are the various instances of recorded and analyzed situations of "culture contact," which occurred both in the recent past and in the present. Among these situations of culture contact the impact of Western civilization on various primitive and traditional societies and cultures should be first mentioned, and also the transplantation of members of various particularistic, traditional societies into a "modern" industrial setting, mostly through migration.[119]

The literature on culture contact, on the impact of Western civilization on primitive peoples, repeatedly describes the disruption of family life which results from this impact. This disruption not only takes on various forms of family disorganization, etc., but always involves a change in the mutual evaluation of the generations as well—some extent of rebellion of the younger members of the family against the social roles imposed on them in relation to the authority of the older members. Within the former traditional social setting they were able to evolve their identity through specific forms of interaction with the members of elder generations; in the new situation, however, this interaction no longer provides them with such security. On the one hand, they may have been given access to various facilities for performance of roles which were barred from them in the traditional setting, or such as are inaccessible to the older generation, e.g., earning money in exacting manual labor, etc. On the other hand, general cultural orientations transmitted from the older members to the younger ones are inadequate for full orientation within the new situation. It may well be that no such fully integrating orientations and principles develop at all; but in any event the old orientations are obviously inadequate, and the elder members are no longer adequate symbols of role disposition within the new setting. The younger people usually start a search for new identification, and at one phase or another this search is expressed in terms of ideological conflict with the older generation as such, of the ideological identification of youth, of young people as a distinct cultural category. Whether this rebellion really gives rise to new integration of the personality, or whether it results in a failure of ego integrity[120] is immaterial at this point of our discussion. The important point is that the transition from a particularistic to a universalistic setting gives rise to a specific "youth" or "age" ideology and identification. The extent to which such identification forms a basis for cohesive social groupings varies, but to some extent it always does form such a basis.

A very important example of such ideological and social transformation may be seen in some processes of social change in modern China, and in the transformation of the traditional Chinese society. Within that society, which constituted one of the most clear-cut examples of a relatively complex society integrated by particularistic kin criteria, the relative seniority of various age groups *within* the family unit was very much emphasized. The whole kinship structure of Chinese society was regulated to some extent by this principle, and differences between the various age grades within the family and kin unit were strongly stressed.[121] These differences were stressed, however, within a setting of mutual interaction. With the transformation of the traditional Chinese society under the impact of Western ideological, economic and military processes, which have necessarily given rise to more individualistic and universalistic ideas and criteria of social action, we witness increasing stress on absolute age, and on the growing common identification of the *ch'ing-nien* (the young adults). This common identification has served as the basis for many active social groupings, which formed parts of the incipient Chinese youth movement and of various social and political movements.

A similar development can be traced in the disintegration of the traditional Jewish community—one of the most familistic societies known—under the impact of emancipation and modern commercial and industrial development. Even in the traditional, familistic society, various youth groups of "bakhurei yeshiva" (youngsters of the college) would be formed in those centers of learning which drew students from many localities and in this way took them out of the familistic setting. With more modern developments within the traditional society, these groups developed even more distinct youth ideology and activities. Later these groups also formed the nucleus of numerous Jewish Socialist and Zionist group activities.[122]

Similar developments can be found in most non-European countries which felt the impact of Western institutions. Most of the nationalistic movements in the Middle East, in India, Indonesia,[123] etc., consisted of young people, quite often students, or young officers who rebelled against their elders, against the traditional familistic setting in which there existed a very strong emphasis on the authority of elders. They tried to develop new social values and groups, and within most of these movements there was a very strong emphasis on a specific youth consciousness and youth ideology. In fact, the need to "rejuvenate" the country was strongly emphasized by these nationalistic movements.

One of the most striking examples of the emergence of youth and age groups through transition from a particularistic to a universalistic social setting may be seen in centers of migration, especially in the United States.

The importance of the "peer group" among immigrant children is a very well-known phenomenon, which usually appears in the second generation of immigrants. It is mainly due to the relative "breakdown," or, rather, shrinkage of the family life of immigrants within the countries of absorption; and the more highly these countries (or those sectors within which the immigrants are absorbed) are industrialized and urbanized, i.e., regulated according to universalistic criteria, the sharper the breakdown. This shrinkage and limitation is due mainly to two interdependent factors: (a) the limitation of the effective capacity of family life and relations caused by the necessity to concentrate most of the available energy on various problems of adjustment to the new country, i.e., the diminished capacity of (mainly) the parents to fulfill adequately their family roles; and (b) the general, more permanent trend of transplantation into a society where (unlike the situation in most of the immigrants' countries of origin, especially that of the peasants) the family does not constitute a basic unit of the division of labor and where its general sphere of activities is much more limited.

From the point of view of the immigrant or second generation child, his family of orientation is inadequate as a general point of orientation towards the new social structure. On the one hand, the parents' status images and cultural orientation generally dif- guidance of their children as the latter need. On the other hand, the parents' status-images and cultural orientation generally dif- fer from those accepted within their new social setting, and even under the most favorable conditions they can serve only as basic, general symbols of role predispositions, and not as guides to con- crete roles and role expectations within the new social setting. The attainment of full ego identity within the new country is, among immigrant children, definitely connected with a detach- ment from the setting of their family of orientation and a stronger identification with the universalistic patterns of the new country.[124] For this reason there arises among some of them a very strong predisposition to join various "peer groups" which may sometimes facilitate their transition to the absorbing society by stressing—both in their composition and in their activities— the more universalistic patterns (and achievement orientation) of the new society or which may express their rebellion against this society. Within such groups a distinctive youth ideology develops, sometimes stressing the distinctiveness of "American- ized" youth in relation to their immigrant parents, or on the other hand, stressing their rebellion against the new society and their rather romantic attachment to their old culture. While the dis- position to participation in "peer groups," "youth cultures," exists in most sectors of American society, it seems to be espe- cially noticeable among immigrant children.[125]

Here, as in the above-mentioned instances of culture contact, these dispositions may give rise either to a new ego integration and identification or to ego and personality breakdown; but what is important for our discussion is the fact that in these cases no adequate ego integrity can be attained within family and age- heterogeneous relations.

The same connection between immigration from particularistic societies to universalistic ones and the emergence of youth movements, etc., is clearly seen in Israel, among the legitimate youth movements and especially among the so-called Oriental Jews, i.e., those who come from the nontraditional and particularistic setting of the Jewish communities of the Ottoman Empire, and among whom the percentage of juvenile delinquency, etc., is greatest.[126]

We have seen above that the development of various types XIV   of youth groups and youth-oriented agencies broadly follows the development of a universalistic, achievement- and specificity-oriented division of labor in modern societies.

But we may go beyond the establishment of such general correlations, based on historical material on the one hand, and studies of culture contact on the other. The material at our disposal, although not always very systematic, lends itself to a more detailed analysis, which is important for the further elaboration of our general hypothesis. We may study the distribution of age (youth) groups in various sectors of modern societies, and analyze the relation between the degrees of their importance and cohesion, etc., and the extent of prevalence of various institutional derivatives of universalistic role allocation. While the general prevalence of such role allocation in modern societies, as compared with other societies, is clear, it does not mean that there exist no significant differences within the various sectors of modern societies. The extent of these differences may best be analyzed by means of comparison between the extent to which the family or kin unit still constitutes at least a semi-autarchic economic unit of production and of transmission of status.

Here we already encounter some other variables—such as specificity, and ascription or achievement—besides the basic difference between particularistic and universalistic criteria. Here, however, these additional variables are not treated and analyzed for themselves, but only in so far as they constitute institutional derivatives of the universalistic criterion. The specific ways in which these variables influence the structure and composition of age groups will be discussed in the following chapter.

If we analyze various sectors of modern society from the standpoint of our comparison, the most important difference is that between rural and urban sectors. It is obvious that within most rural sectors the relative importance of the family as a semi-autarchic unit of production, as the main property-owning unit, etc., is much greater than within urban traditional peasant communities of Europe,[127] French Canada[128] and various sectors of Latin America, while the importance of the family greater than within some more mechanized and market-oriented rural sectors of the United States.[129] When discussing the Israeli Kibbutz we shall see that the importance of the family unit is not necessarily connected with the *technical* requirements of the agriculture, as in the traditional patterning of rural life in Europe and the United States. If we compare, on the one hand, more traditional and less traditional rural sectors, and, on the other hand, rural sectors with urban and urbanized sectors of modern societies, we shall immediately see that the greater the "familism" the smaller the articulation of youth groups and of the "adolescent problem."

In rural sectors family transition at adolescence is not as acute as in urban centers. The life of the adolescent is apt to run within the framework of his family unit or a similar unit, and the postponement of social maturity owing to a long period of preparation is neither a very acute nor a pressing problem. Consequently there does not also arise the consciousness of specific age and youth problems, as in more modernized and urbanized sectors. The age groups that do arise take mainly the form of loose play groups, with very little stability or cohesion. It is only the formally organized age grading of the school that impinges on rural life to a very large extent, claiming, as it were, the dues of belonging to a universalistic society. But it has been shown in many researches that, in so far as the traditional "familism" of rural life maintains its hold, the impact of the age-graded school is not very significant; sometimes it even realizes fully the formal requirements; sometimes—more often—it does not leave any permanent traces on the social life of the community. It is only in proportion as the rural sectors becomes more and more mechanized and market- and achievement-oriented that the school can claim its full due.[130]

In general it may be said that in a period of rapid social mobility, industrialization always gives rise to a great plethora of youth groups, youth agencies and general consciousness of youth as a problem. There is plenty of relevant evidence from the United States of America, the U.S.S.R. and several other European countries. Similar consequences may be noticed when the scope of various universalistic agencies is widened—as for instance, in the raising of the school age in England.[131]

A systematic comparison directly related to our problem is afforded by an analysis of the distribution of various types of age groups and youth movements in the various sectors of Israeli society. It was shown there that the intensity and importance of youth group life is invariably correlated with the extent to which the family is the main unit of economic division of labor and social allocation of roles, and positively correlated with the formalization of the educational system, the prolongation of the schooling period, and the extension of the space between leaving the family of orientation and attaining full status within the family of procreation. Age groups are of almost no importance in the traditional and stable sectors of the Oriental Jews, among whom the community is still constituted, in a way, as a "federation" of extended families and family-centered synagogues. Age groups are still negligible in rural sectors based on private family ownership of land (the *Moshava*), somewhat more articulate in the family-based co-operative settlements (*Moshav Ovdim*), very much emphasized and varied in the urban sectors and in situations of culture contact between the Oriental and the more modern community (see above), and attain their fullest formalization and importance in the Kibbutz. It was also shown that the importance of age groups in the rural sectors has increased considerably with the weakening of their economic self-sufficiency, with the impossibility of settling all the sons on the land, and the necessity for broadening their occupational choices.[132]

Within the framework of rural Israeli society there exists another possibility of testing our hypothesis almost on an experimental level: namely, through comparison of the two main types of co-operative rural settlement in Israel: the communal settlement, the Kibbutz, and the co-operative settlement, the Moshav. Many of their social and economic characteristics may be treated as almost totally equivalent. Both these types of agricultural settlement are about 35-40 years old, and were formed by Zionist pioneers who have striven for the normalization of Jewish economic life and have conceived of work on the land as their highest ideal. In their conception the ideal of return to the land was coupled with that of social justice, of establishment of a social commonwealth—hence the co-operative and communal framework of their settlements, although there exists a stronger collectivist tendency in the communal settlements. The level of the settlements' development is roughly similar, both forms having developed relatively high mechanized techniques of cultivation, and attained similar levels of economic development and standard of living. Both forms have developed rapidly throughout the last 30 years, the number of settlements and members has grown, and a second—and sometimes even third—generation has grown up and stayed on the land. Both also have similar school systems which form part of the general educational system of the Jewish community in Israel. And yet they differ very markedly, both in their family organization (and the place of the family within the total community) and in the prevalence of formalized age groups. We have described earlier the very formalized age grading system of Kibbutz children, connected with and yet distinct from their school. No such parallel systems can be found in the Moshav. There we find the formal age grading of the school and the very informal and loose play groups of children and adolescents. They usually constitute part of the country-wide youth movement, but their participation is very weak and rather ineffective until the "transitional age" before marriage. When compared with that of the Kibbutz, the age group and youth organization of the Moshav is of small social and individual importance. What is the reason for this difference in view of the great basic similarity between the two types of settlement? On the one hand, the difference may be ascribed to different ideological emphases and planning: the establishment of children's groups in the Kibbutz constituted a part of the ideological setup. The existence of this difference cannot, however, be based on ideology alone, and must also be explained in structural terms. It seems that this difference is most clearly connected with the different types of family organization in the two types of settlement, in both of which it is conceived mainly in terms of ideological precepts and values. In the Moshav the family constitutes the basic unit of agricultural production, and agricultural familism constitutes one of its main ideals. The life of the children runs its course mainly within the family unit, in close participation with the parents, all sharing the same roles and performing similar tasks. There exists almost no discontinuity between the world of the parents and that of the children, and it is through participation in age-heterogeneous relations with his parents that the child gradually attains his social and economic maturity. When he grows up he will continue his father's work, either inheriting his farm or receiving a similar one on which he will establish his own family. It is only in relation to school and to some nation-wide activities (necessarily universalistically patterned) that the scope of the family is inadequate. The reverse is true of the Kibbutz. Here the family's social sphere is more restricted than in any other sector of modern society. The family is not a unit of production, nor even of consumption; most meals are eaten in the common dining hall of the settlement. The children usually do not sleep with their parents, but in separate establishments. It is only in the sphere of housing, by sharing a common room, that the family group (the married couple, the parents) forms a formal unit. There exists no institutionalized occupational or specialization continuity or inheritance between generations. In the Kibbutz we find, then, very strongly marked discontinuity between the world of the adults and that of the children; the children live in a world of their own which is somewhat sheltered from the exigencies of adult pioneering life (e.g., children's houses are built when their parents still live in tents). The children meet their parents only for a few hours a day, when the parents try to be "at their best," enacting very distinct, artificial roles. The strong dissociation between parents and children is an outcome of the desire to establish a completely communal life, without personal inheritance of any kind and with a very strong orientation on the common values, which seem to be opposed to any emphasis on family life. And it is within his age group that the child in the Kibbutz is oriented towards this common life, maintaining from the outset a strong identification with it, which, at least formally and officially, outweighs his more emotional identification with his parents. The age groups, especially those of the adolescent period, serve as preparatory stages for full participation in the community, and it is through them that general identification and solidarity with the community is maintained.[133] This semi-experimental comparison constitutes one of the most striking validations of our main hypothesis.

XV   The material on modern societies presented here also validates our general hypothesis, by establishing the correlation between the extent of universalistic social relations and the emergence of age groups (with modern societies, mostly "youth groups") and the consciousness of a youth problem. As in the case of primitive societies, the mere establishment of such a correlation is not enough; it should be supplemented by a more detailed analysis of the types of activities of youth groups and the types of social relations and goals they develop and maintain. We have already alluded to some of these in the course of our discussion, and analysis of some of these characteristics must be relegated to subsequent chapters. Yet we may point out here some of the most general characteristics, particularly those which are important for comparison with the primitive and traditional societies discussed above.

As within primitive and historical societies, there, too, a very strong emphasis is laid on the relation between leaving the family, and achieving social maturity, reaching forward to attain full social status. Even within most of the informal groups of children in modern societies, relative separation from family life is stronger than in primitive societies; the smallness of the family and kin groups does not enable them to encompass these children's groups. The urge of the children to leave the family, to emancipate themselves from the limitations and restrictions of family authority, becomes stronger in adolescence and forms one of the main bases for joining peer and youth groups.[134] One of the most important bases for this urge is the possibility of renouncing the restrictions of family status, the strong emphasis on preparatory activities, and the "preparatory" evaluation of their status. It is the possibility of attaining full equal status within a group that is of crucial importance here.[135]

This emphasis on attainment of status can be seen clearly in the great difference between children's play groups and the adolescent cliques and gangs that develop from them (just as in primitive societies the various age groups and sets develop out of informal children's groups). The adolescent cliques are more than just groups with some common transitory goal. They constitute cohesive primary groups with a very strong mutual identification of the members. Their members are "ego-involved" in them.[136] One of the most interesting and significant indications of this craving for status may be found in the various informal and semi-formal initiation rites which most of these groups evolve. Even if these rites lack the full dramatization and official sanction of the society, yet they imply the strong emotional strivings for maturity and status.[137] This ego involvement is due mainly to their (the group's and its members') importance as objects of the adolescent's need dispositions, particularly his craving for the attainment of status in terms different from those of the family and the school, and different from the obviously "preparatory" character of the roles allocated to him by the adults, both in the family and in the school. These roles are either too much enclosed within the family circle and segregated from wider spheres of social relations, or may have—because of their "preparatory" character, as in the school—very strong instrumental emphasis. It may be said that within these adolescent "peer groups" the adolescent seeks both to transcend the limits of his family roles and the family discipline imposed on him (or her), and to attain some more direct goals and gratifications in interpersonal relations with equals which would counterbalance the strong emphasis on instrumentality throughout his preparatory years.

Within these groups, as in the primitive age groups, new types of discipline, effected through the autonomous participation of the group, entirely different from those of family life, are imposed on the individual adolescent. The main difference lies in the fact that any individual is evaluated, as it were, according to his own worth and not according to his place within a given family; he is judged by universalistic criteria. At the same time his (or her) worth is not judged according to any specific achievement (as, to a great extent in school, in anticipation of his adult specialization), but according to his total personality and its harmony with both group values and goals, or according to diffuse and collectivity-oriented criteria. This diffuse image is defined in terms of new status aspirations and evaluations which emphasize the emancipation from family discipline.

However, unlike in most primitive age groups, in modern society the new status is not fully attained in these youth groups. Participation in them, even if it is legitimate and fully sponsored by the official agencies of the social system, does not confer full status and social maturity, because the youth groups cannot overcome the preparatory nature of most roles allocated to adolescents in modern societies. In modern societies complete harmony does not always exist between age group membership and age role allocation by the society, and consequently adolescents do not necessarily attain full status through participation in these groups.

This characteristic forms one of the most important attributes of modern youth and age groups. In this very important respect, the youth groups and organizations in modern societies seem to differ from that of primitive and historical societies analyzed by us. While, on the one hand, they share with them some of the most basic characteristics of all age and youth groups, on the other hand, some very important differences exist between them.

XVI   In the foregoing pages, we have described and analyzed how various types of age groups emerge in nonkinship, universalistic societies. The age groups which have been described are characterized by a great variety and diversity, a variety and diversity which have already been analyzed in general terms in the second chapter of this book. Despite this diversity some general characteristics common to all types of age groups have clearly emerged, and we might briefly summarize them before proceeding with our analysis.

In all societies age groups are formed at the transitional stage between adolescence and full adulthood, and are oriented towards the attainment and acknowledgment of the full status of their members. Through participation of the group its members develop their identity and self-evaluation, and it is in terms of such evaluation that the common identification and solidarity of the group is evolved and maintained. This strong emphasis on common experience, common values and mutual identification is found in every type of age group, and serves as the essential driving power for its individual members. It is this common characteristic that explains the universal fact that everywhere the nucleus of an age group organization is a small, usually face-to-face, primary group of peers with a strong sense of solidarity and of mutual identification. The main characteristics of such a group have already been defined and analyzed. First, its membership is, in principle, based on general age criteria, i.e., a member may be anyone within the age category (age grade). In practice, however, the strong bonds which evolve between such members become, with the passage of time, more personal, although in principle (and in practice in so far as it is interwoven within an institutionalized age group hierarchy) the group retains most general criteria of membership. Whatever the actual composition of its membership, the common symbols of its identification and its values and ideology bear a strongly universalistic flavor, emphasizing as they do the universal attributes and image of an age, an image common to every member of the society.

Secondly, this image and the value orientations of the age group are necessarily ascriptive and diffuse. This is so by definition, but it may also be explained by their important function for the development of the member's identity and its incorporation into the common identity of the community. As has already been explained several times, this function could not have been fulfilled but for the preponderance of these criteria. It is important to emphasize here that this ascription and diffuseness are not related to any segregated, marginal clusters of roles, but to the most central and crucial aspects of one's roles and activities—those connected with one's overall status and integration within the community.

It is this that explains the third, and last, common characteristic of age groups, namely, their very strong internal solidarity and sometimes also community orientation. This community orientation, when it exists, is not confined only to the solidarity of the nuclear primary age group. It extends then beyond their narrow limits towards the total community and its values. This extension may be fully institutionalized and legitimated, as in most primitive tribes, or be of an outspokenly deviant type as in the German youth movements, but whenever it exists, it forms an important element in the structure of the nuclear primary group and constitutes a basic element of its value system and ideology. It is most clearly related to the status and community-integration aspirations which form the driving power of these groups. Even when such an orientation to the total, or wider, community does exist, all youth groups evince a very sharp *internal* solidarity which, under appropriate conditions, may be extended.[138]

It is clear that all these characteristics bear out the postulates behind the main hypotheses of this work. Beyond them the various types of age groups evince a variety of characteristics and structural arrangements which have been described and briefly classified in this chapter and in the previous one. Until now only the main common characteristics of age groups (and some of their ramifications) have been explained. It is the task of the next chapters to go beyond these common characteristics and to explain their diversity and variety. Our analysis till now has shown that age groups are an agency to which under certain conditions important tasks in the social structure are allocated. The exact nature of these tasks would, however, differ in different societies, according to the extent to which other types of groups perform such tasks. It is with this problem that the next chapter will deal.

CHAPTER IV

Specialization and the
Structure of Age Groups

I In the preceding chapter, the hypothesis that age groups arise in nonkinship, universalistically regulated societies was validated. It was shown, however, that these age groups comprise a great variety of types and characteristics which were enumerated at the end of Chapter II. So far only very few of the differences in the incidence of these characteristics have been accounted for and related to the different degrees to which universalistic criteria regulate and integrate the social system.

In order to be able to account for the additional differences, we must do more than elucidate the general importance of universalistic criteria; we must look for additional variables within the general framework of universalistic societies.

Until now we have not systematically differentiated between various types of universalistic societies, although already the discussion in the previous chapter has indicated, in a general way, that the characteristics of age groups vary in different types of universalistic societies. We shall now proceed to such an analysis. We shall differentiate between various universalistic societies according to the extent of specialization and achievement orientation existing both in their principles of role allocation and of value orientation, and according to the relative strength of collectivity orientations within them. We shall attempt to show, in a systematic way, how such differences are related to variations in the structure and functioning of age groups in these societies.

The starting point of such an analysis will be the hypothesis, submitted in the first chapter, that:

the scope of age groups is confined to the "transitory" sphere between kinship relations and those regulated by the criteria of achievement and specificity.

This hypothesis is derived from the fact, illustrated many times in the preceding chapter, that within the age groups themselves certain definite and fixed principles are at work according to which their membership is patterned and their relations regulated. We have seen that membership in age groups is based on broad ascriptive criteria which may be common to all members of the society, and that the relations between members of age groups, their mutual obligations, are, for the most part, of a diffuse nature.

It has also been shown that age groups evince strong solidarity and collectivity orientation. These characteristics are universal in all age groups, and the place of the age groups within a given society is largely determined by the extent to which the integrative principles of the society are similar to those of the age groups. When such harmony exists, the scope of the activities, tasks and functions allocated to age groups in the institutional structure of the society is large. If no such similarity and harmony exist between the overall integrative principles of the society and those of the age group, i.e., when they are achievement-oriented, individualistic, etc., the scope of age group activities within the institutional structure and within the individual's life history is necessarily diminished. This is the basic supposition which will guide us in this chapter; we shall now attempt to substantiate and elaborate it in greater detail. This hypothesis is closely related not only to the problem of *age groups* as such, but to the more general problem of the importance of the criterion of age for the allocation of roles in a society. We have already postulated in the first chapter of this book that the importance of this criterion is closely related to the degree in which the integrative principles of the society are particularistic, diffuse and ascriptive. In this chapter, therefore, we must compare various universalistic and particularistic societies according to the extent of specificity and achievement orientation that exists within them, and their repercussion on the organization of relations between various age grades. In this way we shall try to show in greater detail that age groups may perform different integrative tasks in different societies, and that these differences are related to the existence and distribution of other groups performing such tasks in a society.

The first problem to be analyzed is the extent to which specialization and achievement orientation within various univevrsalistic societies affects the structure of the age groups. The extent of specialization in a society can best be judged by the number and importance of roles that are segregated from other roles or clusters of roles, that are organized according to distinct criteria and in segregated spheres, and the incumbents of which act towards each other according to the specific obligations of these roles, to the exclusion of other mutual demands.

In order to facilitate the evaluation of the extent of such specialization in any society, we shall employ R. Linton's nomenclature, which distinguishes between universals, specialties and alternatives in the distribution of roles within a social system.[1]

The extent to which there exist many specialties and/or alternatives within a social system constitutes, roughly speaking, an index of the importance of specialization from the point of view of allocation of roles within that system. By "extent," not merely the *number* of such roles is meant, but mainly their importance in the institutional arrangements of the society and the degree to which they serve as criteria of differential status for members of the society. Preponderance of universal roles, which all members perform alike, usually means that specialization is minimal. Both specialties and alternatives can be either ascribed or achieved. There are specialties which are ascribed to various people or groups on the basis of some basic qualities of theirs, and the choice between certain alternatives may be limited to members of a certain group, e.g., members of a caste, religious sect, local group, etc. On the other hand, they may here be achieved, as in the case of most occupational roles in modern society. Although the distinction between ascribed and achieved specialties and alternatives is not always clear-cut in reality—as for instance when only members of a given group can achieve certain occupational roles —it will be of some importance to our further analysis. A further difference which will be important for our discussion is that between universalistic and particularistic specialized and achievement-oriented societies. Our main concern is, of course, with universalistic societies; but for comparative purposes we shall also have to analyze the main types of such particularistic societies.

II   We shall begin by analyzing the extent of specialization among the various primitive tribes:

Among the segmentary tribes which have been discussed in this work (the Nuer, Turkana, Nandi, Galla, Kikuyu, etc.) the number of universals is maximal, especially in those areas not regulated by family, kinship or descent group relations. There are only two or three exceptions. The first is in the distribution of wealth. There are usually some differences in wealth (mainly in cattle) among the various families or groups of families —differences which may sometimes determine the extent of esteem accorded to a man.[2] In these tribes, however, these differences appertain mostly to family and descent groups and are more or less regulated by them, i.e., they do not usually belong to those institutional spheres regulated by universalistic criteria. The second exception may be found in some of these tribes in the field of religious leadership, e.g., among the Guk of the Nuer, the Nandi, Masai, etc.[3] In most of these tribes the most important tribal ritual offices are not vested in kinship groups, and therefore religious offices form definite "specialties" or "alternatives" within the basic framework of universalistic criteria. By their very nature, however, they are very limited in number and therefore cannot affect the life of most members of the society, as only few can attain to these offices. This exception does not, then, really invalidate the preponderance of "universals" in these societies. The third exception is rather an accentuation of certain of the "universals"—the special esteem which is accorded to the exceptionally brave warrior, the particularly wise elder, etc.[4]

The preponderance of "universals" in these tribes does not necessarily mean that all members perform more or less the same roles throughout their entire lifetime. Such a situation occurs mainly in very small, undifferentiated tribes composed of self-sufficient households. This situation does not exist in the majority of the tribes under discussion; the different roles which have to be performed cannot be combined into unsegregated clusters—warriorship, participation in government, etc. These roles are not, however, allocated as specialties or alternatives to different people, but to every man at a different stage of his life. In so far as there is specialization, it is not ascribed to different persons, but only to different age categories which are common to all. It is entirely ascribed, and almost no element of achievement enters into it. Some persons may excel in the performance of these tasks and thus gain special esteem, but this does not involve differential prestige of statuses and positions.

In these tribes, then, almost complete harmony obtains between *all* of the criteria of role allocation and the criteria of age group composition (except, of course, in those spheres regulated by kinship relations). Accordingly, we find that in these tribes the age groups constitute one of the main agencies for the allocation of roles within the social system. This explains several of their characteristics. At this point of our discussion only two of these characteristics should be emphasized: first, that they cover the entire adult life span of the individual; second, the fact that the age groups regulate the behavior of members of the society and stratify the whole population, ascribing to all members of the tribe definite positions in the mutual relations.

III   It is when we come to the various types of primitive tribes composed of noncentralized "villages" that we encounter a totally different picture as far as both specialization and achievement orientation are concerned. Among the Yako, Ibo and certain Yoruba tribes (and probably also among other primitive peasant communities) we find a number of "societies" or "associations" to which large sections of the adult population belong, and which are usually open to all free (nonslave) members of the tribe or village. There are two main types of such associations, which may perhaps be typologically distinct but in reality interconnected. The first is an association (or society) which devotes itself to a more or less specific purpose, e.g., hunting, dancing, etc.

The second type is a titled society, entrance to which is regulated by payment of a special fee, and in which titles of different grades are conferred according to the amount of the fee paid. Its purpose is not very specific; it is usually of a more diffuse character, and constitutes in a way a mutual aid and investment society (as the fees of the new members are distributed among the older ones). These associations also perform various integrative tasks within the society as a whole—such as supervision of public order—and exert great influence in government, etc.

There is no great difference between this and the first type of association, as most of the first also exact entrance fees, and some of them (usually those which do exact such fees) also perform various tasks of government, allocation of economic aid, etc., as for example in the Yako villages. The importance of these associations is not, then, confined to their own members, nor are their activities a purely "internal" affair. The place of the individual in the association, the grade which he attains within it, usually constitutes the most important index of general social status within his tribe; it is through his position within these associations that an individual exerts his influence and power in the whole tribe, mainly because of the various integrative functions which these associations perform in it. The various graded titles and membership positions in these associations are not hereditarily vested in various families, lineages or other descent groups, but are acquired individually, although perhaps with the help of the families. In some cases there are even explicit rules prohibiting inheritance of the father's position by the son.[5] These associations are, then, obviously within the scope of universalistically regulated roles; but at the same time they entail, from the point of view of the allocation of roles, an element both of some specialization and of achievement orientation. The various grades within an association—and the concomitant general status—are not ascribed to all members, but are achieved by certain persons only through special exertions on their part. Thus from the point of view of role allocation, these associations act as a definite counterbalance to the age groups which exist within all of these tribes.

What, then, is the concrete interrelation between the two in these societies? Some general common characteristics may be discerned. First, the importance of age groups diminishes in those age grades (stages in a person's life) in which the individual has to exert himself in competitive activities for the achievement of status in the various associations. This may come about in various ways. Among the Yako the formal organizaztion of the age sets persists over a long period, but the scope of their activities and their importance dwindle in middle age. The age sets no longer perform various important corporate activities which are more or less equally allocated to all members; most of their activities center around internal and recreational affairs, such as assistance at feasts, marriages, funerals, etc. Among some of the Ibo and Ibibio tribes, age sets cease to function altogether in middle adulthood, as they do also among some of the Yoruba tribes.[6] The internal inconsistency between age groups and these associations may here be easily discerned. In so far as corporate activities are concerned, their performance by age groups usually means more or less equal distribution of tasks among all members of the group. Any internal differentiation within the group does not negate this basic quality, but only tends to stress the group's autonomy and solidarity. The element of equal ascription is an essential part of the structure of the group. This equality obviously cannot exist within the associations because of the differentiation of status, nor can the solidarity of the equalitarian age group be wholly maintained within these associations. In many cases senior members of the various associations exert a very pronounced authority over the age group, an authority derived from their differential position. This could not be done if they were still members of the age set organization, participating fully in it. (In that case their authority should be derived from the age group itself, and not from any outside agencies or criteria.) This incompatibility between the two types of groupings may best be seen among certain Yoruba tribes, where everyone up to a certain age attains various grades given on an equal basis to all members of the tribe (or village), with either no entrance fees or only such minimal fees as everyone can afford to pay. After a certain stage, however, the fees become prohibitive, not all members can afford them, and only a few can achieve the higher grades.[7] Exactly at the point where differential fees are exacted, the universality of the age group breaks down, as the grades are no longer ascribed to all members of a tribe but may be achieved by some of them only. All of the grades constitute, as it were, one series; yet the basic difference between "age" and "achieved" grades is clear-cut. In all of these cases we see that at the exact structural point where achievement-oriented and specialized activities begin to rule, the importance of age groups subsides and, in general, age ceases to be a definite and clear criterion for allocation of roles and for the description of an individual's status.

When we compare, then, age groups in these villages to those of the segmentary tribes, we find even at first glimpse several structural differences, which seem to be related to the extent of specialization and achievement orientation. First, there is the limitation of the age span covered by age groups. Second, there is a decrease in the extent of regulation of behavior of members of the tribe. Age group relations regulate here the internal relations of their own members, rather than the overall behavior of all members of society vis-à-vis one another. Thirdly, the scope of their activities is more limited than in nonspecialized tribes, as they perform mainly subsidiary roles, directed by outside, authority-bearing agencies.

Despite these structural differences and variations, and the difference between the structure of age groups and the integrative principles of these societies, we find that age groups both fulfill definite functions within the social system and are closely connected with the various titled associations and central authority-bearing agencies, whether by being regulated by these associations or by performing various tasks in common with them. Usually there is no opposition between the age groups and the official bearers of authority, and their interaction does not generate tensions in the social system. The age groups are also, as we have seen, corporate and legitimate groups, which perform many important tasks within the community, participate in its rituals, and are wholly accepted within it. This structural integration may be connected with the fact that the basic value orientations of these societies are diffuse and collectivity-oriented (and in a way also particularistic), and that the specialized and achievement-oriented allocation of roles takes place within the framework of these values. The various grades of the associations denote differential achievement of a diffuse ideal, not a specific, segregated activity; and they are clearly bound by criteria of collectivity orientation, i.e., are oriented towards the maintenance and furthering of the community's economic resources, ritual well-being, etc. The individual's achievement is bound within the limits of the collectivity. This may be seen in these association's functions as societies for mutual help, in their participation in communal ritual functions, etc. While their principles as role allocators differ from those of the age groups, their basic value orientations are, in a way, harmonious with the basic criteria of age group activities. Therefore the two, despite structural incompatibility, may still be interconnected without generating specific tensions or opposition.

Another interesting case from the point of view of this discussion may be found among the Heiban, Otoro, and mainly the Tira tribes of the Nuba group.[8] Here we find that a person's status is determined by the extent of wealth he can amass and distribute and/or by his physical endurance and prowess. Both wealth and physical endurance have to be proved at special ceremonies, those of *orco*. The attainment of both of these distinctions is obviously a matter of differential individual achievement—which, in the case of the amassing of wealth, involves many years' planning and activities.[9] The attainment of these distinctions is open to everyone, but only a few achieve it. These people, called *romoco* and *urdhini*, enjoy special esteem and various privileges, although they do not perform any concerted activities as a group or necessarily participate in expressly integrative functions (government, etc.). These distinctions, although they emphasize virtues which might be attained by all, are not only accentuations of roles which are ascribed to everyone; they must be specially achieved and constitute, in fact, alternative roles within the society. This type of specialization and achievement orientation has a bearing on the structure of age groups similar to that in the Yako-Ibo type. Among them also the age span of the groups is limited, extending only to the age of 23-26, when achievement orientation activities begin to absorb the individual's energies and time. The age groups cease to function after this age, and the solidarity of the group becomes but a memory in later stages of life. Within the age group the same virtues and roles are extolled—physical prowess, working ability (working on the land), farming skill, etc. But all these roles are organized on an ascriptive and collective basis: the wrestling matches are matches between groups; excelling in work enhances the prestige of the group; and the strong competitive spirit which prevails is bound to the age group as such, ascribed to all its members and demanding the same exertion on the part of all. This basic difference between the collective activities of age groups and individualistic, co-operative, achievement-oriented status aspirations is minimized here by the identity and continuity of value orientations. For this reason we find both full institutionalization of activities of age groups and lack of opposition between age groups and other institutionalized spheres of the social system. At the same time the extent of regulation of behavior by age groups is limited because of the presence of other integrative principles within the social system.

The structural incompatibility between age groups and achievement orientation, and the consequent possibilities of social mobility, may perhaps be most clearly seen in those cases in which the age groups themselves serve as channels of social mobility, as in most centralized, primitive monarchies (Zulu, Swazi, Tswana, etc.[10]). Within these kingdoms most of the roles not allocated on the basis of kinship criteria (such as central political roles appertaining to the royal clan) are of the nature of "universals," which are allocated on the basis of age. Yet the distinctness of the political framework and the "universalistic" type of citizenship entails the possibility of differential socio-political status—becoming a councillor, the king's trusted man, etc.[11] The main avenue to such distinction is service in the age regiment, excellence in the performance of various public tasks, duties, etc.—an excellence which is in a way but an accentuation of the common duties, the universals ascribed to all members of the tribe. However, once such an excellence changes an individual's position and status when he becomes a councillor or some other type of king's "official," he usually leaves his age regiment, and may even assume, in relation to it, a position not based on age, such as that of commander of the age groups, similar in some instances to those of the princes, members of the royal clan.[12]

A similar picture can be found among various Berber tribes in North Africa, who have come within the orbit of a more urbanized way of life. Here also their traditional age groups (about which the available information is not, by the way, very complete) have diminished the scope of their activities and have developed into semi-formalized mutual aid societies, with some secondary ritual functions, but without any fully institutionalized tasks.[13]

IV   One of the most interesting cases for our discussion is that of the Plains Indian age societies. As has been shown above, these groups possess the elements of both age ascription and some type of achievement, exemplified mainly in the purchase of various ceremonial rights, and in the implicit possibility of unwillingness—or inability—to do so. However, at the same time this achievement is always a collective one, effected by the group as a whole and not by an individual. This contradiction between the ascriptive age aspect and the achievement purchase aspect gave rise to a series of discussions in anthropological literature as to whether the Plains Indian societies may really be called "age groups" (or "age sets"[14]). It is proposed here that the solution of this problem may lie in the distinction between the sphere of role allocation and that of value orientation—a distinction which in this case bears a somewhat specific and paradoxical character. It seems that the element of achievement exists mainly in the spheres of value orientation, as exemplified in many Plains societies (even nongraded ones) and among the Pueblos by the "quest" for a "vision," a "dream," etc.[15] This achievement is oriented towards diffuse and particularistic values (the quest for some particular spirit), and in this way firmly anchored in the "traditional" setting of these tribes. This peculiar type of achievement orientation (which may be compared, as it has often been, with some types of religious ecstasy in various sects, and may be clearly seen also in the development of the Peyote cult[16]) is not, however, matched by allocation of roles according to purely achievement-oriented criteria. Although within these tribes such achievement orientation exists to some extent, e.g., in matters of wealth, horse breeding etc., W. F. Whyte's analysis has shown clearly that such status differences exist mainly among those tribes which have no age grades, and even there mainly within the limits of family and kin groups.[17] Among age-graded tribes most roles are allocated on a universalistic and ascriptive basis; that is why age groups continue throughout the individual's adult life, form an autonomous hierarchy, and perform various corporate and integrative activities.[18] At the same time, however, the element of achievement in value orientations must find some expression in the age group's composition, and does so, as it were, in the symbolical process of purchase and acquisition. This purchase does not entail an individual achievement based on the performance of an (individually) specialized role, but is effected (collectively) through the group, each member's place and role usually being *ascribed* according to his position in the group, and only groups as such competing symbolically for the various roles. Unlike the former cases analyzed above, a basic structural similarity and harmony obtains here between age groups and role-allocating agencies. However, there is some difference from the point of view of value orientations, and hence we would suggest the possibility of some element of conflict or opposition (not purchasing, refusing to see the point, etc.). Such a conflict, however, is almost always solved peacefully because of the prevailing basic harmony.

The basic incompatibility between achievement-oriented, competitive distribution of "grades" and statuses and age group organization may also be seen in some Melanesian societies, which are characterized by the well-known system of the *suckwe*, men's clubs with a very complicated system of grades and ranks. In the older literature on age grading this system[19] was often compared to certain age societies, particularly those of the Plains Indians, because of the external similarity of "grades" which youths wish to attain through payment of entrance fees to various "associations." Yet the basic difference has already been succinctly analyzed by R. Lowie in his earlier writings.[20] The Melanesian system constitutes a combination of differential status which is achieved through competitive, achievement-oriented activities, and the limitation of these activities to positions largely hereditary in family groups. Both of these principles are incompatible with age groupings, and indeed we see that here age groups are completely nonexistent, despite some formal similarities of these associations with the grading system of certain age groups.

V   The Nupe state is much more complicated, and forms, in a way, a distinct case among all of the societies within our sample. As we have seen, it is a rather rigidly stratified society in which the extent of "universals" is relatively limited, with a preponderance of various "caste"- and "class"-bound specialities. Yet the various upper classes, the aristocracies of civil and military services, which are distinct from the "commoners," are not rigidly bound to descent groups. Their recruitment is to some extent based on individual achievement and mobility, although it obviously affects only a small part of the population. At the same time some of the basic value orientations are common to *all* strata and emphasize this community. We find here a society in which the social stratification is partly one of *caste*—if by caste is meant the rigid and unalterable distribution of social privileges and resources on the grounds of descent. However, there is also class stratification based on differentiation in power, which permits movement between the strata in accordance with compatibility, with services rendered—especially in war—with work, success and luck, that is, it permits social mobility based on universalistic criteria.

We find here, then, a strong element of diffuse achievement orientation in the sphere of values, with mainly ascriptive specialization in actual role allocation. This ascription is not, however, related universalistically to all members of the society, but differentially to various strata, with a strong possibility of universal mobility. There are various channels of mobility, such as actual recruitment into the various aristocracies, "clientship" and the stratum of Moslem teachers, the *"maalams."* All these channels serve as points of connection between the various strata, and emphasize in various ways the community of their value orientation, despite the strong tendency towards particularistic, ascriptive specialization. The picture here is obviously much more complicated than in the hitherto-discussed societies, especially because of the peculiar blending of ascriptive stratification with community of value orientations and the structurally important channels of universalistic achievement and mobility. These complications have some important effects on the structure and composition of the age groups which have already been described in Chapter II. First, the life span of the age groups is here limited too, and age group activities do not serve (especially in the towns) as main prerequisites of attainment of full adult social status. They are effective mostly during those periods in the individual's life before he is called upon to assume his status, which is more or less ascribed on the basis of class (or caste) position.[21] They do not serve, then, as necessary prerequisites of social status, but as a sort of general preparation for it. Neither do they form a uniform organization cutting through society, but consist mainly of separate groups in each locality, and within each ascriptively specialized group (group guilds, social strata, etc.). This is obviously connected with the fact that despite their legitimacy and institutionalization, no institutionally basic, formal roles or tasks are allocated to them, and their activities are mainly those of recreation and to some extent of participation in religious institutions and festivals. (Within the villages the age groups also perform very important tasks in the realm of agricultural work.)

The extent to which they regulate the behavior of members of the society is still more limited than in hitherto-discussed cases. Their effectiveness is confined to their limited local and class boundaries, and they do not regulate the general behavior of their members in relation to one another and to other members of the society. Their regulation of behavior is a purely internal affair. The most important regulation is effective during the adolescent and early adult stage, although there are also some mutual obligations between age mates which persist after that stage: attendance at family feasts, general friendliness and help, etc. The age groups' main function, as S. E. Nadel's analysis clearly shows, is to uphold the solidarity of each locality and stratum, and to act as a "school of citizenship," inbuing their members with identification with the common values and symbols of their society.

Here we already find a somewhat new type of age group—groups which are mostly concerned with training and preparation, and do not perform any definite tasks within the society. We shall see below that this distinction between training and task-performing age groups is of great importance for the understanding of the various youth groups in modern societies.

VI   We have endeavored to show that the existence of specialization and achievement oreintation within a universalistic society tends to restrict the span of life which the age groups cover and the extent of their regulation of the behavior of all members of the society. These are not, however, the only results of the existence of specialization and achievement orientation within a society. Some additional structural differences may be derived from them, some of which have already been alluded to, particularly in the last section on Ancient Greece, and should now be more fully analyzed.

The extent of specialization wtihin a society has very important repercussions on the internal structure of the age group system as such, and on the interlinking of the various age groups in a unified structural hierarchy. In those "universalistic" tribes where the only specialization is the ascriptive diffuse specialization of the age grades (the Nandi, Masai, Galla, Kamba, Kikuyu, etc.), we find a number of definite structural characteristics which are absent—or transformed—in those societies in which specialization is more complex and based on achievement. First, we usually find here a close correspondence between age grades and age groups (or age sets). Usually a set is organized on the basis of belonging to a given age grade, and if several groups are formed within the grade, they are mostly designed as subgroups of the age grade set.[22] This close correspondence between age grades and age sets is possible only in so far as *all* age grades are assigned exclusive roles and serve as the main categories for the allocation of the most important roles of the social system; it does not exist in "specialized" tribes (just as it does not exist in those tribes, such as the Nuer, etc., in which lineages and kinship units still perform many integrative tasks). Within the "specialized" tribes, villages and societies in which the age span of the age grades is limited, each age group covers but a number of years, usually within one, or at most two, age grades.

Closely connected with this correspondence between age grading and age groups is the structural arrangement of the various age groups into an autonomous, autocephalous, interlinked hierarchy. Among the Yako, Ibo, etc., and among the Swazi, Zulu, in Sparta, etc., the different age groups are organized and connected through the activities and authority of persons outside the age group hierarchy—the village (or ward) officials, the king, or public officials. Each age group is more or less directly connected to this official, and not to any other *age group*. The age group hierarchy as such is not effective in ordering relations between the various age groups; they are regulated "from above." The various roles (which in these cases are basic for the social system) are allocated to each age group separately,[23] and not through internal arrangements between the different age groups. The concrete authority of a senior age group over a junior group— except for very general attitudes of respect, etc.—is rather limited. Thus it may be said that the age groups here are heterocephalous.

In the nonspecialized societies the picture is different. Here all the different age groups constitute a unified, interlinked hierarchy. This hierarchy is autonomous, the relations between the various age groups being regulated by norms applying to them and applied by them. The roles allocated to each age group are regulated by rules upheld by the age groups themselves, rules which form a crucial part of the institutional structure of society and which regulate the behavior of all its members. These internal, autonomous arrangements are most obvious in the "cyclical" type of age sets—the Nandi, Kipsigis, Galla, Meru, etc.— in which each age group is allocated special roles which change automatically with a change of age grades. There are no other outside centers of authority—except some of the religous leaders

—which could help mediate the relations between the different age groups. Each age group is directly linked with other groups, and it is through their respective representatives that their mutual relations are regulated[24] and thus the whole hierarchy is autocephalous.

These attributes of a unified, autocephalous, autonomously and automatically regulated hierarchy are also characteristic of the noncyclical type—such as the Masai—and to some extent also the Plains Indian age groups. Among these groups, the senior age groups are also centers of legitimate concrete authority, which is exerted in relation to the junior sets, and the relations between them are not limited to mere general attitudes of respect.

An important manifestation of these characteristics is the type and order of advancement and succession of the age groups (sets). In the "specialized" societies (and in the centralized kingdoms), each age group advances gradually on the scale of seniority, thus changing its position relative to other age grades, but usually without changing basically its tasks and activities, or assuming new authority; while among the nonspecialized tribes one group succeeds another, inheriting its position and automatically taking over its tasks and activities and acquiring new authority. This is most clearly evident in the buying procedures of the Plains Indian age groups.

Thus we see that in so far as specialization gives rise to integrative agencies outside the fold of age groups, the age group hierarchy loses its unified, autocephalous structure of autonomously and automatically interlinked groups, its internal distribution of authority and its effectiveness in the regulation of age group behavior through automatic succession of absolute status positions.

The situation is somewhat different in those societies within which age groups perform predominantly "preparatory" roles and training functions, and only incidentally tasks and roles which form an integral part of the institutional structure. This situation exists among the Nupe and somewhat less among some of the Nuba tribes, among the urbanized Berbers and to a small extent in Athens. Here, once more, the internal autonomy and autocephaly of the age groups is stronger than in those "specialized" tribes in which real tasks are allocated to the age groups by the bearers of authority. They manage their own internal affairs with little intervention from the outside, and consequently the links between different age groups are relatively strong. One of the leader-sponsors of an age group must be a member of a senior age group, and there is some degree of co-operation between various age groups, particularly on ritual occasions. Among the Nuba tribes there is an even more explicit element of authority of senior over junior age sets, resembling the relation between adjacent and alternate age groups among the Nandi, Kipsigi, etc. Unlike those tribes, however, the span of age group life here is much shorter, and consequently the succession of one age group by another does not constitute (especially among the Nupe) a succession of absolute social status, which holds good in the whole social structure. The succession of age groups is related mostly to their "internal" status system, which does not give them any specific place in the status system of the whole society, although it is modelled on the latter. In these cases the relative autonomy of the age group is not related to the basic institutional structure of the society, but only to a segregated cluster of roles, and is attained at the price of this exclusion and segregation.

These various structural characteristics of age groups in "specialized" primitive societies also have a very interesting repercussion on the relation between the family and the age group. As has been shown in the case of all age groups, the social spheres of the family and of the age group are always distinct. But the sharp opposition between family and age groups observed in several of the nonspecialized tribes (Nandi, Meru, etc.) does not exist here. (In these societies the age groups perform, for instance, important functions in various family festivals.) This may be explained by the fact that in these societies the attainment of full status within the total society is not effected through age groups, but mainly through other, more specialized agencies and groups. Thus the opposition between the particularistic status of the family and the universalistic statuses of the total society is less acutely felt in the age groups than in other associations.

The extent of specialization is also, naturally, inversely related to the structural importance of tasks allocated to age groups. In so far as integratively important roles are concentrated within specialized agencies, the age groups cease to operate in those sectors of the social system, and at those stages of the individual's life career, at which achievement- and specificity-oriented principles regulate the allocation of roles and rewards. In these societies no central political and juridical functions can be vested in the age groups; at most they can perform subsidiary tasks allocated to them by the power-exercising agencies within the society. The scope of concrete, fully institutionalized tasks which are allocated to age groups is thus inversely related to the extent of specialization, i.e., to the extent to which these tasks are concentrated within specialized agencies. The greater the specialization within universalistic achievement-oriented societies, the greater the emphasis on "preparatory" and training tasks allocated to age groups. Within most of the primitive societies hitherto discussed (with the partial exception of urban Nupe) the extent of specialization is not so great as to deprive the age groups of the performance of definite tasks within the society. Such a development took place, however, already in Athens, and will be found to a much greater extent in modern societies. .

VII   The effects of specialization and achievement orientation on the structure of age groups can also be clearly discerned in Ancient Greece.[25] Moreover, the comparison between Sparta and Athens may yield some very interesting results. Both in Sparta and in Athens the main integrative agencies of the society, especially in the political field, were not organized on the basis of ascription—whether age, blood or any other kind. Partial exceptions are, of course, the Spartan kings and to some extent the *Gerusia*. But in the latter case the necessity of election brought in an important element of achievement. Most other political offices in both places were based on some sort of achievement, usually manifested in constant elections and supervision on the part of the Assembly. The various political offices and committees—whether the *ephors* in Sparta or the various magistrates in Athens—constituted special agencies, membership in which was based mostly on achievement and perhaps also, to some extent, on specialization in political affairs. They were entirely outside the scope of any ascriptive group within the social body of free citizens.

Accordingly, we find here some age group characteristics which have already been noted, in one way or another, in the various primitive societies hitherto discussed. First, the age groups cover a relatively shorter age span—in Sparta, most effectively until 30 and to some extent after 60, in Athens, up to 20. At the age of 30 in Sparta, and in Athens, the individual became a full citizen and could enter into the sphere of political and economic achievement and competition. Secondly, the age groups were not autonomous or autocephalous; they were organized and directed by adults, by various official representatives of the society, by their teachers, etc., or to some extent, as in Sparta, by any adult. The strong discipline effected in these groups—especially in Sparta—was maintained by a combination of spontaneous activities of the youths with strong supervision by adults. The hierarchy of age groups existing in Sparta was organized and supervised by adults, by official representatives of the State; and the relations between the different age grades were also organized by them, and not autonomously by the groups themselves. The same applies, although in a much less formal and organized way, to the various schools and the *epheboi* of Athens. We find here, as in many of the achievement and specificity-oriented primitive tribes, a strong emphasis on the internal activities of the age groups and the performance of various tasks allocated to them by the men in authority. But there existed no overall regulation of behavior of members and nonmembers alike by the age groups. Only a general attitude of respect towards elder people was instilled formally in Sparta, much more informally in Athens.

Beyond these similarities, however, we find striking differences between the organization of age groups in Athens and in Sparta. We have already seen the main differences in the former chapter: the uniform and unitary organization in Sparta, extending up to the age of 30; the differentiated and nonunitary organization of different types of schools, gymnasia and *epheboi* in Athens, ending at the age of 20. The Athenian age groups were concerned mostly with training, and only to a very limited extent with the performance of definite institutional tasks. It seems to us that this difference can be plausibly connected with differences in the extent of specialization in these two societies. Specialization among the Spartan citizens was relatively small, and perhaps nonexistent, with the partial exception of variations in agricultural wealth. Thus it may be said that the Spartan citizen body was, from the economic and professional point of view, a largely homogeneous group. This could not be said of Athens, where, especially at the end of the fifth and fourth centuries B.C., economic and professional differentiation and specialization closely connected with processes of familial mobility reached a high degree. Moreover, as we shall see, collectivity orientation was much stronger in Sparta than in Athens. Here a more individualistic spirit prevailed, setting a high value on individual accomplishments, teaching, etc. Hence we find that the period of preparation was much shorter, especially in the case of the poorer classes who did not go beyond primary education; and also that the structure of age and youth groups was less formal and uniform, the differentiation and looseness in their organization much more pronounced. Moreover, there was a rather marked differentiation between the private and individualistic spheres of preparation—the schools—and the public training of the *epheboi* and to some extent also the gymnasia. The strong individualistic emphasis did not negate the existence of the public sphere and of identification with the collectivity, but it did differentiate, to some extent, between it and the more private individualistic spheres of preparation and education.

       This general conclusion must, however, be supplemented VIII   by a more detailed explanation of the functions of age groups in such societies, from the point of view of both the individual personality and the social system.

In the preceding chapters it has been postulated that age groups, owing to their ascriptive, diffuse and collectivity-oriented characteristics, basic emotional support and social solidarity to their members, continue to exist even in a universalistic framework. It was asserted that in so far as various universalistic, specialized, etc., roles are organized within the framework of age groups, the basic solidarity of the age groups provides a framework of such support. In this way, it was shown, instrumental activities are combined, in one cluster of roles, with solidary and expressive gratifications, and the strain of purely instrumental relations is eased.

Such an explanation is entirely feasible for those unspecialized societies (like the Nandi, etc.) in which age groups constitute the basic institutional framework of the society, to whom the most important roles are allocated. In that case the various instrumental roles are performed in relation to them, and they constitute a constant framework of solidarity and expressive integration. Such a situation does not exist, however, in the more specialized societies, where the basic integrative tasks of the society are performed within specialized, achievement-oriented agencies, and the scope of age groups diminishes correspondingly. Can age groups still perform, within such societies, some of the functions attributed to them? Can they still serve as a framework of solidarity, despite the fact that they no longer constitute the basic institutional framework of the society? It seems to us that they still continue to perform some of their functions, from the point of view of both the individual personalities and the social system, although in a somewhat different, transformed manner. In order to be able to understand this problem fully, we shall take up the main characteristics of age groups in the hitherto-discussed specialized societies, and analyze the ways in which they influence the basic functions of the age groups.

We may begin by taking up the limitation of the age span which the activities of these groups cover, a limitation which manifests itself either in the groups' ceasing to function altogether (as among some Ibo, Yoruba, Nuba, Nupe and Athenian groups), or in the limiting of their sphere of activities (as among the Yako). In these societies, the importance of age groups is especially emphasized in the later stages of adolescence and the first stages of adulthood. During this period the age groups perform certain definite functions as regards the individual's personality.

First, they constitute a transitory and preparatory sphere of relations. In all of these societies we find that age group activities include not only various definite tasks allocated them by the bearers of political power in the societies, tasks which constitute, as it were, ends in themselves, but also what may be called definitely preparatory activities. These activities and roles emphasize all of those virtues which may become important later in the achievement-oriented stage of the individual's life, by upholding more or less the same criteria according to which differential status is achieved. These virtues may be military prowess and farming ability, as among some of the Nuba tribes; or economic diligence and ability, as among the Yako and probably also the Ibo, Ibibio and some Yoruba tribes; or, finally, the general inculcation of civil-religious virtues among the Nupe. Similar emphases existed in the military age groups of the Spartans, the age regiments of the Incas and the Aztecs,[26] and in Athens (strong emphasis on the civic virtues). Unlike, for instance, the Nandi group, the Masai, etc., no definite change in the tasks allocated to each age grade and age groups occurs here; but there is a greater continuity and similarity, the younger grades being imbued with goals similar to those they have to uphold in later years.

The institutional arrangement of these activities differs, however, in the age groups in comparison with later stages of the life career. Within the age groups these roles are universally ascribed and definitely bound to the common activities and solidarity of the group, and not dissociated from it as in later stages. At this stage they ensure the individual's full participation in a solidary, primary group, and gratification of his needs for acceptance and affection, thus making him see these various goals as connected with both his emotional, personal security and the sharing of common goals of his society. Thus the strain of the more purely instrumental relations which these activities entail in later stages of the individual's life is eased, because these activities are bound to the common goals and anchored in the individual's primary relations and groups. In other words, it may be said that the re-formation of the individual's identity, at his passing from the age group stage of his life-career to the achievement-oriented stage, does not become an acute problem because (a) the continuity and compatibility of types of activities, and (b) the development of the disposition to perform these roles, have been developed, together with emotional acceptance in a solidary group, in which they become firmly anchored.

Secondly, although the active functioning of age groups ceases at a certain stage, relations between age group members usually tend to continue afterwards, in a more restricted and personal way. We have seen that age mates are required to participate in various familial feasts, ceremonies (marriages, births, funerals), etc., this participation involving definite rights and duties (economic help, eating certain portions of meat, various obligations of mutual help, etc.). The same holds true of Nupe[27] and to some extent of various Ibo villages (the relevant information is not explicit enough[28]). All these relations emphasize mutual, diffuse obligations which are, in a way, a continuation of the more intensive relations within the primary (age) group, and constitute a permanent structural position in which the primacy of expressive and solidary over purely instrumental relations is emphasized. In this way the emotional security attained in such relations is not only a matter of a "reservoir" gathered at a certain point of the individual's life career, but is constantly reactivated on various, definitely structured, occasions. From the point of view of the individual's self-image and identity it means that the overall, diffuse image developed in age groups and centered around age criteria is also constantly reactivated. This usually takes place on occasions connected with kinship and family events, which are, as it were, brought out of their relative segregation, reactivated through the participation of (ex-) age mates, and liked to more instrumentally regulated role clusters.*

The second major characteristic of age groups in "specialized" societies—the small extent of overall regulation of their members' behavior and the greater emphasis on internal relations and solidarity—can be explained in a similar manner. In these societies age groups do not perform overall integrative functions; these are usually performed by other agencies, organized according to

---

* This analysis does not necessarily postulate that ex-age mate relations are the only structural positions through which primary expressive gratification is attained in these societies. There are usually many such situations and relations, such as institutionalized friendship, etc. However, these are beyond the scope of our analysis.

criteria of achievement and specialization, in which the overall regulation of behavior is centered.

Age groups and relations do not in these cases regulate all aspects of the behavior of their members in relation to all other members of the society. They can, however, enhance the security and identification of their members by developing their mutual affection and solidarity and assuring them of its permanency.

This strong emphasis on internal relations and solidarity is very important for the group members, because of the stronger emphasis on instrumental relations in the wider social structure. Age groups often perform functions of mutual economic aid which counterbalance, to some extent, the exigencies of purely instrumental relations, and thus serve as a very important focus of emotional security for their members.

This analysis also indicates the functions of age groups in specialized societies which contribute to the continuity and stability of the social system. It has been shown that both the scope of activities and the extent of autonomy of age groups diminishes in these societies, and they tend to perform subsidiary tasks under the direction of other centers of authority. Despite these limitations, however, they continue to perform tasks which are vitally important for the social system:

First, they serve as agencies through which general role dispositions to identification with the society and its main values are inculcated during the period of greatest educational receptivity.

Secondly, they serve as the main agencies for the allocation of universal, common roles, which are more important and larger in scope than specialized activities. Their importance for the maintenance of the solidarity of the social system is expressed in the strong emphasis which they put on the interconnection between the various instrumental activities and the values of the society, and in the firm binding of these achievements within limits allowed by the basic collectivity orientation of the society. This is especially evident in the role they play in all communal festivals. Thus, for instance, among the Yako we find that, on the one hand, the formation of new age groups and initiation of their members are effected in one of the most important collective rituals of the tribe. On the other hand, the age groups themselves participate corporately in some of the most important communal festivals, e.g., the first-fruit ceremonies. The same is true of the first-fruit ceremonies of the Zulu, and of the central ritual of "strengthening the king" among the Swazi.[29] Among the Nupe one of the central ceremonies, the *Ganni*, which corresponds to some extent to a New Year's ceremony, is primarily the festival of the age groups.[30] Similarly, the Spartan age groups participated actively in the main civil festivals, as did the students of Athenian gymnasia in the various games and competitions. In all these festivals the limitation of purely individual activities within the framework of collective goals is very strongly emphasized. While such limitation is not always successfully emphasized in the various associations (among which some competition for power may arise at any time) and in the purely economic sphere, age group relations emphasizes these boundaries both through their own formal activities and through the more diffuse relation between ex-age mates. They serve as primary groups whose value orientations and goals are harmonious with those of the whole society and oriented towards them, thus fostering the solidarity of the whole society.

In addition to this, the age groups in these societies also uphold a general attitude of respect towards elders and ensure smooth interaction between the different generations. While these relations are not, in these societies, as fully organized within the scope of the age groups as in the nonspecialized primitive societies, they do foster these general attitudes among their members.

Finally, age groups also serve as selective agencies through which the more active leaders and "elite" elements are prepared, chosen and transferred to the adult institutional sphere. This last function emphasized the continuity between some of the basic value orientations of the age groups and those of the other institutionalized sectors in these societies.

Thus we see that the function of age groups within specialized societies is somewhat different from that in nonspecialized societies, although it is also derived from the basic postulates presented in the preceding chapters. The main difference lies in

the fact that the institutional scope of the age groups in specialized societies is more restricted than in nonspecialized ones, and
that therefore the balance between instrumental, solidary and
expressive gratifications provided by them is necessarily limited
to certain occasions and situations in the social system. The age
groups no longer constitute the main institutional framework of
social solidarity. They are confined first, to the preparatory stage;
secondly, to certain restricted relations and activities on behalf
of the authority centers; and thirdly, to certain definite occasions, such as economic need, family rituals, communal festivals,
etc. In these activities and on these occasions their basic solidarity
and the emotional support they give are reactivated, remembered
and enhanced. They constitute, as it were, centers of solidarity
(although not the only ones) to which people turn after excessive
instrumental activity; although they no longer constitute an
overall framework of such solidarity which encompasses and
regulates most instrumental activities.

IX At this point it would seem suitable to present some comparative material which would further validate the hypothesis and also elucidate it. We have hitherto analyzed
universalistic societies with some extent of specialization and
achievement orientation. Both specialization and achievement
orientation may, however, exist and co-exist within particularistic societies. It would be to the point, it seems, to analyze
briefly some societies of that kind and to see what light this
analysis may throw on our problem.

In our previous presentation we have already analyzed some
types of specialization within particularistic societies, based on
more or less rigidly defined descent groups—as among the Tallensi, the Pueblos (especially the Hopi), etc. We have seen that
in these tribes no age groups arise, as all of the individual's life
is bound within the limits of his descent group; and that in such
societies the various informal children's play groups do not crystallize into fully formalized age groups; the individual attains his
full identity and maturity within the family, kinship group, etc.,
and not within these play groups.

Family or descent groups do not, however, constitute the main
unit of social division of labor and specialization in all particu-

laristic societies. Such a situation exists only in more "primitive," less differentiated societies. In more complex and differentiated particularistic societies, such as the main historical societies, there arise distinct orders of political, economic and ritual positions and agencies, which are not identical with the family or descent groups and which are not regulated by kinship criteria alone. There arise distinct groups whose main principles of allocation of roles and rewards, although definitely particularistic, are not identical with the roles enacted with the family unit. These roles may be vested in representatives of family and kin groups, hereditarily confined to them or allocated to them on the basis of differential family status; but they are not merged within or identical with family groups.

Most of the more complex, historical, nonuniversalistic societies are of this kind, and not of the relatively simple kind of primitive society, in which the various kinship groups serve as the only—or main—institutionalized groups. In all such societies the attainment of specialized roles entails removal from the family, either for all or for some of its members. In order to perform some of these roles and enjoy the rewards they carry, the members of the family have to leave it for a certain period of time, or for a definite part of their entire life. It would be interesting to compare such a transition from the family to the specialized group with that effected in universalistic societies through age groups. Limited space prevents a thorough examination of many cases and types of such transition, but some examples related to the type of material we have presented hitherto may be attempted.*

One such comparative example may be the "secret associations" of Sierra Leone and Liberia, the *Poro* and the *Sande* of the Mende,[31] and other tribes of the Liberian hinterland.[32] As among the Ibo and the Yoruba, special associations are here among the most important sections of the political and social structure, playing an important role in the political and ritual life of the

---

* It is interesting to note that relations between age groups and secret associations have been among the central problems of the old literature on age grades. The analysis there was, however, mainly oriented to the establishment of a unitary evolutionary scheme, though the basic incompatibility between the two was already discerned and stressed in that literature.

tribe, and being—sometimes together with the chief (king) and sometimes in opposition to him—the main center of political power. These associations are usually graded, and include all of the male (or female) population of the tribe. Despite this inclusiveness, the sphere of life over which the secret society rules is strongly differentiated from that of the family and the regular daily routine of households, lineages and villages.

This separateness is symbolically manifested in the secret initiation into the *Poro* school, from which both women and youngsters are excluded, and the various ceremonies of coming back into the fold of the family.[33] While this initiation is more or less universal, it enables the individual to become a member of the lowest grades of the society only. The higher grades are hereditarily vested in representatives of various families and lineages; and so, consequently, is membership in the *Poro* council.[34] Thus we find here a particular type of specialization: on the one hand, an inclusive "secret" society; on the other, specialization of political and ritual functions vested in particularistic groups, which also regulate the entire membership of the "secret society." This specialization entails a definite transition from the family and permanent segregation of political roles from those of the kinship units; not only the symbolical and temporary segregation of all initiation ceremonies, but a more real and permanent one.

This transition and segregation are effected in the *Poro* school, where attendance is compulsory for almost all members of the tribe, and both the secret lore of the tribe and various, more specialized technical skills are acquired. Although we have no detailed information about such a school, one thing seems to stand out clearly: although the school necessarily brings people (boys and girls) of the same age together, this is not done in terms of common age homogeneity or in order to establish an age-homogeneous group. The groups are not ideologically described as age groups; i.e., the fact of age homogeneity is only incidental to the main goals of these groups and their symbols of identification, symbols which center around the community of the mysteries of the *Poro,* and which cut across age differences. In so far as age is stressed, emphasis is laid on the com-

plementary age-heterogeneous element of seniority, of the interaction of different generations in a common situation and through
the sharing of common goals and values, and not on absolute
age differences.[35]

Thus transition from the family to another, wider particularistic unit is not effected through a common age group which
emphasizes age differences, but through a stronger reactivation
of and emphasis on both the complementariness of age grades
and their common values and goals. Although the human image
and the identity involved in these situations and schools are
couched in terms of age (grading), they do not involve the
necessity of participating in an age-homogeneous group in order
to develop and maintain these images and identity. This is
attained through the reactivation of the relations of seniority,
and it is in this way that smooth transition is effected.

Parallel instances may be found in many societies whose economic division of labor is organized into specialized units (crafts,
guilds, etc.), which are particularistically built up, either through
hereditary succession or through personal adoption, and which
necessitate some period of preparation—of apprenticeship and
learning. We find such cases among the Maoris,[36] among several
other Polynesian societies,[37] and in the main historical societies
of medieval Europe, China, etc.[38]

In all these cases, transition from the family of orientation to
the new particularistic group is also necessary. Such a transition
may involve the coming together of young people of more or
less similar age; but, again, this does not make them into an age
group. Their most significant relations are those with their
"master," who teaches them their craft and to whom they are
(or become) personally (particularistically) bound in terms of
seniority and on the basis of age complementariness.[39]

Historically the most interesting case of this type may be
found in feudal European society (and also in other feudal societies)[40] as well as in the European urban guild society. The
guild education, on the one hand, and the educational system
of the aristocracy in preparation for knighthood, on the other
hand, are the most vivid examples of this kind. The feudal society
was particularistically defined and regulated. It was organized into

several social strata, relations between which were very largely determined by their relative positions towards one another in respect of prestige, authority and power. The interaction between various members of this society was largely determined by their relative positions on this hierarchy scale, and not by any universalistic criteria equally applicable to all. Most of these particularistic strata and positions were usually also ascribed, although within them some roles had to be achieved, and there also existed some mobility between them. This mobility (with the exception of that effected within the church) was oriented towards the achievement of various particularistic positions, which then once more became ascribed (mostly on a hereditary basis). Many important roles of the ruling class—the feudal aristocracy—necessitated a long period of preparation and of removal from the individual's family of orientation. Throughout this period of education, usually effected at the courts of other knights and princes, the young "apprentice" would usually be placed together with other youths of similar age and position, with whom he would share his life during this period. Their education was usually couched in terms of age grading, and the various grades were sometimes clearly differentiated.

And yet, despite all these facts, these youths did not constitute a full-fledged, age-homogeneous and autocephalous group. Whatever element of age homogeneity existed was but subsidiary to their relations with seniors, and never developed into full common identification. Their basic identification was formed by their relationship to their "lord"—a personal and particularistic relationship—and it was also according to this criterion that their group life and roles were structured and allocated. Here once more the element of particularistic age seniority was preponderant within the framework of the feudal hierarchy.[41] This has been aptly expressed by the great French sociologist and sinologist, M. Granet, when speaking of Chinese feudalism: "On devient *un* homme en devenant l'homme de son père ou de son seigneur." (M. Granet, *La féodalité Chinoise*, Oslo, 1952, p. 189.) In this also the close connection between the familial and the feudal hierarchies is expressed.

A somewhat different, yet basically similar, situation is encountered in those "specialized" particularistic societies in which there exists a strong subsidiary achievement orientation, and in which the attainment of certain particularistic "specialties" is to some extent regulated by achievement. Among many societies, both primitive and historical, this holds true of the achievement of special political positions through education in the king's court or at special royal schools.[42] These schools are usually age graded, and every class is therefore somewhat of an "age group." And yet the element of age homogeneity and age grouping is once more but subsidiary and partial. This is so, first, because it affects only a very small part of the population, and therefore age grouping cannot become important as an indicator of universalistic roles and relations and of general social status. Secondly, the element of age grouping is only transitory, mainly because the positions to which it leads are particularistically defined, and closely connected with definite subsectors of the society, and thus incompatible with a strong emphasis on age-homogeneity. The identity of these students is built up around these particularistic aspirations and orientations, and therefore any emphasis on overall, common age grouping must become subsidiary. Age grouping is operative here in that part of the social system in which roles are allocated according to universalistic criteria; but as this part of the social system is segregated and subsidiary, and the element of common age but a by-product of particularistic achievement orientation, the importance of age grouping to both the personality and the social system is minimal.

The most interesting instance of achievement-oriented education within the framework of a particularistic society is the classical Chinese social and educational system, and, to a lesser extent, various other Southeast Asian educational systems.[43] Chinese society has been aptly described by T. Parsons as one of a "particularistic achievement" type. The classical system of examinations and of acquisition of official posts was, from the point of view of "formal" criteria of role allocation, achievement-oriented. At the same time it was particularistic, since it laid great stress on criteria of the examinee's relation to various hierarchical relations and values, his personal qualities in relation to other groups, and not on various universalistic criteria such as efficiency. In actuality these various roles were also particularistically defined, i.e., in terms of the mutual (hierarchical) relations of various units and groups. These roles were also to a large extent limited to various particularistic groups such as family and kin groups, gentry strata, etc.[44] The knowledge required for success in the official examinations necessitated a long period of study; consequently special schools were established throughout China. These schools were internally age graded, bringing together boys of similar age. And yet no full-fledged age groups developed, mainly because both the value orientation and standards of role allocation prevalent in the most important institutional spheres of the social structure were particularistic, and their preparation was oriented towards the attainment of these particularistic positions and values. On the one hand, the Chinese family system was of crucial importance at all points of this "familial" society, and served as one of the main allocative agencies in all spheres; while, on the other hand, the whole "officialdom" constituted a particularistically oriented stratum, very closely connected with the family system itself.[45] Within this system there was a very strong emphasis on relative age and seniority; even during the period of preparation the young man was bound by this system and oriented towards it, and any development of universalistic age ideology and identification was impossible, despite the existence of age graded groups within the schools.[46]

The same basic personal particularistic relationship between pupils and teachers (masters) can be clearly seen within the framework of the great religious systems and sects. Even in the case of most universal religions, the educational relationship between master and pupil is couched in personal charismatic terms.[47] Even the groups of "bakhurei yeshiva" in the traditional Jewish society, mentioned briefly above, did not form full-fledged, universalistic youth groups, but only groups limited to a very distinct, particularistic setting and value orientations. In this respect these schools are entirely different from the modern school system, with its universalistic premises.

We have already seen in the previous chapter that modern school systems are usually organized on a country-wide basis, and are oriented towards the development of various universalistic achievements. Although it is well known that the school system is unevenly distributed between different social strata, its basic value premises are universalistic and achievement-oriented. This was not the case in the various schools that existed in familistic peasant societies in Europe and Asia, in the caste system of India and Ceylon, in the urban artisans' schools connected with the guilds, or in the aristocratic schools of both the Roman Republic and Empire.[48] These were oriented towards a preparation for various restricted roles within the scope of ascriptive and particularistic groups, and not towards universalistic achievements. A similar situation can also be found, for instance, in the educational system of the Byzantine Empire, both in the secular universities and in the church schools, which were of great importance in the cultural and political life of the state.[49] The modern system itself has developed from such particularistic schools (such as the various country schools, and the 17th and 18th century "public" schools in England); the transition from these systems to the universal education of modern states is very instructive from the point of view of our discussion, as it shows clearly the emergence of a new type and direction of age identification.[50]

Cursory as the presentation in this section has been, it is sufficient, we believe, to analyze the differences between specialization and achievement orientation within particularistic and universalistic societies, the different types of social relations existing with them, and the importance of these differences for the problem of formation of age groups and universalistic age ideology.

The main difference encountered is that in particularistic societies (i.e., those societies whose main criteria of allocation of roles and rewards are particularistically defined) the period of preparation, of transition from the family and the actual meeting with coevals, does not give rise to overall, universal age groups and age group ideology. While it is quite important in the inculcation of some subsidiary universalistic orientations, especially in the intellectual and cultural field, this orientation does not constitute a basic element of these groups. This has been accounted for on several bases. First, in most of these societies (except the Mende, etc.) the preparatory schools do not encompass, either potentially or actually, all the members of a given age grade within this society, but only a very select group. Secondly, the criteria according to which this group is selected and which determine its identification are usually particularistic, and, together with concomitant value orientations, they define the contents of the roles towards which the preparation tends. Thirdly, in most of these situations there is a very strong emphasis on *relative* age, quite often on personal relationships of seniority between teachers and pupils, etc.

The particularistic orientation of their aspirations, the particularistic setting of their roles, and the consequent basic harmony between the structure of their family roles and those of occupational, political, etc., spheres, provide a firm basis of emotional security and of identification. Their status image is securely anchored within these particularistic frameworks, which assure them both primary relations and collective identification, and compatibility between the two. Thus, the "accident" of age homogeneity does not constitute, from the point of view of either the status aspirations of the members or the principles of role allocation, an important focus of identification and community orientation.

X   The analysis of the effects of specialization and achievement orientation in universalistic and particularistic societies brings us to another point which is of general interest to our analysis, and which was already mentioned in the first chapter of this book: the general place of *age* in the main types of societies hitherto discussed. We have until now concentrated on the specific problem of organized age groups. But the problem cannot be fully understood without a brief consideration of the more general problem of the place of age criteria in the value systems, and in the princpiles of role allocation, in a society. Under what social conditions is this criterion of importance in all these respects? In what types of society, even in those which have no age group systems, are significant roles in the political, economic and ritual spheres allocated on the basis of age, and authority and respect given according to the principle of seniority? It seems that our discussion and description of several types of societies enable us to give a systematic answer to this question. In *most* of the primitive societies hitherto discussed, both with and without age groups, age constitutes a relatively important principle in the allocation of roles in most spheres. Thus elders hold important political and ritual offices within most of the lineages and kinship groups of these societies, and the corporate power of these groups in relation to other groups is vested in them. They are also usually incumbents of most of the important offices of the society as a whole. Age and seniority command general respect and exert authority and influence. This is especially so in the various segmentary tribes, in many of the centralized, kinship-organized kingdoms and secret societies and associations. But this picture changes to some extent in some of the achievement-oriented and specialized societies. The preponderance of universalistic achievement restricts to a large extent the importance of age. This is in line with the hypothesis formulated in Chapter I, namely, that the importance of age as a criterion of allocation of roles is related to the extent to which the general value system of a society is harmonious with those of the human image of age. We have seen that age definitions are by their nature ascriptive and diffuse. Hence any strong emphasis on achievement and specialization reduces the importance of the age criterion as a principle of role allocation. Accordingly we find that the relative importance of age and seniority diminishes somewhat in the various associations of Yako, Ibo, etc. And yet even this decline of the importance of the age criterion is relative. Even among these tribes we find that age and seniority command respect and, at least within the sphere of the family and the clans, also positions of authority. While the explicitness of the age criterion in the process of role allocation in the wider spheres of society has become smaller here, and does not apply in several spheres and organizations, this causes no great diminution of the respect given to seniority. Age and seniority still count very much, although in a rather more general and diffuse way, and not always as a *specific* criterion of allocation of roles. It is only in the more specialized societies, e.g., in Athens in the

4th century B.C., that we witness some diminution of this respect and some potential disruptions and unresolved strains in the relations between generations.

The only partial exception to this law are tribes in which there exists a very strong emphasis on military valor, which by necessity diminishes with advanced age. Here, as among the Nandi, Masai, etc., we find a much stronger emphasis on the warrior age grade, and not on elder age and seniority in general, and it is this age grade which commands the greatest authority and prestige. Here also the criterion of age serves as a basic criterion of allocation of roles; but because of the special emphasis on warriorship, there is a shift in the relative evaluation of different age grades.

The situation in the more differentiated, particularistic, specialized and achievement-oriented societies is somewhat more complicated. On the one hand, to the extent that achievement and specialization prevail, the importance of the criterion and value of age necessarily diminishes. In the sectors governed by these orientations, roles are allocated according to principles differing from those of age. And yet age—especially relative age, or seniority—does not lose all of its significance. If we look either at classical China, with its patrimonial bureaucracy, or at the various ecclesiastical hierarchies of Europe and Asia, or generally at feudal and guild societies, we see that seniority plays a very important role in social relations, commands authority and respect, and usually has a strong, even if not always fully articulated, influence on the allocation of roles and on the patterns of behavior within many social spheres. While the general hierarchical principles of a stratified society cut across the criterion of age, at the same time they uphold its importance within each of the strata, and in a general way uphold the value of age—of wisdom and experience—and the respect due it in their value systems and ideology. This is due to the preponderance of the particularistic criteria within them. As we have already seen, these criteria set a definite limit to the scope of achievement and specialization. They encompass, then, the total, diffuse style of living of a given particularistic group, and uphold this traditionalistic style. Hence their strong emphasis on experience, on knowledge of and penetration into the framework of this style of living—all of which tends to emphasize the importance of age and seniority, even if not all roles are allocated on this basis. But even in this way the basic continuous and complementary relations between generations are vigorously upheld.

It seems that our general supposition as to the types of societies in which age is an important criterion of allocation of roles is verified by this analysis. In so far as a diffuse and ascriptive value orientation is maintained, the importance of the age criterion is relatively great. It is necessarily greater in particularistic than in universalistic societies. In the former, even when the basic units of the society are built not on blood ties, but on various hierarchical principles, the importance of age and seniority is maintained in detail within each stratum, and also as a general value of the society. If some achievement- and specificity-oriented activities exist in these societies, they are usually kept within the bounds of traditionalistic units within which seniority is again maintained, even if many roles are not directly related to it. It is only when achievement and specificity orientations take place within the framework of an overall universalistic society— as occurs in most modern societies—that the relative importance of the age criterion changes greatly.

Turning now to the whole complex of modern societies, XI   we find more intensive specialization and achievement orientation than in any other society hitherto analyzed. As in the preceding chapter, we shall have to describe this complex in an "ideal type," necessarily cursory, way, which may, however, suffice for our purposes. The intensity of specialization and achievement orientation in modern society is threefold. First, there exists a great segregation and differentiation between the various social spheres, and the number of "specialties" and "alternatives" becomes very great, especially in the economic field. Most of the economic processes are enacted in specialized agencies and groups distinguished from one another according to their specialized functions. The economic division of labor is based on separation between units of production and consumption, and among the former (and to some extent also among the latter) there is a high degree of internal specialization. The same applies in a somewhat different manner to political, ritual and intellectual activities. Most roles incumbent on members of modern societies, outside the field of family and kinship, are also highly specialized. These roles usually necessitate a long period of preparation and learning, are mostly nonascribed, i.e., must be achieved, and their performance is judged by standards of both specificity and achievement.[51] Secondly, not only are the criteria of role allocation based on specificity, specializaztion and achievement; we find the same standards predominant in the field of value orientations as well. Thirdly, within most modern societies there is also a strong individualistic orientation in the sphere of value orientations; i.e., the sphere in which roles and awards are allocated with respect to individualistic gratification only is larger and stronger than in any other hitherto-discussed type of society. We find here a basic difference from primitive and past historical societies, among which, as has been shown, the various achievement-oriented and specialized principles of allocation of roles were to different degrees bound within the limits of diffuse, ascriptive and sometimes even particularistic value orientations. In modern societies the development of a universalistic society has been historically connected with the development of specific achievement value orientations. Historically, this interconnection goes back to the development of puritanism, modern capitalism and the liberal modern state based on universal citizenship.[52] It should of course be clear, as has already been shown in the preceding chapter, that this has been a gradual development unevenly spread in various sectors of Western societies, and to this day unevenly distributed among them.

This type of social organization, which is prevalent in modern societies, limits the scope and number of roles allocated on the basis of age alone. There exist very few organizations and groups in which roles are allocated expressly on the basis of age. Some organizations—the more achievement-oriented and competitive ones—are to a very large extent opposed to any specific recognition of age or seniority as an important element in their structure. Moreover, in many of these fields middle or advanced ages are looked down upon and feared. Within them there exists potentially strong competition between various age grades and generations, and relations between them are strained. In other organizations there may be somewhat less antagonism towards considerations of age and seniority, although only rarely do they become explicit criteria of role allocation. Considerations of seniority—and sometimes rules of seniority—exist within many formal, bureaucratic organizations like the army, church, universities, etc., although seniority is not always identical here with relative age. Age is also of some value in those spheres which have a more diffuse and collective orientation, and in which considerations of experience and "accumulated" wisdom are of importance. Outstanding examples in the occupational fields are country or family doctors and lawyers; in politics, "elder statesmen." In all these cases considerations of age are of some general importance in social relations, although even then they are not immune from more achievement-oriented criteria, which give greater importance to younger people. In general it may be said that the great emphasis on achievement and specialization limits to a very great extent the importance of age as an explicit criterion of allocation of roles. It does not, however, negate it altogether, nor does it diminish the importance of organizing relations between generations. Its importance becomes perhaps even greater, as in these cases there exist many inherent strains between various generations, and their smooth interaction and continuity may, to some extent, be impaired. It will be one of the most important tasks of our analysis to see how youth and age groups in modern societies affect relations between generations.

We shall now turn to an analysis of the impact of specialization and achievement orientation in modern societies on the structure of their age groups. One of the main outcomes of the process has already been analyzed, namely, the long period of preparation for which special institutional devices—the schools—have been developed. Contrary to the particularistic societies analyzed in the preceding section, this preparation is strongly bound to universalistic and achievement-oriented values which, as has been shown, determine the strong development of "age groups" and of identity based on age criteria.[53]

The preparatory period in school is not, here, usually a transitory period from one particularistic group (or position) to another, but is oriented towards the attainment of specialized roles, the contents of which are usually to some extent both universalistic and achievement-oriented. The modern school system with its strong emphasis on preparatory age grading is strongly related to the high extent of specialization existing within modern societies. However, as has been shown in the preceding chapter, this school system, with its emphasis on instrumental achievements, does not provide an adequate goal for all the needs of the youths and adolescents, and it is this that gives rise to various spontaneous youth groups. In modern societies these youth groups share, together with the school, the "preparatory" sphere; the effects of intensive specialization may also be clearly discerned in the composition and activities of these various age and youth groups, youth agencies, etc. Several of these characteristics are similar to those of age groups in specialized primitive societies, but in these cases they are much more pronounced. We shall present these characteristics as they apply in the most general way to most modern societies.

The first of these characteristics is that limitation of the life span in which youth groups operate is very pronounced in these societies. In most modern youth groups (with the partial exception of the German youth movement), activities are clearly confined to the adolescent and very early adult span, and never extend beyond it. It is of course true that in many youth organizations we find older people performing various directive tasks (e.g., recreation directors, sponsors, semi-official instructors, etc.). However, these people are clearly representatives of adult society, who deal with the young people and guide them, and not "original" members of the group. Original membership is clearly confined to the adolescent and very early adult stage, i.e., the stage before specialization and achievement-oriented activities take up most of the individual's life and energy (and clearly before the establishment of a new family unit). The internal solidarity of the youth group is quickly disrupted, and the group's cohesion and attraction for its members is weakened with the onset of social maturity, preparation for marriage and the need to find a job.* This is as true of the loosely organized groups of "peers" of the United States as of the more formalized youth organizations of Israel and the highly formalized ones of Russia.[54]

The only partial exception to this limitation of the age span may be found among some of the German youth movements, in which, owing to their sectarian and uninstitutionalized character, attempts—mostly unsuccessful—were made to prolong the existence of the movement and its influence beyond the adolescent span. However, this could be attempted only in so far as these movements lacked legitimization and institutionalization, and attempted to be revolutionary movements.

In no other cases are there definite activities or clearly defined mutual rights of youth group members beyond the span of adolescence; although many life-long friendships are established during that period and a general spirit of comradeship is instilled. However, this spirit is not bound to any definite roles or obligations.

Secondly, we find in all modern youth groups, movements and organizations an exceptionally strong emphasis on the internal activities of the group, and an almost complete lack of regulation of the general behavior of members of the society. Even when the youth organization is completely directed and organized by adults, it does not perform any regulative function with regard to the overall behavior of either its own members or other members of the society. The center of its interest and activities is in the internal affairs of the group or organization, and not outside its boundaries.

This very strong emphasis on internal relations also explains one of the most common characteristics of modern youth groups —the great importance of a small, autonomous, primary group as a nucleus of all of these organizations.[55] It has already been shown that such small groups are the basic nuclei of all types of age groups, but in most primitive organizations this nucleus is firmly interwoven with the larger organization and bears its sym-

---

* This accounts for the fact that youth movements and organizations among working class youth usually cover a shorter period of life, and begin early to engage in purely technical, vocational activities.

bols of identification and values. Within modern youth groups such a nucleus enjoys much greater internal autonomy, and between its members there tends to develop a very strong emotional interdependence and intensive mutual identification.[56] This intensity is based mainly on emotional links, which attain a special importance because of the "preparatory," segregated nature of the roles allocated to adolescents, and because of the serious emotional problems connected with the period of adolescence and the reformulation of adolescent ego identity in modern societies.[57] This strong emotional relation may or may not be fully integrated into broader, formalized structures; but it is this emotional strength that makes it possible for these groups to become nuclei of various rebellious and deviant movements and activities.[58]

XII   Thus we see that the general characteristics of age groups in specialized societies are accentuated and intensified in modern youth groups, but are not structurally dissimilar to those of primitive societies. But the picture of specialization and achievement orientation and their repercussions on the structure of youth groups is not uniform in all sectors of modern societies. There exists here a great differentiation between various strata within modern societies, which is strongly connected with the nature and extent of specialization and achievement orientation within them. One of the most important indices of specialization and achievement orientation is the nature and scope of occupational choice within a given sector, and its relation to the general value system of the society and of this sector. The first important variable is, of course, the extent of specialized knowledge and skill that a given occupation or group of occupations demands. This obviously determines to a large extent the length of preparatory education necessary, and also the age at which the young adolescent or adult enters occupational life. But the technical necessities of preparation are not the only factor which determines the length of preparation and education. Many aspects of the educational system are focused on symbolic and intellectual knowledge. Thus a second variable which influences the length of education and the nature of preparation is a given group's attitude towards the various symbolic and intellectual values embodied in the school system.

Thus we find that in most of the lower classes of certain societies the period of organized preparation and education is very short, and corresponds to both the occupational and value patterns of these strata. The occupations of these groups do not demand a very large extent of preparation and education, and no great value is set on such preparation and education. The youngster begins to work relatively early in life (12-16), and little skilled knowledge is required. There is a latent opposition to the demands of the school and its value, and usually only slight supervision by the parents of their children's education. The occupation choices given these children are very limited, and the family does not usually direct them actively towards any definite occupation. It does restrict the possibilities and horizon of choices and aspirations, but does not in itself constitute an effective economic or educational unit. Hence the special characteristics of youth groups within these strata—characteristics which are largely similar in many modern countries. The early beginning of occupational life limits the life span of youth groups; although some of them tend to persist until marriage, and may then develop into informal groups of adults. Thus the discontinuity between family and youth in most modern societies is of shorter duration in these strata than in others. Youth groups, mostly of an unorganized type—"crowds," "gangs," "street corner groups," etc.—lead a very intensive life at a certain period of life, and then gradually develop into formal groups of adults. The pattern of activities and values of these groups and those of the adults of their class are to a great extent similar; although the demarcation line between various age grades is rather strong, and there is little mixing between them. To some extent this pattern is not unlike that found in many peasant societies, to be described in the following chapter. This similarity of values is most clearly seen in the negative attitude towards school and formal education, and in the total dissociation of the youth groups from school life. Thus, in these cases the small extent of specialization shortens the life span of the youth groups, while their attitude towards some of the main values of the society gives rise to some extent of association with adult-sponsored youth agencies. This is especially true of the attitude towards the school, but also to some extent as regards various youth clubs, organizations, etc. The most outstanding exceptions from this point of view are the various types of working-youth movements and organizations. These have been very influential in Continental countries, in Israel, etc.; but even there their greatest influence has been among skilled workers or as far as they served as channels of mobility towards better occupational strata. Here we find attempts to inculcate within the adolescents a feeling of pride in their work, and a strong identification with its values and orientations, which is not the case with youth groups recruited among the lower-class, unskilled groups. But here also we find that the age span which the youth movement or organization covers is rather limited, as the working age is relatively low.

A totally different picture can be found in the various upper classes of modern society—the English and Continental aristocracy and upper business and professional classes, the American "upper-upper" classes and plutocracy, etc. There the extent of specialization, on the one hand, and identification with the various symbolic values of the society, on the other, is very great. The various occupations in which the members of these classes engage demand a long period of preparation, as does their value system. Hence the very long period of preparation in schools and universities. This specialization and achievement orientation in the occupational sphere is, however, of a very special character. It has—especially in England and in some Continental groups—a very strong ascriptive and diffuse bias. Although the individual members of this group are not restricted in their choice of occupation, the choice is relatively limited. This limitation stems from the attitudes as to what the proper occupations are, e.g., business, the professions, academic careers; and the occupational choice is strongly influenced by the values and style of living of these families, with which the young people usually tend to identify themselves. Thus the specialization and achievement orientation of these groups and their concomitant occupational choices are to a very large extent set within the framework of ascriptive and diffuse patterns of their total style of living.

This pattern of specialization has its repercussions on the structure of youth groups recruited within these strata. Formal education is very prolonged, but, unlike among the lower classes, there exists a very strong connection between it and the spontaneous group life of youth. In some cases the spontaneous youth groups find almost full expression within the framework of the schools. Outstanding examples of this are the English public schools, especially in the form they have taken from the first half of the 19th century. They have been aptly described by the French historian, E. Halévy:

> The masters taught their classes, and in cases of serious insubordination they interfered and flogged the offenders. Otherwise they left the boys to themselves. There were no masters like the French *maîtres d'études*, whose province was the continual maintenance of discipline. Discipline was left in the hands of the older boys, the members of the sixth form, which constituted the senate, the ruling aristocracy of the public school. Servants were few or none. The boys, therefore, had to provide their own service. The younger boys, the members of the lower forms, were the fags of the older boys, waxing their shoes, boiling the water for their tea, carrying their cricket balls and bats. An enormous society of boys between the ages of eight and eighteen governed by an unwritten code of its own making, an almost free republic of 100, 200 or 500 members, a club where even before adolescence a boy was imbued with the spirit of an aristocratic nation: such was the English public school.[59]

The extent to which they molded the activities and characters of the young people is amply illustrated in the numerous autobiographies of members of the English aristocracy.[60] To some extent they resemble the various types of schools in particularistic societies described above, although some aspects of the curriculum and general value orientations had a much more universalistic connotation. But the strongly ascriptive basis of their orientation was fully evident in the close relation between the official school system and spontaneous youth activities. This connection can also be found in participation in various officially sponsored youth agencies—the Scouts, youth clubs, etc.—which are sometimes very prominent among the members of their groups and classes. It is only in some specific cases, as for instance among the very authoritarian families of American plutocracy, that we find some sort of youth rebellion among the children.[61]

The difference between these and lower-class children has been clearly summarized in a recent English study by S. M. Spinley:[62]

Slum Experience	Public School Experience
Broken home with much overt conflict	Stable home with little overt conflict
Unplanned child	Planned child
Large family of siblings	Small family
Sibling relations close and rough	Sibling relations less close and more supervised
Father's occupation manual	Father's occupation business or professional
Mother works after birth of child	Mother does not work after birth of child
Young parents	Older parents
Childhood and adolescence spent at home among siblings and with companions of both sexes	Greater part of childhood and adolescence spent away from home in an age-sex group
School standards and ideals conflict with behavior in the home	School standards and ideals largely congruent with behavior in the home
Taught in school by people who believe themselves of higher social status	Taught in school by people who believe themselves of equal or lower social status

Various middle classes of modern societies show some specific patterns. In some European countries the picture is not entirely dissimilar from that of the upper classes, in so far as a strong connection between occupational patterns and a somewhat traditionalistic, diffuse pattern of life and culture are concerned. This seems to be the case in England; even more so in France, with its more traditionalistic bourgeoisie with strong family values; and to a smaller extent in the United States. Obviously the extent of occupational choice and mobility would usually be greater here than in the upper classes, and emphasis on achievement much stronger. Hence also a somewhat greater extent of separation of family life from the occupational and political spheres, and a somewhat greater differentiation in the structure of youth groups. The period of preparation is relatively long (much longer, of course, than in the lower classes, and sometimes as long as in the upper class); but education may be somewhat more specialized (according to the various occupational exigencies)—especially in the later stages—and less oriented to a diffuse pattern of values and to character development. Hence there may be a somewhat greater scope for spontaneous youth groups; but even these groups are usually closely connected either with the school (e.g., in sports activities) or with various adult-sponsored youth agencies and organizations (e.g., the YMCA, Scouts, youth clubs, various political parties and religious organizations, etc.). Spontaneous youth groups may in these cases develop various convivial and sporting activities, leading to the establishment of close friendships between a small number of young people, etc., but not evolving any marked opposition to the adult world.

The situation is somewhat more complex among those sectors of the middle classes in which achievement orientation is more pronounced, and only weakly related to diffuse and collective patterns of life. This is the case in some parts of the American middle class, and generally in many sectors in which very marked individual mobility prevails. Here the extent of specialization and the emphasis on specificity orientations and achievement is very marked, as is also, consequently, the length of preparation demanded from children and adolescents. The school serves as one of the main channels of preparation and mobility, and its preparatory and instrumental aspects are stressed to a very large extent. Consequently, we find here a rather strong dissociation between the formal organization of the school, the various adult-sponsored youth agencies, and spontaneous youth groups. This dissociation may be expressed in non participation in the various agencies and similar organizations organized by the schools, and/or the development of a somewhat subversive "youth culture" with an ambivalent attitude towards the adult world. Thus we see that although all sectors of modern societies are characterized by a separation between family and occupational life, the exact structure of this separation and of the concomitant specialization and achievement orientations differs greatly in various strata of the society, thus affecting the structure of youth groups in various ways.

In all the major structural characteristics hitherto de-
XIII   scribed, there exists, as we have already pointed out, some
similarity between the structure of modern youth agencies and groups and that of primitive and historical societies
in which specialization and achievement orientation prevail. In
spite of these similarities, however, there are within modern
youth groups several characteristics which differentiate them
from age groups of primitive specialized societies. The first
major difference lies in the fact that modern youth groups are
entirely segregated within the preparatory sphere, and consequently no fully institutionalized roles are allocated to them. In
other words, modern youth groups do not engage in fully institutionalized instrumental relations or in the performance of
institutional tasks in the society. There are, indeed, many instrumental activities within the school, but these activities are clearly
of a preparatory and training character. The extent of preparatory instrumental activities in youth groups is much smaller.
Thus modern youth groups lay a stronger emphasis on solidary
and expressive activities. Consequently no fully recognized instrumental activities are regulated by the solidarity of the youth
groups, and there are, as we have seen, few definite relations
between age mates after adolescence. This segregation of solidary
orientation emphasizes the preparatory nature of modern youth
groups.

The type of preparation and the content of preparatory activities vary, of course, from one type of youth group to another.
In the loose peer groups of American "youth culture" this preparation manifests itself in a somewhat subversive imitation of
"strong" adult behavior, in an attempt to behave like adults, etc.
In the more organized and formalized movements, such as the
various youth organizations affiliated to political parties, it is
manifested in the inculcation of civic virtues, of a common ideology and political indoctrination, to prepare the members for
full, active participation in the political life of their respective
communities. In some of these organizations, and particularly
in the *kibbutz*, there are "children's republics" (directed by
adults) in which the children lead a community life of their own,
patterned after that of the adult society and preparing them for

it by means of daily precepts.[63] In all of these cases, however, the activities of the youth groups emphasize the preparatory aspect and segregate the world of the children from that of the adults, even if in this way they stress the autonomy of the children's world. Thus we see once more that the ways in which specialization and achievement orientations affect the structure of youth groups and organizations differ in various sectors and strata of modern societies. But in all of them the basic structural difference from most primitive and historical societies—namely, the confinement of age groups to the preparatory and training sphere—is evident.

Besides these structural differences between modern youth groups and the age groups of specialized primitive and historical societies, there is an even deeper difference. Contrary to primitive societies, in modern societies there does not usually exist full harmony between the value orientations of the age and youth groups and those of the total society. It has been shown that the value orientations of modern societies tend to be, in different degrees, achievement- and specificity-oriented. This entails some potential lack of harmony with the ascriptive and diffuse imagery of age and youth. The emphasis on instrumental relations and goals is very much stronger in modern societies, and these are not fully integrated into systems of expressive gratification and solidary relations. The continuity and harmony of value orientations found in primitive and historical societies do not exist here. Because of this and of the strong emphasis on preparatory activities, there is a certain difference and discontinuity between the self-image and identity of the youth and those of the adult.

We have already seen that the intensity of this difference varies from place to place. The points of difference, however, are usually rather similar. The first difference is that between the diffuse imagery of the youth and adolescent and the stronger emphasis on occupational specialization necessarily existing among adults. This difference may be found everywhere—in the emphasis on sports and general social conviviality of the American youth culture,[64] in the aspirations towards a new type of man in direct communion with nature and folk of the German youth movement,[65] and in the pioneer image of the Israeli youth movement, etc. In the latter it has been found that one of the main emphases, both in the official literature and among the members themselves, is the possibility and the need to develop a fuller personality, not tied to occupational limitations or to economic troubles and exigencies.[66]

The second difference is that between the ascriptive nature of this human image and the necessity to strive towards individual achievement in later life. The full acceptance of a "comrade" or "pal" because of his being a "good fellow," and not just because of some specific achievement, is also stressed in all youth groups. In this respect there is also usually a great difference between the official value system of the school and that of the youth group.

These differences between the ascriptive and collective orientation of the age (youth) group and the individualistic achievement orientation of adult society have been very clearly shown in our investigations of youth movements in Israel. It has been demonstrated that there is a negative correlation between strong aspirations to achievement roles (economic and occupational) and strong identification with youth movements. Those adolescents who set themselves ideals of occupational and vocational advancement either do not join a youth movement or are among the most indifferent members. Similar occurrences are known in other countries.[67]

The third point of difference is in the individual's relation towards the group, his attitude towards the internal solidarity and mutual identification of members of his group. As we have seen, very strong emphasis is laid on such collective group identification in all modern youth groups, and the cohesion, solidarity and loyalty of the group are stressed as constituting one of the main virtues of youth as distinguished from adult society. Even in the formalized collectivity-oriented youth organizations, the broader solidarity and identification inculcated in the members lack the spontaneity and vitality of those of the youth group. In the German youth movements this internal loyalty has always been extolled; in the Israeli movements it has been emphasized as one of the main "educational" values of the movement.[68] This strong emphasis on collectivity orientation and identification differs, of course, from the more individual-istic emphases in the value orientations of adults in most modern societies.

All these differences, inherent in modern youth groups, make the integration of these groups within the social system difficult, and never complete. The full harmony between the individual's aspirations and the official allocation of roles to adolescents, char-acteristic of most primitive and historical societies, is absent here.

Although the groups satisfy many of the young person's developmental needs, the transition to adulthood involves some emotional change and disruption, which may or may not be overcome later.

This transition usually involves several stresses and anxieties. First, the bodily development of the adolescent constitutes a constant problem to him (or her). Since social maturity lags behind biological maturity, the bodily changes of puberty are not integrated with legitimate cultural values, and their evalua-tion is one of the adolescent's main concerns and problems. The difficulty inherent in attaining legitimate sexual outlets and rela-tions at this period of growth makes the adolescent's problem more acute. Consequently the exploration of bodily changes in himself and among peers, exhibition of bodily prowess, and at-tempts to establish heterosexual relations, are among the main activities of his group.[69]

Secondly, the adolescent's orientation towards the main values of his society is also beset with difficulties. Owing to the long period of preparation, and segregation of the children's world from that of the adults, the main values of the society are neces-sarily presented to the child and adolescent in a highly selective way, with "idealistic" emphasis (i.e., usually with emphasis on the common values and on community orientation), and with-out a realistic relation to actual mechanisms of role allocation according to which they will have to achieve their status within society. The relative unreality of these values as presented to them becomes a focus of awareness among adolescents, and the exploration of the actual meaning of these values and of the reality of the social world becomes one of the adolescent's main problems.[70] This exploration may lead in many directions—

cynicism, idealistic youth rebellion, deviant ideology and behavior, or a gradual development of a balanced identity[71]—and
we shall still have to investigate the conditions under which each
of these reactions takes place. But exploration in this direction
is almost universal in the youth groups of modern societies.[72]

Thirdly, the establishment of stable social relations and performance of stable roles is also problematic for youth and adolescents. The main difficulty here is that whatever temporary
balance they achieve between instrumental and expressive activities and relations does not enable them to attain stable, recognized roles, relations and recognition from the adults.

This incomplete institutionalization is seen most clearly in its
relation to and communication with the adult world. In the
various kinds of spontaneous youth groups there exists an "ambivalent" attitude towards the adult world: on the one hand, a
striving to communicate with it and receive its recognition;
on the other hand, certain dispositions to accentuate the differences between them and the adults, and necessarily also their
opposition to the various roles allocated to them by the adults.
While they orient themselves to full participation in this world
and its values, there are always some attempts to "communicate"
with these values in the distinct, special way common to youth.

The various manifestations of lack of full institutionalization
of youth groups in modern society have their parallels in the ideology of youth groups. As was shown in the preceding chapter,
age grouping usually entails a strong ideological element, and
the main focus of this ideology is the problem of the complementariness and continuity of different age groups. Most modern youth groups create an ideology which emphasizes the
discontinuity of youth-adult periods and the uniqueness of the
youth period in opposition to other age spans. The main differences between the orientations of youth groups and those of
adult society, mentioned above, constitute the main foci of this
ideology; although the extent of its explicitness varies from one
sector of modern society to another, its basic elements are present everywhere. It should be emphasized, however, that some
such discrepancy exists even in those modern societies where
the various youth groups are highly organized into corporate,

formalized structures. We have noted the existence of such a discrepancy in the Israeli youth movements,[73] and it has also been reported in connection with youth organizations in Nazi Germany and in the U.S.S.R. Thus in all these cases we find no such smooth and organized transition between generations as we found in the primitive societies; there always exists some potentially unresolved opposition between them.

On the other hand, the existence of this dsicrepancy does not necessarily entail the development of deviant behavior and ideology on the part of the youth groups. In most cases it is gradually resolved through the process of social maturation, in which peer and youth groups fulfill a very important function, although mostly one of "secondary institutionalization." Despite all these differences between youth groups and the structure of adult society, and the incomplete institutinoalization of the former, it would be erroneous to conclude that they do not perform any functions within the society. Although they perform no tasks within the institutional spheres of society, they may fulfill certain functions similar to those of age groups in specialized primitive and historical societies. First, they—both the school and other types of age groups—inculcate the first dispositions to identification with the society, its general values and norms of behavior and collective symbols. Secondly, they serve also as reservoirs of solidarity which can be reactivated in later life. Although no occasions or duties (except for various types of "occasions") are prescribed for such activities, they very often serve as important factors in social life, in maintaining a definite style of living, and in various convivial activities and groups. Thus the solidarity of youth groups may, even in these societies, overflow into broader channels of adult life and counterbalance the exigencies of various instrumental activities in various informal and mostly unstructured ways. Thirdly, there is the fact, strongly connected with the former one, that in most modern societies the various youth groups—with the exception of the explicitly deviant ones—tend to emphasize the attitude of respect towards elders. This is so despite the latent opposition to the adult world. Many of them emphasize the respect due to the diffuse imagery of older people, and not to their daily activities in the occupational, etc., spheres. The various prescriptions which exist in this regard among the Scouts and similar organizations are well known. In this way they attempt—even if rather feebly—to overcome to some extent the discontinuity between the human images of different ages and the strains between different generations inherent in modern societies. Still, these functions are not fully articulated in all modern youth groups, which differ greatly in these respects; some do not perform them at all. This, as well as the general comparison between primitive, historical and modern societies, focuses our attention on a basic difference between various age groups—namely, the extent to which they perform fully integrative tasks in the society. Before we turn to the analysis of this aspect of our problem, we must explain certain structural differences between various types of age groups. There is an additional element in the structure of the various universalistic societies which is of great importance for the understanding of certain variations in the structure of age groups. This is the extent of individualistic, as opposed to collective, orientations and principles of integration. We must see how the differences in these orientations affect the structure of age groups.

XIV Within the scope of primitive societies this problem has not arisen in a clear-cut way. In so far as our knowledge goes, the value systems and integrative principles of stable primitive societies[74] are largely community-oriented, and the scope of individual gratification is kept well within definite collective limits.[75] It is only within the scope of modern societies (in which not only is allocation of roles performed according to universalistic principles, but value orientations are universalistic and specific as well) that the problem arises in an acute form. Within modern societies we find both individualistically and collectively oriented value orientations; although the difference is not always clear-cut (as, for instance, in several European countries, where strong traditional collectivity orientation and identification persist), it can usually be discerned and evaluated. As each of these value orientations entails a different principle of identification and integration, the influence on the structure of age groups varies accordingly. We suggest that the extent of institutionalization and formalization of age groups (i.e., the extent of their corporateness and corporative performance of roles and tasks), the main variable of age group structure not yet accounted for, is a function of the extent of collectivity orientation of the social system to which they belong

We shall first present the data validating this hypothesis, and then attempt to explain them. The main distinction here lies between what may be called the more or less "loose," informal peer groups, and the formalized, corporate age grades and youth movements of various types. As has already been mentioned, information about primitive tribes seems to confirm this hypothesis, but is insufficient as it cannot offer a direct comparison. However, an interesting case is provided by situations of "culture contact." It has been remarked by ethnologists and anthropologists that the age groups are the first to disintegrate under the impact of Western civilization. This has usually been attributed to the weakening of the common goals and the emergence of more individualistic values. It is interesting to note, however, that in these situations the informal, organized age sets and regiments of old give way to formal, unorganized, loose juvenile groups of various types. This has been demonstrated among both the Swazi[76] and the Tswana.[77] A parallel development can be found among German youth after the breakdown of the Nazi Reich.[77a]

In modern societies the data seem to validate our hypothesis to the full. The most organized and institutionalized age groups may be found in Soviet Russia and in the Israeli *kibbutz* (and formerly in Germany and Italy)—all of them societies with a very explicit community orientation in their value systems.[78] In comparison with them, the peer and adolescent groups of Western Europe and the United States, societies in which individualistic orientation is stronger, are looser in their composition and less institutionalized. It is interesting to note that in Europe a greater extent of formalization and institutionalization exists in youth movements which are definitely affiliated with various political parties and social movements, such as various Catholic youth organizations, youth organizations affiliated with Social Democratic parties, etc., and in the United States among those organizations whose goal is to develop the "civic spirit" in general, such as various community organizations, scout movements, etc.[79] It seems that even in these cases the extent of formalization is much larger in the European movements, in which the element of collectivity orientation has always been stronger. An additional support for this hypothesis may be found in the fact that in most modern societies a specific age group (usually 18-21) is organized for the performance of one of the most important collective tasks of the society—the maintenance of a security force—the army. In most modern societies in which a compulsory military service exists, it is necessarily organized on the basis of age grading, which here becomes thoroughly formalized and organized.[80]

Our investigations in Israel also seem to bear out the hypothesis. It has been found that the highest degree of formalization of youth groups exists in the more collectivity-oriented sectors of the community, such as the *kibbutz* and other sectors with a very strong identification with the pioneering values. In the more individualistic ("private") sectors, loosely organized peer groups are more frequent.[81]

A partial exception may perhaps be found in the "free" German youth movements,[82] in which there was a strong element of internal, corporate formalization and organization, which was not, however, fully institutionalized within the social structure. But it seems that this does not invalidate our hypothesis; the corporate organization of the German youth movements derived its character from the very strong collectivity orientation of their ideology, but as this orientation and ideology were of a rebellious, deviant character in relation to the existing society, they could not have been fully institutionalized.

Our material also shows that the formalization of youth groups in collectivity-oriented sectors (or societies) gives rise to wide, unified organizations, and that the formalized, corporate youth groups are not limited to single, local groups, but are usually organized on a country-wide basis and linked in different ways to various fully institutionalized, adult agencies.

This hypothesis also finds full support in the comparison between Spartan and Athenian age groups. Those of Sparta were fully formalized and organized, and closely connected with the strong collective spirit and orientation of Spartan society, performing some of the most important collective tasks. This was not the case in Athens, where a much more individualistic spirit prevailed. Here the age groups were not so organized, were dispersed among many schools, and only at the *ephebic* stage became thoroughly formalized. This formalization was fully oriented to the performance of collective duties, mainly in the military field. It is therefore also characteristic that with the decline of the city-state and its common patriotic spirit and identification, this formalized organization of the *epheboi* gave place to the more "academic-cultural," and less organized and formalized, variety.

How can this hypothesis be explained? As a starting point we should analyze the meaning of formalization and corporate activity, both for the individual and for the social system. For the individual (adolescent), participation in a formalized and corporate group entails a high degree of identification with it, of merging his own identity with that of the group and its symbols of identification. In the "looser" groups there may also be a strong mutual identification between the members, between the "peers," and with the standards set up by the group. Such identification, however, is mostly of the personal, face-to-face type, based on primary personal relations, and usually does not include strong identification with specific symbols of the group or with its collective identity. In the "looser" groups the mutual identification and attachment of the members is of a more individualistic type, the group as such not functioning as a somewhat "super-personal" body. The corporate and formalized group, however, has an identity of its own with which that of the members must be merged.

The formalized groups of the *Komsomol*, the *kibbutz*, etc., always have some strong common symbols of identification—common names, corporate activities, organization, etc.—symbols which to a smaller extent exist in looser groups as well.

The corporate youth group serves also as a selective agency for potential members in various institutionalized groups within the adult sector of society. This selection is effected mainly through the group's strong connections with various organized, official agencies by which it is sponsored and directed.

It is these characteristics that explain the relationship between the corporateness and formalization of the age groups and collectivity orientation, especially in modern, industrial societies with a high degree of specialization and of individualistic achievement geared to this specialization. In so far as individualistc orientation persists, the child's (adolescent's) identification with his parents (particularly the father) and their occupational and economic roles may provide for him a basis for identification with the ultimate values of the society. In these cases the problem of transfer of identification from the family to the wider institutional spheres and to the total social structure is not as acute as in other types of "nonfamilial" modern societies. In the latter societies, too, the necessity for such a transition exists, and the family does not encompass the most important roles of the society. Yet the child's identification with his particular parent-image may constitute a certain, though by no means complete, basis for the role dispositions which are necessary for full membership and social maturity; this is so because, first, the general image of the parent with which the child identifies himself includes from the outset some aspects of extra-familial, achievement-oriented roles; and secondly, because these individualistic role dispositions constitute important—if not the only —manifestations of the ultimate values of the society.[83]

In collectivity-oriented modern industrial societies the picture is different. Among these societies the parent (father) does not appear in his specialized, achieved roles as a full bearer of the ultimate values of the society. Therefore full identification with the individual parent's position and achievement-oriented activities is inadequate, as this position must itself be evaluated through its relation to the common, shared values. Any strong individualistic orientation or role disposition which is to some extent inherent in every modern achievement system is potentially disruptive from the point of view of such a social system. A wider, more inclusive type of identification and role disposition for collectivity orientation must be developed by the child (or adolescent) to enable him to become a full member of society.

These different types of general role dispositions are related to the extent of formalization and corporateness of youth groups. In so far as individualistic value orientations prevail, the adolescent's relation to his peer group and its members, although important for the gratification of various need dispositions and for the practical learning of various patterns of behavior, is not the only one which influences the development of his identity. The attainment of full identity and maturity entails the ultimate leaving of the youth group; the group itself is also valued in so far as it leads beyond itself, making possible the fuller achievement of individualistic status. That is why under these conditions corporate, formalized groups do not serve as proper objects of the individual's need dispositions, and only looser groups succeed in gratifying them.

However, in so far as collectivity orientation exists, the attainment of full social maturity and membership entails the development of a fuller communal identification, which must be accomplished during the period of transition from the family of orientation to the wider society. Hence in these cases the disposition to participate in groups which incorporate and symbolize the common values of the society is stronger, and the individual may, to some extent, merge his identity in them. This does not, of course, mean that all adolescents in such a society have strong dispositions to participate in such more closely knit groups. This is not the case, of course, especially because in such societies there is a tendency to develop many structural inconsistencies which breed potential deviancy and disaffection.[84] This analysis assumes only that in collectivity oriented societies the disposition of most individuals to participate in such groups is usually stronger than in individuallistically oriented communities.

The fact that any strong ideology of "'age" or "youth" is, as we have seen throughout this book, collectivity-oriented, and therefore cannot be fully institutionalized in individualistically oriented societies, may also help to clarify this correlation between corporate age groups and community orientation in the sphere of values.

From the point of view of the social system, the corporate,

formalized age (youth) group also performs an important function in collectivity-oriented, specialized societies. First, it constitutes an excellent strategical position through which the solidarity of a small, primary group may overflow onto the larger system, emphasizing collective value orientation. Secondly, the age group makes possible a strong inculcation with common values during the period of preparation, in this way ensuring some limitation of the tendency towards individualistic achievement inherent in any specialized society. Thirdly, and perhaps most important of all, the formalized age group or youth organization constitutes one of the most important agencies for selection of membership to the elite positions, and therefore for a distribution of rewards. Through this process of selection social mobility and individual achievement are closely connected with performance of community-bound roles; in this way an institutional counterbalance to individualistic orientations is found. The special importance of the youth organization in this respect is manifested in the fact that it can control the transition from the purely preparatory period to that of full adult specialization.[85] These characteristics of formalized youth groups also throw some light on a structural characteristic touched upon earlier—namely, the extent of age group autonomy. It has been shown that a more or less complete age group autonomy exists either when age groups are the main integrative agencies within the social system or, conversely, to the extent that they are segregated from such agencies. Accordingly, the extent of autonomy should be relatively high in modern societies; but it is in inverse ratio to the extent of collectivity orientation and formalization of age groups. As has been shown, such formalization involves some degree of direction by adults—sometimes even complete regimentation.

It may be asked why, if this analysis is correct, do we find, even within the framework of individualistically oriented societies, some degree of formalization in youth organizations (as evinced in the various above-mentioned community organizations in the United States, etc.). It seems that the explanation should be sought in the fact that, as we have already seen and shall see in greater detail below, even in the most individualistically oriented societies some extent of community orientation must be institutionalized in order to maintain the solidarity of the social system.

The inculcation of this collectivity orientaion is especially important during the period of preparation for adult roles; the various youth groups and youth agencies are, as we have seen, used for this purpose, and various definite tasks which symbolize these attitudes are allocated to them in the preparatory sphere. Since such an element of collectivity orientation is inherent even in individualistic societies, it accounts for the permanent tendency towards some formalization in all youth groups, and particularly in youth agencies and organizations.

CHAPTER V

Age Groups
in Familistic Societies

I   In this chapter we shall present the material bearing on and validating the second major hypothesis of this work, i.e., the material related, not to the place of the family and of the descent unit in the total social structure, but to the internal structure of the family, kinship or descent unit. This hypothesis has been formulated in the following way:

Age groups tend to arise when the structure of the family or descent group blocks the younger members' opportunities for attaining social status within the family because (a) the older members block the younger ones' access to the facilities which are prerequisites of full adult roles, and/or (b) the sharpening of incest taboos and restrictions on sexual relations within the family unit postpones the young members' attainment of full sexual maturity.

This hypothesis relates, then, mainly to the authority structure of the family unit and to the extent to which it impedes the attainment of full social status by its junior members.

It should, of course, be quite obvious that age groups which exist under these conditions differ considerably from those existing under the conditions described in the first major hypothesis (i.e., under universalistic criteria of integration of social systems). The main difference is in the extent of their universality and of the emphasis on universalistic criteria. Those age groups which arise because of an authoritarian family structure are seen to be more closely tied to that particularistic structure and have a somewhat narrower universal span than hitherto-discussed age groups. Secondly, since these age groups arise as a result of strong tension between the generations, a somewhat stronger deviant potential is indicated. At this stage, however, we shall refrain from drawing a sharp comparison between the two types of age groups, first presenting the basic material bearing on this second hypothesis. This material is much scarcer than that relating to the first hypothesis, although there exists quite a lot of information bearing indirectly on this problem. The analysis found below is based mainly on material relating to the following societies: the Murngin tribe of Australia,[1] the Tiv Tiv tribe of East Africa,[2] the Nyakyusa age villages of Africa,[3] Irish peasants (mainly of Clare county),[4] and some additional peasant societies.[5] In so far as possible, comparative material will be presented, as well as other material bearing indirectly on some of the problems that arise.

a. The Murngin

II   In the Murngin tribe, which has been brilliantly analyzed by L. Warner,[6] we find a complete and extreme case of gerontocracy, i.e., of preferential allocation of roles to the older people, who hold the most prestige-bearing positions of the social system in the ritual, economic and (quasi-) political (judicial, advisory) fields. Age grading is very explicit and formalized among them, and constitutes a phenomenon with a pronouncedly religious connotation.

This strong age grading has its fullest symbolic expression in the totemic myths of the Murngin, in which the various phases of life and the various *rites de passage* are strongly emphasized and possess a fully ideological and religious connotation. In their myths we find another important emphasis, directly related to the fact of age grading, namely, a very strong dichotomy of the sexes and strong religious and magical emphasis on the necessity of circumscribing the legitimate social relations. This strong dichotomy of the sexes finds its institutional expression in the separation of the sexes at the age of 6-8, when the boys leave for the boys' camp while the girls remain with their families of orientation. There is a very strong "sister taboo," and a very strong prohibition of the boys' witnessing or appraising their parents' sexual relations. These taboos emphasize both the dichotomy of the sexes and the differential sexual indulgence allowed each age grade, which is clearly related to the latter's differential magical and ritual powers. It is also very important for our discussion to emphasize that status in the age grade is very closely tied to the individual's position in the family, as the various age grades are themselves defined in terms of family position and the main *rites de passage* are connected with transition from one family position to another.

This rigid system of age grading, connected as it is with sexual dichotomy and family position, gives rise to definite age grouping during a certain age span, when the boys leave their families of orientation in the general camp and "retreat" to a camp of their own. There, the elders (to whom instruction is entrusted) and the older boys exercise authority over the younger ones, and strong emphasis is laid on the differential authority of the various grades. Age group life ceases when the boys marry, leave their camp and enter the general one. Thus, with the attainment of some of the basic prerequisites of social status, especially in sexual matters, the specific age group life of the Murngin ceases.

b. The Tiv Tiv Tribe

The picture in the Tiv Tiv tribe of East Africa is somewhat more complicated than that among the Murngin, or, for that matter, among the Nyakyusa. The age groups of the Tiv Tiv can be partly related to a nonkinship division of labor, which exists among them to a limited extent and manifests itself mainly in the fact that some (quasi-) political, prestige-bearing offices of leadership are not vested in given lineages.[7] This element of nonkinship division of labor is, however, only a subsidiary one in relation to the Tiv Tiv age sets. One of the most important elements in their social organization is the giving of strong preferential rights and powers to the senior members of the family and lineage unit. This preferential treatment is mainly expressed in two ways. First, the possibility of establishing a legitimate marriage through the payment of a bride-price, or, more usually, through marriage by exchange between groups of kinsmen.

The basic arrangements of this pattern of exchange marriages benefit the elder brother and postpone for a long time the marriage of the younger ones. As Agika, himself a member of the tribe, has put it:

"'If a man had five sons and two daughters, the sons had the use of the *argve* (bride-price) in order of seniority. The elder sons took them (the cattle) first and the younger had to wait their turn. When the elder sons begat daughters they took some cattle and gave them to their brothers who came next after them. But the youngest would still be left. He might be well on in years before his turn came to take an *argve*, and all this time he would remain a bachelor."[8]

This situation gives rise to a very great number of irregular unions, which are very common among the Tiv Tiv, and to the custom of marriage by capture, in which, characteristically, the age mates help capture the bride.[9]

Secondly, the preferential treatment accorded to elders also prevails in the field of acquisition of prestige, through economic exertion (wealth) and/or magical-ritual powers. It is through participation in cults and acquisition of ritual powers that the individual attains prestige and influence. The mastery of the cults is more or less monopolized by the elders, and an individual's slow, gradual advance depends chiefly on his position in the group and his relation to its elders. As long as the older generation is alive, the younger one does not aspire too much to the higher offices, and is dependent on the good will of the elders for other offices as well. An individual would not dare to run the risk of offending one of the senior members of his group or exciting his jealousy (through contracting a "flesh debt") and in this way exposing himself to the "bad," strong magical powers of the elders. The concentration of wealth is effected on more or less the same lines, and it seems that only in exceptional cases and in interlineal matters may a younger man attain any high position. In any event, it seems that the general potential jealousy of the elders towards the younger people is so great in all spheres that the latter can attain position or wealth only through mutual help and organization. It is in this light that the Tiv Tiv age groups can be understood.

The age sets are usually composed of members of a maximal lineage (sometimes subdivided into smaller units of members of minimal lineages), and are so arranged that two brothers never belong to the same set. Each set is gradually formed from the younger children, and is formally organized when it finds a sponsor among some members of the lineage older by 4-5 years, whose name it usually takes on. The members of the set perform various tasks for their sponsor (adviser), mainly in the economic field (farming). There is almost no corporate, formal link between the various sets, and they lead separate lives and existences (except in one part of Tivland, where two adjacent sets usually act together). Yet the sets are more or less parallel in all of Tivland, which enables a man to find those people closest to him wherever he happens to be. Although circumcision is universally practiced in Tivland, it is an entirely individual (or family) affair and does not constitute a prerequisite for entrance into the age set. Age group life is very active and important in late adolescence (18-20) and during the prime of adulthood (until about the age of 40-50 years), but becomes less important in later life, when the solidarity of the age mates and the scope of their corporate activities weakens greatly.

The age sets perform manifold functions in the economic, juridical and ritual fields, but their main emphasis is on mutual help among themselves and a common stand against the elders. The aspect of mutual help is very strong in the economic fields, in the capture of brides, and—perhaps most important of all—in the juridical and ritual fields, where too strong oppression on the part of the elders is feared or suspected. A whole age set, led by its sponsor, may appear at meetings of the elders' council to protect one of its members against magical malevolence on the part of the elders. These activities take on a special importance at approximately the age of 40, when competition for offices becomes more acute. Before this period economic activities predominate. This aspect of mutual help and protection is very important among age mates, and it is significant that its importance wanes with the attainment of elders' status and power. Among age mates there generally prevails a spirit of good will, friendly competition and participation in various *rites de pas-*

sage, but some of the more extreme manifestations of such equality, such as kinship equivalence, lending of wives, etc., do not exist.

The strong element of opposition towards elders should not be construed as one of rift or deviancy. The age set activities constitute the legitimate, or at least semi-legitimate, resolution of the tension between generations, and the age set's very existence eases this tension. The sponsorship of an age set by an elder is a clear indication of this semi-legitimacy, while the importance of the age sets for "letting off steam" by individual members is obvious.

c. The Nyakyusa age villages

The Nyakyusa age villages constitute a unique example in the so far known human societies, a case in which the entire community life of a tribe is based on the differential criterion of age. While there is no known case comparable to this, some of the characteristics of Nyakyusa society are but intensifications of the general indices of "authoritarian" family systems in primitive societies, and it is these characteristics which are most closely related to the unique institution of age villages. While it seems to be impossible as yet to account fully for this unique phenomenon of age villages, these characteristics are sufficient for a broad comparative analysis as far as our hypothesis is concerned.

While Nyakyusa community life is based on age, the distribution of wealth is directed into kinship channels. All important wealth (cattle, which constitute the main item in bride-price) is inheritable within the kinship group (which does not constitute a territorial unit, but is dispersed among numerous age villages). The system of inheritance follows the seniority principle among brothers, then going over to the elder sons of the senior brother.

Cattle are, as mentioned above, the main elements of bride-price, and as polygamy is the ideal of the society there is a very strong potential conflict between elder and younger brothers and between different generations. This potential conflict is rooted in the possibility of the elders' using their cattle for buying themselves additional (young) wives instead of furnishing the bride-price for the younger members of the family (lineage). This also affects an individual's economic independence, as only a married man gets his own fields to till, until which time he has to work for his father (living in a different village from his own). As a result of these arrangements the marriage age of males among the Nyakyusa is relatively high, the younger people having to wait for quite a long period before being provided with the necessary bride-price.

Side by side with these institutional arrangements, we find among the Nyakyusa a very strong emphasis on sexual taboos within the family. According to the Nyakyusa, a growing boy should not be aware of the sexual activities of his parents; therefore he should not sleep at home. Leaving the parents' village is in this way directly connected with decorum. The ramifications of this ideology are, however, much wider. The incest theme is very strong and very much elaborated in Nyakyusa society. It applies not only to mother-son relations, but also, and with great emphasis, to relations between father-in-law and daughter-in-law. Between these two complete avoidance is observed, including avoidance of meeting face-to-face, of accepting mutual hospitality, etc.

The importance of this incest theme can be easily understood in a society in which the avenues to marriage (cattle) are controlled by elder and middle-aged men who may prefer to marry yet another young wife instead of enabling their younger brothers or sons to marry. The danger of seduction of the father's (or brother's) wives, is also probably exaggerated by the custom by which a son may inherit his father's wives (his own stepmothers) as his own wives.

The establishment of age villages is clearly connected with all of these economic and ritual patterns which enable the older men to control cattle and, consequently, wives. Age villages are established when young boys of 9-11 begin to leave their parents' huts for reasons of decorum and establish a village of their own. The formation of such a village usually takes 5-6 years, after which the ranks are closed. Each age village develops out of a particular parents' village, and does not draw its membership from all over the country.

Although there is no formal definition of age, it seems that age reckoning is here—somewhat as in the case of the Murngin—relative to status within the family, and not to an absolute universal age criterion. The lack of such a criterion is seen clearly in the absence of any initiation ceremony; not even circumcision is practiced among the Nyakyusa. Relations between various age villages within the country are not established on the basis of a universal age criterion unifying all the country, but mainly on the basis of relative seniority, according to which the land is distributed in each generation.[10]

The importance of age villages and relations is not confined to the institutional sphere, but find its full expression in the social ideology of the Nyakyusa. "Good company"—eating with age mates, talking with them—is extolled as the highest moral virtue, and the recluse, the "individualist," is strongly derided. Age mate solidarity is highly praised, and there is some indication of semi-homosexual attachment among age mates, especially during the long period of waiting for marriage. Thus we also find among the Nyakyusa an institutionalization of age (homogeneous) groups which serves to ease the tension between generations, a tension engendered because of the elders' monopolization of all avenues to marriage and economic independence. This tension is eased through the establishment of age villages with their own internal strong solidarity, and through the device of handing over political power to each successive generation as it attains social maturity.[11]

Among other African tribes, too, important indications as to the way in which age group formation eases the tension between generations, especially adjacent ones, can be found. This takes place among the Chagga, whose entire educational process has been most brilliantly and succinctly analyzed by O. Raumm[12] and documented by B. Gutmann.[13] Unfortunately, however, the data about the entire social structure of this tribe are insufficient for an adequate analysis, and it would be fruitless to make surmises of any kind. Material about certain Australian tribes, described by Howitt,[14] which resemble the Murngin to a very large extent, is also inadequate.

III The full institutional implications of "delayed" maturity—both in the sexual and the economic spheres—among the various primitive tribes described in the preceding section have been analyzed so far. As for the peasant societies which will next be analyzed, it is the economic implications that are of greatest importance. The best-described example here is the Irish peasant of Clare county, described by Arensberg and Kimball and presented in the second chapter of this book.

The most important feature of the Irish peasants' system of inheritance of property is that the family farm unit usually constitutes an indivisible piece of property, inherited only by one son, and held by the father until a very advanced age; only then does the old father transfer the property to the inheriting son. Until then the son (or sons), who may already have grown children of their own (and sometimes even grandchildren), do not own any property, and are entirely subordinated to their father. This subordination even includes dependence on him for pocket money, let alone food, clothing, etc. It is the father who plans work on the farm, and it is he who participates in the councils of the village and in public affairs. From all these activities the sons—who may be called "boys" until the age of 50-60—are excluded.

Thus we find here a familistic society, defined entirely in terms of kin and descent units, the authority structure of which precludes the attainment of social maturity by many of its younger members. Here marriage does not constitute a full index of social maturity, as a married man continues to be subordinated to his father in economic matters.

This exclusion of the various grades of "boys" from full social participation gives rise to the various informal "age groups," in which they spend their leisure time and which constitute their main social relaxation outside the scope of the family. These groups are not formally demarcated; they form rather informal cliques, but in real life they can be easily distinguished, mainly according to the type of games, etc., in which they indulge. Membership in them is usually acquired not according to the criteria of age, but rather according to position in the authority structure of the family. Unmarried boys form one group, married "boys" another, and the older men, heads of families, yet another distinct clique.

As membership is based mostly on status within the family, a younger man who happens to be a full owner of a farm usually participates in the old men's "cuuyaird."[15] The difference between the various cliques is not confined to types of play, leisure activities, etc.: these differences are but manifestations of a more profound divergence—in extent of authority and in relation to the main values of the familistic society. The old men's "cuuyaird" is the arbiter of public opinion in the village; it is the place where the most important decisions about various communal affairs are made, where every significant item in the life of the village is discussed and, in an informal way, decided upon. The informal meetings of the old men have a definite role in the authority structure of the village. The younger men's cliques do not enjoy any such status, and their preoccupation with informal games, etc., is in a way an indication of their exclusion from the authority structure of the whole community and their need to find some compensation in a social sphere of their own. Within this sphere they maintain a sort of loose solidarity, based on semi-opposition to the elders and their values. While the elders are the repositories of the familistic values of the society, the younger "boys" have a somewhat more critical attitude towards these values and tend, in their games, social evenings, etc., to deride these values a bit and to joke about the elders who uphold them. It seems that tension between the generations is continuous—the older generation accusing the younger of lack of reverence and discipline, and extolling the "good old days," the younger tending to accuse the older of autocratic tendencies.[16] And yet the younger members' opposition to the older ones is not complete. It finds its main expression when they are by themselves, mostly in informal meetings; while on common public occasions all due deference is paid the elders, and their authority in all economic matters is accepted without demur within the family and on the farm.

The opposition of the younger members to the older ones does not culminate in any breakdown of the family unit, or, ultimately, of the authority of the elders. The young men's cliques constitute an "insulated" sphere of social activities which is only partly institutionalized within the social structure of the village. It provides a psychological outlet for the young person's need for a group in which he is a full member, without being subject to any authority but his own; while at the same time it does not undermine the basic values and institutional structure of the society. These values are ultimately accepted by the younger people—as can be seen both in their overt behavior on public occasions, etc., and in the speedy and successful transition from membership in these cliques to those of the elders, with the concomitant change in their authority position in the family.[17] And yet it must be emphasized that the existence of these "age groups" constitutes a constant focus of deviant behavior, albeit one which is insulated and, from the point of view of every individual, a transitory phase in his development. This element of deviancy is evident in the constant ideological tension between the generations, a tension which emphasizes the discontinuity between different age grades.

There exists some comparative material on peasant societies which helps us fully to validate our hypothesis. It is possible to compare the authority structure of the Irish peasant family with that of other peasant groups, such as the Welsh,[18] traditional Chinese,[19] Guatemalan,[20] and French-Canadian peasantry,[21] about which more or less full data are available, as well as many historical European peasant societies. In all these cases we find a rather strict familistic division of labor and society, usually organized on the lines of an extended family (except in the case of the Welsh), and with some degree of paternal authority. The extent of familistic self-sufficiency is greatest among the Chinese peasants, among whom relatively few outside groups are formed; it is smallest, it seems, among the Guatemalan Indian peasants. In all these societies, then, there do not exist nonkinship integrative principles which would give rise to age groups. As has been shown earlier, the formal age grading of the modern school system does not easily strike root in these societies.[22] On the other hand, however, we find here no age groups at all, not even those of the second type (e.g., among the Irish peasants). This is clearly attributable to the different allocation of authority within the family. In all of these societies one can find some sort of institutional arrangement by which the young married adult attains not only legitimate sexual maturity, but also considerable economic and political independence of his father (or of the head of the extended family). The attainment of this independence may be assured immediately upon marriage, or after a specified, short period (the maximum number of years after marriage in our sample is 4). The attainment of maturity manifests itself either in the allocation of a plot of land for the use of the young couple, or in the building of a separate household for them. Although in most of these societies the overall, diffuse authority and prestige of the father and the respect he enjoys constitute an important element of the social structure, this authority does not operate in such a way as to curtail or make impossible the attainment of social maturity by the younger adults. Consequently we do not find here any strongly articulated, formal or informal age groups, or a strong consciousness of opposition between different age grades. On the contrary, a strong complementarity of different age grades exists in every family and descent group. In most of these societies (and especially among the Welsh) we find informal groups of youngsters engaged in common play, recreation and informal social gatherings. These groups are, however, entirely composed of unmarried adolescents, who leave immediately after marriage, when they join the adult family groups.[23] A similar development occurs in the French-Canadian parish of St. Denis. There we find that the greatest intensity of activities in communal and political affairs and the strongest consciousness of belonging to a specific age level is manifested by the unmarried adolescents—already out of school but not yet settled on farms of their own or gone to town.[24] Similarly, in the Israeli *Moshav* and *Moshava* it is the unmarried adolescent group (or the young couples still living with parents) who show the greatest predisposition to join country-wide youth movements.[25]

In all these cases active participation in such groups ceases with marriage, the subsequent attainment of full adult maturity and independence, and absorption in adult duties and activities. Unlike the Irish peasants, among these groups marriage usually brings about such independence and, consequently, no constant age groups arise, there being only transitory groups of adolescents based more on common family status than on any identification on the basis of age. Conditions do not exist here which would be favorable to the development of full-fledged age groups from such embryonic beginnings as transitory bachelors' groups.

The crucial importance of allocation of authority within the family for the emergence of this type of age groups can be clearly discerned, in a negative way, in St. Denis, and probably among all French-Canadian peasants.[26] There we find very strong and formalized age grading, especially in religious and ritual matters (not unlike the Murngin); i.e., it is only with advancing age that the child becomes a full religious personality, as can be seen in various ceremonies—baptism, confirmation, participation in masses, etc. At most of these ceremonies social participation is to some extent arranged according to age groups. These groups do not continue their existence outside the ceremonies. Age grouping is dissolved within the family units, within which independence is assured to the young married people. Only the young bachelors form an informal group of their own. The strong ritual emphasis on old age is not coupled here with institutional arrangements which would curtail the attainment of social independence, and therefore "gerontocratic" age grading does not give rise to strong age grouping, except on ritual occasions.[27]

The importance of these conditions, related to the authority structure of the family (and the closely related emphasis on prohibition of any sexual manifestations within the family) can be shown from yet another point of view. All these conditions (authority, sexual prohibitions, etc.) are in a way but intensifications of certain universal elements existing in every family structure. Some of the results of these conditions—tensions between the generations during the period of growth, of adolescence and of transition from the family of orientation to that of procreation; prohibition of sexual activities within the family; some sort of sexual shyness between the generations, etc.—are probably more or less universal elements in every family structure.[28] All these results entail a certain degree of differential categorization of members of the family unit, and certain institutional arrangements which embody these categorizations. This holds true especially of the period of transition from the family of orientation to that of procreation, and the period of heterosexual exploration. In many societies we find separate lodgings for unmarried adolescent and young adult males—either a hall within the family compound or a house set aside for the bachelors' use. Such lodgings can be found in Southeast Asia, among Scandinavian peasants,[29] as well as in other countries. In all such cases we find that the bachelors (and sometimes also the unmarried girls) form distinctive groups of their own which engage in mutual sexual explorations, "social" evenings, etc. The same phenomenon appears in various Balkan villages,[30] and is also known to exist in many other familistic peasant societies—both historical and contemporary. The custom of assigning separate lodgings to young people upon the attainment of sexual (physical) maturity is also widely prevalent among primitives. The extent to which these arrangements and groups are formalized differs from place to place, and the material at our disposal is inadequate for an analysis of all the degrees of formalization or of the conditions under which they arise. They seem, however, to be very widely distributed and to be more or less inherent in the structure of every family and especially of familistic societies.

Some of the most interesting examples of full institutionalization and formalization are to be found in the various Indian youth dormitories, especially among the Morung of Konyag Nagas[31] and the Ghotul of the Muria; many similar institutions can also be found among the various Naga and other tribes in India.[32] There, the various types of youth dormitories form the nuclei of "children's republics," and constitute the home of the bachelors of the tribe, in which they live and lead their "free" love life, but which they abandon (officially at least) after marriage.

There exists a great variety of these institutions among Indian tribes, which have been aptly described and summarized by Ch. von Fürer-Haimendorf.[33] However, it is still very difficult to analyze the conditions under which the various types of youth dormitories, etc., arise. Once more, only their general significance in the context of our discussion can be indicated here.

All these examples show us that special groups of adolescents, bachelors, etc., are to be found in most familistic societies. But only under very specific conditions—conditions which hinder the attainment of full sexual maturity and social independence— do these groups, in which the age element is entirely subsidiary, develop into age groups of some sort.

A similar pattern can also be found in those sectors of modern societies in which the element of authoritarianism in the structure of the family is strong. Several such examples have already been briefly mentioned. One of them can be found among immigrant families, coming from familistic, peasant societies and entering into the orbit of a modern, industrialized society. We have already seen how this authoritarianism has alienated the younger generation and given rise to various types of youth and peer groups. It is interesting to note that these groups evince most of the characteristics outlined above and that their integration within any youth agency, school, etc., is fraught with difficulties. The same is also true of the development of various types of youth rebellions in modern Germany, from the early 19th century up to the development of the "Free Youth Movement" and the Nazi youth movement.[34] This case will be analyzed in greater detail in the following chapter, but we might mention here that in this case we have a traditional authoritarian family system drawn into the orbit of a universalistic, achievement-oriented society, which undermines the family's authority structure and throws into sharp relief its inability to provide its members with full social status.

Another interesting example can be found in the case of certain sections of the American upper classes and plutocracy— as depicted in several popular novels, e.g., *The Late George Apley*, *Kitty Foyle*, etc. Here the extreme authoritarianism of the family, and especially of the father, has alienated the younger generation, sometimes driving them away from home on various attempts to win economic and family independence. Various psychiatric documents show that such an alienation may even give rise to mental breakdowns. But here the rebellion is usually temporary and usually the younger generation returns to take up the high social status and responsibilities incumbent on them according to the family values.

IV   It may be assumed that age groups which arise under the conditions stated in the second major hypothesis differ from those which arise under conditions of the nonkinship (universalistic) social division of labor. Some of these differences have been implied in the material presented throughout the foregoing discussion, but they shall now be systematically and explicitly stated. These differences are to be seen most clearly in the primitive and peasant societies mentioned above, and, in a somewhat more diluted form, also in modern societies, in various youth dormitories, etc.

(1) The first difference relates to the categorization of members on the basis of age. In most of these societies the age definition is very closely based on the position within the authority structure of the family (or lineage) unit, and age grades are very largely defined in terms of these positions—not as general connotations common to all members of a society. The emphasis on *relative* position (as every authority position, at least within the limits of a concrete social unit, must be) is here stronger than the more universalistic orientations of other age groups. In some cases, as in bachelors' houses, etc., the distinction is blurred, as it may also be in the transition from one group to another (as among the Irish peasants). Consequently the span of life which these groups cover is also usually determined by the transition from one authority position within the family to another (as seen clearly in the fact that among the Tiv, age groups cease to function upon the attainment of the status of elders; in the composition of the Nyakyusa age villages; and in that of the age cliques of the Irish peasants).

(2) The second difference, closely connected with the first, is the fact that in all these cases the composition and organization of age groups is not based on universal membership in the whole

social system, but only on membership in the family or lineage unit (or in a group of such families or lineages). These age groups do not cut across the various kinship and descent groups of which the total society is composed, but are usually contained within them (although in some cases some sort of parallel units exist in the different lineage units). In other words, categorization on the basis of age homogeneity does not apply universally to all members of the total society, but mainly to members of the given family or kinship unit. They never organize any activities common to the whole society. In so far as such activities exist at all, they are organized, as among the Tiv, through various lineages or cult associations. Their most important activities and functions seem to be performed within the limits of the kinship unit, and not outside it.

(3) This can be seen also in the next important characteristic —namely the absence of any unified age group hierarchy. We have seen in previous chapters that such a hierarchy may be absent either because of the limitation which the span of life in which age groups are operative imposes, or because of the weakness of their organization. Here such a unified hierarchy is absent, the age span is relatively long, and the corporate organization of each age group (or age village) is carried to a very high degree. Between the various age groups we do not find, however, any unified organization or hierarchy. There are no common tasks which they perform and no common duties allocated to them. Their social life is entirely separate. In some cases, as among the Tiv, the members of one age set scarcely know the names of members of other age sets of their lineage.[35] They have no common chiefs, and there is no transition from one set to another. An older set has no authority over a younger one, and there are no relations of seniority and juniority specifically regulating relations between different age sets. Each age set leads an entirely separate and independent existence. In so far as any relations are carried on between them, they are necessarily mediated by special persons who themselves are outside the scope of the age set: the village chiefs of the Nyakyusa, the "set advisers" of the Tiv.

Thus we see that these age groups do not constitute a unified organization, either from the point of view of the whole society, or as regards the interrelations between different age groups of any specific lineage group.

(4) This brings us to the fourth structural difference of these age groups from those of the first type—namely, the relatively small extent of overall integrative activities which they perform. This may be seen also in the absence of a unified organization, which clearly shows that in so far as any integrative activities are allocated to these groups, this is done not on the basis of an overall age hierarchy, but mainly as parts of various kinship, descent (and perhaps other particularistic) units. This is clearly seen in the already mentioned fact that such activities (as, for instance, in the economic field among the Tiv and in both the economic and political fields among the Nyakyusa) are supervised not by internal chiefs (or heads) of the age groups, but mainly by persons who stand in some kinship or personal relations to these groups. These are the chiefs, advisers, etc., whose relation to the group is based on common membership in a particularistic descent unit. It is also through these persons that the groups are connected with the overall organization of the society; i.e., they do not form fully autonomous groups within that structure.

(5) The relatively small extent of integrative activities allocated to these groups can also be seen in their nature and internal organization. In the contents of their activities (e.g., economic) no overall differences can be discerned from the other type of age groups. But the significance of these activities varies considerably. First, there is a very strong emphasis on the internal affairs of the group and on the opposition of the group to other groups (mostly elders), rather than on performance of public duties and taking part in general organization. Secondly, although there is the usual emphasis on expressive relations and overall attachment, these do not always constitute a framework for wider instrumental activities which are incumbent on their members by virtue of their relations outside the kinship unit. One may find here a stronger emphasis on expressive relations which are detached from any overall nexus of rights and duties with regard to other members of the society. The activities of these

age groups do not usually have preparatory character, anticipating future, adult activities; as a rule, they differ from the adult activities to a much larger extent than do those of other types of age groups.

(6) This lack of integrative significance from the point of view of the social system of most of the activities of these age groups is parallelled by their dissociation from any status-conferring ceremonies for the individual. Unlike the other types of age groups, membership in these does not indicate the attainment of full social status. This is clearly shown in the fact that in no case is entrance into age groups connected with initiation or circumcision. In some of the societies no such ceremonies exist; while in others they have no connection with entrance into and membership in age groups.

(7) This brings us finally to the most inclusive and important characteristics of these age groups: namely, their very strong deviant tendencies and the emphasis on opposition between the various generations. We have seen that in most primitive societies there is no such full-fledged opposition; wherever such opposition does exist it is resolved through full institutionalization and legitimate regulation, as among the Nandi. In the cases now under discussion, however, this opposition is not fully institutionalized, and the deviant potential is very strong, although not entirely disruptive. Even more important is the opposition—both ideological and structural—which forms the basis of the common identification of the group; even the specific age symbolism is couched mostly in terms of opposition. An ambivalent attitude towards the world of the adults (or of the elders) always prevails, and the basic values of the society are not fully accepted. Not only may different age groups tend to emphasize different aspects of common values—as may well happen in all types of age groups—but there may also exist a nonconforming attitude towards them. This can be seen most clearly among the Irish peasants, and to some degree also among the Nyakyusa. This opposition is not only ideological; it may have various important behavioral manifestations, e.g., self-help and mutual juridical (and economic) support among Tiv age set members, and the

age villagers of the Nyakyusa. In all these cases this mutual help is (especially among the Tiv) directed against the power of the elders.

Within none of the societies discussed above does this opposition and potential deviancy give rise to a complete breakdown of the continuity of the social system (and of the personalities of its members), but only to a partial insulation of these deviant potentialities. This is achieved through some degree of segregation of the relative spheres of conformist and deviant behavior, and consequent splitting-up of ambivalent attitudes, which makes possible at least partial institutionalization of the "segregated" deviant phases. The latter is made possible because: (a) the members of the age groups identify themselves more or less fully with the values of the adult society and aspire towards full social status, thus (b) making the age group period transitional for most of them.

We have now seen the basic differences between age groups which arise under conditions of universalistic principles of role-allocation and those which arise under conditions which block the attainment of status within the family. In the latter type the extent of general, society-wide age identification is relatively weak as a criterion of membership, the span of their activities is usually limited to the limits of particularistic units (family and lineage), and their main function seems to be the easing of tensions between the different generations.

The two types of age groups are analytically distinct. In all of the examples discussed above this analytical distinction is also concrete. In principle there may, of course, exist cases in which the two types coexist; i.e., within a universalistic society there may be a very strong authoritarian family structure. Several typical instances which have been mentioned above can be found in cases of immigration, culture contact, in the development of certain modern revolutionary movements, and in some traditional societies under the impact of industrialization. Under these conditions of utter incompatibility—with the partial exception of the American upper class, which will be analyzed in greater detail in the next chapter—age groups cannot usually perform their functions of easing tensions between generations, and become outrightly deviant and rebellious. While it is difficult to differentiate between the relative influence of the two sets of conditions under which the age groups emerge, it would seem that the combination of these conditions tends to intensify the deviant tendencies of the age groups.

CHAPTER VI

The Functions of Age Groups
in the Social System

(INTEGRATIVE AND
DEVIANT AGE GROUPS)

I   In preceding chapters we have attempted to account for several differences in the structure of age groups by relating them to various differences in the main structural characteristics of the social system and its integrative mechanisms. We have succeeded in fully validating our initial hypothesis in its various details, and in differentiating it greatly by accounting for many additional details. Throughout our analysis, however, we have continuously encountered another difference between various types of age groups, namely, the extent to which they perform integrative or disintegrative functions in the social system; in other words, the extent of occurrence of deviancy in age groups. Unlike other structural differences—e.g., the life span which age groups cover, the differences between task-performing and training age groups, etc.—this difference has not yet been systematically analyzed and accounted for. In other words, we have not yet analyzed either the various types of conformity or deviancy or the social conditions which give rise to them. We shall now turn to these problems. While it will be necessary to repeat some of the material presented in the preceding chapters, we shall do so only to the minimal extent necessary for the forthcoming analysis.

Before we set out to analyze the specific problem of integrative (or disintegrative) functions of age groups, it should be explained more precisely what is meant by integrative functions. To put it very briefly: any group, institution, etc., is seen to perform integrative functions in so far as it contributes to the continuity of the social system. By continuity is meant continuous performance of the main institutional roles and of the most general orientations by members of a society, irrespective of changes in the biological composition of membership (i.e., the interchange of generations). From the point of view of the individual personalities it is the maintenance of the individual member's motivation to perform institutionalized roles and the development of such motivation (or disposition) that constitute the main criteria of an "integrative function."

The previous analysis has clearly shown that age groups may constitute a basic institutional focus as far as the continuity and stability of the social system are concerned, and one of the main channels for the transmission of the social heritage. The extent to which this channel really performs these transmissive tasks is an important, although certainly not the only, index of social continuity.

Before proceeding to the analysis of integrative and disintegrative age groups, we shall inquire how and under what conditions it is possible for age groups to develop deviant tendencies. We shall attempt to explain this possibility in the framework of our general assumptions and hypotheses, and shall then derive from it more specific hypotheses as to the conditions under which age groups develop in one direction or another.

It has been postulated that age groups arise in societies in which the family (or kinship unit) does not constitute the main unit of the social and economic division of labor, and in which the individual must acquire and learn various general role dispositions which cannot be learned within the family. Age groups, which are usually articulated during the period of transition from the family of orientation, may serve as channels for the learning (of some, at least) of these general role dispositions. Thus it may be said that age groups constitute an interlinking sphere between the family and other institutionalized spheres of society (political, economic, etc.)

This statement about the interlinking nature of age groups should be explored a bit further, as it constitutes, in a way, the focal point of the present analysis. In particular should it be explained in greater detail what is meant by an "interlinking sphere" within the social system.[1] Since various institutional sectors within a society are usually regulated according to different integrative principles, it is obvious that the role expectations raised in one of them cannot always be fully gratified within the other. In such cases a lack of motivation for the performance of certain of these roles and frustrations over the impossibility of realizing others may result; and the stability of the social system may be endangered. In order to combat such dangers every social system employs various adjustive mechanisms, and an "interlinking sphere" is one of them. An interlinking sphere is organized in such a way that, on the one hand, it makes possible the gratification of at least some of the role-expectations roused in one institutional sector; while on the other hand it links these gratification of at least some of the role expectations roused in towards the other institutional sectors. Thus it may be said that an interlinking sphere brings out the orientations towards certain sectors of the society latent in another sector. The effectiveness of such an interlinking sphere depends on the extent to which it is permanently interwoven within the institutional structure of the society, so that the gratifications it provides and the aspirations it arouses have the full, normative backing of the society and ensure full gratification within it. Certain religious institutions (such as the Catholic confessional or some Jewish traditional holidays, particularly the Day of Atonement) or central collective rituals bear this characteristic.[2] Thus, for instance, the analysis of many primitive ceremonies has shown that in them the economic, political and ritual spheres of the society are closely interwoven. In these ceremonies the importance of economic activities, of production, is very strongly emphasized. At the same time, however, the purely individualistic or familial aspect of economic activities and achievements, an aspect strongly stressed in everyday life, is subordinated to the collective values and political hierarchy of the society. Thus the attainment of economic prosperity is here conditioned on effective participation in the political sphere and identification with its values.[8]

It is obvious, however, that there may be many such interlinking spheres in any social system. Our previous analysis has shown that age groups constitute such an interlinking sphere (within universalistic societies) between the family and the occupational, political and general value systems of the society. We have seen that within an age group the individual seeks to attain solidary relations and gratifications akin to those of the family, and greatly influenced by the aspirations and orientations raised within the family. At the same time the internal organization of age and youth groups already emphasizes some different types of roles; e.g., its internal allocation of roles is usually more universalistic, there may be within it more competition, etc. These relations are to some extent organized according to criteria existing in the economic, political, etc., spheres of society, and oriented towards and influenced by these spheres and criteria. In age groups such as those of the Nupe, which serve as "schools of citizenship," their orientation towards the general values of the society and its political sphere are obvious. This becomes even more evident in cases where the age groups perform definite tasks in the economic, political and ritual spheres. In all these cases their own solidarity is largely dependent on the successful maintenance of these general orientations and performance of these various tasks. In this way age groups interlink the family sphere, on the one hand, and the economic, political and value systems, on the other. They bring out the latent orientations towards these spheres which exist within the family. This interlinking sphere is of great structural importance within the social system for several reasons. First, it does not interlink segregated, marginal clusters of roles, but those most important from the point of view of the socialization of the individual. Secondly, the role expectations which it attempts to gratify are those oriented towards the attainment of full membership in the community and solidary identification with it (which have been raised in the family and built on the basis of the family's solidarity), and towards the attainment of *full social status* (within the occupational, political, etc., spheres). Thus these role expectations are concerned with the total aspirations and status image of the individual, both in relation to his own self-image and his identification with the community. The attainment of both in one cluster of roles is not possible in all sectors of a universalistic and specialized society, because of the segregation of instrumental solidary and expressive gratifications in different spheres. And it is the function of age (youth) groups to provide a sphere of roles in which a strong solidary orientation towards the community may be interwoven with wider universalistic and instrumental relations.

The attainment of a balance between solidary and expressive identification and instrumental relations within age groups is very important also from the point of view of minimizing any potential hostility or rivalry between generations. In a universalistic and achievement-oriented society, the preponderance of instrumental relations may intensify such rivalry, as the allocation of rewards is not regulated according to clearly ascriptive criteria. The subordination of these instrumental relations to overall expressive community orientations in age groups assures that to some extent this competition will be kept within the bounds of collective solidarity and ascriptive regulation.

Age groups can fulfill their integrative functions only in so far as they succeed in maintaining such a balance between expressive status and community orientations, on the one hand, and instrumental relations of the social system, on the other. The existence of such a combination, however, is not given or automatic; it occurs only under specific conditions. These conditions are closely related to the genesis of age groups as an interlinking sphere between the family and other institutional spheres of society.

If this analysis of age groups as an interlinking sphere between the family and the occupational, etc., structure is valid, it should also explain the conditions under which they perform fully integrative, partly integrative or deviant roles. Accordingly it is postulated that the extent of fulfillment of integrative functions by age groups is related to the extent of harmony between the family and other institutionalized spheres in universalistic societies. Only if the expectations and dispositions raised in the family are not in total disharmony with and opposition to the other institutionalized roles and identifications can age groups fulfill their integrative functions. In other words, it may be said that only in so far as there are present within the family some orientations—latent or manifest—towards the concrete society in which it exists, and its main values, can age groups fulfill this function. Otherwise the discrepancy between role-expectations and community orientations and the possibility of realizing these role expectations is so great that it cannot be bridged. It is only in so far as some compatibility or harmony exist between the structure of values of the family and of other institutionalized spheres of society that the various roles allocated to youth in the transitional, interlinking sphere can be more or less clearly defined by adult society. Otherwise that sphere becomes in a way undefined and unstructured, or rather is defined in contradictory ways, and hence not fully institutionalized.

Both the extent of harmony between the family structure and other institutional spheres of the society and the extent of integrative or deviant tendencies of age groups are, of course, matters of degree. We shall therefore set out the concrete criteria of each, beginning with the criteria of compatibility between the family and other institutional spheres of the society. (It should of course be remembered that our analysis is applied within the basic framework of universalistic societies, in which there is some initial lack of structural compatibility between the family and other spheres.) These criteria seem to be the following:

A. The extent of harmony between the main value orientations (and hierarchy of values) of the family and of other spheres.

B. The extent of compatibility between the authority structures of the different spheres. (This is especially important because of the place of the family in building up the individual's general attitude towards authority.)

C. The extent to which the family performs various tasks and roles within the major institutional spheres of society, i.e., the economical, political, ritual, etc., spheres. Instances can be found to the degree that economic tasks (production), political or ritual functions are allocated, *to some extent,* to the family. Even within nonkinship societies this may take place, although the family here can never become, by definition, the major unit of division of labor.

D. The extent to which the status aspirations and references of the family are compatible with the possibilities existing within the society and its subsectors and with their main value orientations. Of special importance here (mostly, of course, in modern societies) is the problem of the extent to which the family is capable of orienting its children towards realistic occupational choices and the extent to which its general style of living is acceptable—within the society and by its children.

All these criteria spell out, in various ways, the extent to which positive—even if latent—orientations towards the total society exist within the family. Also of special importance in this context is the extent to which harmony prevails between the internal solidarity and community orientation of the family and the overall solidarity of the society. While in universalistic societies family solidarity does not automatically overflow into that of the total society, the extent to which this is possible is very significant.

It is the basic hypothesis of this chapter that the degree of existence of these criteria determines the extent of conformity or deviancy of age groups. Before presenting the material bearing on this hypothesis, however, we have first to proceed and elaborate the concrete indices of these integrative or disintegrative tendencies. We shall begin by explaining them in some detail.

The main test of conformism or deviancy of age groups is the extent to which the objects and roles chosen by age mates are appropriate and adequate for the fulfillment of their general social aspirations; to which the attainment of full, solidary participation in a group of coevals coincides with the roles allocated them by the authority centers of the society. Such harmony may also be defined as the extent to which the preparatory socialization effected in age groups is compatible with the main institutional patterns of symbols, norms and values of the social structure, and to which the transition from preparatory to fully institutionalized spheres is successfully effected.

What, then, are the concrete indices of such harmony or successful transition? It seems that there are three levels of such indices. The first refers to the relation between the values and orientations of the basic, primary age group, and the basic norms of the institutional structure of the society. The problem here is the extent to which the various norms and values of the society constitutes the patterns of symbols to which the age group is oriented. This may be seen in the extent to which the solidarity of the age group overflows into the total society, and the extent to which age group ideology does not stress hostility towards other age groups and generations or towards the values of the total society. The maintenance of all these references and orientations towards the general society implies the existence of effective and smooth channels of communication between primary age groups and the total social structure.

An important point in this respect is the nature of the *internal* allocation of roles within the age group or age group system. To the extent that this allocation is based on universalistic, and in some cases also to some extent achievement criteria, its orientation towards the political, economic, etc., spheres is articulated and its interlocking function can be more successfully fulfilled.

This brings us to the second level or group of indices, the extent to which participation in age groups confers full social status and sexual identity on its members. As we have seen earlier, through membership in an age group an individual develops new psychological attitudes, new personality norms, and a new identity. If this new identity is compatible with the expectation of the general society and confers upon him full social status and legitimization of the establishment of a new family unit, the age groups have performed an integrative function in the social structure.

The third level of compatibility extends beyond the preparatory and training stage, and refers to the extent to which fully institutionalized roles (e.g., economic, political, ceremonial) are allocated to age groups and adequately performed by them.

Cutting across these levels as a general index of the extent to which age groups perform integrative functions for the social system is the nature of intergeneration relations within and between them. In general it may be said that to the degree that an age group is heterocephalous—i.e., directed in one way or another by members of other age grades whose authority is fully accepted —its conformity and integrative functions are greater. This heterocephaly may take the form of autonomy and autocephaly of the total age group hierarchy (as among the Nandi, etc.), whereby the elder age groups command the respect of the younger and exert some authority over them; or it may take the form of the direction of the age groups by older people outside the age group hierarchy. In so far as harmonious interaction exists between generations, and in so far as the age and youth groups inculcate attitudes of respect towards elder generations, they can help maintain the continuity of the social system. When, however, they breed opposition to elder generations and their values, they take on more and more of a deviant character.

We have outlined here three main levels of the extent of harmony between age groups and the general social structure. These levels are: (a) the extent of harmony between the values and orientations of age groups and the basic institutional norms and values of the social structure—compatibility which manifests itself in adequate socialization and smooth interaction with other generations; (b) the extent to which the identity evolved through participation in age groups is adequate for attaining full social status; and (c) the extent to which fully institutionalized roles are allocated to age groups. These three levels have been presented here in an ascending scale-order, i.e., the existence of any of the "higher" levels always implies that of a former one. These levels define the *degrees* of integrative orientations of age groups. Thus there are societies in which only the first level of harmony exists, others in which the first two, and still others in which all three exist. Beyond that there are, of course, deviant or semi-deviant cases in which not even the first level of compatibility exists, and in which age groups engage in outright deviant practices. We shall now examine our material in order to see to what extent it substantiates, elaborates or modifies the hypothesis presented above. We shall first analyze the societies in which age groups perform fully integrative functions, and finally those in which they bear a clearly deviant character.

II   Among most of the primitive tribes discussed in this book (with the exception of the Murngin, Tiv Tiv and Nyakyusa, discussed in Chapter V), we find very strong identity and compatibility between the value orientations of the kinship unit and of the total society.[4] First, there is a common emphasis on identical solidarity and community orientations, and in all cases known we find that the total community, in its symbolic and ritual values, constitutes the main reference group of orientations of the kinship unit. The family has very strong orientations towards the community; this may be seen in the full participation in ritual ceremonies, communal affairs and government, and in the overall preparedness to accept communal jurisdiction and direction. In no case do we find an indication of disposition on the part of the family unit to evolve separatist communal orientation and identification, or to dissociate its status aspirations from the communal framework. Although membership in the family unit is not sufficient for the attainment of full participation in the community, there is no strong opposition to the values of the community.

Secondly, the same harmony may be found in the strong emphasis on collective, diffuse and ascribed values, with only very partial emphasis on role specialization (and achievement) among certain tribes (Yako, Ibo, etc.). Even among these tribes the element of achievement and specialization is important mainly with regard to the principles of role allocation among different members, and (as has been shown in Chapter IV) *not* with regard to the contents and orientations of these roles and the values to the realization of which they are oriented. The main specialized activities are, in these societies, geared to the collective goals, and are usually strongly regulated by communal authorities. At the same time, however, as has been shown in Chapter IV, it is obvious that the higher the extent of role specialization, the smaller the scope of institutionalized roles allocated to the family unit.

In these societies family and kinship units also perform various tasks in several institutional fields. They are usually important units of production. Most of them are also ritual groups, with their own gods and ancestor worship. Even if these are not the most important ritual values of the society, they still have a recognized and legitimate place within it. These groups are usually also jural groups with some mutual responsibility; they also have to perform various political tasks—although they are not the main agencies of political control. The families are also important status units, and usually help the individuals (e.g., by economic help in becoming a member of an association) to attain that status which is not purely ascribed.

Although few specific data exist on this point, it seems that a great extent of compatibility may be found between the authority structure of the kinship unit and the total society—compatibility which finds one of its expressions in the clearly paternalistic attitude of chiefs and kings in the more centralized kingdoms, and in the general transformation and extension of respect attitudes towards seniors within the kin system which we find in most other tribes. Among some of the Yoruba and Ibo tribes, for instance, we find the gradual emancipation of the child from his economic dependence on the father, while he is still living within the family of orientation and being actively assisted by the father to gain the prerequisites of independence and authority which will become important in his adult life.

This basic harmony between the value orientations and authority structure of the family and of the total society facilitates transition from one sector to another. Such a transition does not entail entirely contradictory roles and behavior, but is effected within a framework of common values and value orientations. These two spheres are very strongly connected in respect to the balance between instrumental and expressive gratifications; the primacy of expressive and solidary community orientation and participation exists also in the total society, although the scope and importance of instrumental orientation is greater in other sectors of the society than within the kinship system. Therefore transition from the family (or kinship) unit to other institutionalized spheres and participation in them do not necessarily entail loss of solidarity with the community; and thus there is a great extent of harmony between the role-dispositions of the individual (with the strong emphasis on com-

munity orientation engendered in the family) and the roles allocated to him within the social system.

Accordingly, we find that in all of these tribes age groups can
easily interlink the family sphere and the political, economic,
etc., spheres, and fulfill fully integrative functions, as may be
judged by applying all the criteria of integrative functions set
out in the first section of this chapter.

Within these tribes we usually find complete correspondence
between the individuals' propensity to join age groups and participate in them, and the official, legitimate roles which are allocated to them by the bearers of authority: the individuals are most
eager to perform those roles which are allocated to the age
groups.[5] The existing data fully warrant the assumption that no
structural tendencies towards deviancy can be discerned in these
age groups, although it may well be that cases of purely individual deviancy do exist. The fullest expression of this correspondence is found in the fact that in all these societies entrance
into age groups is connected with the attainment of full, mature
social status, usually through initiation; there is scarcely any
other way of attaining social status except through initiation
and membership in an age group. In some of the tribes not only
initial adult status is attained through membership in age groups;
the same holds true of attainment of further, more differentiated
status grades, which in these cases are more or less synonymous
with age grades.

In these tribes most of the universally ascribed status grades
are based on age grades, and can be attained only through participation in age groups. This is most evident in the fact that
transition from one age grade to another is not an individual
affair, but must be effected in a corporate group, in this way
linking the solidarity of the group with that of the total social
system (on whose behalf the various statuses are allocated).

Within all these tribes membership in age groups, and particularly entrance into the "active" section of the age group hierarchy, is closely connected also with the attainment of sexual
maturity and the undertaking of legitimate heterosexual relations. Such relations are usually allowed only after initiation,
and in some cases special sexual privileges are given to the mem-

bers of the most active grade—the warriors.[6] In some tribes the pursuit of heterosexual flirtations and relations constitutes one of the main age group activities.

Thus in all these tribes the development and attainment of full personal identity and membership in the total community is conditioned on membership in the age group hierarchy, and cannot be achieved outside of it. Age group membership and the status achieved upon initiation into an age group are the main symbols of the individual's status and self-identification. It is through participation in age groups that an individual develops general dispositions for activities and roles which he has to fulfill within the society, and becomes capable of performing them.

The same harmony may be traced in all of these societies between the values and solidarity of the primary group nucleus of the age group and those of the total community. This harmony finds important expression in certain structural arrangements which exist in one form or another in almost all of these primitive tribes: (a) The proclamation of a new age set and/or the promotion and succession of age groups are usually ceremonial communal affairs in which the whole community or its main representatives participate. (b) The individual age group receives its emblems and symbols of identification from the official representative of the tribe. (c) Age groups serve as the main educational agency of the society, through which both technical and ritual knowledge are imparted to its members. (d) Age groups are an important agency of social control within the village or tribe. (e) Age group activities and formation enjoy full ritual sanctions in these societies.

In all of these primitive tribes, however, there is not only basic harmony between the values of age groups and those of the total society; age groups are also fully accepted bearers of roles and tasks allocated to them within the social systems. In all of them we find that age groups are among the most important agencies for the performance of fully institutionalized, central, integrative, juridical tasks, etc. Among the Nandi, etc., they are the main agencies for the performance of these roles. Among the Yako, etc., they are directed by other agencies in which the power and authority of the society are vested, and which in their

turn perform various roles—especially those relating to government, law, etc.—thus limiting the extent of age group activities.
Among the Swazi, etc., age group activities are also directed by
an outside agency which holds the monopoly of political power
—the king. In all of these societies the extent of institutionalized
roles performed by the age group is inversely related to the
extent of specialization, based on either family and descent
groups or special, achievement-oriented agencies and groups. In
all of them, however, definite institutionalized roles are performed by age groups, thus making them one of the most important institutionalized fields of the social structure. Their roles
and groups are generally acknowledged by both members and
nonmembers; the norms deriving from their group structure
and values are also generally acknowledged, binding, and crucial
in their conduct; and their boundaries and tasks are clearly and
precisely defined.

Within these primitive societies the high extent of institut-
tionalization of age groups is manifested in the important role
which members of other age groups and/or generations fulfill
within any given age group. In all of them any given group is
closely related to others, either through an autonomous and
automatic division of functions between different age groups
or through direction by members of age grades other than its
own. Among the Yako, Ibo, Ibibio and some Yoruba tribes, all
age group activities are directed by persons to a large extent
outside of the age group hierarchy, i.e., belonging to a different
generation. It is through this direction, and abiding by the rules
set down and applied by the authority of these persons that
age groups receive their recognition and the possibility of participating fully in the community. Among the Nandi, etc., relations between age groups are regulated through automatic succession, by virtue of which each age group is closely related to
the whole hierarchy. Among the Nuer, Bantu Kavirondo, Gusii,
etc., where no corporate age groups exist, the maintenance of
attitudes of respect towards elders is one of the main tenets of
the entire age group system, which finds its most salient manifestations on ritual occasions. In all these cases the strong interlinking of age groups and generations provides for continuity

between generations, and mitigates or nullifies any potential strain, competition or hostility in connection with rewards within the social system. Among the Nandi group (with the exception of the Suk) this potential hostility between generations is institutionalized and sanctioned in various rituals of succession, in which it finds symbolic expression and through which it is fully legalized. Thus in all these societies the transition from childhood to adulthood is effected through agencies either identical with age groups or closely related to them.[7]

Among all of the so-called primitive societies and age groups, the Nupe provide an interesting partial exception, or perhaps a marginal case, between the formerly discussed primitive societies and more complex (particularly modern) societies. Among the Nupe the relation between the family structure and the total society is more complicated than in other primitive societies. This is due mainly to the special blending of relatively rigid stratification with strong emphasis on common universalistic values and consequent social mobility—all of which have been analyzed in great detail in former chapters (III and IV). As a result of this special situation there is seemingly strong harmony between the main value orientations of the family and those of the general social structure, but no parallel compatibility between the family structure and universalistic elements in the general social structure. The relation between the family and the general social structure differs also within various strata, as well as between rural and urban sectors, as has been shown in our previous analyses.

These relations between the family structure and the general social structure have their repercussions on the extent of integrative functions fulfilled by age groups. Because of strong and rigid specialization and stratification, age groups hardly ever perform definite tasks within the total society. (In the villages they perform several roles important from the point of view of the community.) The only partial exception is in the field of religious and ritual institutions, in which age groups perform important tasks in several communal religious festivals. Otherwise, age groups constitute a relatively segregated sphere, performing mainly "preparatory" tasks as "schools for citizenship."

Thus, from the point of view of fully institutionalized roles the Nupe age groups perform but limited integrative functions. On the other hand, however, we find full harmony between the values of the age group and those of the society which have a distinct universalistic connotation. The education for citizenship provided by age groups means the development of identification with the common universal values of the society and its main symbols of identification. These values and the institutional structure in which they are embedded constitute the main symbol patterns to which age groups are oriented. The diversified internal status system of age groups is modelled after that of the total society. They are thus a very important preparatory channel for members of the society, and it is here that their main integrative functions may be seen. One of the indications of the importance of age groups as preparatory channels in these societies is the fact that within these groups we quite often find that the *internal* allocation of roles is based on universalistic and sometimes—although very rarely—also achievement criteria. These criteria, indicative of certain future (adult) roles, are bound here within the limits of ascriptive and diffuse relations. In this way successful interlinking between the family and other institutional spheres is effected.

It is only within those primitive tribes among which the authority structure of the kinship unit is incompatible with the attainment of full social maturity that we find a strong deviant tendency within the age groups. This has been analyzed for the Tiv Tiv, Nyakyusa and Murngin in Chapter V, and is mentioned here only as additional proof of the importance of the authority structure of the kinship unit.

III   The picture in ancient Sparta[8] is very similar to that described for the various primitive tribes. We find here a rather complete harmony between the orientations of the family and the general values and status criteria of the community. Most of our indices apply here very clearly: the family was an integral part of the community; it performed various integrative tasks, especially in the economic field, identified itself with the values of the society and participated in its main ceremonies. There are some indications that the women were not always as fully amenable to the official discipline as were the men, but there are no indications, until the decline of Sparta, of overt opposition to the values of the community. Accordingly we find that age groups performed fully integrative tasks and succeeded in their function as an interlinking sphere between the family and other spheres of the social structure. Here also all the main indices apply fully. Full harmony and correspondence existed between the values of age groups and of the society. The education and socialization effected in these groups was oriented entirely towards the future military life of the Spartans, and fully identified with it. Although there were probably instances of lack of discipline, apathy, etc., they did not undermine the system as such. The internal allocation of roles within these groups, with its emphasis on universalistic competition, etc., is also indicative of their orientations towards their future roles. It was also true that only through participation in age groups could a Spartan receive full social status as a citizen, and be initiated into manhood. Throughout his participation in the age groups he was directed by members of other age groups and generations, and interacted with them continuously, accepting their authority and the discipline they imposed on him. Finally, age groups performed important—mostly military—tasks in the society. Although most of the integrative functions of the society were not fulfilled by them, they did, however, perform those tasks allocated to them by the bearers of authority. Their fully integrative functions could also be seen in the important part they took in all public festivals and ceremonies.

The picture in Athens[9] is in many aspects similar, although differing in details and complexity. As we have already seen in the former chapters, it was, in a way, a forerunner of the situation to be found in modern societies, which will be discussed presently. It seems that here also, basic harmony existed between the status orientations of most families and the values of the society. However these orientations and values were, as we have already seen, much more differentiated than in Sparta. There was a greater differentiation between the private, individualistic orientations and the more communal and patriotic ones. It is well known that the relations between the two occupied a most prominent place in Greek social and political thought, especially during the period of the decline of the city-state. But it seems that on the whole during the 6th and 5th centuries B.C there was a great degree of harmony between these various orientations and values, even if they were not equally distributed among all classes of citizens and their families. In general there was a distinct feeling of the existence of an encompassing way of life, so powerfully expressed in Pericles' funeral speech.

Accordingly, we find also that the various age groups, schools, etc., performed mostly integrative functions, although usually much more within the preparatory and training sphere than in the performance of definite tasks. The values of the various schools and gymnasia were fully compatible with those of Athenian society and culture in general, and they trained their pupils to absorb these values and fully identify themselves with them. Although there was but little state supervision of schools, both their pupils and those of the gymnasia were trained to participate in the various festivals, competitions, etc., organized by the State. It was also only through participating in the formalized, official age group and undergoing the training of the *epheboi* that the young Athenian was fully initiated into manhood and became a full citizen of his state. In these groups he also performed some definite military tasks—the only ones officially allocated to age groups in Athens. In the schools, the gymnasia and the *ephebic* groups alike, the young people were directed by members of elder age groups, whose authority was on the whole accepted. But the fact that "private" and "public" age groups were so markedly differentiated in Athens made it possible for them sometimes to become foci of social and cultural change. Thus it seems that most of the cultural and philosophic movements of the 4th century B.C were closely related to certain of the schools, and Socrates was accused of corrupting youth. The social system of Athens was much more given to inherent change than that of Sparta, and the youth groups usually constituted one of the important foci of such change. With the decline of the city-state the public age groups also disappeared, and only the more private groups, the schools of various types, continued to exist, mainly within the fold of the upper classes.

IV   Within the framework of various modern societies there exists nowhere such great harmony or compatibility between the value orientations and structure of the family and the main integrative principles of the society as within the primitive societies. Several basic structural incompatibilities have been outlined in the preceding chapters. The modern family, despite—or perhaps because of—the great limitation of the scope of its activities, strongly emphasizes diffuse, particularistic collective values and relations. The family solidarity and emotional interdependence of its members are centered around these value orientations, which constitute the main symbols of identification of the family group. In this respect, therefore, there is a basic difference between the structure of the family and the integrative principles of modern societies, which are oriented more towards universalistic, achievement and individualistic values.[10] The basic structural discrepancy between the family and the occupational structure is a universal fact in modern societies, and is much more acute than in any primitive universalistic society. Such a discrepancy does not necessarily mean total rejection by the family of the achievement, etc., and values of the society as its basic common values and as status orientations for its members. Such total rejection of the values of the society occurs only under very specific limited conditions (which will be analyzed below).

Most modern families maintain strong orientations towards the general status criteria of the society and mould some of their activities accordingly. These orientations may be only latent in the internal activities of the family and in daily relations between parents and children. But they are usually very strongly emphasized in the father's occupational activities and in his general human image, and to some extent also in the value patterns inculcated by the mother. This status orientation is most clearly seen in the occupational direction which the family may give to its children and in the parents' attempts to influence their future occupation and style of living. It is in this orientation that a very strong link may exist between the life and values of the family and those of the general social structure. Yet even within these orientations and aspirations some strong internal discrepancies may be present. These discrepancies are due both to the structural differences between the family and other social spheres, and to the fact that the transition from one to the other involves a relatively sharp change in patterns of behavior and values.

Among these discrepancies another merits special attention—namely, that between the family structure and the integrative principles of modern societies with regard to the relative importance of individualistic and collectivity orientations and standards. Here the problem is a double one. First, in all modern societies the preponderance of achievement and specificity orientations necessarily entails a very strong individualistic tendency, especially in respect of criteria of occupational choice, and to some extent also those of status allocation. The family unit always has a much stronger collectivity orientation with relation to itself, and sometimes even to the total community. It is within the family that the first and basic role dispositions to accept the general moral standards and community identifications are developed and corresponding role expectations evolved. Transition to the more individualistic sectors of society necessarily involves some frustration of these role expectations. This does not mean however, that in those modern societies with a strong collectivity orientation this discrepancy is totally overcome. Here the second aspect of the problem arises. The individualistic element is inherent in any framework of (family) status aspirations in any modern society, and a too strong collectivity emphasis may become opposed to such status aspirations, which are borne by every family, through its emphasis on *its* own advance and achievement.

Thus in no modern society does complete correspondence exist between the structural principles and values of the family and those of the total society. Within modern societies, despite strong links between the family and other social spheres, most strongly expressed in the status aspirations of the family, the full realization of solidary orientations is not always possible in the economic, occupational, and even the political spheres. While personal and familial relations play a great part in engendering and supporting orientations towards the *general rules* of moral behavior, so important in the consensus of modern societies, they are not fully adequate in themselves in this respect because of the various discrepancies analyzed above. Therefore the transition from family to total society is necessarily fraught with severe emotional difficulties, as it necessitates redefinition and transformation of the individual's role expectations.

These emotional difficulties are paralleled by some additional structural consequences. Owing to the structural discrepancies between the family and the total social system, the development of hostility and competition between generations is always possible. In these cases this hostility cannot always be easily kept within the bounds of communal solidarity, since this solidarity is weakened by the various basic structural differences.[11]

Owing to all these reasons, interlinking the family sphere with other spheres of the society is not as easy here as in primitive societies, and it is divided between two or three channels—the schools, youth agencies and age (youth) groups. In modern societies the rise of youth groups is due, as has been shown earlier, to the relative inadequacy, from the point of view of the adolescent's needs, of the more official channel—the school. But precisely for this reason the youth groups themselves are never fully adequate as an interlinking sphere, and cannot fulfill fully integrative functions. This can be clearly seen through the application to them of the main criteria of integration.

As has been shown in the preceding chapters of this book, none of the age groups in modern societies can be said to perform fully sanctioned tasks within the main institutional spheres of the social system. Age groups and youth movements do not usually perform *routine* tasks within the institutional sphere of "adult" modern society; at most they perform various symbolical activities which emphasize their identification with the ultimate values of the society, such as taking part in various ceremonies, etc. Even in those societies such as the *kibbutz*, where children perform various tasks akin to those of adult society, such as working in the fields and gardens, etc., the meaning of these roles is different from that in adult society, and is mostly of a preparatory nature and symbolic value.

Therefore we also see that in these societies membership in age (youth) groups does not necessarily or automatically bestow upon the individual full social status, or enable him to develop his full identity, his sexual image and capability of maintaining legitimate and stable heterosexual relations. It is true that one of the main "attractions" of age groups for the individual members lies in their expectation of fulfilling their aspirations for full status, heterosexual experience, etc., through membership in these groups. We have seen the importance of their informal initiation ceremonies in this connection. However, these expectations, as we have seen earlier, are not fully gratified in any modern age group, although the extent of their gratification differs from one type to another. In no modern society do we find any ceremonials or rituals which bestow on members of an age group full social status and the right to enjoy heterosexual relations. In all modern societies the attainment of such full status is ultimately dependent on the performance of various roles within the specialized, achievement-oriented spheres outside the fold of the artificial preparatory world of youth. Membership in an age group may serve as a good preparatory channel for the *future* (even the near future) attainment of such maturity; it does not automatically bestow it.

As Erikson's analysis of development of identity in various modern societies shows, in none of them is maturity or integrated ego identity attained fully through participation in the preparatory stage alone; this development is conditioned on participation in spheres beyond the preparatory stage. Neither is full heterosexual maturity attained in a youth group; it may be attained only beyond the exploratory stages of youth groups. In many cases clear-cut incompatibility exists between the solidarity of the small nuclear primary age group and the development of heterosexual attachments.[12]

The same applies, as we have already seen, to harmony between the values and ideology of age groups and those of the total society. In most modern societies there is no full identity or harmony between the two. In many places a special ideological emphasis is laid on the period of youth as a special stage of life, during which there are special, more direct relations to the ultimate common values of the society than in later stages of life, involving participation in the institutionalized spheres of society. In many modern age groups and youth movements, especially in the more organized or formal ones—even in those belonging to sectors and societies with strong collectivity orientation—a belief prevails that the period of youth is, or should be, more strongly collectivity-oriented than adulthood. In most modern youth movements and agencies there is some degree of romantic "idealization" of youth, of the belief in its more idealistic attitude and spirit.[13] This idealization constitutes one of the basic elements of modern youth ideology everywhere, and emphasizes the distinctiveness and relative discontinuity between youth and adulthood.

The same seems to apply to interaction between generations in modern age groups. In many of them, except for the outright deviant and rebellious groups, such as the German Youth Movement, delinquent groups, or the most informal type of "crowd" or "corner gang," there may be some extent of adult participation and direction, whether in the form of informal direction of leaders of youth agencies, teachers, etc., or in the formal direction of collective youth organizations. In none of these cases, however, are these adult leaders completely accepted. There is always some opposition to them, based on the alleged autonomy of youth, on the strong mutual identification of the small youth group with its strong emphasis on its own ideology.[14] It seems that some tension between the nuclear group and the officially sponsored leader is inevitable in all of these groups, as is also the disposition to accept leaders with charismatic, nonformal authority based on full acceptance and symbolization of the values of the youth group.[15]

For all these reasons the transition from the nuclear primary youth group to the total community in most modern societies is not effected through fully institutionalized and stable channels which assure smooth transition. In most cases some element of anomie, of potential deviancy and rebellion sets in because the transition from one set of roles to another is not supported by full official, ceremonial sanctions.

The extent to which this transition is effected through channels and agencies closely interlinked with the youth groups therefore becomes a very important index of the integrative functions of age groups in these societies. In this way these groups may maintain some function as selective agencies through which some, at least, of their members are oriented towards their adult roles. Because of all these factors, great emphasis should be laid in our analysis on interrelations between the educational (school) system of a given society and its various youth groups and organizations. We have seen in the preceding chapters of this book that the family, school and youth groups of a given society should be seen as one—even if differentiated—system. Within it the educational system serves as a link between the other two, as within it the society's expectations in regard to the children are most fully articulated. The extent to which this system is capable of co-operating, in one way or another, with the spontaneous groups and expectations of youth is of very great importance for the understanding of the extent to which youth groups perform integrative or semi-integrative functions in the society.

Thus we see that in modern societies age groups, in so far as they do not develop outright deviant tendencies, usually evince only the first kind of integrative indices, i.e., general harmony between their value orientations and those of the society. Even such harmony is not always complete, and these youth groups usually serve as necessary, though insufficient, preparation for the attainment of full social status; although they themselves do not usually confer such status. In addition, no fully institutionalized roles are allocated to them. Thus they cannot be said to constitute a fully institutionalized sphere within the social structure; at best they constitute a sphere of "secondary institutionalization,"[16] i.e., a limited and segregated sphere within which there exists relative permissiveness for the performance of certain patterns of behavior differing from the official, fully sanctioned roles of a society.

Let us explain in greater detail the meaning of "secondary institutionalization." It develops when certain patterns of behavior and value orientations differing from the official patterns of a given society arise under certain conditions inherent in the social structure—conditions which cannot be nullified and which are in a way important to the stability of the system. Secondary institutionalization is an adjustive mechanism through which these patterns of behavior may be realized in a certain limited, segregated sphere of society; thus, on the one hand, it insulates potentially deviant tendencies, while on the other hand, it maximizes the gratification of the members and through this their solidarity with the social system.*

According to our analysis most youth groups in modern societies (except for the outright deviant, rebellious cases) fulfill such functions of "secondary institutionalization." Age groups constitute a segregated sphere—with few fully sanctioned roles allocated to it—which emphasizes value orientations different from the fully institutionalized ones. At the same time, however, the role expectations related to these orientations always arise in these societies, and, as they are so closely related to the development of the personality and of identification with the community, their realization is important for the maintenance of personal integrity and solidarity with the total society. Their segregation in a specific sphere at once minimizes certain frustrations due to their nonrealization in some of the institutional spheres of the society, and makes possible the gradual maturation of the personality and gradual preparation for adult roles and transition to them, through a continuous maintenance of some basic collectivity orientation. In so far as age group relations are reactivated in later stages of life, on various occasions, they serve as a reservoir of potential solidarity with the social system.

From the previous analysis, a very important characteristic of modern youth groups can be derived. Through membership in such groups the individual develops his personality: he attains psychological maturity and develops his identity. But all these psychological processes of maturation are to a very large extent

---

* An interlinking sphere may under certain conditions, but not always, become one of the mechanisms of secondary institutionalization.

divorced from the prescription and performance of any definite roles. Thus the individual is, in these groups, mainly oriented towards general norms, values, etc., and not to any specific roles. It is true that within the different youth and peer groups various roles are "acted out"—roles which already have some universalistic and achievement orientations. But, first, these roles are still confined within the limits of the solidary primary groups. Secondly, most of them are only acted out and tried, and no specific choices or commitments are made as yet. In general, the period of adolescence in modern societies has been aptly defined by Erikson as a period of "moratorium" from the point of view of the choice of definite occupational, political, etc., roles and a definite commitment to this choice.[17] This is, of course, very closely related to the multiplicity of alternative roles within modern society, and to the necessity of maintaining some *general norms* according to which these alternatives are chosen. Thus it may be said that the success of the secondary institutionalization of modern youth groups may be measured to the extent that during this period of moratorium they develop within its members the basic psychological attributes of maturity, of ability to choose between these various alternatives according to the general moral norms and values, and to evince general emotional and behavioral stability.

V   The previous section contained a description of the most general features of relations between the family structure and the main integrative principles of modern societies, and an analysis of their repercussions on the functioning of youth groups within modern societies. It is obvious, however, that within this general framework there is a great extent of variability and difference, from the point of view of both the relations of the family to the total social structure and the functioning of age groups. It is now our task to see whether this variablility may also be accounted for within the general framework of our hypothesis. We shall first analyze those societies in which age (youth) groups perform various integrative or semi-integrative functions, and second, those whose groups are outright rebellious or deviant. The following analysis will necessarily be couched in abstract terms, and will proceed, to some extent, in an "ideal-type" way. It should be obvious that in reality the distinction between the various types is not as clear-cut as presented here, as a large extent of overlapping always takes place. The limitations of space, the nature of our material and the paucity of systematic research, however, make this rather abstract method necessary.

Apparently the greatest extent of harmony between family structure and the total social structure—within the basic framework of discrepancies between the two in modern societies—occurs in stabilized, collectivity-oriented societies or subsocieties such as the U.S.S.R., in the Israeli *Kibbutz*, and to a much lesser extent Japan, Italy and Germany.[18] It may seem so because, first, strong community orientation is more or less wholly institutionalized within the official framework of these societies; from this point of view there may be a basic continuity between the family and the total community, although there may be great differences in emphasis. Secondly, this strong collective emphasis may also mitigate, to some extent, the institutional emphasis on specificity, as this last element is often embedded within the framework of diffuse collective achievements and universalistic-ascriptive membership in the community. However, this constitutes only a relative mitigation of the emphasis on instrumental activities, as such relations are necessary in an industrial society.

But despite these factors of continuity, there are several basic discrepancies and strains in such societies between the family structure and that of the official, collectivity-oriented sectors. First, the demands of the collectivity may easily encroach on the private sphere of the family, its solidarity and stability. This is found in all societies of this kind.[19] Secondly, in many families a strong orientation may exist towards instrumental rewards in the various occupational spheres, which are necessarily organized according to various criteria of achievement and specificity and in which numerous careers are open to the individual. While lip-service to the communal ideals must be paid in all these spheres, real identification with them may be very small and a more cynical or "realistic" approach may be predominant. This is, of course, more frequent in large-scale societies such as the U.S.S.R., etc., than in a small community like the *kibbutz*.[20] Thirdly, within many of the lower strata of these societies utter apathy is felt towards the official collective values.[21]

Thus it may be said that while some of the structural differences and discrepancies between the family structure and the values of the society are, from the point of view of official ideology, minimized, there are many other tensions and discontinuities, manifesting themselves in apathy towards the official values, and sometimes in the development of secondary orientations and values. These tensions are due to the fact that in these societies there is a tendency to minimize entirely the relative segregation inherent in the complicated division of labor of modern societies. This minimization is effected in most of these societies (with the exception of the *kibbutz*) by means of an autocratic use of power which may quite often bring about an opposite effect: maximization of tensions and strains.

These official attempts to minimize the discrepancy between the family structure and the total society correspond to the relatively high degree of integrative functions of the official youth groups and organizations. In these formal, collective youth organizations the various integrative possibilities existing within the framework of a "preparatory" segregated sphere seem to be utilized as fully as possible. Members enjoy the fullest measure of participation in various collective rituals and ceremonies of the total society, and symbolic fulfillment of various tasks and roles which are evaluated as important contributions to its welfare and progress. Through such participation and contribution they also enjoy the feeling of being accepted as *potential* full members of the society, and of attaining the various prerequisites of such membership. In these cases the youth organizations are used as legitimate and fully accepted preparatory channels for the acquisition of full status, although this acquisition as such is clearly beyond them. This can be seen in several ways: first, in the strong ritualization of their activities; second, in their serving as channels for the recruitment of future elite members of the society; and third, in their importance for future careers of various types.[22] The special ideological emphasis on youth bears a somewhat less deviant character here than in other cases, mainly because of the strong element of collectivity orientation in the official value system of the society, which emphasizes its accordance with the inherent collectivity orientation of the youth group, and tries to shed it of its specifically rebellious utopian element. And yet it may quite often be oriented against the main values of the family and its internal solidarity.

In the sectors of these societies in which collectivity orientation is strong, transition from the family to the total society is on the formal level as complicated as in other modern societies or sectors of them, and youth and age groups can better fulfill their interlinking function. Within their own organization they attain some balance between semi-institutionalized instrumental and expressive solidary gratification, and are closely interlinked with the collective symbols of identification and with expressive participation within the community. Because of their clearly "preparatory" nature, they also constitute a segregated sphere in the social system; but the transition from this to the fully institutionalized sphere is effected through channels and agencies which have a recognized place within their own structure (such as official party leaders and party agencies, or communal committees which supervise the youth organizations). It is also within these youth groups that the formal direction and supervision by representatives of the total society is most fully established and accepted. This may be clearly discerned also in the fact that the extent of opposition between the school and the youth organization is minimal, as the two form parallel parts of the same formal, unitary organization.[23] This pattern of youth groups and organizations exists, in these societies, mainly in the official, formalized sphere. The youth organizations themselves serve in these societies as a training ground for the elite, and are very selective. Within many of the lower, more apathetic strata, youth organizations are not very effective. We know little of the various informal children's groups in these sectors, but there is some indication of their existence and even of their potentially deviant—or at least apathetic—tendencies. Moreover, within the formal youth groups themselves quite a degree of apathy develops side by side with various "realistic" career orientations. Thus it seems that these organizations are most effective in the upper strata of the society, where they succeed in fulfilling their various interlinking functions. In other strata they may serve as channels of mobility, and in this way may quite often intensify the potential conflict between the family and the political structure. In small communities like the *kibbutz* they are of course much more effective; although here also quite a great degree of apathy and private orientations seems to develop. In most strata the strong collectivity orientation of these movements runs counter to the inherent internal solidarity of the family, and their rigid formal organization only tends to intensify the tensions between the family and the political spheres of the regime.

But even the relatively stable functioning of youth organizations in the official spheres of collectivity-oriented societies is possible only in so far as there exists more or less complete identity in the nature and contents of the community orientations of the family and the total society; i.e., in so far as these social systems are more or less stabilized, even if their functioning involves severe strains, among them strains on the family structure. Most of these collectivistic movements may well arise in the form of rebellious, revolutionary movements, out of a social setting many sectors of which do not share their basic common goals and identifications. This is how most of these movements have arisen (with the partial exception of the Isràeli *kibbutz* and other "pioneering" youth movements, which have transplanted themselves into an entirely new social setting). In these stages the formal youth organizations created by these movements, although fully identified with their goals, are very strongly oriented against the existing identifications and orientations of the families; one of their main aims is, not to bridge over the gap between the family and the total social structure, but rather to destroy the existing family order.

VI   In most other modern societies and their sectors there exist some collective orientations which counterbalance the purely individualistic emphasis inherent in an achievement-oriented, specialized system. These collective orientations may be of a semi-traditionalistic nature, emphasizing mostly certain patterns and styles of living; or they may be closely connected with certain political parties, religious groups, various types of communal activities, or even a general, diffuse feeling of patriotism. Their relative strength differs in various societies and sectors thereof. We have analyzed some such cases in Chapter IV, and have seen that they seem to be much more pronounced in various sectors of European societies than, for instance, in the corresponding strata of the United States (unless they are based on a strong ethnic identification). In most cases, however, they form part of the general pattern of living of various social strata (with the partial exception, perhaps, of some of the lowest classes) and of the general criteria of status. While they do not usually negate to any large extent the strong emphasis on achievement and specificity, they imbue it with a more diffuse social orientation. In these societies the school system usually represents this collective emphasis to some extent. A good example of this—besides the English public schools, which have already been discussed—is the *école normale* and the role it played in the social and cultural life of the Third Republic.

The relation between the structure and values of the family and of the general society (or some of its main subgroups) in these societies may be somewhat complex. From a certain point of view it would perhaps be possible to divide these societies into three sectors: (a) the collective sector, in which families identify themselves with collective values (as in the fully collectivized societies); (b) the purely individualistic sector, in which families identify themselves with individualistic values only; and (c) the transitory sectors, where there is no such identification. Such a division, however, would be inadequate, as it postulates the total segregation of these sectors. In fact, however, such total segregation does not exist, and both orientations (individualistic and collectivistic) are interwoven in all sectors, although to different degrees. Thus there may be great complexity here in the relations between the various families and other institutionalized spheres. This is so for the following reasons:

(a) There is an unequal distribution of collective and individualistic orientations, either among the various sectors of

Consequently, correspondence does not necessarily exist between the orientations of a family and those of a given institutional sector to which its members may belong.

(b) Because of (a), neither the individualistic nor the collective "sector" or criterion has a monopoly of status conferral within society, and full participation and membership in the social system cannot be attained through one sector only. So, for instance, the urban member of a pioneering labor party in Israel cannot entirely neglect achievement criteria in the economic and occupational field, the attainment of which is necessary for the maintenance of his social status, even if it runs counter to some aspects of his party ideology.

(c) Consequently, different families have a greater number of possible status positions from which to choose and to which to orient their children; although they must take into account both orientations, they can to some extent choose which of them to emphasize. Thus, on the one hand, there may be many families whose status orientations are more or less harmonious with the collective orientations of their respective sectors. In such cases the communal participation of the family is very strongly emphasized, and tends to lessen, to some extent, its segregation from the various occupational and civic activities. On the other hand, there may be many families whose status orientations are not so harmonious with the status criteria of its sectors, or who overemphasize certain status criteria. They may have either stronger collective or individualistic orientations. In these cases some internal contradictions and discrepancies may arise within the families, and within the general dispositions they hand over to their children.

Within the more outspokenly individualistic sectors of modern societies, the relation between the family and the total society is in a way simpler. In these sectors there is a maximal structural difference between the two spheres, and a consequent maximal extent of segregation between fields of expressive and instrumental gratifications. The field of family life is largely, although perhaps not entirely, segregated from that of the occupational and civic life of the parents (fathers), and the transition between the two necessarily entails very strong discontinuity. At the same time the family identifies itself with individualistic status criteria and emphasizes some of these values as the *common* values of the society, and the normative rules which uphold these values as the main moral rules incumbent upon its members. In this way a basic harmony between the values of the family and those of the society is maintained.

The functions fulfilled by age groups within these sectors and types of modern societies correspond to the relations existing between the family and the total social structure. In the "mixed" sectors we find the more formally organized youth groups and organizations of the various European and American political parties, religious groups, civic and communal youth organizations and the various Israeli youth movements. In some cases, already analyzed in Chapter IV, youth life is centered around various special types of schools, such as the English public school system. In none of these cases do we find such close interlinking with adult-sponsored agencies or such close communal participation as in the official sectors of the collective societies. Membership in these organizations is not a necessary prerequisite for attaining full social status, and although these groups tend to participate in various communal activities and celebrations, etc., their place within them is not as fully articulated or sanctioned as within the collective sector. Membership in them alone does not assure full participation in the community, and there is a very strong tendency to emphasize the ideological discontinuity between the "youth stage" and the adult world. In this connection there is also a strong emphasis on youth's more direct relation to the collective values of the society, collective values which, unlike those in the more collectivized sectors, are not fully embedded within the institutionalized structure of society.

The transition to full adulthood and the allocation of fully sanctioned roles is only in part effected through agencies connected with and directing youth organizations. In many cases it is effected without any relation to age groups, and only to the degree that an individual aspires to roles within the purely collective sectors (e.g., to political roles in a party or movement, or to a communal settlement) can this transition be realized to some extent through such agencies. In other cases, youth groups have a self-dissolving character, as their identity and activities are discontinued in the adult world.*

Yet, because of the strong emphasis within these groups on collective goals and their strong attachment to the collectivity-oriented sector of the community, they perform various selective functions within the society. In the collective sectors they maintain the stability and continuity of the society, their function being somewhat akin to that of the formalized youth groups of collective societies. At the same time, adolescents coming from more individualized sectors, having more individualistic orientations, may also find within them a temporary repository of collective identifications. In this way the groups are important for the maintenance of overall solidarity with the social system and a balance between individualistic and collective orientations. In many cases (e.g., in Israel) we find that youth movements with different extents of collectivity emphasis are distributed *more or less* equally among the various sectors according to their value orientations, thus helping to maintain the balance between the sectors and the basic social orientation of each sector. But such correspondence can never, of course, be full, as there is necessarily some mobility between the sectors, and the various youth movements may serve as one of the channels of this mobility. If this occurs they serve, not as agencies through which the internal balance and continuity of the social system is maintained, but as potential "disrupters" of such a balance. (They may become similar to some of the appendages of revolutionary movements to be analyzed shortly.) From Israeli research we know that many members who come from families opposed to the collective pioneering values of the *Yishuv* show a greater tendency to emphasize the specificity and discontinuity of the "youth stage" in relation to adult society, and to evolve a more aggressive identification with their group, than do members who come from families with a positive orientation to these values.[25] In many cases it may be that a too strong aggressive identification with a

---

* An interesting case of special, self-dissolving youth groups, participation in which is an important prerequisite to attaining adult status, is that of the "societies" of debutantes in various upper-class sectors in Europe and the United States.[24]

given youth movement or organization may limit the youth's occupational choice and put him in a rather difficult position from this point of view. Very intensive participation in a youth movement may impair his education and preparation for an occupation, and may orient him only to very selected spheres with but limited opportunities, i.e., the political sphere. On the other hand, it may well happen that some of the more collectivity-oriented organizations, e.g., those implementing various citizenship programs, do not succeed in reaching many strata of youth, which remain entirely apathetic to wider collectivity loyalties and center their activities in a very narrow circle of family, friends, work, etc.[26]

There are many such examples of youth movements organized by various political, nationalistic or ethnic parties and groups, developing very aggressive symbols of identification, participating in the political struggle and constituting an important channel of social and political change. A very pertinent description of such a situation is given for French Canada,[27] and many similar examples may be found elsewhere.[28] In these cases the similarity of these youth organizations to the various appendages of outright rebellious parties and movements (described below) is very strong.

One of the main aspects of youth groups in these societies and sectors is their interrelation with the school systems. We have already analyzed in Chapter IV the various types of interrelation between school systems and youth groups. It is worth-while to emphasize here an additional aspect of the problem—namely, the influence which the various youth movements and their ideology have exercised on the school systems of various countries. In many European countries, such as the Netherlands, the Scandinavian countries, etc., they have influenced the curriculum directly or indirectly by introducing various sports activities, excursions, etc. Their influence on the various trends of so-called progressive education has also been manifold. It could be seen in the establishment of many new types of schools in the Weimar Republic, as well as in several Central European countries.[29] In this way they helped—mostly through teachers and educators who themselves were members of such organizations—to effect important changes in the educational system and to bring it closer to the expectations of youth and the spontaneous youth groups. They thus became agents of continuous social change within the accepted framework of society.

A similar effect of these various youth groups can also be found in other spheres of life, particularly in political and social organizations. Not only do various political parties and social organizations initiate many of these youth groups and youth clubs; but they in their turn influence the activities of these parties, intensify their youth consciousness, make them more aware of the necessity to find outlets for the political aspirations of the young people. In many cases we find special political clubs for young people—e.g., Young Conservative Associations, etc.

This function of many types of modern youth groups can also be seen in their relations to older people and in their general place in intergenerational relations. We have already seen that in most of these organizations the acceptance of adult authority is only partial. But at the same time various age grades do interact here, and general and diffuse attitudes of respect towards the elders are usually inculcated. Although these attitudes are not fully prescribed or institutionalized, they do have some general effect on the behavior of children and adolescents, and mitigate the potential intergenerational strife inherent in most achievement-oriented societies. This is especially effective in the sectors in which the family pattern of life includes various orientations harmonious with the criminal, etc., activities of youth groups. In these cases the secondary institutionalization of youth groups tends to facilitate greatly the transition from childhood to adulthood. This may be seen also in the fact that participation in the various youth groups also aids in the psychological development of youth by developing within them the ability to maintain stable relations with various people, to participate in spontaneous activities, to choose between various roles, to face changes in social relations and patterns of activities, and to maintain general identification with the main norms and rules of social life. But all these functions can be fulfilled by these youth movements only if, first, they succeed at all in reaching various strata of apathetic youth; and, second, they do not develop the above-mentioned potentially aggressive attitudes. These attitudes may to some extent impair the personality development of the members, and give it an aggressive and authoritarian bent.

The picture of youth groups within the almost purely individualistic sectors and types of modern societies is somewhat similar to that described above, but the extent of segregation of youth groups within the social structure is greater. In these groups emphasis on the psychological need dispositions of the individual which do not find full gratification within the officially ascribed youth roles of adult-sponsored organizations is somewhat more explicit than in all formerly cited cases. Membership in peer groups is of great importance for the personality development of the individual, and satisfies many of his needs and cravings. Numerous researches have shown that without participation in such peer groups the individual's psychological development is seriously impaired, giving rise to various pathological manifestations;[30] yet in all these cases peer group membership is but a stage in the youth's emancipation from family dependence, a stage which itself must be overcome before he attains full social and heterosexual maturity.

The pattern of relationships and groups evolved at this stage, as we have already seen in former chapters, differs in several crucial points from the institutional allocation of roles in adult society, and sometimes also from that of the adult-sponsored youth organization, despite the fact that in all of them strong emphasis is laid on development of the individual's character and personality and on his civic duties as one of the central goals of action. To some extent the romantic idealization of youth finds a very salient expression here, both in ideological emphasis on the discontinuity between the youth and adult stages, and in the actual patterning of relations. Tension between the autonomous group and its adult sponsors may be quite high, frequently taking the form of direct evasions and refusal to obey;[31] and the ultimate transition to adult society is disconnected from the life of the peer group, entailing its decomposition and abandonment. Of all the cases discussed so far, this is clearly the type which is most segregated from any given institutional sphere of society, and not directed by its authorized agents or bearers of authority.

Thus it would seem that the main functions of these youth groups, perhaps more than others, are to enable the individual to develop a personality capable of choosing between various adult roles, at the same time maintaining some minimal collectivity orientation and loyalty to the main moral norms of the society. In this way they may help the individual to adapt to a rapidly changing society. But the extent of their success in this respect differs greatly according to various, sometimes accidental, circumstances.

VII   Hitherto we have analyzed those cases in which the various youth groups perform, despite their institutional segregation, at least semi-integrative functions within the social system—whether through outright regulation of relations between generations, role allocation, or preparation of the members for the performance of future roles. However, among the various types of age groups there are also outright deviant types, i.e., those who engage in totally nonconformist behavior which disrupts transmission of the social heritage and the continuity of the social system.

In cases of such deviant age groups there is a total discrepancy between the expectations and aspirations of the youth group and its members and the expectations extended towards them by the adults. The reference group and patterns of symbols of the primary age group are totally opposed to the existing social system, and the group maintains no effective communication with the adult society.

In these cases the age groups do not entirely succeed in attaining a balance between the instrumental relations inherent in the main institutionalized spheres of the social structure and full solidary participation within the actual community; thus they usually tend to evolve a new primary identification, which (a) cannot fully organize the instrumental relations within the framework of the existing community, and therefore (b) orients itself to a new, deviant community.

It is very characteristic that in all cases of deviant youth groups there is a very marked opposition between the official, adult-sponsored youth organizations and roles, particularly the school, and the spontaneous youth groups. While some discrepancy between them exists in all modern societies, in the case of deviant youth groups it becomes full articulated and develops into outright opposition, usually synonymous with conflicts between the generations. In these cases any continuity between the different generations is abruptly broken, and the younger generation neither sees itself as in any way related to the older, nor has any expectations of developing according to the human image of the older people. Synonymously, it maintains no attitudes of respect towards the older people; in this way it also undermines harmonious interaction between the generations.

We shall now turn to an analysis of the main types of deviant age groups and the conditions under which they arise. We shall attempt to see whether their deviancy can also be explained through the relations between the structure of the family and that of the total society.

For the purpose of our analysis we shall divide the various deviant age (youth) groups into four main categories:

(a) Unorganized groups of youth delinquents arising in situations of "culture contact";[32]

(b) Juvenile delinquent groups of different degrees of organization and cohesion;[33]

(c) Youth organizations of revolutionary movements and parties;[34]

(d) Rebellious youth movements (mainly the German youth movement in one of its main phases).

(a) We shall first briefly analyze the various instances of unorganized youth groups in situations of culture contact, such as have been described among the Sioux.[35]

In most of these cases the youth camps do not even evolve a strong common identity and ideology, nor do they help their members to develop or integrate their ego identity. In most of them we find that (a) the members' families have been disorganized for quite a long period, failing to transmit to the children any coherent system of values or even any most general orientations, or to furnish them with minimal emotional security after the first years of childhood;[36] and that (b) the families themselves have usually lost any orientation towards full participation in a community, and have thus become totally apathetic in this respect. Both of these characteristics are usually related to extreme situations of culture contact through which various indigenous tribes are deprived of the basic framework of their life. This may help to explain the totally negative and disorganized nature of this youth group deviancy. It is mostly of a regressive, unorganized type, and is clearly related to the lack of any orientation to a wider, total, actual community, and of any hope of participating within such a community. It is also very strongly connected with the family's opposition to the school system and the very strong alienation of the children from it.

(b) The deviancy of the more organized types of delinquent groups, with stronger group cohesion and deviant youth ideology, is of a different character. It is oriented mostly against the institutionalization of normative *means* of a society, and not directly against its ultimate values. Although institutionally these groups are entirely disconnected from the legitimate adult world and rebel against it, their goal orientations are usually within the framework of their social structure. Their anomie is mostly what Merton calls the innovatory type.[37] They usually arise in a situation in which orientation to a community is possible; but a basic lack of harmony and compatibility prevails between the main patterns of symbols and values of the family and its authority structure, on the one hand, and the actual community, its values and authority structure, on the other. One of the most usual of such conditions is that of families who have migrated from traditional to industrialized societies.[38] In these cases the family orientation is usually particularistic, ascriptive and traditional, with a strong authoritarian system; while the actual community is universalistic and achievement-oriented. At the same time, however, there is not usually total regression from the community (as may happen in the former case), but a difference of emphasis and evaluation. For the family the actual total community does not constitute an object of primary identification or a status-conferring agency, but only a means for the continuance of physical existence; and the family evinces a strong tendency to maintain its old ways of life. In such cases not only are the parents unable to direct their children to various specific,

concrete roles; but they do not even evince any positive identification towards their new setting. Many researches, especially
in the United States and Israel, show the close relation between
these conditions and the rise of delinquent groups.[39]

Some of the main characteristics of these delinquent groups
may also be explained by the nature of the discrepancy between
their family background and the new social setting. Among
them we usually find not total, organized denunciation of the
new setting, but mainly emphasis of achievement of the community's main goals regardless of the legitimate, institutionalized
means of this achievement. Usually coupled with this is strong
emphasis on various symbolical and "phraseological" aspects of
adult behavior—overdressing, indiscriminate spending of money,
and illegitimate sexual relations.[40] The strong deviant "youth"
ideology is, in these cases, focused to a very large extent on
exaggeration of these symbolical aspects of adult behavior, thus
emphasizing both non acceptance of the fully institutionalized
roles of the adult world, and the coveting of these goals.

A very important aspect of these delinquent groups and their
families is their ambivalent attitude towards the school system of
their community. There are, in this respect, two main possibilities. There may be, on the one hand, a strong rejection of the
school system and its values, and of the very long period of
preparation it entails. In this respect the picture is similar to that
in most of the lower-class groups already described, except that
the discrepancy is much stronger. The extent of this discrepancy
may also become greater because of the inability of these families
to direct their adolescent children to any appropriate occupation choices—either because of the disorganization of the family
itself or because this would raise the children's level of aspirations beyond the existing institutional possibilities. In such cases
it may also be that the parents want the children to attend grades
in school which are advanced far beyond their real possibilities
or beyond their interests (they may have a more realistic ap-
praisal of their abilities); in this way the conflict is intensified.[41]

A somewhat similar type of delinquency seems to arise in the
interstices of various social strata and groups in which there is a
similar attitude on the part of the family towards the institutional

structure of the society. This attitude may be very closely connected to various types of thwarted mobility. The various researches on delinquency, though numerous, do not provide systematic material which would enable us to differentiate clearly between various types of delinquent youth formations and their relation to various types of relations between the family and the total society. Nor do we know yet to exactly what extent various types of delinquency arise without direct relation to family structure and orientation (although this does not generally seem to occur among organized deviant youth groups), or what conditions of family disorganization give rise to other types of deviancy besides deviant youth groups. Although many data have been accumulated in this connection, they are hardly amenable to systematic analysis.

From various researches on trends of delinquency, etc., it is known only that these groups tend to rise under such conditions as war, both parents' working outside of the home, etc., which minimize the family's effective socializing functions and/or enlarge the scope of unusual, uninstitutional opportunities before the adolescents, thus emphasizing once more their distinctiveness from the "settled" order of adult society.[42] K. Davis has rightly pointed out that the "parent-children" conflict is intensified during periods of accelerated social change.[43] During such periods the society offers, as it were, many opportunities beyond the stable status aspirations of the family. The potential discrepancy which exists in all modern societies between the structure of the family and that of the total society is maximized, thus giving rise to intensified conflict between generations. This conflict may give rise either to various forms of organized rebellion, which will be discussed below, or to various forms of social apathy and estrangement from certain collective values of the older generation. Researches on postwar German youth seem to indicate this clearly.[44] Much further research will have to be carried out before it is possible to substantiate any systematic propositions on this problem. At present only the very general connection between the family, its relations towards the social structure, and the formation of juvenile delinquent groups can be established.

(c) The third type of deviant age (youth) group is composed of the youth organizations of various revolutionary movements and parties. In most such European movements and parties of the nineteenth and twentieth centuries, and in nationalistic and social movements among non-European (Colonial) peoples, there has been a special youth organization and/or a very distinct youth ideology. In some cases the movement was composed of young people, students, etc., and styled itself accordingly. Mazzini's Young Europe, the Young Turks, the various nuclei of students in most social and national movements of the nineteenth and twentieth centuries in Europe and Asia—all are outstanding examples of this kind. A detailed social analysis of all of these movements is yet to be written; only when this is done will a fully systematic analysis within the framework of our hypothesis be possible. But even at this stage some broad outlines may be indicated.

Two facts are most significant from this point of view: first, that almost all such modern movements have developed a special "youth ideology." The essence of these ideologies (from the point of view of our analysis) is that the changes which they advocate and struggle for are more or less synonymous with rebellion against the "old" order and generation—a rebellion of youth, a manifestation of the *rejuvenation* of national and social spirit. In them the usual modern emphasis on youth as bearers of the common values of the community—in these cases of the *new* type of values—is accentuated and geared to realization of the movements' political and social goals. In some cases, as has already been indicated above, the whole movement identifies itself with such a romantic ideology and values.

Secondly, among most such political movements with a strong political-collective orientation, there is a universal tendency to form special youth organizations with whose aid they might muster youthful energies against the old order. A purposeful attempt usually takes place to disconnect the young people from their families, to turn them against the latter and the order they represent, and to intensify the conflict between the generations. This tendency is intensified when these movements are on the verge of success and achievement of political power and try to consolidate a new social order which would entirely abolish the old one. In all of these cases special, revolutionary youth formations of a distinct rebellious type are organized. The most indicative examples of this are the youth organizations developed by the Nazi party, the Soviet regime in Russia, and the new popular democracies of Eastern Europe.[45]

In all of these cases spontaneous youth groups are firmly interwoven within more general organizations, some of which are composed of adults and young people alike, while some include only youthful groups, as was the case in some of the Russian revolutional parties, or in certain nationalistic movements in the Near East. In a way these movements may be compared to the formalized youth organizations of the collectivity-oriented societies, and it is usually because of their strong collective emphasis that the formalization and organization of youth groups take place. However, unlike the youth groups of stabilized collective societies, these groups bear a strong deviant, revolutionary character. But this deviancy is not of a purely "youth" nature. It is part and parcel of a more general rebellion, and even the special youth ideology is a part or manifestation of a more general revolutionary ideology.

The important fact, then, which calls for an explanation is that almost every modern revolutionary movement has to develop such youth ideology and youth organizations, and most processes of social and political change must, to some extent, be realized through such channels and with such an ideological emphasis. The starting point of an explanation of this fact should be certain more or less universal characteristics of these modern movements:

(1) Most of them bear an outspoken *collective* orientation and ideology in which particularistic and universalistic elements are very strongly and ambivalently interwoven. While these groups organize themselves on a strong particularistic basis and emphasize very strongly both their own internal solidarity and symbols of identification and the strong attachment to their national collectivity, they also usually tend to emphasize some strong universalistic values and standards. But these are mostly transferred to the future, utopian stage; at the same time, however, they

constitute an important part of the ideology of the movements, and are especially emphasized in their proselytizing campaigns.

(2) These movements usually rebel against either a particularistic authoritarian (traditional) society or a combination of the latter with certain universalistic and individualistic traits, and they aspire to establish an entirely new collectivity.

(3) Their ideology and programs are usually couched in secular and social terms, thus emphasizing the problems of reorganization of the social system in ideological terms.

Because of all these characteristics, particularly (1) and (3), these movements must cope with problems of reorganization of the whole social system in terms of universalistic and secular values—thus necessarily emphasizing universal, social categories —and they are bound to muster social forces around such symbols of identification.

As their rebellion is oriented against the social order in its totality in terms of universal secular values, they must necessarily focus their attention on those *universal social groups* within the society which can be mustered and in whose name the rebellion can be effected. Hence the strong emphasis on youth and on a rebellious organization of youth groups. It is important to note that in other types of social change and movements, in which there is no emphasis on *total* rebellion in secular and universalistic terms, no such emphasis on youth emerges.[46]

This analysis of the basic characteristics of modern rebellious and revolutionary movements already throws some light on the conditions of their development, and especially on their relation to the family structure. As in the case of other deviant youth groups, so their deviancy can also be explained through the lack of harmony between the family structure in which their members grow up and the total society of which the family constitutes a part. This discrepancy has here some special characteristics which can be related to the specific traits of these youth groups.

Most of these movements arise in societies in which a traditional social order is undermined by the impact of modern, universalistic, social, political and economic developments—either through internal developments or through the penetration of foreign, European groups and interests. Significantly enough, in most of these countries the political and intellectual development has been much more advanced than the economic. Economically only very few sectors—commerce, public works, communications —have developed to some extent, while industrial development has lagged behind. For this reason the economic and professional opportunities open to young people are inadequate, and the ability of families to direct and promote the occupational development of their children is limited and quite often inadequate. This is especially true of the more intellectual youth, various groups of students, young officers, etc. The multiplication of these groups, which constitute the most important nuclei of all these revolutionary movements, has been symptomatic of the uneven development of the various spheres of society.[47]

In most of the societies (or sectors of societies) in which these youth groups arise, the family with its values and authority structure stands as a symbol of the general social order against which they rebel. Thus the family is not, here, as in the case of the former types of deviant youth groups, opposed to the total existing society, but is rather identified with its "conservative" part, against which another part rebels. The community orientation of the family and its status symbols and aspirations are seen as inadequate and "reactionary." In their place new collective symbols of identification are proposed by the revolutionary movement and by its various youth groups. These symbols of identification are oriented against those to which the family system is attached and with which it is identified, and which, because of their universalistic and social connotation, must emphasize rebellion against the family and its values. Such an emphasis is especially important, as otherwise these new symbols cannot forge the younger generation's identification with the new values.

Because the family is opposed here mainly as a symbol of the existing social order, the youth rebellion is not couched in purely autonomous terms, but constitutes part of a more general rebellion, usually sponsored by certain counter-elites within the society. These counter-elites, among whom some of the young students may play a prominent part, aim at the disruption of social continuity and the establishment of a new secular social order; they must therefore give special emphasis to youth. This emphasis is strengthened by the fact that they themselves are usually composed of young people. But it is laid not in the specific autonomous terms of a youth culture, but mainly in terms of general values with which the rebellious movement identifies itself. This rebellion against the family, and the intensification of conflict between generations in terms of an overall social rebellion, are also strongly connected with a negative attitude towards the school systems of these societies. Quite often these school systems are of a very traditionalistic pattern, strongly emphasizing the social and political hierarchy of their countries and supervised by their main centers of authority. Usually they are confined to the upper middle social strata and entirely bound by their values. The teachers themselves are either members of these groups, entirely identifying themselves with their values, or of lower-class origin, looked down upon by the parents of pupils themselves. The Russian teacher as depicted in the Russian classics amply bears witness to this situation, and a similar pattern can be found in many other countries where these rebellions have taken place. Thus it can be understood that in most of these movements the rebellion against the older generation is very often pointed at the school system, sometimes even more than at the family. Many of these rebellious groups start life clandestinely in schools, military academies and universities, and these institutions are usually among their most important targets.

This explains also the point that in so far as these rebellious and revolutionary movements are successful in overthrowing the existing social order and creating a new one, the nature of their youth groups is quickly transformed. As soon as a new social hierarchy and family structure are established which identify themselves with the new social order, these youth groups entirely lose their rebellious, deviant characteristics and usually become transformed into legitimate, collectively organized groups. Only in so far as the rebellious movement becomes a permanent element of the society against which it rebels do its youth movement continue in their deviant character and serve as channels through which the various deviant personalities are selected and mobilized.

It is of course obvious that such lack of harmony between "old" and "new" exists in almost all cases of social change, and that in such cases opposition to "elders," etc., always sets in. But full identification of the family with a certain society and strong opposition to it occur only in those types of movements of social change that bear the above-enumerated characteristics. A sharpening of the conflict against the values of the family as such must occur mainly in such secular universalistic and communal movements, which aim at a total reorganization of society.

(d) The fourth type of rebellious, deviant youth movement is exemplified in the German youth movement, the development of which was described in Chapter II. This type constitutes without doubt the clearest example of a revolutionary sectarian movement,[48] entirely focused on youth consciousness and ideology. This consciousness and ideology served as a center for total rebellion against the existing social order in its entirety, particularly against its common values and symbols of identification. It was believed that through full articulation of the distinctness of youth a new community would arise, a true *"Gemeinschaft,"* which would supersede the existing "bureaucratic," artificial order, and do away with all of its negative aspects. Not only did there exist in the ideology of this movement discontinuity between the values and institutional arrangements of the nuclear primary age groups and those of the total society (as in other types of deviant groups); but the primary groups evolved active orientations to new types of reference groups which were in total opposition to the existing ones. In principle a tendency predominated towards a complete discontinuation of communication with the existing adult society. Both the activities and ideology of the movements clearly showed their conception in a spirit of acute status anxiety and personal insecurity: total rejection of achievement and specificity-oriented activities, emphasis on primitive romanticism (shown in the strong emphasis on life in nature, style of dress, etc.), and a strong tendency towards male eroticism and ambivalent attitudes towards girls and women.[49] These attitudes were coupled with total rejection of any adult, institutionalized authority, and a strong disposition towards charismatic youth leadership. The manifest aim of the movement was to establish an adult society of its own, so as not to be compelled to effect the transition to adulthood within the framework of the established social order. As was shown earlier, this point was the most critical in the history of the movement, as the paradox and impossibility of focusing a revolutionary movement on the transitory criterion and stage of *youth* became evident. This paradox gave rise, on the one hand, to manifold influences in the sphere of education, etc., and, on the other hand, to a continuous stream of unresolved tensions and unsuccessful rebellions, which constituted part of the background for the rise of the Nazi movement but never in themselves succeeded.

The conditions which gave rise to this movement are of great importance to our analysis, which is closely based on the broader analyses of T. Parsons,[50] H. Becker,[51] Erikson,[52] Jungmann[53] and others.[54] The German youth movement arose at a time when the patriarchal and authoritarian German society, closely bound to ascriptive status (*ständisch*) positions, was under the impact of swift industrial development (during the Bismarckian era) which undermined the economic bases of the traditional, ascriptive order and opened up wide spheres of instrumental achievement. Unlike the various "underdeveloped" societies analyzed above, the tempo of industrial development here was very rapid and the occupational opportunities increased accordingly. At the same time, however, this industrial development did not give rise to an individualistic achievement society, nor to a social order in which economic achievement ("progress") was closely bound to collective goals (i.e., in which collectivity was the bearer and object of economic advancement), as for instance in the U.S.S.R. The German industrial society of the Bismarckian and post-Bismarckian era developed within a traditionally ascriptive political framework which was to some extent opposed to the rising industrial society, and which resolved to curb it or keep it within limits, from the point of view of both political power and status conferral. One of the main results was the development of a very formalized, ascriptively oriented, bureaucratic structure.

One of the most important fields where bureaucratic and authoritarian structures developed was education. As in many other modern societies, we witness a very rapid development of formal schooling and school systems. Here, however, this system was built up according to the most authoritarian premises and was envisaged as one of the main channels for the training of good soldiers for the State and king. It was one of the most centralized and government-controlled educational systems, and its whole atmosphere was focused on precepts of obedience to authority. Historically it was connected with both the *Aufklärung* and the Romantic movement which idealized the State, and was used in this spirit by the State. It was also very closely related to the "*Ständisch*" order of German society, and inculcated total identification with its values and very articulated hierarchy. Among all the educational systems of Modern Europe it was the most formal and rigid, leaving almost no place for spontaneous youth activities. It was also used as one of the main social agencies to counter the "bad," demoralizing effects of modern industrialism and liberalism.

Because of all these trends there developed a basic, though complicated, discrepancy between the family structure and the total social structure, as well as a very severe rift within the structure of the family itself. On the one hand, the family was still based internally on a relatively strong authoritarian and ascriptive value, and strongly oriented towards the old traditional collectivity images. On the other hand, its ascriptive status orientation could not be fully upheld in the occupational (more achievement-oriented) sphere. Thus the father's authority became undermined in a way, and he could not serve as a full model for status aspirations; yet his authority was still strongly upheld by the formalized, bureaucratic structure and by the formalized educational system. Internal tensions within the family became very strong, both between the "authoritarian" father and the submissive mother, on the one hand, and between them and the children, on the other. The children could not fully identify themselves with the father, whose authority was thrust upon them, nor with the mother, whose image was highly ambiguous because of the mixture of "love" (towards the children) and submissiveness (towards the father). This internal tension was one of the main reasons for the lack of development of a fully integrated sexual image or the capacity for heterosexual relations, which manifested itself, as has been shown, in the development of the German youth movement.

The tension and discrepancy were not, of course, limited to the family. They were necessarily connected with a parallel discrepancy in orientation towards participation in the general community and status attainment within it. The orientation of the typical middle-class family was to a large extent bound to the old ascriptive particularistic order, and not to the new industrial (achievement) order, nor to the new universalistically ascriptive community upheld by the *Junker* bureaucracy and the *Kaiser*. (It should of course be emphasized that, for obvious reasons, this entire analysis applies mainly to the middle classes, and not to the aristocracy or the working classes.) Thus the family could orient its children neither towards attainment of achieved status, nor towards full, expressive participation in a total community, as there was no compatibility between the expectations of such community aspirations and the possibilities of their realization within the institutional structure. It should be emphasized that the main discrepancy was between a particularistic, ascriptive value orientation and a universalistic ascriptive one, and between the two and an institutional structure based to a large extent on achievement-oriented values and allocation of roles. It seems that because of this type of discrepancy the specific form of a youth rebellion developed here. This discrepancy between the family structure and the total social structure could be resolved by the youth neither through identification with a "revolutionary," universalistic adult society (as there existed some identity between the communal identification of the family and the existing social order), nor through purely individualistic (delinquent) activities; as there could not be found among the middle-class sectors unequivocal acceptance of the achievement goals connected with money and business, or a total rejection of the common symbols of identification of the society.

Because of all these factors, the youth who had to leave the family and enter adult society evinced a very high extent of tension, which could not always find release within a sphere of secondary institutionalization or within an adult rebellious movement. Thus developed the revolt of youth whose main focus became youth in itself.

The main characteristics of this rebellious youth movement, outlined above, may also be understood from its genesis in internal family tension and in tension between the family and the total community. The strong rejection of adult society, the homosexual leanings and the strong yearning for the establishment of a new community (*Gemeinschaft*) which would overcome, as it were, the "materialistic," "formalistic" trimmings of the existing order—all these may be clearly related to the above-outlined analysis.

Within the German youth movement, the potential deviant force of modern age groups was most clearly demonstrated; but so, also, were its limitations. Disconnected from any organized group, whether legitimate or revolutionary, it showed the futility of a purely youth rebellion. Its influences were manifold. Some of the youth groups and their leaders tried to find a legitimate place in society mainly by influencing the educational system and reforming schools. In this pursuit they were partly, but only partly, successful, after the fall of the Empire. Some of them attached themselves to various political and social movements during the Weimar Republic and tried to imbue them with a new spirit of youth and vigor. But the energy and vitality of the "free" youth "movement"—which was only helped by the continuous social and economic upheavals of the Weimar Republic—were not spent in these manifold attempts; neither could they find any fully legitimate outlet within the changing and unstable circumstances of the Republican period. While there existed and developed in Germany many organized youth movements which were like those in other modern countries, there remained a continuous residue of unresolved tension among German youth, which formed one of the main backgrounds of the rise of the Nazi movement and which was utilized, exploited and harnessed by that movement and regime.

The analysis presented above has distinguished between several distinct types of deviant age groups and the conditions under which they arise. It has been shown that different structural conditions may account for the different types and structures of deviancy. Sometimes these conditions have been defined in very broad terms, since at the present date of research we could not go beyond them. But it should be clear that the analytical distinctness of these conditions (and of types of deviancy) does not necessarily entail a complete, concrete differentiation. The conditions analyzed above are, in a way, inherent in the structure of modern societies. Since in every modern society there are many different sectors and strata, it is quite possible that several or all types of these conditions may co-exist within them and give rise to several types of deviant age groups, as well as to various overlappings with more integrative youth groups. These types of conditions may sometimes even merge with one another and change into one another.

It should also be clear that, both for reasons of space and shortage of adequate systematic researches, we cannot deal here with all the concrete cases and shades of deviant youth groups of modern societies. We cannot dwell on the development of the various types of youth rebellion or of accentuation on youth ideology in literature, art, patterns of fashion, etc. We have dealt only with general structural analyses, through which our hypothesis has been verified and elaborated. Many more systematic and comparative researches are needed before we can go beyond this rather general analysis of the place of age and youth culture in processes of social change.

We have thus come to the end of our quest. We have
VIII   seen how in all societies age-heterogeneous relations, and in different universalistic societies age-homogeneous groups, constitute one of the most important channels for the transmission of the social heritage and maintenance of social continuity, and of the main foci of social continuity, or discontinuity. It has been demonstrated that in all universalistic societies this transmission must be effected either through autocephalous or heterocephalous age groups; its failure to do so is manifest in the deviant orientation of age group activities and identification.

This transmission of the social heritage is not, however, organized in exactly the same way in all (universalistic) societies, and a brief glimpse at the main differences may throw some light on the more general problem of conditions of stability of social systems. It has been shown that in some societies (such as the Nandi, etc.) the whole mechanism of transmission of the social and cultural heritage is centered in the institution of age groups. This transmission is effected through the most rigid prescription of roles at every stage of life, and through a most thorough linking of the individual's need dispositions and personality development to the official allocation of roles in the social system. The element of choice is very small, and the most concrete roles are completely interwoven with the general role-disposition evolved through the process of socialization.

In the more differentiated and specialized societies, this interconnection between need dispositions and role prescription, between general role dispositions and concrete role allocations, no longer exists, either in the general social system or in the structure of the age groups. Here the transmission of the social heritage is focused more or less on the development of an autonomous personality without a very precise prescription of roles. The scope of the choice becomes larger and more important, and social continuity is more dependent on the maintenance of the basic rules of choice and of the universe of choice than on the prescription of any detailed roles. This is most clearly seen in the growing emphasis on the "preparatory" activities of age groups, and in their relative institutional segregation. Thus the weakening of the fully institutionalized, integrative functions of age groups and their relegation to the sphere of secondary institutionalization do not necessarily denote the emergence of an unstable social system, but of a system whose continuity is focused on the maintenance of a universe of choices (alternative roles). In such a system the main emphasis is on the maintenance of the basic rules of choice and the society's general symbols of identification. Such a system is necessarily more dependent on the full psychological maturity and autonomy of its members than on any detailed role prescription: hence the greater emphasis in these age groups on the "psychological" preparation of their members.

At the same time, however, it is clear that such a system involves a much stronger element of change, and perhaps even of instability, than those systems in which transmission of the social heritage is effected through rigid role prescription. Thus age groups also become foci of potential deviancy and change, and the borderline between change and instability is very fine. The lack of any rigid prescription of roles, of any clear definition of the roles of youth by adults in modern societies, necessarily makes youth groups one of the most important channels through which the numerous changes of modern societies take place, and sometimes develops them into channels of outright rebellion and deviance. The crucial importance of age relations in all societies and of age groups in all universalistic societies is clearly seen in the fact that the smooth transmission of social heritage, various attempts at change and various manifestations of discontinuity are largely, even if not wholly, effected through them.

CHAPTER VII

Archetypal Patterns of Youth

Youth constitutes a universal phenomenon. It is first of all a biological phenomenon, but one always defined in cultural terms. In this sense it constitutes a part of a wider cultural phenomenon, the varying definitions of age and of the differences between one age and another.[1] Age and age differences are among the basic aspects of life and the determinants of human destiny. Every human being passes through various ages, and at each one he attains and uses different biological and intellectual capacities. At each stage he performs different tasks and roles in relation to the other members of his society: from a child, he becomes a father; from a pupil, a teacher; from a vigorous youth, a mature adult, and then an aging and "old" man.

This gradual unfolding of power and capacity is not merely a universal, biologically conditioned, and inescapable fact. Although the basic biological processes of maturation (within the limits set by such factors as relative longevity) are probably more or less similar in all human societies, their cultural definition varies from society to society, at least in details. In all societies, age serves as a basis for defining the cultural and social characteristic of human beings, for the formation of some of their mutual relations and common activities, and for the differential allocation of social roles.

The cultural definitions of age and age differences contain several different yet complementary elements. First, these definitions often refer to the social division of labor in a society, to the criteria according

From *Daedalus*, Vol. 91, No. 1, 1991, of the Proceedings of the American Academy of Arts and Sciences.

to which people occupy various social positions and roles within any society. For instance, in many societies certain roles—especially those of married men, full citizens, independent earners—are barred to young people, while others—as certain military roles—are specifically allocated to them. Second, the cultural definition of age is one important constituent of a person's self-identity, his self-perception in terms of his own psychological needs and aspirations, his place in society, and the ultimate meaning of his life.

Within any such definition, the qualities of each age are evaluated according to their relation to some basic, primordial qualities, such as vigor, physical and sexual prowess, the ability to cope with material, social, and supernatural environment, wisdom, experience, or divine inspiration. Different ages are seen in different societies as the embodiments of such qualities. These various qualities seem to unfold from one age to another, each age emphasizing some out of the whole panorama of such possible qualities. The cultural definition of an age span is always a broad definition of human potentialities, limitations, and obligations at a given stage of life. In terms of these definitions, people map out the broad contours of life, their own expectations and possibilities, and place themselves and their fellow men in social and cultural positions, ascribing to each a given place within these contours.

The various qualities attributed to different ages do not constitute an unconnected series. They are usually interconnected in many ways. The subtle dialectics between the unfolding of some qualities and the waning of others in a person is not a mere registration of his psychological or biological traits; rather, it constitutes the broad framework of his potentialities and their limits throughout his life span. The characteristics of any one "age," therefore, cannot be fully understood except in relation to those of other ages. Whether seen as a gradually unfolding continuum or as a series of sharp contrasts and opposed characteristics, they are fully explicable and understandable only in terms of one another. The boy bears within himself the seeds of the adult man; else, he must as an adult acquire new patterns of behavior, sharply and intentionally opposed to those of his boyhood. The adult either develops naturally into an old man—or decays into one. Only when taken together do these different "ages" constitute the entire map of human possibilities and limitations; and, as every individual usually must pass through them all, their complementariness and continuity (even if defined in discontinuous and contrasting terms) become strongly emphasized and articulated.

The same holds true for the age definitions of the two sexes, although perhaps with a somewhat different meaning. Each age span is defined differently for either sex, and these definitions are usually related and complementary, as the "sexual image" and identity always constitute basic elements of man's image in every society. This close connection between different ages necessarily stresses the problem of transition from one point in a person's life to another as a basic constituent of any cultural definition of an "age." Hence, each definition of age must necessarily cope with the perception of time, and changes in time, of one's own progress in time, one's transition from one period of life to another.

This personal transition, or temporal progress, or change, may become closely linked with what may be called cosmic and societal time.[2] The attempt to find some meaning in personal temporal transition may often lead to identification with the rhythms of nature or history, with the cycles of the seasons, with the unfolding of some cosmic plan (whether cyclical, seasonal, or apocalyptic), or with the destiny and development of society. The nature of this linkage often constitutes the focus round which an individual's personal identity becomes defined in cultural terms and through which personal experience, with its anguish, may be given some meaning in terms of cultural symbols and values.

The whole problem of age definition and the linkage of personal time and transition with cosmic time become especially accentuated in that age span usually designated as youth. However great the differences among various societies, there is one focal point within the life span of an individual which in most known societies is to some extent emphasized: the period of youth, of transition from childhood to full adult status, or full membership in the society. In this period the individual is no longer a child (especially from the physical and sexual point of view) but is ready to undertake many attributes of an adult and to fulfill adult roles. But he is not yet fully acknowledged as an adult, a full member of the society. Rather, he is being "prepared," or is preparing himself for such adulthood.

This image of youth—the cultural definition of youth—contains all the crucial elements of any definition of age, usually in an especially articulated way. This is the stage at which the individual's personality acquires the basic psychological mechanism of self-regulation and self-control, when his self-identity becomes crystallized. It is also the stage at which the young are confronted with some models of the major roles they are supposed to emulate in adult life and with the major symbols and values of their culture and community. Moreover, in this phase the problem of the linkage of the personal temporal transition with cosmic or societal time becomes extremely acute. Any cultural definition of youth describes it as a transitory phase, couched in terms of transition toward something new, something basically different from the past. Hence the acuteness of the problem of linkage.

The very emphasis on the transitory nature of this stage and of its essentially preparatory character, however, may easily create a some-what paradoxical situation. It may evolve an image of youth as the purest manifestation and repository of ultimate cultural and societal values. Such an image is rooted first in the fact that to some extent youth is always defined as a period of "role moratorium," that is, as a period in which one may play with various roles without definitely choosing any. It does not yet require the various compromises inherent in daily participation in adult life. At the same time, how-ever, since it is also the period when the maximum identification with the values of the society is stressed, under certain conditions it may be viewed as the repository of all the major human virtues and primordial qualities. It may then be regarded as the only age in which full identification with the ultimate values and symbols of the society is attained—facilitated by the flowering of physical vigor, a vigor which may easily become identified with a more general flowering of the cosmos or the society.

The fullest, the most articulate and definitive expression of these archetypal elements of youth is best exemplified in the ritual dramati-zation of the transition from adolescence to adulthood, such as the various *rites de passage* and ceremonies of initiation in primitive tribes and in ancient civilizations.[3] In these rites the pre-adult youth are trans-formed into full members of the tribe. This transformation is effected through:

1. a series of rites in which the adolescents are symbolically di-vested of the characteristics of youth and invested with those of adult-hood, from a sexual and social point of view; this investment, which

has deep emotional significance, may have various concrete manifestations: bodily mutilation, circumcision, the taking on of a new name or symbolic rebirth;

2. the complete symbolic separation of the male adolescents from the world of their youth, especially from their close attachment to their mothers; in other words, their complete "male" independence and image are fully articulated (the opposite usually holds true of girls' initiations);

3. the dramatization of the encounter between the several generations, a dramatization that may take the form of a fight or a competition, in which the basic complementariness of various age grades—whether of a continuous or discontinuous type—is stressed; quite often the discontinuity between adolescence and adulthood is symbolically expressed, as in the symbolic death of the adolescents as children and their rebirth as adults;

4. the transmission of the tribal lore with its instructions about proper behavior, both through formalized teaching and through various ritual activities; this transmission is combined with:

5. a relaxation of the concrete control of the adults over the erstwhile adolescents and its substitution by self-control and adult responsibility.

Most of these dramatic elements can also be found, although in somewhat more diluted forms, in various traditional folk festivals in peasant communities, especially those such as rural carnivals in which youth and marriage are emphasized. In an even more diluted form, these elements may be found in various spontaneous initiation ceremonies of the fraternities and youth groups in modern societies.[4] Here, however, the full dramatic articulation of these elements is lacking, and their configuration and organization assume different forms.

The transition from childhood and adolescence to adulthood, the development of personal identity, psychological autonomy and self-regulation, the attempt to link personal temporal transition to general cultural images and to cosmic rhythms, and to link psychological maturity to the emulation of definite role models—these constitute the basic elements of any archetypal image of youth. However, the ways in which these various elements become crystallized in concrete configurations differ greatly from society to society and within sectors of the same society. The full dramatic articulation of these elements in the *rites de passage* of primitive societies constitutes only one—perhaps the most extreme and articulate but certainly not the only—configuration of these archetypal elements of youth.

In order to understand other types of such configurations, it is necessary to analyze some conditions that influence their development. Perhaps the best starting point is the nature of the social organization of the period of adolescence: the process of transition from childhood to adulthood, the social context in which the process of growing up is shaped and structured. There are two major criteria that shape the social organization of the period of youth. One is the extent to which age in general and youth in particular form a criterion for the allocation of roles in a society, whether in politics, in economic or cultural activity—aside from the family, of course, in which they always serve as such a criterion. The second is the extent to which any society developed specific age groups, specific corporate organizations, composed of members of the same "age," such as youth movements or old men's clubs. If roles are allocated in a society according to age, this greatly influences the extent to which age constitutes a component of a person's identity. In such cases, youth becomes a definite and meaningful phase of transition in an individual's progress through life, and his budding self-identity acquires content and a relation to role models and cultural values. No less important to the concrete development of identity is the extent to which it is influenced, either by the common participation of different generations in the same group as in the family, or conversely by the organization of members of the same age groups into specific, distinct groups.

The importance of age as a criterion for allocating roles in a society is closely related to several major aspects of social organization and cultural orientation. The first aspect is the relative complexity of the division of labor. In general, the simpler the organization of the society, the more influential age will be as a criterion for allocating roles. Therefore, in primitive or traditional societies (or in the more primitive and traditional sectors of developed societies) age and seniority constitute basic criteria for allocating social, economic, and political roles.

The second aspect consists of the major value orientations and symbols of a society, especially the extent to which they emphasize certain general orientations, qualities, or types of activity (such as physical vigor, the maintenance of cultural tradition, the achievement and maintenance of supernatural prowess) which can be defined in terms of broad human qualities and which become expressed and symbolized in specific ages.

The emphasis on any particular age as a criterion for the allocation of roles is largely related to the concrete application of the major value orientations in a society. For instance, we find that those primitive societies in which military values and orientations prevail emphasize young adulthood as the most important age, while those in which sedentary activities prevail emphasize older age. Similarly, within some traditional societies, a particular period such as old age may be emphasized if it is seen as the most appropriate one for expressing major cultural values and symbols—for instance, the upholding of a given cultural tradition.

The social and cultural conditions that determine the extent to which specific age groups and youth groups develop differ from the conditions that determine the extent to which age serves as a criterion for the allocation of roles. At the same time, the two kinds of conditions may be closely related, as we shall see. Age groups in general and youth groups in particular tend to arise in those societies in which the family or kinship unit cannot ensure (it may even impede) the attainment of full social status on the part of its members. These conditions appear especially (although not uniquely[5]) in societies in which family or kinship groups do not constitute the basic unit of the social division of labor. Several features characterize such societies. First, the membership in the total society (citizenship) is not defined in terms of belonging to any such family, kinship group, or estate, nor is it mediated by such a group.

Second, in these societies the major political, economic, social, and religious functions are performed not by family or kinship units but rather by various specialized groups (political parties, occupational associations, etc.), which individuals may join irrespective of their family, kinship, or caste. In these societies, therefore, the major roles that adults are expected to perform in the wider society differ in orientation from those of the family or kinship group. The children's identification and close interaction with family members of other ages does not assure the attainment of full self-identity and social maturity on the part of the children. In these cases, there arises a tendency for peer groups to form, especially youth groups; these can serve as a transitory phase between the world of childhood and the adult world.

This type of the social division of labor is found in varying degrees in different societies, primitive, historical, or modern. In several primitive tribes such a division of labor has existed,[6] for example, in Africa, among the chiefless (segmentary) tribes of Nandi, Masai, or Kipigis, in the village communities of Yako and Ibo, or in more centralized kingdoms of the Zulu and Swazi, and among some of the Indian tribes of the Plains, as well as among some South American and Indian tribes.

Such a division of labor likewise existed to some extent in several historical societies (especially in city states such as Athens or Rome), although most great historical civilizations were characterized mainly by a more hierarchical and ascriptive system of the division of labor, in which there were greater continuity and harmony between the family and kinship groups and the broader institutional contexts. The fullest development of this type of the social division of labor, however, is to be found in modern industrial societies. Their inclusive membership is usually based on the universal criterion of citizenship and is not conditioned by membership in any kinship group. In these societies the family does not constitute a basic unit of the division of labor, especially not in production and distribution, and even in the sphere of consumption its functions become more limited. Occupations are not transmitted through heredity. Similarly, the family or kinship group does not constitute a basic unit of political or ritual activities. Moreover, the general scope of the activities of the family has been continuously diminishing, while various specialized agencies tend to take over its functions in the fields of education and recreation.

To be sure, the extent to which the family is diminishing in modern societies is often exaggerated. In many social spheres (neighborhood, friendship, informal association, some class relations, community relations), family, kinship, and status are still very influential. But the scope of these relations is more limited in modern societies than in many others, even if the prevalent myth of the disappearance of the family has long since been exploded. The major social developments of the nineteenth century (the establishment of national states, the progress of the industrial revolution, the great waves of intercontinental migrations) have greatly contributed to this diminution of scope, and especially in the first phase of modernization there has been a growing discontinuity between the life of the children, whether in the family or the traditional school and in the social world with its new and enlarged perspectives.

Youth groups tend to develop in all societies in which such a division of labor exists. Youth's tendency to coalesce in such groups is rooted in the fact that participation in the family became insufficient for developing full identity or full social maturity, and that the roles learned in the family did not constitute an adequate basis for developing such identity and participation. In the youth groups the adolescent seeks some framework for the development and crystallization of his identity, for the attainment of personal autonomy, and for his effective transition into the adult world.

Various types of youth organizations always tend to appear with the transition from traditional or feudal societies to modern societies, along with the intensified processes of change, especially in periods of rapid mobility, migration, urbanization, and industrialization. This is true of all European societies, and also of non-Western societies. The impact of Western civilization on primitive and historical-traditional peoples is usually connected with the disruption of family life, but beyond this it also involves a change in the mutual evaluation of the different generations. The younger generation usually begin to seek a new self-identification, and one phase or another of this search is expressed in ideological conflict with the older.

Most of the nationalistic movements in the Middle East, Asia, and Africa have consisted of young people, students, or officers who rebelled against their elders and the traditional familistic setting with its stress on the latter's authority. At the same time there usually has developed a specific youth consciousness and ideology that intensifies the nationalistic movement to "rejuvenate" the country.

The emergence of the peer group among immigrant children is a well-known phenomenon that usually appears in the second generation. It occurs mainly because of the relative breakdown of immigrant family life in the new country. The more highly industrialized and urbanized that country (or the sector absorbing the immigrants) is, the sharper the breakdown. Hence, the family of the immigrant or second-generation child has often been an inadequate guide to the new society. The immigrant child's attainment of full identity in the new land is usually related to how much he has been able to detach himself from his older, family setting. Some of these children, therefore, have developed a strong predisposition to join various peer groups. Such an affiliation has sometimes facilitated their transition to the absorbing society by stressing the values and patterns of behavior in that society—or, on the contrary, it may express their rebellion against this society, or against their older setting.

All these modern social developments and movements have given rise to a great variety of youth groups, peer groups, youth movements, and what has been called youth culture. The types and concrete forms of such groups vary widely: spontaneous youth groups, student movements, ideological and semipolitical movements, and youth rebellions connected with the Romantic movement in Europe, and, later, with the German youth movements. The various social and national trends of the nineteenth and twentieth centuries have also given impetus to such organizations. At the same time there have appeared many adult-sponsored youth organizations and other agencies springing out of the great extension of educational institutions. In addition to providing recreative facilities, these agencies have also aimed at character molding and the instilling of civic virtues, so as to deepen social consciousness and widen the social and cultural horizon. The chief examples are the YMCA, the Youth Brigades organized in England by William Smith, the Boy Scouts, the Jousters in France, and the many kinds of community organizations, hostels, summer camps, or vocational guidance centers.

Thus we see that there are many parallels between primitive and historical societies and modern societies with regard to the conditions under which the various constellations of youth groups, youth activities, and youth images have developed. But these parallels are only partial. Despite certain similarities, the specific configurations of the basic archetypal elements of the youth image in modern societies differ greatly from those of primitive and traditional societies. The most important differences are rooted in the fact that in the modern, the development of specific youth organizations is paradoxically connected with the weakening of the importance of age in general and youth in particular as definite criteria for the allocation of roles in society.

As we have already said, the extent to which major occupational, cultural, or political roles are allocated today according to the explicit criterion of age is very small. Most such roles are achieved according to wealth, acquired skills, specialization, and knowledge. Family background may be of great importance for the acquisition of these attributes, but very few positions are directly given people by virtue of their family standing. Yet this very weakening of the importance of age is always connected with intensive developments of youth groups and movements. This fact has several interesting repercussions on the organization and structure of such groups. In primitive and traditional societies, youth groups are usually part of a wider organization of age groups that covers a very long period of life, from childhood to late adulthood and even old age. To be sure, it is during youth that most of the dramatic events of the transition from one age to another are manifest, but this stage constitutes only part of a longer series of continuous, well-defined stages.

From this point of view, primitive or traditional societies do not differ greatly from those in which the transition from youth to adulthood is not organized in specific age groups but is largely effected within the fold of the family and kinship groups. In both primitive and traditional societies we observe a close and comprehensive linkage between personal temporal transition and societal or cosmic time, a linkage most fully expressed in the *rites de passage*. Consequently, the transition from childhood to adulthood in all such societies is given full meaning in terms of ultimate cultural values and symbols borne or symbolized by various adult role models.

In modern societies the above picture greatly changes. The youth group, whatever its composition or organization, usually stands alone. It does not constitute a part of a full institutionalized and organized series of age groups. It is true that in many of the more traditional sectors of modern societies the more primitive or traditional archetypes of youth still prevail. Moreover, in many modern societies elements of the primitive archetypes of youth still exist. But the full articulation of these elements is lacking, and the social organization and self-expression of youth are not given full legitimation or meaning in terms of cultural values and rituals.

The close linkage between the growth of personality, psychological maturation, and definite role models derived from the adult world has become greatly weakened. Hence the very coalescence of youth into special groups only tends to emphasize their problematic, uncertain standing from the point of view of cultural values and symbols. This has created a new constellation of the basic archetypal elements of youth. This new constellation can most clearly be seen in what has been called the emergence of the problems and stresses of adolescence in modern societies. While some of these stresses are necessarily common to adolescence in all societies, they become especially acute in modern societies.

Among these stresses the most important are the following: first, the bodily development of the adolescent constitutes a constant problem to him (or her). Since social maturity usually lags behind biological maturity, the bodily changes of puberty are not usually given a full cultural, normative meaning, and their evaluation is one of the adolescent's main concerns. The difficulty inherent in attaining legitimate sexual outlets and relations at this period of growth makes these problems even more acute. Second, the adolescent's orientation toward the main values of his society is also beset with difficulties. Owing to the long period of preparation and the relative segregation of the children's world from that of the adults, the main values of the society are necessarily presented to the child and adolescent in a highly selective way, with a strong idealistic emphasis. The relative unreality of these values as presented to the children—which at the same time are not given full ritual and symbolic expression—creates among the adolescents a great potential uncertainty and ambivalence toward the adult world.

This ambivalence is manifest, on the one hand, in a striving to communicate with the adult world and receive its recognition; on the other hand, it appears in certain dispositions to accentuate the differences between them and the adults, to oppose the various differences between them and the adults and to oppose the various roles allocated to them by the adults. While they orient themselves to full participation in the adult world and its values, they usually attempt also to communicate with this world in a distinct, special way.

Parallel developments are to be found in the ideologies of modern youth groups. Most of these tend to create an ideology that emphasizes the discontinuity between youth and adulthood and the uniqueness of the youth period as the purest embodiment of ultimate social and cultural values. Although the explicitness of this ideology varies in extent from one sector of modern society to another, its basic elements are prevalent in almost all modern youth groups.

These processes have been necessarily accentuated in modern societies by the specific developments in cultural orientations in general and in the conception of time that has evolved in particular. The major social developments in modern societies have weakened the importance of broad cultural qualities as criteria for the allocation of roles. Similarly, important changes in the conception of time that is prevalent in modern societies have occurred. Primordial (cosmic-mythical, cyclical, or apocalyptical) conceptions of time have become greatly weakened, especially in their bearing on daily activities. The mechanical conception of time of modern technology has become much more prevalent. Of necessity this has greatly weakened the possibility of the direct ritual links between personal temporal changes and cosmic or societal progression. Therefore, the exploration of the actual meaning of major cultural values in their relation to the reality of the social world becomes one of the adolescent's major problems. This exploration may lead in many directions—cynicism, idealistic youth rebellion, deviant ideology and behavior, or a gradual development of a balanced identity.

Thus we see how all these developments in modern societies have created a new constellation of the basic archetypal elements of youth and the youth image. The two main characteristics of this constellation are the weakened possibility of directly linking the development of personality and the personal temporal transition with cosmic and societal time, on the one hand, and with the clear role models derived from the adult world, on the other.

In terms of personality development, this situation has created a great potential insecurity and the possible lack of a clear definition of personal identity. Yet it has also created the possibility of greater personal autonomy and flexibility in the choice of roles and the commitment to different values and symbols. In general, the individual, in his search for the meaning of his personal transition, has been thrown much more on his own powers.

These processes have provided the framework within which the various attempts to forge youth's identity and activities—both on the part of youth itself and on the part of various educational agencies— have developed. These attempts may take several directions. Youth's own activities and attempts at self-expression may first develop in the direction of considerable autonomy in the choice of roles and in commitment to various values. Conversely, they may develop in the direction of a more complete, fully organized and closed ideology connected with a small extent of personal autonomy. Second, these attempts may differ greatly in their emphasis on the direct linkage of cultural values to a specific social group and their view of these groups as the main bearers of such values.

In a parallel sense, attempts have been made on the part of various educational agencies to create new types of youth organizations within which youth can forge its identity and become linked to adult society. The purpose of such attempts has been two-fold: to provide youth with opportunities to develop a reasonably autonomous personality and a differentiated field of activity; and to encompass youth fully within well-organized groups set up by adult society and to provide them with full, unequivocal role models and symbols of identification. The interaction between these different tendencies of youth and the attempts of adult society to provide various frameworks for youth activities has given rise to the major types of youth organizations, movements, and ideologies manifested in modern societies.

These various trends and tendencies have created a situation in which, so far as we can ascertain, the number of casualties among youth has become very great—probably relatively much greater than in other types of societies. Youth's search for identity, for finding some place of its own in society, and its potential difficulties in coping with the attainment of such identity have given rise to the magnified extent of the casualties observed in the numerous youth delinquents of varying types. These failures, however, are not the only major youth developments in modern societies, although their relatively greater number is endemic in modern conditions. Much more extensive are the more positive attempts of youth to forge its own identity, to find some meaningful way of defining its place in the social and cultural context and of connecting social and political values with personal development in a coherent and significant manner.

The best example in our times of the extreme upsurge of specific youth consciousness is seen in the various revolutionary youth movements. They range from the autonomous free German youth movements to the less spectacular youth movements in Central Europe and also to some extent to the specific youth culture of various more flexible youth groups. Here the attempt has been made to overcome the dislocation between personal transition and societal and cultural time. It is in these movements that the social dynamics of modern youth has found its fullest expression. It is in them that dreams of a new life, a new society, freedom and spontaneity, a new humanity and aspirations to social and cultural change have found utterance. It is in these youth movements that the forging of youth's new social identity has become closely connected with the development of new symbols of collective identity or new social-cultural symbols and meanings.

These movements have aimed at changing many aspects of the social and cultural life of their respective societies. They have depicted the present in a rather shabby form, they have dubbed it with adjectives of materialism, restriction, exploitation, lack of opportunity for self-fulfillment and creativity. At the same time they have held out hope for the future—seemingly the not very far off future—when both self-fulfillment and collective fulfillment can be achieved and the materialistic civilization of the adult world can be shaken off. They have tried to appeal to youth to forge its own self-identity in terms of these new collective symbols, and this is why they have been so attractive to youth, for whom they have provided a set of symbols, hopes, and aims to which to direct its activities.

Within these movements the emphasis has been on a given social group or collectivity—nation, class, or the youth group itself—as the main, almost exclusive bearer of the "good" cultural value and symbols. Indeed, youth has at times been upheld as the sole and pure bearer of cultural values and social creativity. Through its association with these movements, youth has also been able to connect its aspiration for a different personal future, its anxiety to escape the present through plans and hopes for a different future within its cultural or social setting.

These various manifestations have played a crucial part in the emergence of social movements and parties in modern societies. Student groups have been the nuclei of the most important nationalistic and revolutionary movements in Central and Eastern Europe, in Italy, Germany, Hungary, and Russia. They have also played a significant role in Zionism and in the various waves of immigration to Israel. Their influence has become enormous in various fields, not only political and educational but cultural in general. In a way, education itself has tended to become a social movement. Many schools and universities, many teachers, have been among the most important bearers of collective values. The very spread of education is often seen as a means by which a new epoch might be ushered in.

The search for some connection between the personal situation of youth and social-cultural values has also stimulated the looser youth groups in modern societies, especially in the United States, and to some extent in Europe as well—though here the psychological meaning of the search is somewhat different. The looser youth groups have often shared some of the characteristics of the more defined youth movements, and they too have developed an emphasis on the attainment of social and cultural change. The yearning for a different personal future has likewise become connected with aspirations for changing the cultural setting, but not necessarily through a direct political or organized expression. They are principally important as a strong link with various collective, artistic, and literary aspirations aimed at changing social and cultural life. As such they are affiliated with various cultural values and symbols, not with any exclusive social groups. Thus they have necessarily developed a much greater freedom in choice of roles and commitment to values.

Specific social conditions surround the emergence of all these youth groups. In general, they are associated with a breakdown of traditional settings, the onset of modernization, urbanization, secularization, and industrialization. The less organized, more spontaneous types of youth organization and the more flexible kind of youth consciousness arise when the transition has been relatively smooth and gradual, especially in societies whose basic collective identity and political framework evince a large degree of continuity and a slow process of modernization. On the other hand, the more intensive types of youth movements tend to develop in those societies and periods in which the onset of modernization is connected with great upheavals and sharp cleavages in the social structure and the structure of authority and with the breakdown of symbols of collective identity.

In the latter situation the adult society has made many efforts to organize youth in what may be called totalistic organizations, in which clear role models and values might be set before youth and in which the extent of choice allowed youth is very limited and the manifestations of personal spontaneity and autonomy are restricted. Both types of conditions appeared in various European societies and in the United States in the nineteenth and early twentieth centuries, and in Asian and African societies in the second half of the twentieth century. The relative predominance of each of these conditions varies in different periods in these societies. However, with the progress of modernization and the growing absorption of broad masses within the framework of society, the whole basic setting of youth in modern society has changed—and it is this new framework that is predominant today and in which contemporary youth problems are shaped and played out.

The change this new framework represents is to some extent common both to the fully organized totalistic youth movements and to the looser youth groups. It is connected mainly with the institutionalizing of the aims and values toward the realization of which these movements were oriented, with the acceptance of such youth organizations as part of the structure of the general educational and cultural structure of their societies.

In Russia youth movements became fully institutionalized through the organization of the Komsomol. In many European countries the institutionalizing of youth groups, agencies, and ideologies came through association with political parties, or through acceptance as part of the educational system—an acceptance that sometimes entailed supervision by the official authorities. In the United States, many (such as the Boy Scouts) have become an accepted part of community life and to some extent a symbol of differential social status. In many Asian and African countries, organized youth movements have become part of the nationalistic movements and, independence won, have become part of the official educational organizations.

This institutionalizing of the values of youth movements in education and community life has been part of a wider process of institutionalizing various collective values. In some countries this has come about through revolution; in others, as a result of a long process of political and social evolution.

From the point of view of our analysis, these processes have had several important results. They have introduced a new element into the configuration of the basic archetypal elements of youth. The possibility of linking personal transition both to social groups and to cultural values—so strongly emphasized in the youth movements and noticeably to some extent even in the looser youth culture—has become greatly weakened. The social and sometimes even the cultural dimension of the future may thus become flattened and emptied. The various collective values become transformed. Instead of being remote goals resplendent with romantic dreams, they have become mundane objectives of the present, with its shabby details of daily politics and administration. More often than not they are intimately connected with the processes of bureaucratization.

All these mutations are associated with a notable decline in ideology and in preoccupation with ideology among many of the groups and strata in modern societies, with a general flattening of political-ideological motives and a growing apathy to them. This decline in turn is connected with what has been called the spiritual or cultural shallowness of the new social and economic benefits accruing from the welfare state—an emptiness illustrated by the fact that all these benefits are in the nature of things administered not by spiritual or social leaders but, as Stephen Toulmin has wittily pointed out, "the assistant postmaster." As a consequence, we observe the emptiness and meaninglessness of social relations, so often described by critics of the age of consumption and mass society.

In general, these developments have brought about the flattening of the image of the societal future and have deprived it of its allure. Between present and future there is no ideological discontinuity. The present has become the more important, if not the more meaningful, because the future has lost its characteristic as a dimension different from the present. Out of these conditions has grown what Riesman has called the cult of immediacy. Youth has been robbed, therefore, of the full experience of the dramatic transition from adolescence to adulthood and of the dramatization of the difference between present and future. Their own changing personal future has become dissociated from any changes in the shape of their societies or in cultural activities and values.

Paradoxically enough, these developments have often been connected with a strong adulation of youth—an adulation, however, which was in a way purely instrumental. The necessity of a continuous adjustment to new changing conditions has emphasized the potential value of youth as the bearers of continuous innovation, of noncommitment to any specific conditions and values. But such an

emphasis is often couched in terms of a purely instrumental adaptability, beyond which there is only the relative emptiness of the meaningless passage of time—of aging.[7]

Yet the impact on youth of what has been called postindustrial
society need not result in such an emptiness and shallowness, although
in recent literature these effects appear large indeed. It is as yet too
early to make a full and adequate analysis of all these impacts. But it
should be emphasized that the changes we have described, together
with growing abundance and continuous technological change, have
necessarily heightened the possibility of greater personal autonomy
and of a flexible yet stable identity during the period of youth.

These new conditions have enhanced the possibility of flexibility in
linking cultural values to social reality; they have enhanced the scope
of personal and cultural creativity and the development of different
personal culture. They have created the possibility of youth's developing what may be called a nonideological, direct identification with
moral values, an awareness of the predicaments of moral choice that
exist in any given situation, and individual responsibility for such
choices—a responsibility that cannot be shed by relying on overarching
ideological solutions oriented to the future.

These new social conditions exist in most industrial and post-industrial societies, sometimes together with the older conditions that gave
rise to the more intensive types of youth movements. They constitute
the framework within which the new configuration of the archetypal
elements of youth and the new possibilities and problems facing youth
in contemporary society develop. It is as yet too early to specify all
these new possibilities and trends: here we have attempted to indicate some of their general contours.

NOTES

1. A general sociological analysis of the place of age in social structure
has been attempted in S. N. Eisenstadt, *From Generation to Generation*
(Chicago: The Free Press of Glencoe, Illinois, 1956).

2. The analysis of personal, cosmic, and societal time (or temporal
progression) has constituted a fascinating but not easily dealt with focus
of analysis. For some approaches to these problems, see *Man and Time*
(papers from the Eranos Yearbooks, edited by Joseph Campbell; London:
Routledge & Kegan Paul, 1958), especially the article by Gerardus van der

Leeuw. See also Mircea Eliade, *The Myth of the Eternal Return*. Translated by W. R. Trask. New York: Pantheon Books, 1954 (Bollingen Series).

3. For a fuller exposition of the sociological significance of initiation rites, see Mircea Eliade, *Birth and Rebirth* (New York: Harper & Brothers, 1985) and *From Generation to Generation* (ref. 1).

4. See Bruno Bettelheim, *Symbolic Wounds, Puberty Rites and the Envious Circle* (Chicago: The Free Press of Glencoe, Illinois, 1954).

5. A special type of age groups may also develop in familistic societies. See *From Generation to Generation* (ref. 1), ch. 5.

6. For fuller details, see *From Generation to Generation*, especially chs. 3 and 4.

7. For an exposition of this view, see Paul Goodman, "Youth in Organized Society," *Commentary*, February 1960, pp. 95-107; and M. R. Stein, *The Eclipse of Community* (Princeton: Princeton University Press, 1960), especially pp. 215 ff.; also, the review of this book by H. Rosenberg, "Community, Values, Comedy," *Commentary*, August 1960, pp. 150-157.

CHAPTER VIII

Contemporary Student Rebellions—Intellectual Rebellion and Generational Conflict

Beyond many features which contemporary student currents share with other types of youth movements, the contemporary student movements evince also some new ones. Of these, two are perhaps most outstanding. There is, first, that probably for the first time in history at least some parts of these movements tend to become entirely dissociated from broader social or national movements, from the adult world, and do not tend to accept any adult models or association—thus stressing intergenerational discontinuity and conflict to an unprecedented extent.

Second, many of these movements tend also to combine their political activities with violence and destructive orientation which go much beyond the anarchist or bohemian traditions of youth or artistic, intellectual subcultures and with a very far-reaching general and widespread alienation from the existing social order.

These new features of youth rebellion and student protest are analyzed as a result of the convergence and mutual reinforcement of the two major sets of conditions or processes, namely,

Reprinted from *Acta Sociologica* 14 (1971), No. 3.

of widespread intellectual antinomianism on the one hand, and of generational discontinuity and conflict, and of their simultaneous extension to the central zones of a society and to very wide groups and strata alike.

I

Student rebellions and adolescent violence are not new in the history of human society. Student violence had been reported already in the middle ages while student rebellions and movements—especially as parts of wider social and national movements—have been an integral part of the history of modern societies.

Similarly, various types of adolescent rebellions or deviance, rooted to no small degree in generational discontinuity or conflict, can be found throughout the history of human society.[1]

In some cases these two phenomena—youth deviance or violence and student rebellions—have tended to converge and some element of intergeneration and conflict has probably been present in many student movements.[2]

Most of such features which could have been discerned in the types of youth rebellion or student movements throughout history and modern history in particular, can also be found in many of the contemporary expressions of youth rebellion and student radicalism.

But beyond these features, contemporary student movements evince also some new ones. Of these, two are perhaps most outstanding. There is, first, as Edward Shils has noted, that probably for the first time in history at least some parts of these movements tend to become entirely dissociated from broader social or national movements, from the adult world, and do not tend to accept any adult models or association—thus stressing intergenerational discontinuity and conflict to an unprecedented extent.[3]

Second, many of these movements tend also to combine their political activities with violence and destructive orientation which go much beyond the anarchist or bohemian traditions of youth or artistic, intellectual subcultures and with a very far-reaching general and widespread alienation from the existing social order. Although these *new* specific characteristics are certainly not the only ones to be found in the contemporary youth scene, and they certainly do not obliterate many older types of youth cultures, youth rebellion and student protest—yet they are indeed among the most salient new features on this scene.

Many explanations of these new features have been offered and it would not be possible to repeat or summarize them all here.

Rather, we would like to propose that part, at least, of the explanation of these new features of youth rebellion and student protest lies in the convergence and mutual reinforcement of the two major sets of conditions or processes, namely, of widespread intellectual antinomianism on the one hand, and of generational discontinuity and conflict, and of their simultaneous extension to the central zones of a society and to very wide groups and strata alike.

II

Intellectual antinomianism is not something new in the history of mankind. It constitutes an extreme manifestation of the tensions and ambivalence between intellectuals and authority which to a large extent are given in all human societies. These tensions and ambivalence are rooted in two distinct yet strongly interconnected bases.

One is the close relation between the activities and orientations of intellectuals and those of the authorities and holders of power in the formation and crystallization of the specific cultural and social contours of the charismatic orientations and symbols of any society or civilization and of its tradition and centers.

The second is the close relations between some at least of the skills and technical knowledge of some groups of intellectuals and the organizational exigencies of the exercise of power and authority in any society.[4]

This tension is due not only to the antithesis, often stressed in Western thought, between organization and exercise of power and participation in the maintenance of broad socio-cultural order—although this antithesis may indeed constitute an important basis of this tension. Beyond this tension is also inherent in the fact that the charismatic qualities of social order—and the quest to participate in them—are not focused or centered in only one institutional sphere, and that they become dispersed, albeit differentially, in all institutional spheres. This in itself tends to explain to some extent both the existence of a plurality of authorities in any society, and the "natural" predilection of the holders of political power to attempt to monopolize and regulate the central institutions of the society and its charismatic orientations and their ultimate impossibility to do so.

The problematics and variety of such tensions can perhaps most clearly be seen in the symbolism of political power and authority that can be found in most civilizations.

In all cultural traditions, one of the major foci of political symbols and thought is the concern with the relations between the political order and the other types of "symbolic-institutional"—cosmic, moral and social—orders and especially with those orders which are conceived in the tradition of a given society or culture as the most central and important delineators of its basic cultural and collective identity, and as the most important parameters of human existence.

The problematics of this relation are usually conceived in terms of the mutual symbolic and organizational relevance of these orders, of their legitimation, autonomy and responsibility. Are the other ("non-political") orders highly relevant to the political one; and whatever the degree of their relevance, how are they conceived and how are these relations perceived and organized?[5]

This tension is also rooted in the structural interdependence and relations between the intellectual and the powers.

Political authorities need the basic legitimation and support which can be provided mostly by intellectuals, by religious or secular intellectual élites. The intellectuals and intellectual organizations tend to need the protection and help of the political institutions for the establishment and maintenance of their own organizations and positions.

Hence the continuous tensions and ambivalence on the symbolic and structural levels alike, between the intellectuals and the holders of power or authority, focuses around the respective nature, scope, and relative autonomy of participation of the intellectuals and the political powers in the socio-political and cultural orders and is rooted in their continuous mutual interdependence.

Political authorities may naturally attempt to control entirely the activities of the intellectuals and to claim for themselves the sole right to represent the major religious and cultural symbols of the society, and they also expected the intellectual organizations to assure a certain level of political activity and involvement in central political activities which their respective regime may need.

Against this the intellectual élites would often attempt to be able to become the sole or major representatives of the pure social and cultural orders, to usurp central political offices and to remove their organizations from the political control and influence of the rulers.[6]

III

The potentially "antinomian" tendencies of intellectuals become especially articulated in so far as the tensions between them and political authorities tend to converge with some of the major themes of protest, rebellion and heterodoxy. Such themes have been continuously recurring in the history of human societies and civilizations and have been largely rooted in the tensions inherent in any process of institutionalization of social life in general, and of authority in particular.

Among these themes is first, the tension between the very complexity and fragmentation of human relations inherent in any institutional division of labor, as against the possibilities of some total unconditionality of participation in the basic social and cultural order.

Parallel to this are also the tensions inherent in the temporal dimension of human and social condition, in the tensions between the deferment of gratification in the present as against the possibility of their attainment in the future.

Hence many movements of protest tend to emphasize the suspension or negation of the structural and organizational division of labor in general, and to emphasize the idea of "communitas" of direct, unmediated participation in the social and cultural orders.

They tend also to emphasize, together with such participation, the suspension of the tensions between "productivity" and "distribution" and tend to merge these two together through a basic commitment to the unconditional participation in the community.

Similarly, many such movements contain a strong emphasis on the suspension of the differences between various time-dimensions—between past, present and future—and of the relation between such dimensions to patterns of gratification and allocation of rewards.

The two institutional-symbolic foci around which the ambivalence to traditions and orders tend to converge are first those of authority, especially as vested in the various political and cultural centers, and second, the system of stratification in which the symbolic dimensions of hierarchy are combined with structural aspects of division of labor. It is thus that symbols of authority and of hierarchy constitute the most common objects of ambivalence and foci for demands for change in any society.

These various tendencies to heterodoxy, antinomy and rebellion are most clearly articulated by intellectuals—but it would be wrong to assume that they are oriented only against the political authority. They may also be oriented against intellectual authority and it is perhaps in this fact that the antinomian tendencies of intellectuals may tend to become most clearly articulated.

Needless to say, such antinomianism is only an extreme phenomenon, very often found within small groups of intellectuals, which tends to develop under very specific conditions. Yet it may also be an important ingredient of the orientations of wider groups of intellectuals—an ingredient which under certain conditions may indeed become more widespread.

Such conditions conducive to a more pervasive spread of such antinomian attitudes and dispositions have been indeed most prevalent in modern societies in general and in contemporary ones in particular, and they are closely related to the very spread of modernity, of its structural characteristics and of its ideological premises and symbols.[7]

The revolutionary orientations, which were at the roots of most breakthroughs to modernity, have been, whatever their concrete contents, oriented towards a complete transformation of the nature and contents of the centers of the social and cultural orders, of the rules of participation in them and of access to them, and of the relations between these centers and the periphery.

From the point of view of contents of these centers, the major transformation concomitant with modernity has been in the growing secularization of the centers and of the "opening up" of their contents, i.e., the non-acceptance of the givenness of these contents, the spread of the assumption that these contents can indeed be formulated anew.

This was closely connected with changes in the structure of the centers and the relations among them; with the growing autonomy of such centers—the political, cultural, societal centers; with the growing interpretation and independence among them as autonomous units; and above all with changes in the relations between the centers and the periphery.

Modern social orders have been characterized by the growing impingement of the periphery on the center and by the opening up of access to the center for the periphery; by the permeation of the periphery by the center and by the concomitant tendency to the obliteration of the difference between center and periphery and making membership in the collectivity tantamount to participation in the center.

This impingement on the center could be best seen in the political field. The broader groups and strata of society tended more and more to impinge on its central institutions, not only in making various concrete demands on it, but also by developing the aspirations to participate in the very crystallization of the center, its symbols and its institutional contours. The major social movements that have developed with the onset of modernization—be they national, social or cultural—all of them manifest, in varying degrees and scope, this tendency.

These processes were, of course, closely connected with the second major trend concomitant with modernization—namely that of growing structural differentiation in general, and of the spheres of intellectual, scientific and professional endeavor in particular. The development of specialized scientific and technological roles and institutions and the growing impact of these on the occupational structure is too well known to need any lengthy specification.

IV

But perhaps the most important change related to these developments from the point of view of our discussion was in the social organization of the educational sphere. In most pre-modern societies the process of education was usually divided into several rather compartmentalized aspects. The central educational institutions were oriented mainly toward the education of an elite and upper strata, and to the upholding and development of the central cultural tradition in its varied manifestations.

The local educational institutions, which were usually only loosely connected with the central ones, were oriented chiefly to the maintenance of some general, diffuse and rather passive identification of the various strata with the overall symbols of society, without, however, permitting them any closer participation in the central political and cultural activities, and of provision of some technical know-how which would be appropriate to their position in society. Between the two were several educational institutions which served as either channels of restricted "sponsored" mobility into the central spheres of society, or of some specific vocational preparation.

On the whole, the educational system in these societies was geared to the maintenance and perpetuation of a given, relatively unchanging cultural tradition, and did not serve either as a channel of widespread occupational and social mobility, or of overall active participation of the broader strata in the cultural and political order and of their respective center. The type of education given to different classes was greatly, although not entirely, determined by their social-economic position and not vice-versa.

This began to change with the onset of modernity. Education started to deal with problems of forging new national communities and their common symbols, access to which tended to become more widely spread among different strata. At the same time, it began to serve increasingly as a channel of more general occupational and allegedly achievement-based selection. Moreover, the system of education tended to become more centralized and unified, thus assuring its permeation into wider strata of society.

V

This societal unification of the education system, when combined with the continuous developments of the structural and symbolical aspects of modernity, gave rise to a series of social and cultural contradictions and discontinuities which have become, on the one hand, extremely widespread throughout the society, while, on the other, they tended to become more and more focused around its very central symbols.

Most of these contradictions and discontinuities tended to focus around the tension between the premises of plenitude and full participation inherent in the symbolism of modernity and the various actual structural limitations on the realization of these premises which tended to develop with the spread of modernity.

These problems and tendencies have developed in all the social spheres, and in the literature special emphasis was given to the occupational and economic sphere.

Thus it was often emphasized that the most important such developments in the economic fields were the bureaucratization of most types of economic markets and the growth of bureaucratization, specialization and professionalization in the occupational structure, increasing the close interrelationship between attainment and occupational placements.

These developments gave rise to problems and discontinuities in areas such as those of social mobility, educational selection and above all in the special service occupations which organized in bureaucratic settings the selection to which was based on meritocratic criteria.

But beyond these developments in the occupational and economic field, parallel processes developed also in the cultural field, and it is on these that we would like to focus our analysis here.

Perhaps the most important single overall development in this field— which, in a great variety of ways, has been common to many different countries—has been the transfer of emphasis from the creation and participation in the future-oriented collective value, to the growing institutionalization of such values.

This has been very closely related with a very important shift in the whole pattern of protest in modern societies. Here, as in so many other cases, when many of the initial charismatic orientations and goals have indeed become—through the attainment of political independence, broadening of the scope of political participation, revolutionary changes of regimes or the development of welfare state policies and the like—at least partially institutionalized, they give rise to new processes of change, to new series of problems and tensions, and to new foci of protest.

It is important to emphasize that the same has been true of youth movements and activities, when the goals and values toward whose realization these movements aim become institutionalized through the acceptance as part of the structure of their societies. This has indeed happened in most modern societies. Thus, in Russia youth movements became fully institutionalized through the organization of the Komsomol. In many European countries the institutionalizing of youth groups, agencies, and ideologies came through association with political parties, or through acceptance as part of the educational system. In the United States, many (such as the Boy Scouts) have become an accepted part of community life and, to some extent, a symbol of differential social status. In many Asian and African countries, organized youth movements have become part of the official educational organizations.

All these changes have also been associated with a marked decline of ideology in the traditional nineteenth and early twentieth century sense, and a general flattening of traditional political-ideological interest. This decline, in turn, has been connected with the growth of the feeling of spiritual or cultural shallowness in the new social and economic benefits accruing from the welfare state or from the "consumers society."

This tendency is intensified by the fact that in many such countries, be they the New States of Asia and Africa or Russian post-revolutionary or European welfare states, the new generation of youth and students face not only reactionary parents but also successful revolutionaries who have become part of a new "establishment," creating a new collective reality which youth has to face, a reality that evinces all the characteristics of a bureaucratized establishment, but at the same time presents itself as the embodiment of revolutionary collective and spiritual values.

This tendency was also reinforced by the weakening of the ideological dimensions of the Cold War and by the consequent loss of the negative images and symbols.

VI

Within this general framework of developments of the cultural sphere several special developments or processes stand out. One such development is what may be called the breakdown of continuity of historical consciousness or awareness.

It is not only that the new generations have not experienced such events as the depression or the two World Wars which were crucial in the formation of their parents. What is more significant is that, probably partly due to the very process of the institutionalization of the collective goals of their parents on the one hand and the growing affluence on the other, the parent generation failed to transmit to the new generation the significance of the meaning of these historical events.

The very emphasis on the new goals has increased a tendency to stress the novelty of the world created by the parents—a tendency taken up and reinforced by the younger generations.

Another cultural process—closely related to the preceding one, and especially prominent in Western societies in general and in America in particular—has been the reversal of the hitherto existing relation between the definition of different age-spans and the possibilities of social and cultural creativity.

Unlike in the—even not so distant—past, youth became more and more seen not only as preparation for the possibilities of independent and creative participation in social and cultural life, but as the very embodiment of permissive, often unstructured creativity—to be faced later on with the constraints of a relatively highly organized, constrictive, meritocratic and bureaucratic environment.

It was probably not these constraints as such—which in themselves certainly were probably not greater than those in most societies—but rather the discrepancy between the permissive premises of family and educational life and the realities of adult life which tended to create the feeling of frustration and disappointment. Moreover, these feelings were often shared by many members of the parent generation and reinforced by its guilt-feeling about the incomplete realization—because of their very institutionalization –of the goals of their own youth and of the movements in which they participated.

VII

As a result of all these trends there tended to develop, in many contemporary societies in general and in the highly developed and industrialized in particular, a whole series of structural and symbolical discontinuities—all related to the spread and development of the institutional and symbolic dimensions of modernity, and all of which gradually converged around both intergenerational conflicts and widespread intellectual antinomian tendencies.

These discontinuities were much more variegated than those between a relatively closed traditional familial structure and more specialized and universalistic occupational and political system, which have given rise, in many societies in general and in the first stages of modernity in particular, to various types of interpregenerational conflicts.[8]

They tended to become transposed beyond the direct opposition between family, on the one hand, and educational and occupational sectors on the other—to the different sectors of the society through which youth passes, and that therefore the foci of such discontinuity tend to become, in modern societies in general and in contemporary societies in particular, much more diversified. They may include discontinuity between the family and the educational and occupational spheres; between the family and educational institutions on the one hand, and the occupational sector on the other; between the productive and the consumer roles in the economic sector; between the values and orientations inculcated in the family and the educational institutions and the central collective symbols of the society; between the premises of these symbols and the actual political roles of the parents and younger people alike—thus cutting across family roles themselves. These new types of discontinuities tended to impinge most intensively on the social and cultural situation of youth and on the concrete manifestations of youth problems and protest.

Here several such repercussions can be singled out. One is that the span of areas of social life that the specific youth or student culture encompasses has tended to expand continuously. First, it has extended over longer periods of life, reaching, through the impact of the extension of higher education, to what before was seen as early adulthood. Second, it tends more and more to include areas of work, of leisure time activity, and of many interpersonal relations. Third, the potential and actual autonomy of these groups, and the possibility their members have of direct access to work, to marriage and family life, to political rights, and to consumption have greatly increased, while their dependence on adults has greatly decreased.

Because of this, paradoxically enough, the growing direct access of young people to various areas of life has given rise to a growing insecurity of status and self-identity and to growing ambiguity of adult roles.

This insecurity and ambiguity tends to be enhanced first by the prolongation of the span between biological and social maturity and by the extension of the number of years spent in basically "preparatory" (educational) institutions. Second, it is enhanced by the growing dissociation between the values of these institutions and the future—especially occupational and parental-roles—of those participating in them.

Third, it is enhanced by the fact that for a long period of time many "young" people may as yet have no clear occupational roles—or responsibilities may be dependent on their parents or on public institutions for their economic needs—while at the same time they constitute an important economic force as consumers and certainly exercise political rights.

In turn this situation may become intensified or aggravated by the fact of the growing demographic preponderance of the "young" in the whole population and by the increasing possibilities of ecological mobility.[9]

These discontinuities very often tended to culminate in a crisis or weakening of authority evident in the lack of development of adequate role-models, on the one hand, and the erosion of many of the bases of legitimation of existing authority on the other.

As a result of all these processes the possibilities of linking personal transition to social groups and to cultural values alike, to societal and cosmic time, so strongly emphasized in the youth movements and observable, to some extent, even in the earlier looser youth culture, has become greatly weakened. In general, these developments have depressed the image of the societal and cultural future and have deprived it of its allure. Either the ideological separation between present and future has become smaller, or the two have tended to become entirely dissociated. Out of the first of these conditions has grown what Riesman has called the cult of immediacy; out of the other, a total negation of the present in name of an entirely different future—both in principle, totally unrelated to any consciousness of the past.

VIII

These various processes analyzed above gave rise to a shift in the orientations and foci of protest in modern societies, and it is in this shift that the antinomian tendencies of intellectual protests can be most clearly discerned.

Unlike the older classical movements of protest of early modernity—the major social and national movements, all of which tended to assume that the framework and centers of the nation-state constituted the major cultural and social reference points of personal identity and of the charismatic orientations to some socio-cultural orders, and that the major tasks before modern societies was to facilitate the access of broader strata of the society to these centers—the new movements of protest are characterized by their scepticism toward the new modern centers, by their lack of commitment to them, and their tendency toward lack of responsibility to the institutional and organizational frameworks of these centers.

The foci of protest tend to shift from demands for greater participation in national-political centers or from attempts to influence their socio-economic policies to new directions. The most important of these directions seem to be: first, attempts to "disrobe" these centers of their charismatic legitimacy and perhaps of any legitimacy at all; second, continuous searches for new loci of meaningful participation beyond these existing socio-political centers and the concomitant attempts to create new centers which would be independent of them; third, attempts to couch the patterns of participation in their centers not so much in socio-political or economic terms, but more in symbols of primordial or of direct social participation.

Thus it seems that these developments touch not only on some of the most important structural developments in post-modern societies, but also on the relations of these developments to some of the basic symbolic constituents of these societies—to basic components of the definition of their socio-cultural orders as well as of their cultural, collective and personal identities.

Significantly enough, many of these new orientations of protest were also directed not only against the bureaucratization and functional rationalization connected with growing technology but also against the supposed central place of science and scientific investigation as the basis—or even one of the bases—of the socio-cultural order.

They all denote an important aspect of what has been called by Weber the demystification of the world—demystification which here becomes focused around the possibility that the attainment of participation in these centers may indeed be meaningless, that these centers may lose their mystery, that the King may be naked indeed.

This demystification may well be related to the relative success of the demand for access to these centers and to participation in them and to the obliteration of the symbolic difference between center and periphery. This in its turn may give rise to a new type of social alienation focused not only around the feeling of being lost in a maze of large-scale, anonymous organizations and frameworks, but also around the possibility of the loss of the meaning of participation in these political and national centers.

Or, in other words, these centers may be losing their special place as loci of the participation in a meaningful socio-cultural order, and as the major social and cultural referents of personal identity. There tends to develop here a growing feeling of dissociation and of lack of congruence between the quest for participation in the charismatic dimension of human and social existence and these specific types of social and political centers.

But it is not just the contents of these antinomian tendencies that is important and new, but the convergence of these contents with the spread and location of these tendencies.

It is highly significant, from the point of view of our analysis, that this type of protest is not borne only by small closed intellectual groups but by widespread circles of novices and aspirants to intellectual status, who constitute—given the spread of the modern educational system and the parallel effects of the spread of media of mass-communication—a very large part of the educated public on the one hand, while on the other hand, for the same structural reasons they impinge on the centers of intellectual creativity and cultural transmission and become integral, even if transient, parts thereof.

It is indeed owing to these processes that these institutions in general and universities in particular have become the loci in which the convergence of intergenerational conflict with potential intellectual protest and antinomianism has taken place.

It is this also which explains why the University is chosen as one of the focal symbols and objects of such total attack against the existing order.

It is not that the various bureaucratic or meritocratic features are necessarily much more developed in the University than in organizations and institutions, but rather in the social and cultural orders they tend to become more salient and articulated. The University is being here perceived as the major locus of the possibility of such participation, and as the very place in which the quest for such creativity could be institutionalized. In this way the University has tended to become the major focus of legitimation of modern social order, and the attack on it indicates not only dissatisfaction with its own internal arrangements or even with the fact that it serves also as one mechanism of occupational and meritocratic selection. The choice of the University as the object of such attack rather emphasizes the denial that the existing order can realize these basic premises of modernity: to establish and maintain an order which could do justice to the claims to creativity and participation in the broader social order, and to overcome the various contradictions which have developed within it from the point of view of these claims.

It is, of course, very significant that this denial is also often shared and emphasized by many of the faculty itself which evinces here some of the guilt feelings alluded to above, of the parent generation in general and of the intellectuals among them in particular.

It is perhaps in the attack on the University that the new dimension of protest—the negation of the premises of modernity, the emphasis on the meaninglessness of the existing centers and the symbols of collective identity, become articulated in the most extreme—although certainly not necessarily representative—way.

It is also here that basic themes of youth rebellion become very strongly connected with those of intellectual antinomianism. It is here that the rebellion against authority, hierarchy and organizational framework, directed by the dreams of plentitude and of permissive unstructured creativity, tends to become particularly prominent, especially as the University serves also as the institutional meeting point between the educational and the central cultural spheres of the society.

Perhaps the most significant fact about these movements against the University is that they develop throughout the world in macrosocietal situations which are structurally basically different—in the centers of highly developed modern, as well as in those of developing and underdeveloped ones—but which are at the same time perceived by those participating in them as symbolically similar.

Those participating in them tend to develop rather similar attitudes toward the symbolic aspects, toward the premises and promises of modernity and the similar *perceptions* of being placed in situations of relative deprivation with regard to these premises and promises of modernity.

The fact that the bases of such deprivation or discontinuity differ greatly—that for instance, in the underdeveloped countries they are mostly those between traditional and modern sectors, in the Communist regimes between an authoritarian regime and those who want to extend the realism of liberty, and in the highly industrial societies mostly between the sons of affluence and the structural-organizational aspects of their affluent society—does not necessarily abate their symbolic affinity which cuts across different historical and social situations (in a sense this symbolic affinity is reinforced by such broad structural variety) connected with the similarity in the place of the University in the spread of the vision of modernity.

It is in the attack on the University and from within the University that these new extreme postures of rebellions and protest—due to the convergence of generational conflict and intellectual antinomianism—tend to become especially prominent.

Needless to say, these are indeed only extreme postures and they certainly do not constitute the whole picture of contemporary youth or the intellectual scene.

Their relative importance and strength, both for social organization and in the life-spans of individuals may greatly vary, and it is indeed one of the tasks of social research—a task which indeed is being more and more discharged[10]—to attempt to identify some of the specific conditions which tend to give rise in the modern setting, to these, as against other manifestations of youth rebellion and intellectual protest.

But whatever the specific conditions which give rise in the contemporary scene to these, as against other types of youth rebellions, the very novelty of this phenomenon can at least partially be explained in terms of the conditions leading to the convergence of intergenerational conflict and intellectual antinomianism.

IX

We now come to the problem of the possible impact of all these developments on the format of modern society.

It is, of course, difficult to predict the long-range impact of these new types of protest in general, and of youth and student rebellion in particular, on the structure of modern social, political, and cultural orders. Some may see them as the harbingers of an entirely new civilization, of the same order as the various sects which developed at the end of the Roman Empire, and which ushered in the Christian era. But even if one made no such extreme prediction, there can be no doubt that these developments will have several important repercussions on the structure of modern societies.

Perhaps the most important thing is to recognize both the continuous ubiquity as well as the changeability of the conditions giving rise in modern and modernizing societies to continuously changing and new types of youth rebellion, protest, organizations and activities.

Second, it should not be forgotten that especially in industrial societies active age-groups or youth rebels are only a minority in their respective age-spans—minorities which tend to crystallize in the rather specific conditions outlined above.

Thus it seems quite true that despite the great upsurge of continuous youth rebellions, it is doubtful whether youth in modern, industrial societies will develop into a continuous organized political force capable of continuous organized political activities within the established political frameworks. It is only in very exceptional circumstances of the early closure of a new political system and the consequent lack of availability of adequate openings that the political struggle will become couched—as it tends to be in some African states—entirely in terms of "generational groups." But even there with regard to any specific generation it will be a passing—although continuously recurring—phenomenon.

Similarly, it will probably be only in relatively few cases, like in some rapidly urbanizing and industrializing countries such as parts of Latin America, or in Italy, where there may develop conditions not dissimilar to those of the early European industrializing societies—that parts at least of these movements may become allied with some of the existing leftist parties.

Thus, given their orientations they will on the whole find it rather difficult to find continuous allies or to ally themselves to continuously organized political parties—although they may indeed perhaps be swallowed by some new movements which will then obliterate their own distinctiveness—as happened within the right and left wing authoritarian movements of the past.

Rather their impact on existing political frameworks will be mostly manifest by shifting the focus of political issues, influencing the selected candidates and the pattern of their activities, influencing public opinion and often changing its climate.

Beyond this they may probably also exacerbate the cleavages and polarization within these systems and possibly give rise to various extreme reactions.

X

But whatever the direct impact of these movements on the working of existing political systems, organizations and groups, some other long-range repercussions of theirs may indeed be—even if tentatively—discerned.

One such impact will be the development of new foci of continuous protest which will add, in both organizational and symbolical terms, to the available reservoir of models and of traditions of protest in modern societies. It indicates a very important shift in the foci of protests in modern societies. As already indicated above, the major shift here is from greater participation in national political centers or attempts to influence socio-economic policies toward new directions. The most important of these seem to be first, attempts to strip these centers of their charismatic legitimacy—and perhaps of any legitimacy at all; second, continuous search for new loci of meaningful participation beyond these existing centers, and concomitant attempts to create new centers which would be independent of existing ones; third, attempts to couch the patterns of participation in these centers not so much in socio-political or economic terms, but in symbols of primordial relations or of direct social participation.

Truly enough, in a sense, these new foci of protest go back to anarchist and romantic traditions in which protest orientation was not focused around participation in the political center or was at least ambivalent to it. But as these movements of protest do arise from the very process of institutionalization of the former goals which assumed some congruency between the charismatic social, political and cultural centers, and their economic activities, they may already denote new dimensions of change in modern societies.

It seems that the more extreme of these movements, and especially those of the students, will constitute continuous reservoirs of new types of revolutionary activity—a revolutionary activity which will be fed and reinforced by the continuous spread of modernity throughout the world and by the problem and aspiration it raises.

Most of these movements and ideologies will be leftist oriented—thus continuing the predominant leftist orientation of most modern student movements, but the degree of their organizational proximity to leftist, socialist parties will greatly vary—and on the whole will probably be rather ambivalent and discontinuous.

However, given their great predilection against any "establishment" centers and organizations as their basic ideological and antinomian orientations, most fully seen, as has been mentioned above, in their revolt against the University, and the transitory nature of their members, it will be only in some of the exceptional conditions that these revolutionary groups and activities will develop into full fledged organized, continuous, political organizations or parties, working within the existing political frameworks.

They will, however, constitute nuclei of new international enclaves of various political and cultural subcultures with a highly mobile and changing population cutting across national and state boundaries and providing rather continuous "irritants" to the existing frameworks.

XI

But the spread of such varied types of youth cultures and rebellions will probably not be limited only to the more spectacular, nor will the spectacular be always found within the political sphere proper.

On a less dramatic and centrally visible plane, but probably more widely pervasive one, they may also constitute reservoirs of continuously changing new cultural or ideological movements, fashions and activities, be they in the sphere of dress, of artistic styles or new patterns of leisure time activity.

It may well be that one of the most lasting of their effects will be in the development and extension—reinforced by the growing number of young people—of new, loosely, yet continuously connected, expressive sub-cultures—of which that of the Hippies is at present the most prominent but certainly not the only one.[11]

The development of such sub-cultures may provide an indicator of some broader and long-range shifts in the sphere of values and orientations.

In general they indicate a shift to what has been called "humanistic" or "sensate" orientations, a general attitude to the more "this-worldly" asceticism values derived from the Protestant Ethic and especially their later organizational and institutional derivatives, or rebellion against them.[12]

But it is rather doubtful whether these movements will be able also to destroy the organizational bases of those structures, although in their more destructive manifestations they may indeed seem to be very forceful, especially with regard to the Universities.

Rather their effect might probably be more in the direction of more limited, yet probably quite far-reaching structural effects.

One such effect may be the development within modern societies of areas of permissiveness closely related to some of the new subcultures alluded to above—areas in which some people may participate fully, others in a more transitory fashion, areas which will institutionalize the possibility of the extension of individuality beyond the more bureaucratized meritocratic occupational and administrative structures.

Within the framework of some, at least, of these bureaucratic organizations, there may develop also a marked shift toward greater participation of their constituent groups, as well as of broader (community or political) unity in the definition of their goals, in some cases giving rise to far-reaching restructuring of such goals by the incorporation of new social community or "societal" goals and orientations.

It will probably be in the educational sphere in general and in the structure of universities in particular that these developments might indeed create some of the most far-reaching changes. Such changes may take place not only in the details of the internal governance of the University;[13] they may also push toward some dissociation between the various activities—research, undergraduate and graduate teaching, which have coalesced in most modern universities, as well as between some of their major contemporary societal functions—the general-educational, that of professional preparation and occupational selection.

Another effect of these developments may be a redefinition of many roles and role clusters—especially the occupational and citizenship roles—the beginning of which can already be discerned in many places. In the occupational spheres there tends to develop, first, the growing infusion or community of "service"—components into pure professional and occupational activities.

Second, there tends also to develop, as is witnessed already in Japan and to some degree in the U.S. and Western Europe, a growing dissociation between high occupational strata and "conservative" political and social attitudes, creating generations of high executives with politically and cultural "leftist views" and with orientation to participation in some of these new "permissive enclaves" or subcultures. They attest to the development of new continuous international networks and enclaves which share some basic symbolic and social attitudes, which cut across the existing political and social orders, while at the same time their incumbents may indeed have different positions in their respective base societies.

These developments may both institutionalize and reinforce some of the structural and symbolic discontinuities analyzed above, and weaken the importance of the occupational dimension in the status system of modern societies.

In the political sphere, in the definition of the citizenship role they may give rise to the redefinition of boundaries of collectivities, they may lead to growing dissociation between political centers and the social and cultural collectivities, and to the development of new nuclei of cultural and social identity which transcend the existing political and cultural boundaries.

Many of these tendencies may be contradictory, many mutually reinforcing—and which of them will indeed become predominant depends on the specific constellations of the various conditions specified above.

But whatever the specific constellation of such conditions, given the general trends of development inherent in the spread of modernity, these movements and their repercussions will be with us for a long time, even if, of course, with continuous ups and downs. These ups and downs and the concomitant diversity of activities and influences of these groups will vary greatly according, on the one hand, to the degree of types of discontinuity that will develop in various sectors of the society, and, on the other hand, with the extent to which new authority patterns and role-models will become successfully accepted and institutionalized.

But whatever their exact strength, they tend to denote, as we have indicated above, the development of some new important social processes which constitute some breakdown of the relative exclusiveness of the older socio-political movements of the nation-state as the only major framework of societal analysis.

They are one result of the specific constellation, in modern societies in general and in industrial ones in particular, of the general conditions under which age and youth groups arise and in which youth become an important focus and symbol of protest as well as a reservoir of some partial institutional change.

NOTES

1. See on this in greater detail: S. N. Eisenstadt, *From Generation to Generation* (New York: The Free Press, 1956 and 1962).

2. See on this: K. Feuer, *The Conflict of Generations* (New York: Basic Books, 1969).

3. See Edward Shils, "Dreams of Plenitude, Nightmares and Scarcity," in S. M. Lipset and F. B. Altbach (eds.), *Students in Revolt* (Boston: Houghton Mifflin Co., 1969), pp. 1-35.

4. See, for instance, Edward Shils, "Intellectuals," *Encyclopedia of the Social Sciences* (New York, 1968); K. Mannheim, *Ideology and Utopia* (London, 1933); and *Man and Society in an Age of Reconstruction* (London, 1934); and the selections in G. B. de Hussar (ed.), *The Intellectuals. A Controversial Portrait* (New York, 1960).

5. See on this in greater detail: S. N. Eisenstadt, "The Scope and Problem of Political Sociology," in idem (eds.), *Political Sociology* (New York: Basic Books, 1970).

6. For analysis on one such historical case, see S. N. Eisenstadt, *The Political Systems of Empires* (New York: The Free Press, 1964 and 1969), esp. ch. VIII. Also: S. N. Eisenstadt, "Religious Organization and Political Process in Centralized Empires," *The Journal of Asian Studies*, Vol. XXI, May 1962, pp. 74-94.

7. For a fuller analysis of these varied aspects of modernity, see: S. N. Eisenstadt, *Modernization and Change* (New Jersey: Prentice Hall, 1966), and S. N. Eisenstadt, "The Scope and Problem of Political Sociology," op. cit.

8. See S. N. Eisenstadt, *From Generation to Generation*, op. cit.

9. See A. Sauvy, *La montée des jeunes*, Paris, 1966.

10. See, for instance, among many others: P. Abrams, "Rites de Passage: The Conflict of Generations in Industrial Society," *Journal of Contemporary History*, Vol. 5 (1970), No. 1, pp. 175-180. Also, M. Brewster Smith, Norma Haan and Jeanne Block, "Social-Psychological Aspects of Student Activism," *Youth and Society*, Vol. 1 (1970), No. 3, pp. 261-289.

11. See Jerome Pitts, "The Hippies as Contemporary Dissent," *Youth and Society*, Vol. 1 (1970), No. 4, pp. 328-338.

12. See Barbara G. Meyerhoff, "New Styles of Humanism: American Youth," *Youth and Society*, Vol. 1 (1969), No. 2, pp. 151-179.

13. See on this the Winter 1970 issue of *Daedalus* on "The Embattled University."

CHAPTER IX

Youth, Generational Consciousness, and Historical Change

AGE, YOUTH, AND GENERATIONS IN HUMAN SOCIETIES

Introduction

There are certain features that are common to all human societies—among them historical change, the tension between generations, and the concept of the age group or set—in particular the youth group—as a special social category with its own distinct self-consciousness. But it is only in very specific civilizational and historical circumstances that these features come together. Only in special circumstances does historical change become articulated in terms of generational consciousness in general, and that of youth in particular.

It was, of course, Karl Mannheim—as well as J. Marias and J. Ortega y Gassett[1]—who emphasized the apparent universality of generational consciousness or at least posed it as a major problem of research; but this tendency was indeed very closely connected to rather specific civilizational traditions—the European ones—and to specific historical circumstances in the development of this civilization.

How can we then explain such circumstances? Under what conditions does historical change become articulated in terms of generational consciousness in general and that of youth in particular?

Reprinted from *Perspectives on Contemporary Youth*, J. Kuczynski, S. N. Eisenstadt, Boubakar Ly, and L. Sarkar (eds.), The United Nations University, 1988.

THE CULTURAL DEFINITIONS OF AGE AND OF YOUTH

It might first of all be worthwhile to specify the general conditions under which specific age groups and generational tensions and consciousness develop in human societies.[2]

Age differences in general and youth in particular constitute a universal phenomenon. They are first of all a biological phenomenon. Indeed, age and age differences are among the basic aspects of human life in society and in the determinants of human destiny. Every human being passes through various ages, and at each one he attains and uses different biological and intellectual capacities. At each stage he performs different tasks and roles in relation to the other members of his society: from a child, he becomes a father; from a pupil, a teacher; from a vigorous youth, a mature adult, and then an aging and "old" man.

In this sense such definition constitutes a part of a wider cultural phenomenon, the varying definitions of age and of the differences between one age and another.

This gradual unfolding of power and capacity is not merely a universal, biologically conditioned and inescapable fact. Although the basic biological processes of maturation (within the limits set by such factors as relative longevity) are probably more or less similar in all human societies, the definition of age differences in general and of youth in particular is always cultural. Their cultural definition varies from society to society, at least in its details. In all societies, age serves as a basis for defining people's cultural and social characteristics, for the formation of some of their mutual relations and common activities, and for the differential allocation of social roles.

The cultural definitions of age and age differences contain several different yet complementary elements. First, these definitions often refer to the social division of labor in a society, to the criteria according to which people occupy various social positions and roles; for instance, in many societies certain roles—especially those of married men, full citizens, independent earners—are barred to young people, while others—such as certain military roles—are specifically allocated to them. Second, the cultural definition of age is one important constituent of a person's self-identity, his self-perception in terms of his own psychological needs and aspirations, his place in society, and the ultimate meaning of his life.

Within any such definition, the qualities of each age are evaluated according to their relation to some basic, primordial qualities, such as vigor, physical and sexual prowess, the ability to cope with material, social, and supernatural environment, wisdom, experience, or divine inspiration. Different ages are seen in different societies as the embodiments of such qualities. These various qualities seem to unfold from one age to another, each age emphasizing some out of the whole panorama of such possible qualities. The cultural definition of an age-span is always a broad definition of human potentialities, limitations, and obligations at a given stage of life. In terms of these definitions, people map out the broad contours of life, their own expectations and possibilities, and place themselves and their fellow men in social and cultural positions, ascribing to each a given place within these contours.

The various qualities attributed to different ages do not constitute unconnected sets of attributes. They are usually interconnected in many ways, constituting a series of sorts. The subtle dialectics between the unfolding of some qualities and the waning of others in a person is not a mere registration of his psychological or biological traits; rather, it constitutes the broad framework of his potentialities and their limit throughout his life-span. The characteristics of any one "age," therefore, cannot be fully understood except in relation to those of other ages. Whether seen as a gradually unfolding continuum or as a series of sharp contrasts and opposed characteristics, they are fully explicable and understandable only in terms of one another. The boy bears within himself the seeds of the adult man; else, he must as an adult acquire new patterns of behavior, sharply and intentionally opposed to those of his boyhood. The adult either develops naturally into an old man, or decays into one. Only when taken together do these different "ages" constitute the entire map of human possibilities and limitations; and, as every individual usually must pass through them all, their complementariness and continuity (even if defined in discontinuous and contrasting terms) become strongly emphasized and articulated.

The same holds true for the age definitions of the two sexes, although perhaps with a somewhat different meaning. Each age-span is defined differently for either sex, and these definitions are usually related and complementary, as the "sexual image" and identity always constitute basic elements of man's image in every society. This close connection between different ages necessarily stresses the problem of transition from one point in a person's life to another as a basic constituent of any cultural definition of an "age." Hence, each definition of age must necessarily cope with the perception of time, and changes in time, of one's own progress in time, one's transition from one period of life to another.

The stress on such different primordial qualities does not refer only to physical or intellectual capacities. It is always closely related to the basic images of the cosmos and of the place of men within it, to the major cultural orientation values—especially those which are seen as the most important for the formation of collective and personal identity, connecting physical age with various virtues or capacities, as well as with the flow of cosmic and societal time.[3]

Hence the personal transition or temporal progress, or change, tends to become closely linked with what may be called cosmic and societal time—with the rhythms of nature or history, the cycles of the seasons, the unfolding of some cosmic plan (whether cyclical, seasonal, or apocalyptic), or the destiny and development of society. The nature of this linkage often constitutes the focus round which an individual's personal identity becomes defined in cultural terms and through which personal experience, with its anguish, may be given some meaning in terms of cultural symbols and values.

YOUTH AS A LIMINAL, TRANSITORY PHASE

The whole problem of age definition and the linkage of personal time and transition with cosmic time become very often accentuated in that age-span usually designated as youth—the most liminal of age definitions.

However great the differences between various societies, there is one focal point within the life-span of an individual which in most— even if not all—known societies is to some extent emphasized: the period of youth, the transition from childhood to full adult status, to full membership in the society. In this period the individual is no longer a child (especially from the physical and sexual point of view) and is ready to undertake many attributes of an adult and to fulfil adult roles. But he is not yet fully acknowledged as an adult, a full member of the society. Rather, he is being "prepared," or is preparing himself for such adulthood.

This image of youth—the cultural definition of youth—contains all the crucial elements of any definition of age, usually in a specially articulated way, and often in confrontation with other age categories. This is the stage at which the individual's personality acquires the basic psychological mechanism of self-regulation and self-control, when his self-identity becomes crystallized. It is also the stage at which the young are confronted with some models of the major roles they are supposed to emulate in adult life and with the major symbols and values of their culture and community. Moreover, in this phase the problem of the linkage of the personal temporal transition with cosmic or societal time becomes extremely acute. Any cultural definition of youth describes it as a transitory phase, a transition toward something new, something basically different from the past. Hence the acuteness of the problem of linkage.

The very emphasis on the transitory nature of this stage and on its essentially preparatory character, however, may easily create a somewhat paradoxical situation. It may evolve an image of youth as the purest manifestation and repository of ultimate cultural and societal values. Such an image is rooted first in the fact that to some extent youth is always defined as a period of "role moratorium," that is, as a period in which one may play with various roles without definitely choosing any. It does not yet require the various compromises inherent in daily participation in adult life. At the same time, however, since it is also the period when the maximum identification with the values of the society may be stressed, under certain conditions it may be viewed as the repository of all the major human virtues and primordial qualities. It may then be regarded as the only age in which full identification with the ultimate values and symbols of the society is attained—facilitated by the flowering of physical vigor, a vigor which may easily become identified with a more general flowering of the cosmos or the society. Hence youth becomes often a very liminal situation.

The fullest, the most articulate and definitive expression of these archetypal elements of youth and of their liminal potentials is best exemplified in the ritual dramatization of the transition from adolescence to adulthood, such as the various *rites de passage* and ceremonies of initiation in primitive tribes and in ancient civilizations.[4] Hence the youth period and its symbolism, and the liminal situations in which it becomes expressed, may become the focus both of continuity of the social order as well as of protest against it, and of its change.

In all these situations there develop potentialities of protest. Given these liminal characteristics of youth, it is but natural that these symbols should become foci of social or cultural protest.

Most of these dramatic and potential protest orientations can also be found, although in somewhat more diluted forms, in various traditional folk festivals in peasant communities, especially those such as rural carnivals in which youth and marriage are emphasized. In an even more diluted form, these elements may be found in the various spontaneous initiation ceremonies of the fraternities and youth groups in modern societies.[5] Here, however, the full dramatic articulation of the elements is lacking, and their configuration and organization assume different forms.

The transition from childhood and adolescence to adulthood, the development of personal identity, psychological autonomy, and self-regulation, the attempt to link personal temporal transition to general cultural images and to cosmic rhythms, and to link psychological maturity to the emulation of definite role models—these constitute the basic elements of any archetypal image of youth. However, the ways in which they become crystallized in concrete configurations differ greatly from society to society and within sectors of the same society. Their full dramatic articulation in the *rites de passage* of primitive societies constitutes only one—perhaps the most extreme and articulate but certainly not the only—configuration of these archetypal elements of youth.

In order to understand other types of such configurations, and above all the extent to which they become foci of social continuity or of change, it is necessary to analyze some conditions that influence their development. Perhaps the best starting–point is the nature of the social organization of the period of adolescence: the process of transition from childhood to adulthood, the social context in which the process of growing up is shaped and structured. There are two major criteria that shape the social organization of the period of youth. One is the extent to which age in general and youth in particular form a criterion for the allocation of roles in a society, whether in politics or in economic or cultural activity—aside from the family, of course, in which they always serve as such a criterion. The second is the extent to which any society develops specific age groups, specific corporate organizations, composed of members of the same "age," such as youth movements or old men's clubs. If roles are allocated in a society according to age, this greatly influences the extent to which age constitutes a component of a person's identity. In such cases, youth becomes a definite and meaningful phase of transition in an individual's progress through life, and his budding self-identity acquires content and a relation to role models and cultural values. No less important for the concrete development of identity is the extent to which it is influenced, either by the common participation of different generations in the same group, as in the family, or conversely by the organization of members of the same age groups into specific distinct groups.

It is of great interest to our analysis that recently, in the last two or three decades, there has also developed—especially in the Western industrialized countries, perhaps above all in the United States—a growing stress on such age consciousness at the other end of the life-span—in old age.

But it is not just old age as a biological phenomenon that is crucial in the shaping of this phenomenon.[6] It is rather its relations, which depend very much on the major orientations and symbols of the society, especially with regard to work, that are crucial in such a definition. It is significant, from the point of view of our analysis, that the social and cultural conditions which account for such developments are not dissimilar from those which are connected with age and youth groups—although, needless to say, they work in rather different directions in each case.

THE SOCIAL AND CULTURAL CONTEXTS OF DIFFERENT PATTERNS
OF YOUTH SYMBOLISM AND ORGANIZATION

Age as a Criterion of Role Allocation and of Organization of Specific Groups

The importance of age as a criterion for allocating roles in a society is closely related to several major aspects of social organization and cultural orientation. The first aspect is the relative complexity of the division of labor. In general, the simpler the organization of the society, the more influential age will be as a criterion for allocating roles. Therefore, in primitive or traditional societies (or in the more primitive and traditional sectors of developed societies) age and seniority constitute basic criteria for allocating social, economic, and political roles.

The second aspect consists of the major value orientations and symbols of a society, especially the extent to which they emphasize certain general orientations, qualities, or types of activity (such as physical vigor, the maintenance of cultural tradition, the achievement and maintenance of supernatural prowess) which can be defined in terms of broad human qualities and which become expressed and symbolized in specific age-spans.

Thus the emphasis on any particular age as a criterion for the allocation of roles is largely related to the concrete specification of the major value orientations in a society. For instance, we find that those primitive societies in which military values and orientations prevail emphasize young adulthood as a very important—sometimes even as the most important—age, while those in which sedentary activities prevail emphasize older age. Similarly, within some traditional societies, old age may be emphasized if it is seen as the most appropriate one for expressing major cultural values and symbols—for instance, the very upholding, symbolization, and perpetuation of a given cultural tradition. This may be especially important in pre-literate societies where older people may serve as important "storers" of collective memory.

The social and cultural conditions that determine the extent to which specific age groups and youth groups develop differ from the conditions that determine the extent to which age serves as a criterion for the allocation of roles. At the same time, the two kinds of conditions may be, in some situations or societies, closely related.

Age groups in general and youth groups in particular tend to arise in those societies in which the family or kinship unit cannot ensure (it may even impede) the attainment of full social and political status on the part of its members. These conditions appear especially, although not uniquely, in societies in which family or kinship groups do not constitute the basic units of the social division of labor. Several features characterize such societies. First, the membership in the total society (citizenship) is not defined in terms of belonging to any such family, kinship group, or estate, nor is it mediated by such a group.

Second, in these societies the major political, economic, social, and religious functions are performed not by family or kinship units but rather by various specialized groups (political parties, occupational associations, etc.), which individuals may join irrespective of their family, kinship, or caste. In these societies, therefore, the major roles that adults are expected to perform in the wider society differ in orientation from those of the family or kinship group. The children's identification and close interaction with family members of other ages does not assure their attainment of full self-identity and social maturity. In these cases, there arises a tendency for peer groups to form, especially youth groups; these can serve as a transitory phase between the world of childhood and the adult world.

Lately Meyer Fortes, in one of his last papers, has elaborated and systematized this point, by stressing that the emergence of distinct age organization and consciousness lies in the political realm, in the search and definition of citizenship beyond the family sphere and not through the family, while generational differences are mostly elaborated in the structure of the family and kinship unit.[7]

AGE ORGANIZATION IN TRIBAL AND HISTORICAL SOCIETIES

The type of social division of labor and of political and cultural symbolism that generates such conditions is found, as we have seen above in ch. VII,[8] in varying degrees in different societies—primitive, historical, or modern.

To be sure, the extent to which the family is diminishing in its scope in modern societies has been often exaggerated and lately it has been more and more emphasized that in many social spheres (neighborhood, friendship, informal association, some class relations, community relations), family, kinship, and status are indeed very influential and continuously reconstructed. But the scope of these relations is more limited in modern societies than in many others, even if the prevalent myth of the disappearance of the family has long since been exploded. The major social developments in the nineteenth century—the establishment of national states, the progress of the Industrial Revolution, the great waves of intercontinental migrations—have greatly contributed to this diminution of the scope of the family and kinship relations. This was especially true in the first phase of modernization, where there developed a relatively sharp discontinuity in the lives of the children between the family or the traditional school and the social world with its new and enlarged perspectives.

In most modern—as well as in some historical—societies, there developed, unlike in many pre-literate and other historical societies, a certain dissociation between organizations of groups based on age and the symbolic distinction between different age categories, as well as between generations which do not go together throughout one's lifetime but tend to crystallize only in specific age-spans, of which youth has till now been the most important.

These developments have given rise, first, to far-reaching differences between age groups and generational sets—as has been lately shown in great detail by anthropologists[9]—and, second, to a much fuller articulation of the dialectics between, on the one hand, the "rebellious" protest-oriented aspects of youth organization and generational consciousness, and, on the other hand, the continuity-oriented aspects.

Here again it is significant that in some of the industrial societies these dimensions are again coming together among the older people—that is, those who have retired from work—often finding distinct social and political articulation.

It is, in this context, of great interest that in most pre-literate and historical societies these youth organizations and patterns of youth consciousness only rarely developed as movements of protest and foci of change; it is only in modern societies that these developments have taken place.

GENERATIONAL AND YOUTH SYMBOLISM AND CONSCIOUSNESS IN MODERN SOCIETIES

Generational Consciousness in Modern Society

The generational consciousness, about which Mannheim, Marias, and Ortega y Gassett and many other modern writers wrote, is of a different order. It is far from being fully formalized within the familial structure. Rather, it denotes the general consciousness, the self-consciousness of generations, which is, as Meyer Fortes has indicated, rooted in the family, being taken out into the public realm—whether the realm of politics or of culture—and it contains very strong potentialities of social, political, or cultural protest.

This is indeed connected, in a rather paradoxical way, with the fact that in modern societies the development of specific youth organizations is linked with the weakening of the importance of age in general and youth in particular as definite criteria for the allocation of roles in society.

The extent to which major occupational, cultural, or political roles are allocated in modern societies according to the explicit criterion of age—at least up to retirement—is on the whole very small, except with respect to retirement from work. Most such roles are achieved according to wealth, acquired skills, specialization, and knowledge. Family background may be of great importance for the acquisition of these attributes, but very few positions are directly given people by virtue of their family standing. Yet this very weakening of the importance of age, as a criterion of allocation of roles, has been connected with intensive development of youth groups and movements—and lately also, as we have seen, of sets of other "retired" people.

Indeed, the youth group, whatever its composition or organization, usually stands alone. It does not constitute a part of a fully institutionalized and organized series of age groups. It is true that in many of the more traditional sectors of modern societies the more primitive or traditional archetypes of youth still prevail. Moreover, in many modern societies elements of the primitive archetypes of youth still exist. But the full articulation of these elements is lacking, and the social organization and self-expression of youth are not given full legitimation or meaning in terms of cultural values and rituals.

The close linkage between the growth of personality, psychological maturation, and definite role models derived from the adult world has become greatly weakened. Hence the very coalescence of youth into special groups only tends to emphasize their rather special, often problematic standing from the point of view of cultural values and symbols.

It is because of these developments—some incipient phases of which can be also discerned in different literate, historical societies, but which have not been studied adequately[10]—that in modern societies there also arises the possibility of the development of very strong generational consciousness in general, and of the articulation of such consciousness in terms of youth in particular.

HISTORICAL CHANGE, GENERATIONAL AND YOUTH CONSCIOUSNESS, AND REVOLUTIONARY ORIENTATION

The development in modern societies of such a dissociation between generations, and the concomitant possibility of the development of a special type of generational consciousness, are due not only to the complex division of labor that characterizes these societies. They are also closely connected to the relatively quick tempo of historical change, and above all to the consciousness of such change—a consciousness which is often connected with change in cultural values and orientations and which has been basically rooted in the nature of the construction of modern civilizations, of modern social and cultural orders, and in the revolutionary characteristics of this civilization.

The revolutionary orientations which were at the root of most breakthroughs to modernity—and which have later on been incorporated into these modern civilizations—have been, whatever their concrete contents, oriented towards a far-reaching transformation of the nature and contents of the centers of the social and cultural orders, of the rules of participation in them and of access to them, and of the relations between these centers and the periphery.[11]

From the point of view of the contents of these centers, the major transformation concomitant with modernity has been in the growing secularization of the centers and the "opening up" of their contents, that is, the non-acceptance of the givenness of these contents—in the spread of the assumption that these contents can indeed be formulated anew.

This was closely connected with changes in the structure of the centers and the relations between them, with the growing autonomy of such centers—whether political, cultural, or societal—with their growing interpretation and independence as autonomous units, and above all with the changes in the relations between the centers and the periphery.

Modern social orders have been characterized by the growing impingement of the periphery on the center, by incorporation of orientations of protest into the center, and by the opening up to the periphery of access to the center through the permeation of the periphery by the center and the concomitant tendency for the difference between center and periphery to be obliterated, making membership in the collectivity tantamount to participation in the center. The major social movements that have developed with the onset of modernization—be they national, social or cultural—all of them manifest, in varying degrees and scope, this tendency.

DEVELOPMENT IN THE EDUCATIONAL SPHERE

These processes were, of course, closely connected with the growing structural differentiations which have been briefly mentioned above.

But, from the point of view of our discussion, perhaps the most important change related to these developments was that in the social organization of the educational sphere. In most pre-modern societies the process of education was usually divided into several rather compartmentalized aspects. The central educational institutions were oriented mainly to the education of an élite and of the upper strata, and to the upholding and development of the central cultural tradition in its varied manifestations.

The local educational institutions, which were usually only loosely connected with the central ones, were oriented chiefly to the maintenance of some general, diffuse, and rather passive identification of the various strata with the overall symbols of society—without, however, permitting them any closer participation in the central political and cultural activities—and to provision of some technical know-how which would be appropriate to their position in society. Between the two were several educational institutions which served as channels either of restricted "sponsored" mobility into the central spheres of society or of some specific vocational preparation.

This began to change with the onset of modernity. Education started to deal with the problems of forging new national communities and their common symbols, access to which tended to become more widely spread among different strata. At the same time, it began to serve increasingly as a channel for more general occupational and allegedly achievement-based selection. Moreover, the system of education tended to become more centralized and unified, thus assuring its permeation of wider strata of the society.

This societal unification of the educational system, when combined with the continuous developments of the structural and symbolical aspects of modernity, gave rise to a series of social and cultural contradictions and discontinuities which have become, on the one hand, extremely widespread throughout the society and, on the other, more and more focused around its central symbols; and it is the combination of the revolutionary characteristics of modern civilization, together with these discontinuities, that created some of the most important background conditions for the development of new types of generational and youth consciousness and protest.

HISTORICAL EXPERIENCE, GENERATIONAL CONSCIOUSNESS AND YOUTH SYMBOLISM, AND MODERN YOUTH MOVEMENTS

The possibility of the development of such consciousness is enhanced by the occurrence of quick historical changes or ruptures, the consciousness of which is shared by members of the same age group or age cohort. But needless to say, while historical change is particularly rapid and the consciousness of such change very widespread in modern societies, it does not always create generational consciousness—although probably to some degree such consciousness is both more common than previously supposed and less confined to the symbolism and ideology of youth.

Such consciousness, including generational consciousness, is more often set in terms of basic historical experience, be it national or cultural, or in terms of unique historical events—wars, changes of regime, and the like.[12]

It is only in rather special historical circumstances and situations that such generational consciousness becomes expressed in terms of youth symbolism.

Among such situations in modern societies two are probably of special importance.[13] One was developed at the end of the nineteenth and the beginning of the twentieth century, and found its fullest expression in the free German youth movements, though it was also present in the less spectacular youth movements of Central Europe and to some extent in the specific youth culture of various more flexible youth groups. In all these movements a very strong attempt was made to overcome the dislocation between personal transition and societal and cultural time. It was in these movements that the social dynamics of modern youth found one of its first full expressions. It was in them that dreams of a new life, a new society, freedom and spontaneity, a new humanity, and aspirations to social and cultural change found utterance. It was in these youth movements that the forging of youth's new social identity became closely connected with the development of new symbols of collective identity or new social-cultural symbols and meanings, which thus become foci of protest aimed at the reconstruction of society and culture.

These movements aimed at changing many aspects of the social and cultural life of their respective societies. They depicted the present in a rather shabby light; they censured it for its materialism, restriction, exploitation, and lack of opportunity for self-fulfilment and creativity. At the same time they held out hope for the future—seemingly the not very far-off future—when both self-fulfilment and collective fulfilment could be achieved and the materialistic civilization of the adult world shaken off. They tried to appeal to youth to forge its own self-identity in terms of these new collective symbols, and this is why they have been so attractive to youth, for whom they provided a set of symbols, hopes, and aims to which to direct its activities.

One of the major characteristics of many, probably most, of these movements was, indeed, that in their ideology the symbolism of youth was very closely connected with that of the new modern collectivities that were being constructed at the period, and among their aims the reconstruction of such collectivities—national, social, or cultural—was central.

Within these movements the emphasis was on a given social group or collectivity—nation, class, or the youth group itself—as the main, almost exclusive bearer of the pristine cultural value and symbols. It was through its association with these movements that youth was also able to connect its aspirations for a different personal future, its anxiety to escape the present, to plans and hopes for a different future within its cultural or social setting.

The influence of such movements and orientations has become enormous in various fields, not only political and educational, but cultural in general. In a way, education itself has tended to become a social movement. Many schools and universities, many teachers, have been among the most important bearers of collective values. The spread of education itself is often seen as a means by which a new epoch might be ushered in.

While some of these orientations could be found in many of the youth groups that developed in most modern societies—be they in

England or the United States—they developed most fully in situations where these groups became closely interconnected with different social movements oriented at the reconstruction of the centers and symbols of their respective societies. Such movements were most powerful when they were strongly connected with relatively strong primordial and historical—as against religious—orientations, and with strong changes in the patterns of division of labor—above all with growing industrialization and social mobility.

Thus it was above all in the major nationalistic and revolutionary movements in Central and Eastern Europe, in Italy, Germany, Hungary, and Russia, or in the Zionist movement, that these orientations and student movements played a crucial role.

THE ROUTINIZATION OF REVOLUTIONARY MOVEMENTS AND YOUTH AND STUDENT REBELLION OF THE 1960s

The second historical situation in modern societies in which generational consciousness, couched in the symbolism of youth, became very prominent was the development in the late 1960s and early 1970s that became most fully manifest in the various student rebellions and movements.[14]

In this situation the combination between the symbolism of youth and collective symbolism was already of a different order from the one that developed in the various movements analyzed above.

The background to these new developments was a combination of the growing institutionalization of many of the collective values of the social, national, and youth movements discussed above, and the continuous spread of education and changes in occupational structure.

The process of institutionalization of these values was strongly emphasized in the youth movements and noticeable to some extent even in the looser youth culture, and has become greatly weakened. The social and sometimes even the cultural dimension of the future may thus become flattened and emptied. The various collective values become transformed. Instead of being remote goals resplendent with romantic dreams, they have become mundane objectives of the present, with its shabby details of daily politics and administration. More often than not they are intimately connected with the process of bureaucratization.

All these changes were initially closely associated with a notable decline in ideology and preoccupation with ideology among many of the groups and strata in modern societies, with a general weakening of political-ideological motives and a growing apathy to them. This decline was in turn connected with what has been called the spiritual or cultural shallowness of the new social and economic benefits accruing from the welfare state—an emptiness illustrated by the fact that all these benefits are in the nature of things administered not by spiritual or social leaders but, as Stephen Toulmin has wittily pointed out, "the assistant postmaster." As a consequence, we observe the emptiness and meaninglessness of social relations, so often described by critics of the age of consumption and mass society.

In general, these developments have brought about the flattening of the image of the societal future and have deprived it of its allure. No ideological discontinuity is conceived between present and future. The present has become the more important, if not the more meaningful, because the future has lost its characteristic as a dimension different from the present. Through these developments youth has been robbed of the full experience of the dramatic transition from adolescence to adulthood and of the dramatization of the difference between present and future. Their own changing personal future has become dissociated from any changes in the shape of their societies or in cultural activities and values.

Paradoxically enough, these developments have often been connected with a strong adulation of youth—an adulation, however, which was in a way purely instrumental. The necessity of a continuous adjustment to new changing conditions has emphasized the potential value of youth as the bearers of continuous innovation, of non-commitment to any specific conditions and values. But such an emphasis is often couched in terms of a purely instrumental adaptability, beyond which there is only the relative emptiness of the meaningless passage of time—of aging.

THE DEMYSTIFICATION OF THE WORLD: YOUTH REBELLION AND WITHDRAWAL FROM THE CENTER

This transfer of emphasis from the creation and participation in the future-oriented collective values to the growing institutionalization of such values became closely related with a shift in the orientations and foci of protest in modern societies, and it is in this shift that the antinomian tendencies of intellectual protests can be most clearly discerned.

Unlike the older classical movements of protest of early modernity—the major social and national movements—all of which tended to assume that the framework and centers of the nation-state constituted the major cultural and social reference points of personal identity and of the charismatic orientations to some socio-cultural orders, and that the major task before modern societies was to facilitate the access of broader strata of the society to these centers—unlike them, the new movements of protest are characterized by their scepticism toward the new modern centers, by their lack of commitment to them, and by their tendency toward lack of responsibility to the institutional and organizational frameworks of these centers.

The foci of protest have tended to shift from demands for greater participation in national political centers or from attempts to influence their socio-economic policies to new directions. The most important of these directions seem to be: first, attempts to "disrobe" these centers of their charismatic legitimacy and perhaps of any legitimacy at all; second, continuous searches for new loci of meaningful participation beyond these existing socio-political centers and the concomitant attempts to create new centers which would be independent of them; third, attempts to formulate the patterns of participation in their centers not so much in socio-political or economic terms but more through symbols of primordial or of direct social participation.

Thus it seems that these developments touch not only on some of the most important structural developments in postmodern societies, but also on the relations of these developments to some of the basic symbolic constituents of these societies—to basic components of the definition of their socio-cultural orders as well as of their cultural, collective, and personal identities.

Significantly enough, many of these new orientations of protest were also directed not only against the bureaucratization and functional rationalization connected with growing technology but also against the supposed central place of science and scientific investigation as the basis—or even one of the bases—of the socio-cultural order.

They all denoted, as we have seen, an important aspect of what has been called by Weber the demystification of the world—

demystification which here becomes focused around the possibility that the attainment of participation in these centers may indeed be meaningless, that these centers may lose their mystery, that the king may be naked indeed.

This demystification may well be related to the relative success of the demand for access to these centers and participation in them and to the obliteration of the symbolic difference between center and periphery. This in its turn may give rise to a new type of social alienation focused not only around the feeling of being lost in a maze of large-scale, anonymous organizations and frameworks, but also around the possibility of the loss of the meaning of participation in political and national centers.

In other words, these centers may be losing their special place as loci of the participation in a meaningful socio-cultural order, and as the major social and cultural referents of personal identity. There tends to develop here a growing feeling of dissociation and of lack of congruence between the quest for participation in the charismatic dimension of human and social existence and these specific types of social and political centers.

These developments have often been connected to what may be called the breakdown of continuity of historical consciousness or awareness.

It is not only that the new generations have not experienced such events as the Depression or the two world wars, which were crucial in the formation of their parents. What is more significant is that, probably partly due to the very process of the institutionalization of the collective goals of their parents on the one hand and growing affluence on the other, the parent generation failed to transmit to the new generation the significance of these historical events.

Paradoxically enough, this very process of the institutionalization of the image of the future and its consequence provided the background for the emergence of a new type of generational consciousness, focused on youth symbolism but of a different order from the one that developed in the late nineteenth and early twentieth century.

Such development was connected with the spread of new educational and occupational trends that took place in so-called post-industrial societies. As a result of these trends there tended to develop, in many contemporary societies—especially in the highly developed and industrialized ones—a whole series of structural and symbolical discontinuities—all related to the spread and development of the institutional and symbolic dimensions of modernity, and all of which gradually converged around both intergenerational conflicts and widespread intellectual antinomian tendencies.

These discontinuities were much more variegated than those between a relatively closed traditional familial structure and a more specialized and universalistic occupational and political system, which have given rise, as we have seen, in many societies in general and in the first stages of modernity in particular, to various types of intergenerational conflicts.

These discontinuities tended to go beyond the direct opposition between family, on the one hand, and educational and occupational sectors on the other, to affect the different sectors of the society through which youth passes, and therefore the foci of such discontinuity have become, in modern and particularly in contemporary societies, much more diversified. They may include discontinuity between the family and the educational and occupational spheres; between the family and educational institutions, on the one hand, and the occupational sector on the other; between the productive and consumer roles in the economic sector; between the values and orientations inculcated in the family and the educational institutions and the central collective symbols of the society; and between the premises of these symbols and the actual political roles of the parents and younger people alike, in which case they cut across family roles themselves. These new types of discontinuities have impinged most intensively on the social and cultural situation of youth and on the concrete manifestations of youth problems and protest.

Here several such repercussions can be singled out. One is that the area of social life that the specific youth or student culture encompasses has tended to expand continuously. First, it has extended over a longer period of life, reaching, through the impact of the extension of higher education, to what before was seen as early adulthood. Second, it tends more and more to include areas of work, leisure time activity, and many interpersonal relations. Third, the potential and actual autonomy of these groups, and the possibility their members have for direct access to work, marriage, and family life, to political rights, and to consumption, have greatly increased, while their dependence on adults has greatly decreased.

Because of this, paradoxically enough, the growing direct access of youth people to various areas of life has given rise to a growing insecurity of status and self-identity and to a growing ambiguity of adult roles.

This insecurity and ambiguity is enhanced, first, by the prolongation of the time-span between biological and social maturity and by the extension of the number of years spent in "preparatory" (educational) institutions, and, second, by the growing dissociation between the values of these institutions and the future—especially in terms of occupational and parental roles—of those participating in them. A third factor is that for a long period many "young" people may as yet have no clear occupational roles or responsibilities and may be dependent on their parents or public institutions for their economic needs, while at the same time they constitute an important economic force as consumers and certainly exercise political rights.

In turn this situation may become intensified or aggravated by the growing demographic preponderance of the "young" in the whole population and by the increasing possibilities of ecological mobility.

These discontinuities very often culminate in a crisis that involves both a weakening of authority—evident in the lack of development of adequate role-models—and the erosion of many of the bases of legitimation of existing authority.

As a result of all these processes, the possibility of linking personal transition to social groups and cultural values alike—to societal and cosmic time—which was so strongly emphasized in the youth movements and observable to some extent even in the earlier, looser youth culture, has become greatly weakened.

At the same time, however, the search for some such link for new loci of charismatic symbols and activities persisted, even if often in a muted form. This search could indeed become articulated in certain historical situations, especially in conjunction with the intensification and convergence of the various structural and symbolic discontinuities analyzed above.

The search was epitomized by the student movements of the late 1960s and early 1970s. In these movements there developed a new configuration of youth symbolism and generational consciousness with a very strong antinomian bias.

It is not just the contents of these antinomian tendencies that are important and new, but the convergence of these contents with the spread and location of the movements—above all, with the fact that this type of protest was not confined only to small, closed intellectual groups but involved widespread circles of novices and aspirants to intellectual status, who constitute, given the spread of the modern educational system and the parallel effects of the spread of mass-communication media, a very large part of the educated public, and yet impinge, for the same structural reasons, on the centers of intellectual creativity and cultural transmission and become integral, even if transient, parts thereof.

This rather unique combination of intellectual antinomianism with youth rebellion gave rise to a new type of youth ideology that was connected to the reversal of the hitherto existing relation between the definition of different age-spans and the possibilities of social and cultural creativity.

Unlike in the past—even the not-so-distant past—youth became more and more seen not only as a preparation for independent and creative participation in social and cultural life, but as the very embodiment of permissive, often unstructured creativity—to be faced later on with the constants of a relatively highly organized, constrictive, meritocratic, and bureaucratic environment. Thus youth now became, even more than before, the transmitters and symbols of a continuous confrontation between the pristine values it embodies and a demystified social reality.

It will still be a long time before the impact of the student movement on the restructuring of various aspects of life in modern societies can be fully and critically evaluated. But there can be no doubt that this impact has indeed been manifold, and that one of its most important aspects has been the growth of generational youth consciousness in many modern societies.

While the intensity and the concrete manifestation of this consciousness will naturally change from one situation to another, the consciousness itself seems to have become more and more prevalent and to contain within itself the various antinomian tendencies analyzed above.

The preceding analysis has indicated some general tendencies which influence different aspects of the development of the symbolism, ideology, and consciousness of youth that bear out our initial premise—namely, that while age difference and youth are universal aspects of human life, their specific cultural and social manifestations depend very much on social, cultural, and historical conditions.

NOTES

1. J. Marias, *El metodo historico de las generaciones* (Revista del Occidente, Madrid, 1949); "Generations," *International Encyclopedia of the Social Sciences,* vol. 6 (Macmillan Free Press, New York, 1968), pp. 88-91; K. Mannheim, "The Problem of Generations," *Essays on the Sociology of Knowledge* (Oxford University Press, New York, 1952), pp. 276-360; J. Ortega y Gasset, *The Modern Theme* (Norton, New York, 1932).

2. A general sociological analysis of the place of age and youth in the social structure has been attempted in S. N. Eisenstadt, *From Generation to Generation* (Free Press of Glencoe, Ill., 1956), and "Archetypal Patterns of Youth," in E. H. Erikson (ed.), *Youth: Change and Challenge* (Basic Books, New York, 1963), pp. 24-43.

3. The analysis of personal, cosmic, and societal time (or temporal progression) has constituted a fascinating but not easily dealt with focus of analysis. For some approaches to these problems, see Joseph Campbell (ed.), *Man and Time* (papers from the Eranos Yearbook, Routledge & Kegan Paul, London, 1958), especially the article by G. van der Lieuuw. See also Mircea Eliade, *The Myth of the Eternal Return,* trans. W. R. Trask (Pantheon Books, New York, 1954).

4. For a fuller exposition of the sociological significance of initiation rites, see Mircea Eliade, *Birth and Rebirth* (Harper, New York, 1958) and S.N. Eisenstadt, *From Generation to Generation* (see note 2 above).

5. See Bruno Bettelheim, *Symbolic Wounds, Puberty Rites and the Envious Circle* (Free Press of Glencoe, Chicago, Ill., 1954), and "The Problem of Generations," in E. H. Erikson (see note 2 above), pp. 54-93.

6. J. E. Birren and K. Wazner Schaie, *The Handbook of the Psychology of Aging* (Van Nostrand, New York, 1972); B. Neugerten, *Middle Age and Aging: A Reader in Social Psychology* (University of Chicago Press, Chicago, Ill., 1968); M. W. Riley (ed.), *Aging from Birth to Death* (Balders Westview Press, Boulder, Colo., 1976); M. W. Riley and Anne Foster (eds.), *Aging and Society* (Russell Sage Foundation, New York, 1968-1974), 3 vols.

7. See M. Fortes, "Age, Generation and Social Structure," in D. Kertzer and J. Keith (eds.), *Age and Anthropological Theory* (Cornell University Press, Ithaca, N.Y. 1984), pp. 99-123.

8. For greater detail see S. N. Eisenstadt (note 2 above).

9. See R. Baxter and U. Almagor (eds.), *Age, Generation and Time— Some Features of East Africa Age Organizations* (St. Martin's Press, New York, 1968); J. La Fontaine (ed.), *Sex and Age as Principles of Social Differentiation* (Academic Press, New York, 1978).

10. See, for instance, L. L. Nash, "Concepts of Experience, Greek Origins of Generational Thought," *Daedalus,* Fall 1978, pp. 1-23.

11. For a fuller analysis of these varied aspects of modernity, see S. N. Eisenstadt, *Modernization, Protest and Change* (Prentice-Hall, Englewood Cliffs, N.J., 1966).

12. See *Daedalus*, Fall 1978; S. N. Eisenstadt (note 2 above); and E. H. Erikson (note 2 above).

13. See S. N. Eisenstadt (note 2 above), chaps. 4 and 6.

14. The literature on student rebellions is, of course, immense. See, for instance, S. M. Lipset, *Student Politics* (Basic Books, New York, 1967); and G. Altbach and R. S. Laufer, *The New Pilgrim—Youth Protest in Tradition* (David MacKay, New York, 1972).

Notes

CHAPTER I

1. R. Linton, *The Cultural Background of Personality*, London, 1947, pp. 43-45. See also Ch. Bühler, *Der Menschliche Lebenslauf als psychologisches Problem*, Leipzig, 1933.

2. The terms "age grade" and "age group" have been formally defined most succinctly by A. R. Radcliffe-Brown in "Age Organisation Terminology," *Man*, 1929, No. 13. According to this definition, which will be used throughout this book, an age grade is "the recognised division of the life of the individual as he passes from infancy to old age."

3. The problem of discontinuous definitions of age grades was first clearly pointed out and analyzed by R. Benedict in "Continuities and Discontinuities in Culture Conditioning," *Psychiatry*, I, 1938, pp. 161-7, and was also emphasized by K. Davis in "Adolescence and the Social Structure," *The Annals of the American Academy of Political and Social Science*, Vol. 236. 1944, pp. 3-17, and in "The Sociology of Parent-Youth Conflict," *American Sociological Review*, Vol. 5, 1940, pp. 523-35. See also Ch. Bühler, *op. cit.*

4. This problem has been infinitely stressed in the relevant literature. A good summary may be found in K. Davis, *Human Society*, New York, 1950, pp. 24-52, 195-234. For its importance to social theory in general, see T. Parsons and E. Shils, "Values, Motives and Systems of Action" in Parsons and Shils (ed.), *Towards a General Theory of Action*, Harvard, 1951, pp. 61 ff.

5. T. Parsons, *The Social System*, Glencoe, 1951, chap. VI.

6. T. Parsons, *op. cit.*

7. This summary analysis of the process of socialization follows that of Parsons and Shils (*op. cit.*, pp. 125 ff. and 227 ff.), and is also based on J. Bowlby's brilliant analysis in *Why Delinquency*, London, 1949, pp. 33-7.

8. This point has been emphasized by R. Linton, *The Cultural Background of Personality*, *op. cit.*, and by K. Davis, "Adolescence and the Social Structure," *op. cit.*

9. For the fullest discussion of the problem of kinship-terminology extension see: G. P. Murdock, *Social Structure*, New York, 1949, pp. 31-184; A. R. Radcliffe-Brown, "Introduction" in A. R. Radcliffe-Brown and

D. Forde, *African Systems of Kinship and Marriage*, Oxford, 1950, pp. 1-86.

10. This assumption is analyzed in Parsons and Shils, *op. cit.*, pp. 150-1, and in K. Davis, *Human Society, op. cit.*, pp. 215-8. Davis' argument is related to and based on that of J. Piaget, *The Moral Judgment of the Child*, London, 1932.

11. J. Piaget, *op. cit.*, pp. 326 ff. For concrete illustrations of such children's groups in various societies see: M. Fortes, *Social and Psychological Aspects of Education in Taleland*, Oxford, (I.A.I. Memoranda), 1938; O. Raumm, *Chaga Childhood*, Oxford (International African Institute).

12. K. Davis, "The Sociology of Parent-Youth Conflict," *op. cit.*, and R. Linton, *op. cit.*

13. A. van Gennep, *Rites de passage*, Paris, 1904.

13a. The psychological aspects of Initiation and Puberty rites have been lately analyzed by B. Bettelheim, *Symbolic Wounds*, Glencoe, 1954.

14. The fullest and best account of initiation rites known to the author can be found in O. Raumm, *Chagga Childhood, op. cit.*, pp. 150 ff. and in G. Wagner, *The Bantu of North Kavirondo*, Oxford, 1949, pp. 334-82. Anthropological literature abounds in such descriptions, which can be found in most anthropological monographs.

15. See A. Varagnac, *Civilisations Traditionelles et Genres de Vie*, Paris, 1948, pp. 138-82. R. Thurnwald in *Die Menschliche Gesellschaft*, B. II, Leipzig, 1931, pp. 281-4, has already emphasized that among peasants marriage and family rites become more important than initiation rites. See also for full documentation of one society: L. Löw, *Lebensalter in der Jüdischen Literatur*, Szegedin, 1875.

16. On the articulation of personality system and social system see Parsons and Shils, *op. cit.*, pp. 146 ff.

17. See H. Brunswick, *La Crise de l'Etat Prussien du XVIIIe Siècle et la Génese de la Mentalité Romantique, Paris, 1949*.

18. See, for instance, Bascom, "The Principle of Seniority in the Social Structure of the Yoruba," *American Anthropologist*, XLIV, 1942, pp. 37-46.

18a. See on this T. Parsons' analysis in Parsons, Bales *e,t al.*, *Family, Socialization and Interaction Process*, Glencoe, 1955.

19. K. Davis, *Human Society, op. cit.*

20. See G. P. Murdock, *op. cit.*, chaps. 1, 5.

21. A. R. Radcliffe-Brown, "The Mother's Brother in South Africa," *South African Journal of Science*, XXI, 1924, reprinted as ch. I of *Structure and Function in Primitive Society*, London, 1952.

22. A brief theoretical discussion of concrete cases of such extension is given by E. E. Evans-Pritchard in "The Study of Kinship in Primitive Societies," *Man*, Nov. 1929, and "The Nature of Kinship Extensions," *Man*, Jan. 1932. Some of the general assumptions are analyzed by G. P. Murdock, *op. cit.*, chaps. 1, 6, 7.

23. The complementary nature of kinship relations and descent groups has been brilliantly analyzed by M. Fortes, *The Dynamics of Clanship among the Tallensi*, Oxford, 1945, and in *The Web of Kinship among the Tallensi*, Oxford, 1949. A succinct analysis of this problem was made by M. Fortes in his lecture in Chicago at the meeting of the American Anthropological Association: "The Structure of the Unilineal Descent Group," *American Anthropologist*, Vol. 55, 1953: and can also be found in F. Eggan's analysis of the Hopi system in "The Hopi and the Lineage

Principle," in *Social Structure Studies presented to A. R. Radcliffe-Brown* (ed. M. Fortes), pp. 120-44, and in *The Social Organization of the Western Pueblos*, Chicago, 1951.

24. This problem has been fully discussed by Parsons and Shils, *op. cit.*, pp. 234 ff., and by T. Parsons, *The Social System*, *op. cit.*, pp. 176-80. See also T. Parsons, "Age and Sex in the Social Structure," in *Essays in Sociological Theory*, Glencoe, 1949, pp. 218-33, and R. Williams, Jr., *American Society*, New York, 1951, pp. 36-78, and see also Ch. Bühler, *op. cit.*

25. See O. Raumm, *Chagga Childhood*, *op. cit.*; Stayt, *The BaVenda*, Oxford (I.A.I.).

26. The integrative principles of overall kinship systems have been most fully analyzed by C. Levi-Strauss in *Les Structures Elementaires de la Parenté*, Paris, 1949.

27. The problems of function and disfunction have been analyzed by R. K. Merton, "Manifest and Latent Functions," *Social Theory and Social Structure*, Glencoe, 1949, pp. 21-83.

28. The term "primary" is meant here in the sense usually used in "primary groups." See K. Davis, *Human Society*, *op. cit.*, pp. 289 ff., and E. A. Shils, *The Present State of American Sociology*, Glencoe, 1948, pp. 40 ff.

29. The most interesting case of such avoidance can be found among the Nyakyusa. See M. Wilson, *Good Company*, Oxford, 1951, and see in greater detail, the analysis in ch. V of this book.

30. For exact definition of these terms see T. Parsons, *The Social System*, chap. VII.

31. We do not assume that any discontinuous definition of the roles of children and adults (as defined by R. Benedict, *op. cit.*) entails the emergence of more or less formalized age groups. Such a discontinuity has often been stressed as one of the main determinants of the insecurity of the adolescent period in various cultures (e.g., in the various works of M. Mead). For a good summary of such evidence see M. Sherif and H. Cantril, *The Psychology of Ego Involvement*, New York, 1946, chaps. 8, 9.

Not everywhere, however, does adolescent insecurity necessarily give rise to strong age-homogeneous groups. According to our hypothesis this takes place only in "nonkinship" societies. In "kinship" societies such insecurity is resolved within the family unit, aided by various initiation rites. For an instance of this see J. Whiting, *Becoming a Kwoma*, New Haven, 1951.

CHAPTER II

1. The most important literature on the Nuer are the following works of E. E. Evans-Pritchard: (a) "The Nuer Tribe and Clan," *Sudan Notes and Records*, vol. XVI, p. 1, XVII, pt. I, p. 1; (b) "The Nuer, Age Sets," *Sudan Notes and Records*, 1933-5, vol. XIX, pt. II; (c) *The Nuer*, Oxford 1940; (d) *Marriage and Kinship Among the Nuer*, Oxford, 1951; (e) "Kinship and the Local Community Among the Nuer," in A. R. Radcliffe-Brown and D. Forde, *African Systems of Kinship and Marriage*, International African Institute (Oxford), 1950.

The description given here is adapted from E. E. Evans-Pritchard, (b) and (e) pp. 257-61.

2. The most important literature on the Nandi is: A. C. Hollis, *The Nandi, Their Language and Folklore*, 1909; G. W. B. Huntingford, "Miscellaneous Records Relating to the Nandi and Kory Tribes," *JRAI*, 1927; G. W. B. Huntingford, "The Nandi Pororiet," *JRA*, 1935; G. W. B. Huntingford, "The Political Organization of the Nandi," B.Sc. Thesis, University of Oxford, 1947 (unpublished), and the same, *The Nandi of Kenya*, London, 1953.

An excellent analysis of the political structure of some tribes of the Nandi type is given in E. E. Evans-Pritchard, "The Political Structure of the Nandi-speaking People of Kenya," *Africa*, XIII, 1940, pp. 250-68. The description given here is based on most of these sources, and especially on the various papers by G. W. B. Huntingford.

3. The literature on Plains Indians is abundant, but there exist very few full analyses. The fullest details and discussion may be found in: R. H. Lowie (ed.), "Plains Indian Age Societies—Historical and Comparative Summary," *Anthropological Papers of the American Museum of Natural History*, XI, Part XIII. Among the most important papers in this volume are: C. Wissler, "Blackfoot Societies"; R. H. Lowie, "Societies of the Hidatsa and Mandan Indian"; A. Skinner, "Societies of the Iowa Indian." See also: A. Bowers, *Mandan Social and Ceremonial Organization*, Chicago, 1950; H. Elkin, "The Northern Arapaho of Wyoming" in R. Linton (ed.), *Acculturation Among Seven Indian Tribes*, New York, 1940, pp. 207-59; L. Hanks and J. Richardson, *Tribe Under Trust*, Toronto, 1950.

There exists an interesting comparative analysis by W. F. Whyte, "Age Grading of the Plains Indians," *Man*, June, 1944, No. 56. This description follows mains R. Lowie, *Primitive Society*, which already contains some comparative material.

4. The references on the Yako are D. Forde's following papers and books: (a) "Kinship in Umor," *American Anthropologist*, vol. 41, 1939; (b) "Government in Umor," *Africa*, XII, 1939; (c) "Marriage and the Family Among the Yako in Southeastern Nigeria," *L.S.E. Monographs in Anthropology*, 1941; (d) "Ward Organization Among the Yago," *Africa*, vol. XX, 1950; (e) "Double Descent Among the Yago," A. R. Radcliffe-Brown and D. Forde, *op. cit.*

The description follows D. Forde (b) and (d).

5. The best literature on the Swazi is that by H. Kuper (Beemer): (a) "The development of the Military Organization in Swaziland," *Africa*, 1937; (b) *An African Aristocracy*, Oxford (International African Institute), 1947.

The description follows H. Beemer (a), pp. 67 ff.

6. The main authority on the Nupe are S. F. Nadel's works: (a) *A Black Byzantium*, Oxford, 1942; (b) "The Ganni Ritual of Nupi, A Study in Social Symbiosis," *Africa*, XIX, 1949.

The description here is based on: "The Ganni Ritual," pp. 177-79; *Black Byzantium*, pp. 394 ff.

7. On the Nyakyusa see: G. Wilson, "An Introduction to Nyakyusa Society," *Bantu Studies*, X (1936); G. Wilson, "Introduction to Nyakyusa Law," *Africa*, X (1937); G. Wilson, *The Land Rights of Individuals Among the Nyakyusa*, Rhodes-Livinstone Institute, paper 1; M. Wilson, *Good Company, op. cit.*

This description follows that of M. Wilson, "Nyakyusa Age–Villages," *JRAI*, vol. 79 (1951).

8. The description of Irish peasant life is based here on: C. Arensberg and S. Kimball, *Family and Community in Ireland*, pp. 132 ff., and C. Arensberg, *The Irish Countryman*, New York, 1950, pp. 107 ff.

9. The descriptive material is abundant. See for instance: R. Landis, *Adolescence and Youth*, New York, 1947; K. Davies, *Modern American Society (Readings in the Problems of Order and Change)*, 1948, pp. 627-667; H. Bell, *Youth Tell Their Story*, Washington, 1938; N. McWill and E. Matthews, *The Youth of New York City*, New York, 1940.

The best systematic descriptions are those of: A. B. Hollingshead, *Elmtown's Youth*, New York, 1949; R. L. Havighurst and H. Taba, *Adolescent Character and Personality*, New York, 1949; K. Davis, "Adolescence and the Social Structure," *op. cit.*

10. See *op. cit.* and W. F. Whyte, *Street Corner Society*, Chicago, 1943.

11. See J. Bossard, *Parent and Child*, New York, 1953, and B. Bettelheim, *Symbolic Wounds*, *op. cit.*, especially pp. 98-100.

12. See Hollingshead, *op. cit.*; Havighurst, *op. cit.*; W. F. Whyte, *op. cit.*

13. Adapted from R. Y. Havighurst and H. Taba, *op. cit.*, pp. 35-41.

14. T. Parsons, "Age and Sex in the Social Structure of the United States," in *Essays in Sociological Theory*, Glencoe, 1949.

15. On literature on working-youth movements, see in detail ch. III, note 112.

16. See on this: W. F. Whyte, *Street Corner Society, op. cit.*; A. Davies and J. Dollard, *Children of Bondage*, Washington, 1940.

The literature on English and European Youth is mostly descriptive. See for instance: B. Reed (ed.), *Eighty Thousand Adolescents, A Study of Young People in the City of Birmingham*, 1950.

Most relevant material is summarized in M. Fleming, *Adolescence*, London, 1948.

17. On juvenile delinquency and delinquent groups in general, see: Tappan, P. W., *Juvenile Delinquency*, New York, 1949; Reckless, W., *The Crime Problem*, New York, 1950; Sellin, Th., *Culture Contact and Crime*, New York, 1938.

One of the first vivid descriptions is the famous book by F. Trasher, *The Gang*, Chicago, 1927.

An interesting analysis is to be found in: S. Kobrin, "The Conflict of Values in Delinquent Areas," *American Sociological Review*, vol. 16 (1951), pp. 653-61.

18. See on this R. Merton, "Social Structure and Anomie," in *Social Theory and Social Structure*, *op. cit.*, pp. 125 ff.

19. The Israeli material is based on researches of the Research Seminar in Sociology of the Hebrew University, Jerusalem. The first phase of the research have been summarized by the author in S. N. Eisenstadt, "Youth Culture and Social Structure in Israel," *The British Journal of Sociology*, June, 1951. The second phase has been summarized by J. Ben-David, "Participation in Youth Movements and Social Status," *Megamoth*, 1954 (Hebrew). Further reports will be published subsequently.

20. The literature on German youth movements is boundless. The following should be consulted at this stage: H. Becker, *German Youth, Bond*

or Free, London, 1946; R. Schmid, German Youth Movements, A Typological Study, Ph.D., University of Wisconsin, 1939; Ch. Lütkens, *Die Deutsche Jugendbewegung*, Frankfurt/Main, 1927; H. Blueher, *Der Charakter der Jugendbewegung*, Lauenberg, 1921.

21. H. Kohn, "Youth Movements," *Encyclopedia of the Social Sciences*.

22. The term "Jugendkultur" has been coined by G. Wyneken. See, for instance, G. Wyneken, *Schule u. Jugendkultur*, Jena, 1919.

23. This phase is fully analyzed by H. Becker, *op. cit.*, ch. II.

24. The description of the Kibbutz age-grades is adopted from the author's *Age Groups and Social Structure, an analysis of some aspects of socialization in the communal and cooperative settlements in Israel*, Jerusalem, 1950, pp. 56.

25. The description here is adapted from H. Fainsod, "Youth Under Dictatorship," *American Political Science Review*, 1951.

CHAPTER III

1. In this respect our procedure differs to a certain extent from that employed in the various researches of the Cross-Cultural survey of Yale. We try to rely mainly on the fullest descriptions of given societies, using all other material only in a subsidiary way, and not assigning to informations of different value the same weights as statistical units.

2. See below, chapter IV.

3. On the various Nilo-hamitic tribes see: L. F. Nalder, *Survey of Mongolia Province*, Oxford (I.A.I.), 1937; C. G. and S. B. Seligman, *Pagan Tribes of the Nilotic Sudan*, New York, 1953; C. G. and S. B. Seligman, "The Social Origin of the Latuko," *Sudan Notes and Records*, VIII, 1925; A. C. Beaton, "The Bari, Clan and Age-Class System," *Sudan Notes and Records*, XIX, 1936, pp. 109-47; H. Driberg, *The Lango*; T. T. S. Hayley, *The Anatomy of Lango Religion and Groups*, Cambridge, 1947; and a general survey: A. Butt, *The Nilotes of the Anglo-Egyptian Sudan and Uganda*, Survey of Africa, London, 1952.

4. On the Karamajong cluster see: P. Gulliver, "The Karamajong Cluster," *Africa*, vol. XXII, 1952, pp. 1-22; P. Gulliver, *A Preliminary Survey of the Turkana Communities*, School of African Studies, vol. 26, Capetown, 1951.

5. On the main tribes of the Nandi group see (in addition to the literature on the Nandi given in chap. II): J. G. Peristiany, *The Social System of the Kipsigis*, London, 1939; J. G. Peristiany, "The Age-Set System of the Pastoral Pokot," *Africa*, XXI, 1951, pp. 188-206; 279-302; J. Beecher, *The Suk*, Oxford, 1911.

The extensive bibliography may be found in I. Schapera, *Some Problems of Anthropological Research in Kenya Colony*, I.A.I. Memorandum XXIII, Oxford, 1949; and see also the brilliant summary of E. E. Evans-Pritchard, "The Political Structure of the Nandi-speaking Peoples of Kenya," *Africa*, XIII, 1940, pp. 250-68.

6. On the Masai see: M. Merker, *Die Masai*, Berlin, 1904; R. S. B. Leakey, "Some Notes on the Masai of Kenya Colony," *J.R.A.I.*, vol. 60, 1930, pp. 185-209; D. S. Fox, "Further Notes on the Masai of Kenya Colony," *J.R.A.I.*,

vol. 60, 1930, pp. 447-467; D. S. Fox, "An Administrative Survey of the Masai Soc. System, *Tankanaika Notes and Records,* 1951.

7. On the Meru, Kamba, Kikuyu see: C. Cagnolo, *The Akikuyu,* Nyeri, 1933; K. R. Dundas, "The Kikuyu Rika" (age sets), *Man,* 1908, vol. 8, pp. 180-82; J. Kenyatta, *Facing Mount Kenya, The Tribal Life of the Gikuyu,* London, 1938; J. F. Middletown, Systems of Land Tenure among the Bantu of East Africa, PSC Thesis, Oxford, 1949; J. F. Middletown, *The Kikuyu and Kamba of Kenya,* Ethnographic Survey of Africa, London, 1953; N. Larby, *The Kamba,* Nairobi, 1944; K. G. Lindblom, *The Okamba in British East Africa,* Uppsala, 1920; W. M. Laughton, *The Meru,* Nairobi, 1922; E. M. Holding, "Some Preliminary Notes on Meru Age Grades," *Man,* XLII, 1942, No. 31.

8. The literature on the Galla is not very systematic. The best accounts, from the point of view of our analysis, are those of A. Werner, "The Galla of East African Protectorate, *Y. Afr. Soc.* 13, pp. 121-42; 262-87; E. Cerulli, *Studii Etiopici,* Roma, 1936; and also see E. Jensen, *Im Lande des Gada,* pp. 315-35, 335-83.

H. Driberg, in his comparative study of age groups (see "Age Grades," *Enc. Britannica*) alludes to the Galla as the originators of the "cyclical" system, but does not provide us with any additional references.

See also, J. H. Driberg, *At Home with the Savage,* London, 1938.

A recent very good comparative description of some of the age set systems of some of these tribes is to be found in A. H. J. Prins, *East African Age-Class System* (Galla, Kipsigis, Kikuyu), Groeningen, 1953.

9. On the Murle see: B. A. Lewis, The Murle Political System, B.Sc. Thesis, Oxford, 1950.

10. We do not know of any full account of the Chagga. Raumm's analysis (*Chagga Childhood*) is very extensive on their educational system, but does not give any full description of the whole society. Some information may be found in: Ch. Dundas, *Kilimanjara and Its People,* London, 1924; B. Guttmann, *Recht der Dschagga,* München, 1931.

11. On the Bantu-Kavirondo, the best account is: G. Wagner, *The Bantu of North Kavirondo,* Oxford (Intern. African Institute), 1951, and his paper in M. Fortes and E. E. Evans-Pritchard (ed.), *African Political Systems,* 1940.

12. On the Gussi (Kissi) see: P. Meyer, *The Lineage Principle in Gussi Society,* I.A.I Memor. XXIV, Oxford, 1949; P. Meyer, "The Joking of Pals in Gussi Society," *African Studies,* vol. X, 1951, pp. 27-41.

13. On the Dorobo see: G. W. B. Huntingford, "The Social Institutions of the Dorobo," *Anthropos,* XLVI, 1951, pp. 1-49; G. W. B. Huntingford, "The Social Origin of the Dorobo," *African Studies,* I, 1942, pp. 183-99.

On the Pokomo see: A. H. J. Prins, *The Coastal Tribes of N. Eastern Bantu,* Ethnogr. Survey of Africa, I.A.I., London, 1952.

14. On the various tribes of the Nuba Group see: S. F. Nadel, *The Nuba,* Oxford, 1947.

15. On the Eskimo see: J. Mirsky, "The Eskimo of Greenland," in M. Mead, *Cooperation and Competition among Primitive Peoples,* N.T., 1937, pp. 51-87.

16. See Allan R. Holmberg, *Nomads of the Long Bow,* Smithsonian Institution, Inst. of Social Anthropology, 10, 1950; K. Oberg, *The Terena and*

the *Caduero of the S. Monto Grosso*, Smithsonian Institutions, 1949; J. Henry, *Jungle People*, New York, 1951.

Many similar cases may be found among North American tribes like the Ojibwa, Papago, etc., and in the simplest Australian tribes. See for instance A. Elkin, *The Australian Aborigines*, 1932 and A. R. Radcliffe-Brown, *The Social Organization of Australian Tribes*, Oceania Monographs, 1931.

17. *Ibid.*

18. On the Tonga see: E. Colson, "The Plateau Tonga," in E. Colson and M. Gluckman, *Seven Tribes of British Central Africa*, Oxford (Rhodes-Livingstone Institute), 151, pp. 94-164.

19. See P. Gulliver, *The Preliminary Survey, op. cit.*

20. *Ibid.*, pp. 194-95.

21. The excellent material on the Tallensi we owe to the various works and books of Prof. Fortes: *Web of Kinship Among the Tallensi*, 1943; *The Dynamics of Clanship Among the Tallensi*, 1945; *Social and Psychological Aspects of Education in Taleland*, Oxford (I.A.I.), 1938, and his lecture on "The Structure of the Unilineal Descent Groups," *American Anthropologist*, vol. 66, 1953, pp. 17 ff., which touches on more general problems and to which this analysis is heavily indebted.).

22. For such cases see, for example: F. Eggan, *The Social Organization of the Western Pueblos*, Chicago, 1951; Ch. Wisdom, *The Chorti Indians of Guatemala*, Chicago, 1947; W. Goodwin, *The Organization of the Western Apache*, Chicago, 1943.

Many similar instances can be found in other parts of the world such as the Trobriands, The Tikopia, The Malekula, etc. See: B. Malinowski, *Coral Gardens and their Magic*, London, 1935; B. Malinowski, *Sex and Repression in Savage Society*, London, 1937; R. Firth, *We, The Tikopia*, London, 1936, especially ch. XII, XIV; B. Deacon, *Malekula* (ed. by C. Wedgewood), London, 1934. And see also, for additional comparative material, R. Redfield, *The Folk Culture of Yucatan*, Chicago, 1943; D. Mac Rae Taylor, *The Black Carib of British Honduras*, New York, 1951; T. Gladwin and S. B. Sarason, *Truk-Man in Paradise*, New York, 1953; G. P. Murdock and W. W. Goodenough, "Social Organization of Truk, *SJA*, III, 1947; A. R. Radcliffe-Brown, *The Andaman Islanders*, Cambridge, 1933; E. and P. Beaglehole, "Ethnology of Pukapuka," *Bulletin of the Bishop Museum*, CL, 1938; R. Williamson, *Social and Political Systems of Central Polynesia*, Cambridge, 1924.

For the material on traditional Jewish Society, I am indebted to my colleague Dr. J. Katz for his *Traditional Jewish Society* (Hebrew, mimeographed, Jerusalem, The Hebrew University, 1954).

23. *Ibid.*

24. See E. E. Evans-Pritchard, "The Nuer, Age Sets," *op. cit.*

25. P. Meyer, *The Lineage Principle in Gussi Society, op. cit.*; A Wagner, *op. cit.*

26. This analysis of the Nandi group is heavily indebted to the following account of E. E. Evans-Pritchard, "The Political Structure of the Nandi-speaking People," *op. cit.* On Pokomo, etc., see A. H. J. Prins, *op. cit.* The new interpretation of the Meru-Kamba group is suggested by J. Middletown, *op. cit.*

27. B. Lewis, *op. cit.*

28. P. Meyer, "The Joking of Pals," *op. cit.*

29. See S. F. Nadel, *The Nuba, op. cit.*

30. For the meaning of symbiotic clanship see: S. F. Nadel, "Social Symbiosis and Tribal Organization," *Man*, 1938, No. 85.

31. On the Yakö see the literature mentioned in Chapter II. On the Ibo and Ibibio see: C. K. Meek, *Law and Authority in a Nigerian Tribe*, Oxford, 1937; M. M. Green, *The Ibo Village Affairs*, London, 1948; P. A. Talbot, *The Peoples of Southern Nigeria*, Oxford, 1926; P. A. Talbot, *Tribes of the Niger Delta*, London, 1932; P. A. Talbot, *In the Shadow of the Bush*, London, 1922; D. Forde and G. I. Jones, *The Ibo and Ibibio-speaking People of S.E. Nigeria*, Ethnographic Survey of Africa, I.A.I., London, 1950; M. S. W. Jeffreys, "Age Groups among the Ika and Kindred People," *African Studies*, vol. IX, 1950.
On the various Yoruba tribes see: N. A. Fadipe, The Sociology of the Yoruba, Ph.D. Thesis, London, 1939 (unpublished Ms.); W. R. Bas-com, "The Principle of Seniority in Social Structure of the Yoruba," *Amer. Anthrop.* XLIV ,1942, pp. 37-46; D. Forde, *The Yoruba-speaking Peoples of S. Western Nigeria*, Ethnographic Survey of Africa, I.A.I., London, 1951.

32. On the structure of the Ibo and Ibibio settlements see: Green, *op. cit.*, pp. 75, 124; Meek, *op. cit.*; Talbot (1922), pp. 311 ff.; Forde and Jones, *op. cit.*, pp. 12-15, 15-24, 69-70, 71-76; Jeffreys, *op. cit.*; H. K. Offonry, "Age-Grades, Their Power and Influence in Village Life," *W. Afr. Review*, vol. 19, Dec. 1948, pp. 1978-9.

33. There exists but little systematic analysis of African peasant communities. One of the best overall descriptions can be found in: H. Labouret, *Paysans D'Afrique Occidentale*, Paris, 1941, pp. 120 ff., pp. 172-6 ff. And see also: D. Paulme, *Organisation Sociale des Dogons*, Paris, 1940, pp. 377, 469; and D. Tait, "An Analytical Commentary on the Social Structure of the Dogon," *Africa*, vol. XX, 1950, pp. 175-199.
See also, for a kinship-centered peasant society D. Paulme, *Les gens du riz*, Paris, 1953.

34. On these more specialized activities see: Forde, Warde Organization, *op. cit.*; P. A. Talbot, *Peoples of Southern Nigeria*, Oxford, 1926, pp. 530-51; Meek, *op. cit.*, pp. 115 ff.; Labouret, *op. cit.* Generally this system of authority has been well analyzed by P. Brown, "Patterns of Authority in West Africa," *Africa*, XXXI, 1951, pp. 261-78.

35. For such a comparison of the Yoruba, see: Fadipe, *op. cit.*, pp. 772-74; Cpt. J. Bridel, Notes on Yafba Age-Grades (unpublished Ms., courtesy of the I.A.I.); P. G. Harris, Notes on the Age-Gades among the Owe Yoruba (unpublished Ms., courtesy of the I.A.I.); Talbot, *ibid.* And see also Basden, *The Niger Ibos*, 1938, p. 139.

36. See Fadipe, *op. cit.*; Talbot, *ibid.*; D. Forde, *The Yoruba-speaking People, op. cit.*, pp. 16-21.

37. C. Bascom, The Principle of Seniority, *op. cit.*

38. See on these, K. Little, *The Mende of Sierra Leone*, London, 1951, in which all the previous publications of the author are summarized; E. Schwab, "Tribes of Liberian Hinterland," *Papers of the Peabody Museum of Am. Arch. and Anth.*, Vol. XXXI, Harvard, 1947.
A more detailed discussion of these societies and their bearing on problems will be found in chapter IV: D. Westerman, *Die Kpelle*, Goettingen,

1921; M. McCulloch, *Peoples of Sierra Leone Protectorate*, Ethnographic Survey of Africa (I.A.I.), London, 1951. And see also a good summary in A. Hoebel, *Man in Primitive World*, pp. 302 ff.

39. See Bascomb, "The Sociological Role," *op. cit.*; Little, *ibid.*

40. See W. F. Whyte, "Age-Grading of the Plains Indians," *Man*, May-June, 1944, No. 56, and R. Lowie, *The Crow Indians*, New York, 1935, *passim*; Jane Richardson, *Law and Status among the Kiowa Indians*, Mon. of the Am. Eth. Society, I, 1940; B. Mishkin, *Rank and Warfare among the Plains Indians*, Mon. of the Am. Eth. Society, 1941.

41. See M. Bowers, *Mandan Social and Ceremonial Organization*, Chicago, 1950, p. 38.

42. This similarity and historical interconnection has been fully analyzed by R. Lowie, "Plains Indians, Age-Societies, Historical and Comparative Summary," *Anthrop. Papers of the Am. Inst. of Natural History*, XI, part XIII.

43. See H. Elkin, "The Northern Arapaho of Wyoming," in R. Linton (ed.), *Acculturation in Seven Indian Tribes*, New York, 1940, pp. 207-59.

44. See F. Eggan, *Social Organization of the Western Pueblos*, Chicago, 1951. Eggan's analysis does fully show that the degree of integration in such a lineage-centered society may be very small, especially if the comolementary of kinship are weak. See on this, in greater detail, M. Titiev, "Old Oraibi," *Papers of the Peabody Mus. of A. Arch. and Eth.*, Harvard, vol. XXII.

45. P. Drucker, "Rank, Wealth and Kinship in Northwest Coast Society," *Am. Anthrop.*, LXI, pp. 55-56; A. H. Goughton, "Yokuts and Western Mono Social Organization," *Am. Anthrop.*, XLVII, 1945.

See also E. Colson, *The Makah Indians*, Manchester, 1953.

See also, for comparative analysis, D. G. Mandelbaum, "The Plains Cree," *Anthropological Papers of the American Museum of Natural History*, vol. XXXVI, pt. II, New York, 1940, and, C. D. Forde, *Ethnography of the Yuma Indians*, University of California Publications in American Archeology and Ethnology, XXVII, 1931.

46. *Ibid.*

47. On the Swazi see the publications of H. Kuper, mentioned in chapter II, as well as: H. Kruper, *The Swazi*, Ethnographic Survey of Africa, London, 1952.

48. On the Zulu see: M. Gluckman, *The Kingdom of the Zulu in Afri can Political Systems*, *op. cit.*, pp. 25-26; E. J. Krige, *The Social System of the Zulu*, London, 1936; T. Bryant, *The Zulu People*, 1949, pp. 461-97, *et passim*.

48. G. W. K. Mahlobo and E. J. Krige, "Transition from Childhood to Adulthood amongst the Zulus," *Bantu Studies*, VIII, 1934, pp. 157-93.

See also the very interesting comparison by W. S. Ferguson, "The Zulus and Spartans, A Comparison of their Military System," *African Harvard Studies*, II, 1918, pp. 197-224.

49. On the Tswana groups see I. Shapera, *A Handbook of Eswana Law and Custom*, Oxford, I.A.I., 1940; I. Shapera, "The Political Annals of a Tswana Tribe," *Communications from the School of African Studies*, N. 18, November, 1947, Cape Town; I. Shapera, "The Ngwato," in *African Political Systems*, *op. cit.*, pp. 56-83.

50. I. Shapera, "The Bakxatla Baxatela," *Africa*, VI, 1933.

51. On the Ashanti, see the classic work of Rattray on *Ashanti Law and Constitution*, 1929; and the modern summary analysis of K. Busia, *The Position of the Chief Among the Ashanti*, Oxford (Intern. Afric. Institute), 1951.

52. On the Bemba see: A. Richards, "The Bemba," in *African Political Systems*, *op. cit.*, pp. 83-121; A. Richards, "The Bemba," in *Seven Tribes of British Central Africa*, *op. cit.*, pp. 164-91; E. Whiteley, *Bemba and Related Peoples of N. Rhodesia*, Ethn. Surv. of Africa, I.A.I., London, 1951.

53. On the Pondo see: M. Hunter, *Reactions to Conquest*, Oxford Cronin, *The Banut Tribes*, very valuable for comparisons from the point of view of our analysis.

54. On the Xhosa group: G. P. Lestrade, "Some Notes on the Political Organization of Certain Khoisa-speaking Tribes, *African Roy. Soc.*, XXIV, 1937. For similar comparisons, see also: I. Shapera, *The Khoisan Peoples of South Africa*, London, 1930; G. P. Lestrade, "Some Notes on the Political Organization of the Bechuana," *S. Afr. Journal of Science*, XXV, 1925, pp. 427-32; H. G. Luttig, *The Religious System and Social Organization of the Herero*, Utrecht.

55. The fullest analysis of the Lozi is given by: M. Gluckman, "The Lozi," in *Seven Tribes of British Central Africa*, *op. cit.*, pp. 1-94.

56. On the Lobedu see: E. and J. Krige, *The Realm of the Rain Queen*, Oxford (I.A.I.), 1943.

57. The fullest up-to-date account of the Basuto is that of: H. Ashton, *The Basuto*, Oxford (I.A.I.), 1951.

58. See S. F. Nadel, *The Nuba*, *op. cit.*

59. See Mr. Hershkovits, *Dahomey*, New York, 1937.

60. See I. Shapera in *African Pol. Systems*, *op. cit.* And G. P. Lestrade, 1937, *op. cit.*

61. See M. Hunter, *op. cit.*, pp. 383 ff. A. Richards in *African Political Systems*, *op. cit.* And the work cited in Notes 51 and 54.

62. M. Hunter, *op. cit.*, p. 395 ff.

63. The best description of the Kgotla can be found in: I. Shapera, *op. cit.*, and I. Shapera, "Value and Opportunity of the Bechuanaland Kgotla," *London Times*, August, 1951.

64. See M. Gluckman, *op. cit.*

65. J. and E. Krige, *The Realm of the Rain Queen*, *op. cit.*

66. S. F. Nadel, *The Nuba*, *op. cit.*

67. The material on the Inca and the Aztec Empires which is pertinent to our problem is summarized in: W. P. Murdock, *Our Primitive Contemporaries*, New York, 1949, pp. 402-50; C. Wissler, *The American Indian*, New York, 1938; E. Valliant, *The Aztecs*, Pelican Books, 1949.

67a. The fullest account of the Nupe is given by S. F. Nadel, *Block Byzantium*, Oxford (I.A.I.), 1943.

67b. *Op. cit.*, pp. 115-47.

67c. A type of age group which seems to be similar to those of Nupe has been reported by R. Delacrozier, "Les Institutions Politiques et Sociales des Populations dites Bamileke," *Etudes Cameronnaises*, Numeros 25-6, 27-8, 1949. The data are, however, too vague to allow for any detailed comparison.

67d. See H. Miner, *The Primitive City of Timbuctoo*, Princeton, 1953, pp. 151-75.

68. The material on Spartan age groups is very abundant and most explicitly stated in Plutarch's life of Lycurgus. The best summaries of modern research on Spartan social organization in general and on the age groups in particular is to be found in: K. T. M. Chrimes, *Ancient Sparta*, Manchester, 1949; and H. Michell, *Sparta*, Cambridge, 1951. See also Rutherford, U. T., "The Public School of Sparta," *Greece and Rome*, III, 1934.

69. *Op. cit.*

70. The material on the social and political structure of Athens is, of course, abundant. G. Glotz's classic *The Greek City* is still the best single account. See also the appropriate chapters in the *Cambridge Ancient History*, vol. V, and P. Cloche's, *La Democratie Athenienne*, Paris, 1950.

71. A good general description of education in Greece can be found in K. Freeman, *The Schools of Hellas*, Cambridge, 1911, as well as K. Grasenberger, *Erziehung und Unterricht im Klassischen Altertum*. The best modern treatise is H. I. Marrou, *Histoire de l'education dans l'antiquité*, 1950. For the summaries of recent research it is useful to consult the articles on education and epheboi in the Oxford Classical Dictionary, 1948, and for fuller discussion in Pauly-Wissowa-Kroll, *Real-Encyclopädie*.

72. An interesting hypothesis on the development of the ephebia from tribal initiation ceremonies, which is not, however, fully validated, may be found in G. Thompson, *Aeschylus and Athens*, London, 1941, especially ch. VII.

73. On the Hellenistic cities see A. J. M. Jones, *The Greek City*, Oxford, 1940.

74. On the Roman political system, see: E. Meyer, *Römischer Staat und Staatsgedanke*, Zürich, 1948; R. Syme, *The Roman Revolution*, Oxford, 1939. G. E. M. De Ste. Croix, "Suffragium, from Vote to Patronage," *British Journal of Sociology*, March, 1954.

75. On Roman education see: Marrou, *op. cit.*, pt. III, ch. I, II, IV, V, VI, VII, and also T. L. Jarman, *Landmarks in the History of Education*, London, 1951, ch. II. Main sources are Tacitus, *Dialogus de Oratoribus*, chap. 28-32; Plutarch's life of Cato; Cicero, *De Republica*.

76. See Quintillian's *Institutio Oratoria*, ed. by F. H. Colson, Cambridge, 1924, chap. III.

77. See above, chapter I.

78. See, for instance, E. E. Evans-Pritchard, "The Nuer, Age-Sets," *op. cit.*

79. See, for instance, G. W. Mahlobo and E. J. Krige, *op. cit.*

80. J. H. Driberg, "The Institution of Age-Grades," *Congres de l'Institute International des langues et des civilisations africaines*, Paris, 1931, pp. 199-208.

81. See E. M. Holding, *op. cit.*

82. On women's age groups see most of the material presented above, and especially: H. Kuper, *African Aristocracy*, *op. cit.*; Huntingford, *Social and Political Organization of the Nandi*, *op. cit.*

83. Bridel, *op. cit.*

84. On the best friend, see for instance, M. Herkovits, *op. cit.* On the difference between friendship and age group relations see: S. F. Nadel, *Black Byzantium*, *op. cit.*, pp. 398-99.

85. P. Meyer, "The Joking of Pals," *op. cit.*, p. 30.

86. See E. E. Evans-Pritchard, "The Nuer, Age-Sets," *op. cit., passim;* G.

Wagner, *op. cit.;* D. Forde, "Marriage and the Family Among the Yako," *op. cit., passim.*

87. See, for instance: D. Forde, *ibid.;* E. M. Holding, *op. cit.;* C. K. Meek, *op. cit.;* and the materials on various primitive peasant communities.

88. The self-discipline enacted by the age group is described in most of the material on age groups. See especially the material on the Yako and Swazi, in chapter II, and in even greater detail the material on the Nupe and the Kikuyu, and on all the African peasant communities; and see also A. Tessier, "Les societes d'enfants et l'enseignement local," *Bull. de l'enseignement de l'A.O.F.,* 1941, No. 105. See also, obviously, the abundant material on Sparta.

89. See H. Kuper, *op. cit.;* J. Krige, *The Social System of the Zulu, op. cit., passim.;* L. S. D. Leakey and D. S. Fox, *op. cit., passim.*

90. See, for instance, M. Fortes, the various works on the Tallensi cited above and F. Eggan, *op. cit.*

91. On some peasant societies and material bearing on our problems see: H. Fei, *Peasant Life in China,* London, 1940; J. Embree, *A Japanese Village,* London, 1944; R. Firth, *Malay Fishermen,* London, 1946; and a more general discussion in R. Firth, *Social Organization,* London, 1951.

92. This point has been stressed by A. R. Radcliffe-Brown in his Introduction to *African Systems of Kinship and Marriage, op. cit.,* pp. 28-29.

93. It is difficult to evaluate the existing materials fully from this point of view, as most ethnographers did not put to themselves this question. The general impression, however, is that such a compatibility did exist. See especially: S. F. Nadel, *Black Byzantium, op. cit., passim;* O. Raumm, *Chagga Childhood, op. cit., passim;* and the material on the Masai given in Note 6.

94. See, for instance, H. Kuper, *op. cit.*

95. For excellent descriptions of the part of age groups in integrative ceremonies, see: S. F. Nadel, *Black Byzantium, op. cit.;* D. Forde, "Integrative Aspects of the Yako First Fruit Rituals," *JRAI,* LXXIX, 1949, pp. 1-91; H. Kuper, *op. cit.*

96. The concept of "modern society" is used here in a very broad way, following mainly T. Parsons' various discussions (especially of Max Weber).

97. Obviously the different trends characteristic of "modern society" are not distributed equally among various concrete societies and the discussion here is mainly given in an "ideal type way." See also J. Schumpeter, *Capitalism, Socialism and Democracy.* A good collection of material on modern American society can be found in K. Davis *et al.* (ed.), *Modern American Society,* New York, 1948.

98. Our assumption here is that loyalty to any given community has a very strong particularistic connotation. See T. Parsons, *The Social System, op. cit.*

99. See on this, in general, K. Folsom, *The Family and Democratic Society,* London, 1945; W. Waller and R. Hill, *The Family,* New York, 1950; K. Davis *et al., op. cit.,* pt. IX; J. Bossard, *Parent and Child,* Pennsylvania, 1953.

100. See T. Parsons, "Age and Sex in the Social Structure," *op. cit.,* pp. 218-33; R. Williams, *American Society,* New York, 1951, Chapter 4.

101. The problem of discontinuity has been analyzed by R. Benedict, "Continuities and Discontinuities in Culture Conditioning," *Psychiatry,* I,

1938; K. Davis, "The Sociology of Parent-Youth Conflict," *Am. Soc. Review*, Vol. 5, 1940.

102. See T. Parsons, "The Kinship System of the Contemporary United States," in *Essays, op. cit.*, pp. 233-51.

103. See Notes 68-76, above.

104. A good analysis of educational institutions can be found in R. Williams, *American Society, op. cit.*; Ll. Warner *et al., Who Shall Be Educated*, New York, 1945. A general survey of the evolution of modern education in relation to various social movements is found in N. Hans, *Comparative Education*, London, 1947. And see also H. Kruckenberg, *Die Schulklasse als Lebensform*, Leipzig, 1927.

105. See K. Davis, "Adolescence and the Social Structure," *The Annals of the American Academy of Political Science*, Nov. 1944, and the May 1948 issue of the *Journa lof Educational Sociology* on "School Culture and Group Life." See also V. Mallison (ed.), *The Adolescent at School*, London, 1949.

106. T. Parsons, *op. cit.*

107. On the problem of adolescent ego identity in modern society in general and in its relation to school see: M. Sherif, *An Outline of Social Psychology*, New York, 1948, pp. 315-39; E. Erikson, *Childhood and Society*, London, 1950, pts. III, IV.

108. See A. Hollingshead, *Elmtown's Youth, op. cit.*; A. Havighurst and H. Taba, *Adolescent Character and Personality, op. cit.*

109. On the English public schools see in greater detail the references in ch. IV.

110. A good general survey of such agencies can be found, among other places, in the Nov. 1944 issue of the *Annals of the American Academy, op. cit.* On political, party and youth organizations in various countries, see: A. C. Percival, *Youth Will Be Led*, London, 1951; W. M. MacEager, *Making Men—The History of Boys' Clubs and Related Movements in Great Britain*, London, 1953; *Eighty Thousand Adolescents, A Study of Young People in Birmingham*, directed by B. Held, London, 1950; *Youth Organisations of Great Britain*, 2nd Issue, 1949; L. A. Meneffee and M. M. Chambers, *American Youth*, Washington, D.C., 1938; the Nov. 1937 issue of the *Annals of the American Academy of Pol. and Soc. Science* and the survey on *Danish Youth* by the Danish Gov't Youth Commission. See also H. Hartman, *Die Junge Generation in Europa*, Berlin, 1930.

111. See one of the textbooks on juvenile delinquency and prevention, such as those by Tappan, Reckless, etc.

112. On working youth movements see: G. Dehn, *Proletarische Jugend*, Berlin, 1929; K. Korn, *Die Arbeiterjugendbewegung*, Berlin, 1923; K. Bendarik, *Der junge Arbeiter von Heute*, Stuttgart, 1953. On some specific problems of working youth see the surveys of the Danish Youth Commission and also the forthcoming publication on youth movements in Israel.

See also H. E. O. James and F. T. Moore, "Adolescent Leisure in a Working Class District," *Occupational Psychology*, vol. XIV (July 1940) and vol. XVIII (Jan. 1944). And see also T. Ferguson and J. Cunnison, *The Young Wage Earner*, Oxford, 1951.

113. Taken from A. C. Percival, *op. cit.*, p. 69. For programs of these various organizations see mainly the literature mentioned in Note 110. See also G. Coyle, *Group Work with American Youth*, New York, 1945.

114. See on this, K. Davis, "Adolescence and the Social Structure," *op. cit.*, and C. M. Fleming, *Adolescence*, London, 1948.

115. A general survey of this problem may be found in G. Watson, *Youth after Sonflict*, New York, 1947, and in G. Eichbaum, *Die Krise der modernen Jugend im Spiegel der Dichtung*, Erfurt, 1930.

116. See S. Hall, *Adolescence*, New York, 1908, and K. Mannheim, "The Problem of Generations," in *Essays*.

117. See some of the textbooks on history of modern education, e.g., T. H. Jarman, *Landmarks in the History of Education*, London, 1951, ch. XIII.

118. H. Brunswick, *La Crise de l'état Prussien de XVIIIème siècle et la genese de da mentalité romantique*, Paris, 1948. For the genesis of youth movements see: F. Jugman, "Autorität und Sexual Moral in der freien bürgerlichen Jugendbewegung," in M. Horkheimer (ed.), *Studien über Autorität und Familie*, 1936, pp. 669-706; H. Becker, *German Youth, Bond or Free, op. cit.*, pt. I; Ch. Luetkens, *Die Deutsche Jugendbewegung*, Frankfurt am Main, 1925.

119. For general material on migrations from this point of view see: W. Thomas and F. Znaniecki, *The Polish Peasant in Europe and America*, New York, 1927, and a general summary in S. N. Eisenstadt, "Delinquent Group Formation among Immigrant Youth," *British Journal of Delinquency*, Vol. II, 1951, pp. 34-45.

120. On these different possibilities inherent in situations of culture contact see: A. I. Hallowell, "The Psychosociological Aspects of Acculturation," in R. Linton, *The Study of Man in the World Crisis*, New York, 1946; S. N. Eisenstadt, "The Oriental Jews in Palestine," *Jewish Social Studies*, July 1950.

121. See M. Levy, *The Family Transition in Modern China*, Harvard, 1949, pt. II, and also O. Lang, *Chinese Family and Society*, New Haven, 1946, especially ch. XX.

122. On this see the work of J. Ben-David (Gross), On the Decompositions of the Traditional Jewish Community in Hungary, M. A. Thesis, Hebrew University (in Hebrew), published in the *Hebrew Historical Quarterly*, Zion, 1953. See in general, on this, the anthology *On Youth Problems in Israel* (Hebrew), Tel Aviv, 1937.

123. See K. M. Pannikar, *Asia and Western Dominance*, London, 1953, especially pp. 45 ff.; H. Th. Fisher, *Kinderaantal en Kinderleven in Indonesie*, Den Haag, 1950, ch. III; J. M. Pluvier, *Overzicht van de Ontwikkelig der Nationalistische Beweging in Indonesie*, Den Haag, 1953, pp. 158-55; W. H. Kiang, *The Ideological Background of the Chinese Student Movement*, Columbia, 1948; Wendel Wermann, *Aus dem Südslavischen Resorgimento*, Gotha, 1921.

124. See I. Childe, *Italian or American?* New Haven, 1943; W. L. Whyte, *Street Corner Society*, Chicago, 1943.

125. Generally on peer-culture in its relation to immigrant children see: I. Bossard, *Sociology of Child Development*, New York, 1949, pp. 493-520.

126. See the author's discussions in: S. N. Eisenstadt, "The Oriental Jews in Palestine," *op. cit.*

127. On European rural society see in R. Maspetiol, *L'ordre eternal des champs*, Paris, 1947, and G. Friedmann (ed.), *Villes et Campagnes*, Paris, 1953.

128. E. H. Huges, *French Canada in Transition*, London, 1945; H. Miner, *St. Denis, A French Canadian Parish*, Chicago, 1939.

129. On rural society in the U.S.A., and for a general theoretical discussion of rural societies see: J. H. Kolb and E. S. Brunner, *A Study of Rural Society*, New York, 1952, pp. 244-56, 313-36, and also K. Davis *et al.,.Modern American Society, op. cit.*, pt. IX.

130. H. Miner, *op. cit.*

131. See K. Davis, "Adolescence and the Social Structure," *op. cit.*, who summarizes the evidence. For developments in England see H. C. Dent, *Growth in English Education*, 1946-52, London, 1954.

132. A full discussion and analysis of the distribution of age groups in various sectors of Israel society is given in S. N. Eisenstadt, "Youth Culture and Social Structure in Israel," *British Journal of Sociology*, June, 1951.

133. The comparison between the Moshav and the Kibbutz is based on S. N. Eisenstadt, *Age Groups and Social Structure: A Comparison of Some Aspects of Socialization in the Cooperative and the Communal Settlements in Israel*, Jerusalem, 1950.

134. See K. Davis, "Adolescence and the Social Structure," *op. cit.*

135. See H. Dimock, *Rediscovering the Adolescent*, New York, 1949; C. Zachry, *Emotion and Conduct in Adolescence*, New York, 1940; P. Blos, *The Adolescent Personality*, New York, 1941; and the survey on Birmingham youth cited in Note 100.

136. See M. Sherif and H. Cantril, *The Psychology of Ego Involvement*, New York, 1947; E. H. Erikson, *Childhood and Society, op. cit.*; C. M. Fleming, *Adolescence*, London, 1948.

137. See J. H. Bossard, *Parent and Child*, Philadelphia, 1953, ch. XIV.

138. See E. Biolds and E. Josephson, *op. cit.*, for a full illustration of this problem among American youth.

CHAPTER IV

1. See R. Linton, *The Study of Man*, 1936, pp. 272 ff.

2. See, on these tribes, the various works mentioned in Ch. II. Most of the references in this chapter are identical with those in the former chapters and for details (date, etc.) the reader is referred to those chapters.

3. See E. E. Evans-Pritchard, *The Nuer, op. cit.*; G. B. Huntingford, *The Nandi, op. cit.*

4. *Ibid.*, and the other relevant literature mentioned above.

5. See C. K. Meek, *Law and Authority in a Nigerian Tribe, op. cit.*; W. J. Bridel, "Notes on Yagba Age Grades," *op. cit.*; and P. L. Harris, "Notes on Age Grades among the Owe Yamba," *op. cit.*

6. See D. Forde and G. I. Jones, *The Ibo and Ibibio-speaking People, op. cit.*; W. J. Bridel, *op. cit.*; and P. Harris, *op. cit.*

7. W. J. Bridel, *op. cit.*; P. C. Harris, *op. cit.*

8. See S. F. Nadel, *The Nuba, op. cit.* Ch. VII.

9. *Ibid.*

10. See H. Kuper, *An African Aristocracy, op. cit.*; I. Schapera, *Handbook of Tswana Law, op. cit.*; E. and J. Krige, *The Social System of the Zulu, op. cit.*

11. H. Kuper, *op. cit.*
12. *Ibid.*
13. M. Miner, *The Primitive City of Timbuctoo, op. cit.*
14. See on this R. Lowie, *Primitive Society, op. cit.,* Chs. X, XI; and A. Hoebel, *Man in the Primitive World,* New York, 1949, Ch. XXI.
15. W. La Barre, *The Peyote Cult,* Yale University Studies in Anthropology.
. 16. *Ibid.*
17. W. F. Whyte, "Age Grading of the Plains Indians," *op. cit.*
18. *Ibid.*
19. See R. Lowie, *Primitive Society, op. cit.,* Ch. X; and W. H. R. Rivers, *History of Melanesian Society,* Cambridge, 1914, vol. I, pp. 138 ff., vol. II, pp. 250 ff.
20. R. Lowie, *op. cit.,* and also his earlier discussion in "Plains Indians Age Societies," in *Papers of the American Museum of Natural History, op. cit.*
21. S. F. Nadel, *Black Byzantium, op. cit.*
22. See Peristiany's analysis of the Pogot (Suk) in "The Age Set System of the Pokot," *op. cit.;* and also A. H. J. Prins, "East African Age Systems," *op. cit.*
23. See D. Forde, "Ward Organization Among the Yako, *op. cit.;* H. Kuper, *An African Aristocracy, op. cit.*
24. See, for instance, W. B. Huntingford, *op. cit.;* A. H. J. Prins, *op. cit.;* and any other description of age groups of these societies cited above.
25. See the literature on Ancient Greece listed in Notes to ch. III.
26. See the Summary in G. P. Murdock, *Our Primitive Contemporaries,* New York, 1949, Chs. XIII, XIV.
27. S. F. Nadel, *Black Byzantium, op. cit.*
28. D. Forde and G. Jones, *The Ibo and Ibibio, op. cit.* and C. K. Meek, *Law and Authority, op. cit.*
29. See M. Gluckman, *Rituals of Rebellion, in S.E. Africa,* Manchester, 1954, as well as H. Kuper, *On African Aristocracy, op. cit.*
30. See S. F. Nadel, *Black Byzantium, op. cit.*
31. See K. L. Little, *The Mende of Sierra-Leone, op. cit.*
32. G. Schwab, *Tribes of Liberian Hinterland, op. cit.*
33. See R. Lowie, *Primitive Society, op. cit.*
34. K. L. Little, *op. cit.*
35. See, in addition to the literature mentioned above, also D. Westerman, *Die Kpelle, op. cit.*
36. E. Beaglehole, "The Polynesian Maori," *Journal of the Polynesian Society,* 43, 1940; and see E. and P. Beaglehole, *Some Modern Maoris,* Wellington, 1946.
37. See, for instance, M. Mead, "Social Organizations of Manua," *Bishop Museum Bulletin* 76, 1930; E. and P. Beaglehole, "Ethnology of Pukapuka," *Bishop Museum Bulletin* 150, 1938; G. McGregor, "Ethnology of Tokwan Island," *Bishop Museum Bulletin* 146, 1937; B. Quain, *Fijan Village,* Chicago, 1948.
38. See H. Pirenne, "Guilds, Medieval," in the *Encyclopedia of the Social Sciences,* and also his more general discussion of it in *Social and Economic History of Medieval Europe,* 1936; and also W. Morse, *The Guilds of China,* London, 1916.

39. *Ibid.*

40. See the various articles on feudalism in the *Encyclopedia of Social Sciences,* and for detailed discussion, M. Bloch, *La Societe Feudale,* Paris, 1940; H. Ganshof, *Feudalism,* London, 1952; M. Granet, *La Feodalite Chinoise,* Oslo, 1952.

41. See, for instance, A. Lagnon, *La vie en France au Moyen Age,* Ch. II, the text by Philliphe de Navare, "Quatre Ages de l'homme."

42. See, for instance, J. Field, *The Social System of the Ga People,* London, 1940; A. Chadwick, *Ubena of the Rivers,* London, 1937; and the vast literature on the Mamluks, especially D. Ayalon, *L'eslavage de Mamluk,* Jerusalem, 1951.

43. See J. Furnivall, *Educational Progress in Southeast Asia,* New York, 1943.

44. T. Parsons, *The Social System,* pp. 195 ff.; M. Levy, *The Family Transition in Modern China, op. cit.;* H. Fei, "Peasantry and Gentry," *American Journal of Sociology,* 1946; H. Fei, *China's Gentry,* Chicago, 1953.

45. *Ibid.*

46. M. Levy, *op. cit.,* and the numerous historical analyses of W. Eberhard, mainly his *Conquerors and Rulers,* Leiden, 1952.

47. See the analysis of J. Wach in *Meister and Jünger,* Leipzig (no date), and in a more general way in his *Sociology of Religion,* Chicago, 1944.

48. See H. Marrou, *L'education dans l'antiquité, op. cit.*

49. See L. Brehier, *La Civilisation Byzantine,* Paris, 1950, ch. XIII, and A. A. Vasiliev, *History of the Byzantine Empire,* Manchester, 1952, *passim.*

50. See T. L. Jarman, *Landmarks in the History of Education,* London, 1951, Chs. X, XII, XIV, and N. Hans, *New Trends in Education in the 18th Century,* London, 1951.

51. See on this the various sociological analyses of modern societies, such as R. Williams, *American Society, op. cit.,* or T. Parsons, *Essays in Sociological Theory, op. cit.*

52. See M. Weber, *The Protestant Ethic, Gesammelte Aufsätze zur Religionssoziologie;* English translation by T. Parsons, London and New York, 1930. See also R. H. Tawney, *Religion and the Rise of Capitalism,* 1927.

53. See, for instance, the various analyses in E. H. Erikson's *Childhood and Society, op. cit.*

54. See T. Parsons in *Essays, op. cit.;* M. Fainsod, "The Komsomol," *American Political Science Review, op. cit.; and* the forthcoming full reports on the researches on Israeli youth movements as well as S. N. Eisenstadt's "Youth Culture and Social Structure in Israel," *op. cit.*

55. See the literature cited above as well as the very illuminating study, E. F. Piefay's "Boys' Clubs and Their Social Patterns," *British Journal of Delinquency,* vol. II, No. 3, 1952.

56. See the various case studies in the studies of adolescents by Fleming, Blos, Zachry, etc., as well as the literature on the German Youth Movement, for instance, H. Blueher, *DOer Charakter der Jugenbewegung,* 1921; *idem, Wandervogel, Geschichte einer Bewegung.*

57. See E. H. Erikson, *op. cit.*

58. See, for instance, F. Thrasher, *The Gang, op. cit.,* or W. F. Whyte, *Street Corner Society, op. cit.*

59. See E. Halévy, *A History of the English People in 1815* (Pelican edition), vol. 3, p. 163.

60. See, for instance, the autobiography of W. Churchill, and many similar examples. See in detail also B. Darwin, *The English Public School*, London, 1929.

61. See, in greater detail for this problem, the discussion in ch. V.

62. S. Spinley, *The Deprived and the Privileged*, London, 1953, p. 131. And see also the literature cited in ch. II, and in Note 58 above. A recent interesting discussion of this problem can be also found in E. B. Olds and E. Josephson, *Young People and Citizenship*, New York, 1953, National Social Welfare Assembly (mimeographed). See also some of the literature on postwar German and American youth, e.g., K. Bendarik, *Der junge Arbeiter von heute—ein neuer Typ*, Stuttgart, 1953.

63. S. N. Eisenstadt, *Age-groups and Social Structure, op. cit.*

64. See the analysis of T. Parsons cited in ch. II, as well as A. H. Hollinghead, *Elmtown's Youth, op. cit.*

65. See H. Blueher, *op. cit.;* Ch. Leutkens, *Die Deutsche Jugendbewegung, op. cit.;* H. Becker, *German Youth, Bond or Free, op. cit.*

66. See the forthcoming report on Israeli youth movements.

67. *Ibid.*

68. See the literature in Notes 65-67.

69. See on this in great detail, E. H. Erikson, *Childhood and Society, op. cit.;* M. Sherif and H. Cantril, *op. cit.;* as well as the voluminous documentary evidence in the many books on adolescence mentioned in ch. IV.

70. *Ibid.* and K. Davis, "The Sociology of Parent-Youth Conflict," *op. cit.*

71. See on this the thesis of Robert C. Schmid, *German Youth Movement*, written under Prof. H. Becker at the University of Wisconsin, 1939 (unpublished).

72. *Ibid.*

73. The material on the Israeli youth movements will be published in full in the near future.

74. As distinct from those primitive societies undergoing various changes under the impact of "culture contact," which will be analyzed shortly.

75. See on this R. Firth, *Elements of Social Organization*, London, 1951.

76. H. Kuper, *The Uniform of Colour*, Witwarsand, 1947, pp. 150 ff.

77. I. Schapera, *Married Life in an African Tribe*, London, 1945, pp. 265-74.

77a. See K. Bendarik, *op. cit.;* H. Schelsky, *Arbeitslosigkeit und Berufsnot der Jugend*, Köln, 1952.

78. See the relevant literature on each of these countries which was referred to in the former chapter, as well as L. Minio-Paluello, *Education in Fascist Italy*, London, 1946.

79. See S. Scheidinger, "A Comparative Study of the Boy Scout Movement in Different Social Groups," *American Sociological Review*, vol. 13, 1948. And see also E. B. Olds and E. Josephson, *Young People and Citizenship, op. cit.;* A. Hollinghead, *op. cit.;* Th. Winslow and F. Davidson eds.), *American Youth*, 1940; K. Bendarik, *op. cit.*

80. This fact is, of course, very well known. Some of the sociological implications of universal conscription which bear in our problem can be found in H. Speier, *Social Order and the Risk of War*, New York, 1952,

R. Caillois, *Quatre Essais de Sociologie Contemporaire*, Paris, 1951, ch. **IV**.

81. S. N. Eisenstadt, "Youth Culture and Social Structure in Israel," *op. cit*. And S. Andrzejewski, *Military Organization and Society*, London, 1954.

82. See the description of this movement in Ch. II.

83. See on this D. F. Aberle and K. Naegele, "Middle Class Fathers' Occupational Role and Attitudes Towards Children," *American Journal of Orthopsychiatry*, vol. XXII, April, 1952, as well as the interim reports on the Harvard Mobility Study in T. Parsons, F. Bales and E. Shils, *Working Papers Towards A Ttheory of Action*, Glencoe, 1953, Ch. V.

84. See Fainsod's analysis of the Komsomol, *op. cit.*, and also A. Inkeles, *Public Opinion in Soviet Russia*, 1951, and H. Becker's analysis in *German Youth, op. cit.*

85. Fainsod, *op. cit.*

CHAPTER V

1. See W. Ll. Warner, *A Black Civilization*, New York, 1937, and a short summary in W. Goode, *Religion among the Primitives*, Glencoe, 1951, pp. 79 ff., 128 ff., 174 ff.

2. See Capt. R. M. Dawnes, *The Tiv Tiv Tute, Kadima* (Nigeria), 1937, Agika's Story, *The Tiv Tiv Tribe as seen by one of its members*, translated and annotated by R. East, I.A.I., 1939.

The fullest analysis of the Tiv, for which we are greatly indebted, is that of Laura A. Bohannan, A Comparative Study of Social Differentiation, Primitive Society, D. Phil. Thesis, Oxford, 1951. See also L. and P. Bohannan, *The Tiv of Central Nigeria*, Ethnographic Survey of Africa, London, 1953.

3. See Wilson, G., "An Introduction to Nyakyusa Society," *Bantu Studies* X, 1936; Wilson, G., "Introduction to N. Law, *Africa*, X, 1937; and Wilson, M., *Good Company*, Oxford (I.A.I.), 1951.

4. C. Arensberg and S. Kimball, *Family and Community in Ireland*, Harvard, 1948.

5. See, for references, Notes 8-22 and 24-30 of this chapter.

6. W. Ll. Warner, *op. cit.*

7. Argika's Story, *op. cit.*, p. 106.

8. *Ibid.*, p. 127 ff.

9. M. Wilson, *op. cit.*, pp. 82 ff., 160 fff., 173 ff.

10. *Ibid.*, pp. 27 ff.

11. *Ibid.*

12. O. Raumm, *Chagga Childhood*, Oxford, 1937.

13. B. Guttman, *Recht der Dschagga*, München, 1928; B. Guttman, *Die Stammeslehren der Dschagga*, München, 1932.

14. Howitt, A. W., *The Native Tribes of South East Australia*, London, 1904.

15. C. Arensberg and S. Kimball, *Family and Community in Ireland, op. cit.*, Chs. VI, X.

16. *Op. cit.*

17. *Op. cit.*

18. A. D. Rees, *Life in a Welsh Village*, Cardiff, 1950, pp. 82 ff.

19. See H. Fei, *Peasant Life in China*, Ch. II; M. Yang, *A Chinese Village*.
20. Ch. Wagley, "The Social and Religious Life of a Guatemalan Village," *American Anthropologist*, Memoir No. 71, 1949, Chs. II, IV. See also M. Tumin, *Caste in Peasant Society*, Princeton, 1953.
21. H. Miner, *St. Denis—A French Canadian Parish*, Chicago, 1939; E. Hughes, *French Canada in Transition*, London, 1946.
22. See H. Miner, *op. cit.*, pp. 182-2.
23. A. D. Rees, *op. cit.*, pp. 59 ff.
24. H. Miner, *op. cit.*, pp. 59 ff.
25. S. N. Eisenstadt, *Age Groups and Social Structure*, *op. cit.*
26. H. Miner, *op. cit.*
27. See G. P. Murdock, *Social Structure*, Chaps. I, II.
28. See, for instance, R. F. Spencer and S. A. Barett, "Notes on a Bachelor House in the South China Area," *American Anthropologist*, vol. 50, No. 3, 1948.
A most comprehensive analysis is to be found in K. Rob V. Wikman, *Die Einleitung der Ehe*, Abö, 1937. See also, K. G. Izkowitz, *The Community House of the Lamet, Ethos*, vol. VIII, 1943.
29. Wickman, *op. cit.*
30. See, for instance, I. T. Sanders, *A Balkan Village*, University of Kentucky Press, 1949.
31. See Ch. v. Fuerer Haimendorf, "The Morung System of the Konyag Nagas, Assaun," *JRAI*, LXVIII, 1938.
32. See, for instance, Roy Chandra, *The Oraons of Chota Nagpur;* Sarat Roy Chandra, *The Birkas*, Ranchi, 1915; J. Hutton, *The Sema Nagas*, London, 1942; J. P. Mills, *The Aa-Nagas*, London, 1926.
33. The fullest comparative analysis can be found in his "Youth Dormitories and Community Houses in India," *Anthropos*, XLV, 1950.
34. On materials on the German youth movements see Notes to Ch. II and Ch. VI.

CHAPTER VI

1. We hope to be able to elaborate this concept in a special publication.
2. This analysis of the function of some religious institutions is implied in the classic Durkheimian analysis of festivals. We hope to deal with it in greater detail in the future.
3. See M. Gluckman, *Rituals of Rebellion in S.E. Africa*, Manchester, 1953.
4. See the numerous literature mentioned in the former Chapters. For a more general analysis see R. Firth, *Social Organization, op. cit.*
5. See, for instance, in E. E. Evans-Pritchard, "The Nuer, Age Sets," in *Sudan Notes and Records, op. cit.*, and in J. Peristianyi, *The Social System of the Kipsigis, op. cit.* Parallel instances can be found in the literature on all other tribes.
6. See, for instance, L. S. B. Leakey, "Some Notes on the Masai," *op. cit.;* J. Kenyatta, *Facing Mount Kenya, op. cit.*
7. *Ibid.*
8. See H. Michell, *op. cit.*

9. See the literature on Athens mentioned in Notes to chs. III and IV, and especially H. Marrou, *op. cit.*

10. See, on this, T. Parsons, "The Kinship System of the Contemporary United States," in his *Essays, op. cit.*, pp. 233 ff.; W. Waller and R. Hill, *op. cit.* See also K. Mannheim, "The Social Problems of Generations," in *Essays in the Sociology of Knowledge,* London, 1952, and "The Problem of Youth in Modern Society," in his *Diagnosis of Our Time,* London, 1943.

11. See K. Davis, "The Sociology of Parent-Youth Conflict," *op. cit.*

12. See P. Landis, *Adolescence and Youth,* New York, 1947, and T. Parsons, *op. cit.*

13. A statement on this can be found in the literature on modern youth movements presented in the former chapters, and specially in that on the German and Israeli youth movements, and on American youth culture.

14. See Fainsod's paper on the Komsomol; H. Becker, *German Youth, Bond or Free, op. cit.*; V. Winkler-Hermaden, *Psychologie des Jugendfuehrers,* Jena, 1927; and the forthcoming publication on the research on Israeli youth movements.

15. *Ibid.*

16. See, on this, T. Parsons, *The Social System, op. cit.*, pp. 110, 305 ff. Our analysis follows closely in this respect that of Parsons.

17. See E. H. Erikson, *Wachstum und Krisen der gesunden Persönlichkeit,* Stuttgart, 1953.

18. See S. N. Harper, *Civic Training in Soviet Russia, Chicago,* 1929; R. Schlesinger, "Changing Attitudes in Soviet Russia," *The Country,* London, 1949; S. N. Eisenstadt, *Age Groups and Social Structure, op. cit.*; J. Embree, *The Japanese Nation,* New York, 1945; J. Embree, *A Japanese Village,* London, 1946; and the literature on Germany cited above.
· A penetrating analysis of youth in Russia can be found in K. Davis, *Human Society,* pp. 229 ff.

19. See Fainsod's analysis of the Komsomol; A. Inkeles, *Public Opinion in Soviet Russia, op. cit.*; W. W. Rostow, *The Dynamics of Soviet Society,* New York, 1953, especially chs. 13, 14; and M. Fainsod, "Controls and Tensions in the Soviet System," *American Political Science Review,* XLIV, No. 2, June 1950, pp. 266-83.

20. S. N. Eisenstadt, *Age Groups and Social Structure, op. cit.*

21. See J. Olds and E. Josephson, *op. cit.*

22. M. Fainsod, *op. cit.*; S. N. Eisenstadt, *op. cit.*

23. *Ibid.*

24. See J. Bossard, *Parent and Child, op. cit.* There are but few full analyses of these societies. The best are to be found in historical studies.
See, for instance, W. Thompson, *Democracy in France,* London, 1952, or D. W. Brogan, *The English People,* 1942. See also all the literature on these countries referred to in earlier chapters, and E. M. Earle (ed.), *Modern France,* especially chs. 4, 5, 17, 19.

25. See the forthcoming publication on the Israeli youth movements.

26. Olds and Josephson, *op. cit.*

27. See E. H. Hughes, *French Canada in Transition, op. cit.*

28. See, for instance, H. Wendel, *Aus dem südslavischen Risorgimento,* Gotha, 1921; W. H. Kiang, *The Ideological Background of the Chinese Student Movement,* Columbia, 1948.

29. See, for instance, B. A. Knoppers, *Die Jugendbewegung in den Niederlanden,* Emsdetten, 1931; G. Thomson, The Influence of Youth Movements on German Education, unpublished Ph.D. Thesis, University of Glasgow, 1934; R. Ulich, "Germany," *Educational Yearbook,* New York, 1936; R. H. Samuel and R. Thomas, *Education and Society in Modern Germany,* London, 1949; P. Picard, *L'Action Sociale de la jeunesse Française de l'apres Guerre,* Paris, 1933; P. Peterson, *Die neureouropäische Erziehungsbewegung,* Weimar, 1926.

30. See the very illuminating analysis of J. N. Demarath in his Ph.D. Thesis (unpublished), Harvard Univ., 1942, Adolescent Status and the Individual.

31. See, for instance, A. Hollingshead, *Elmtown's Youth, op. cit.*

32. See, for instance, M. Mead, *The Changing Culture of an Indian Tribe,* New York, 1932; G. MacGregor, *Warriors Without Weapons,* Chicago, 1946; E. Hellman, *Problems of Urban Bantu Youth,* Johannesburg, 1940; A. Joseph (ed.), *The Desert People,* Chicago, 1949-50, and the various studies on Negro Youth, published by the American Council on Education, such as W. Lloyd Warner (ed.), *Color and Human Nature,* Washington, 1941; A. Davies and J. Dollard, *Children of Bondage,* Washington, 1940; F. Frazier, *Negro Youth at the Crossroads,* Washington, 1940.

33. See the main textbooks on juvenile delinquency; P. W. Tappan, *Juvenile Delinquency,* New York, 1949; W. Reckless, *The Crime Problem,* New York, 1950; and also such analyses as M. Merrill, *Problems of Child Delinquency,* London, 1947.
See also the interesting analysis of J. B. Mays, "A Study of Delinquent Community," *British Journal of Delinquency,* July, 1952; and S. Kobrin, "Conflict of Values in Delinquency Areas," *American Sociological Review,* Oct. 1951, (vol. XVI).
A recent statement of a systematic approach to juvenile delinquency, very much in line with the general argument of our book, is to be found in A. K. Cohen, *Delinquent Boys: The Culture of the Gang,* Glencoe, 1955. Free Press, 1955.

34. H. Wendel, *Aus dem südslavischen Risorgimento, op. cit.;* T. C. Wang, *The Youth Movement in China,* New York, 1927; Hans Kohn, *Imperialismus und Nationalismus im Vorderen Orient,* 1930.

35. M. Mead, *The Changing Culture of an Indian Tribe, op. cit.*

36. *Ibid.*

37. See R. Merton, *Social Theory and Social Structure,* 1949, ch. IV.

38. W. Thomas and F. Znaniecki, *The Polish Peasant in Europe and America,* New York, 1927; J. Childe, *Italian or American?,* New Haven, 1944; the studies of Negro youth cited in Note 26; and also D. Tooth, *Report on Juvenile Delinquency in the Gold Coast,* 1946.

39. See, for a summary of these researches: S. W. Tappan, *Juvenile Delinquency, op. cit.,* pp. 133-40; H. V. Henting, *The Criminal and the Victim,* 1948, pp. 359-97; N. Reckless, *The Crime Problem, op. cit.,* pp. 71-73; Th. Sellin, *Culture Conflict and Crime,* 1938; and S. N. Eisenstadt, "Delinquent Group Formation Among Immigrant Youth," *British Journal of Delinquency,* July, 1951.

40. See S. N. Eisenstadt, "The Oriental Jews in Israel," *Jewish Social*

Studies, 1950; and N. D. Humphrey, "The Stereotype and the Social Types of Mexican American Youth," in *Journal of Social Psychology*, 1945, pp. 22.

41. See the evidence in the literature cited in the two former Notes.

42. See the various analyses in the Nov. 1944 (Adolescents in Wartime) and Jan. 1949 (Juvenile Delinquency) issues of the *Annals of the American Ac. of Pol. and Social Science*.

43. See K. Davis, "Adolescence and the Social Structure," *op. cit.*; E. H. Bell, "Age Group Conflict and Our Changing Culture," *Social Forces*, vol. 12, 1933; K. Mannheim, *op. cit.*

44. See K. Bednarik, *op. cit.*, and H. Schelski, *op. cit.*

45. See, in addition to the literature cited above, the very interesitng report in the *London Times* of August 17, 1951: "The Jamboree and Its Rivals, Challenge of Dictated Youth Movements."

46. One can compare it, for instance, with the transition effected in Japan at the Meji restoration. See H. Norman, *Japan's Emergence as a Modern State*, 1946.

47. See, for example of good case studies and analyses: J. Furnivall, *Colonial Policy and Practice*, Cambridge, 1948; R. Emerson, L. A. Mills and V. Thompson, *Government and Nationalism in S.E. Asia*, New York, 1942; R. Troutton, *Peasant Renaissance in Yougoslavia, 1900-1950*, London, 1952; H. Kohn, *Die Europäisierung des Orients*, Berlin, 1934; H. Kohn, *Nationalismus und Imperialismus im Vorderen Orient*, Frankfurt am Main, *op. cit.*; K. M. Pannikar, *op. cit.*; M. Levy, *op. cit.*; and for a somewhat different pattern: H. Norman, *Japan's Emergence as a Modern State*, *op. cit.*

48. It was aptly defined in this sense by H. Becker, in *German Youth, Bond or Free*, *op. cit.*

49. See on this especially H. Bluehere, *Die Deutsche Wandervogelbewegung also erotisches Phenomenon*, Berlin, 1912. And Jungman, *Autorität und Sexualmoral in der freien deutschen Jugendbewegung*, *op. cit.*

50. T. Parsons, Chs. XII, XIV, in *Essays*, *op. cit.*

51. H. Becker, *German Youth, Bond or Free*, *op. cit.*

52. E. H. Erikson, in *Childhood and Society*, *op. cit.*, the chapter "Hitler's Imagery and German Youth,."

53. F. Jungman, *op. cit.*, *Autorität und Sexualmoral*, *op. cit.* Some interesting comparisons between American and German youth which have some direct bearing on the subject can be found in: D. V. McGraham, "A Comparison of Social Attitudes Among American and German Youth," *Journal of Abnormal and Social Psychology*, vol. 41, and H. S. Lewin, "A Comparison of the Aims of the Hitler Youth and the Boy Scouts of America," *Human Relations*, vol. I, 1947.

54. See, for instance, H. Lichtenberger, *Germany and Its Evolution in Modern Times*, New York, 1913, and R. H. Samuel and R. Thomas, *Education and Society in Modern Germany*, London, 1949.

Additional Bibliography:

Since this manuscript was finished several new publications on different African societies dealt with in this book have been published by the

Ethnographical Survey of Africa. Among these the most pertinent for our purpose are the following:

G. W. B. Huntingford, *The Northern Nilo-Hamites.*
A. Butt, *The Nilotes of the Anglo-Egyptian Sudan and Uganda.*
P. Gulliver & P. U. Gulliver, *The Central Nilo-Hamites.*
I. Schafera, *The Tswana.*
H. Kuper, *The Swazi.*

Index

(Chapters vii-ix are not included in index)

[418]

Ollscoil na hÉireann, Gaillimh

3 1111 40091 5268